U.S.
Trade Policy
and
Global
Growth

U.S. Trade Policy and Global Growth

New Directions in the International Economy

Robert A. Blecker

editor

Economic Policy Institute

M.E. Sharpe
Armonk, New York
London, England

Library of Congress Cataloging-in-Publication Data

U.S. trade policy and global growth : new directions in the international economy /
Robert A. Blecker, editor
p.   cm.—(Economic Policy Institute series)
Includes bibliographical references and index.
ISBN 1-56324-530-2 (alk. paper).—ISBN 1-56324-531-0 (pbk.)
1. International economic relations.
2. United States—Commercial policy.
3. Developing countries—Commercial policy.
4. Competition, International.
I. Blecker, Robert A., 1956–
II. Series: Economic Policy Institute (Series).
HF1359.U25   1995
382′.3′0973—dc20
95-9028
CIP

Printed in the United States of America

The paper used in this publication meets the minimum requirements of
American National Standard for Information Sciences—
Permanence of Paper for Printed Library Materials,
ANSI Z 39.48-1984.

Recommended citation for this book is as follows:
Blecker, Robert A., editor.
U.S. Trade Policy and Global Growth: New Directions in the International Economy.
Economic Policy Institute series. Armonk: M. E. Sharpe, Inc., 1996.

∞

MV (c)   10   9   8   7   6   5   4   3   2   1
MV (p)   10   9   8   7   6   5   4   3   2   1

For my wife,
Elizabeth J. Greenberg

CONTENTS

PART IV: TRADE POLICIES IN THE DEVELOPING COUNTRIES

LIST OF TABLES AND FIGURES

Tables

Figures

PREFACE

This volume brings together a collection of essays offering critical perspectives on current issues in the international economy. While the primary emphasis is on issues of relevance to American trade policy, attention is also given to global macroeconomic issues and to trade and financial policies for the developing countries. Four chapters (chapters 1, 4, 6, and 9) include material previously published by the Economic Policy Institute (EPI) as separate studies; all of these were revised and updated to a greater or lesser extent for inclusion in this book. The other five chapters were newly written for this volume, although most of them reflect research in which their authors have been engaged for some time. Like all EPI publications, this book is intended to be accessible to anyone who is interested in economic policy issues, not just academic specialists.

The authors of the chapters in this book are a diverse group in both interests and inclinations. The authors differ in the degrees to which they would let market forces operate or endorse selective government interventions in particular areas of international trade and finance—and even in the degrees to which they believe that exchange rate adjustment can solve macroeconomic trade imbalances. While all the authors have responded to suggestions from the editor, no effort has been made to enforce a uniform policy perspective. Each author is responsible only for the views expressed in his or her own chapter or chapters—and the editor takes sole responsibility for the views expressed in this preface.

Nevertheless, in spite of the diversity of views represented here, some important common themes emerge. All the authors reject the dogma that pure free market policies should be accepted as articles of religious faith, either in the trade arena or internally. All of them are united in a search for trade and macroeconomic policies that can achieve balanced growth with high employment and an equitable distribution of income both in the United States and in the rest of the world.

This book is being completed at a time when free trade policies are clearly in ascendance globally, at least in rhetoric if not always in reality. Following the consolidation of the European Union into a single market area with harmonized standards, the United States and other nations have been rushing into ever-broader and more all-encompassing agreements to reduce barriers to international trade and protect the rights of international investors. The year 1994 began with the implementation of the North American Free Trade Agreement (NAFTA) with Canada and Mexico and ended with U.S. congressional approval of the Uruguay Round of the General Agreement on Tariffs and Trade (GATT), which creates a new World Trade Organization (WTO). Flush with these victories and undaunted by the Republican sweep of the 1994 congressional elections, President Bill Clinton flew to Indonesia to promote the Asian-Pacific Economic Cooperation (APEC) free trade initiative, and to Miami to endorse the Free Trade Area of the Americas—both of which are supposed to be negotiated by the early twenty-first century (but neither of which yet entails any specific commitments).

As this scenario unfolded, some economic forecasters managed to produce ever more optimistic forecasts of the benefits that these trade agreements would achieve. American families were promised gains in the thousands of dollars each by the early 2000s, if only they would put up with some minor "adjustment costs" in the short run. Long-established economic theories that predict significant redistributive effects of trade liberalization were abandoned by some free trade enthusiasts, who claimed that these trade agreements would be a virtual "free lunch" with no losers (at least in the long run). Ordinary citizens suffering from two decades of falling real wages and stagnant family incomes (maintained only by family members working longer hours) were skeptical, but policy elites insisted that they knew what was good for everyone else. Anyone who questioned the wisdom of the trade agreements currently being negotiated was branded a "protectionist" beholden to "special interests" (especially, supposedly overpaid American workers).

There is no question that the growth of world trade in the post–World War II era has contributed to overall economic growth and that excessive forms of interventionist trade policies have often backfired and stymied national economic development. There is also no question that new technologies (especially in the areas of communication and transportation) have brought the nations of the world closer together, making some form of increased global integration inevitable. But it is a big leap from these conclusions, which are widely shared, to the deduction that completely unregulated trade and capital flows are a necessary or sufficient condition for economic growth and equitable development. Nor is there clear evidence, from an objective reading of the historical record, that throwing a nation's borders open to untrammeled foreign competition and investment is the best way to promote national economic interests. Quite the contrary, the record indicates that selective government interventions to control imports and promote exports have often been used by some of the most successful trading nations, especially the export dynamos of East Asia.

The sudden enthusiasm for free trade agreements is especially ironic in light of the revolutionary new developments in international trade theory over the past fifteen years. New models of international trade have shown that the case for perfectly free trade is at best a special case, which applies only under very stringent conditions that are not necessarily found in the real world. Factors such as economies of scale, "imperfect" competition (e.g., oligopolistic markets), and opportunities for technological learning imply a potentially positive role for appropriate government policies in enabling nations to take maximum advantage of their international trade relations. Yet some of the new trade agreements would severely restrict, if not prohibit, national governments from experimenting with the types of policies that are potentially beneficial according to these new theories.

Even in the traditional models of trade, it was always recognized that trade liberalization could create losers as well as winners. In nineteenth-century Britain, free traders could comfort themselves with the thought that abolishing trade barriers would injure only the landed aristocracy (since most British protection was for agricultural products). Today, both economic logic and common sense suggest that the likely victims of free trade in the United States are ordinary workers with average skills and training, whose products must increasingly compete with those made by much lower-paid workers (often working in factories owned by the same companies or with similar up-to-date equipment) in less developed countries (LDCs). Of course, the solution to such a distributional dilemma is not necessarily to maintain permanent trade protection; education and retraining are often suggested as alternatives. But the prospects for any kinds of sensible policy solutions are not enhanced by efforts to deny that the problem exists.

At the macroeconomic level, the 1980s and 1990s have been a time of recurrent international imbalances and crises. Starting with the U.S. recession and the Latin American debt crisis of the early 1980s, the world economy was then revived by the motor of U.S. fiscal expansion that contributed, along with deeper structural factors, to a pattern of trade imbalances that is unprecedented in the postwar era. The United States has run chronic trade deficits for more than a decade, turning this country into the world's largest net debtor nation and forcing it to rely on capital inflows from other nations—especially the surplus countries of East Asia. Massive currency realignments have thus far failed to eliminate these global imbalances, especially in the case of Japan.

Meanwhile, the early 1990s saw first the United States and then Japan and Western Europe plunge into prolonged recessions, with political systems paralyzed and unable to respond with effective stimulative policies. Overall, global growth is being actively constrained by the tight monetary policies of central banks, starting with the U.S. Federal Reserve and the German Bundesbank. The same types of policies are in place in developing nations, often promoted by the International Monetary Fund (IMF) and the World Bank as well as the U.S. government in response to the debt crisis. While these policies have brought inflation under control, they have done so at a severe real cost in lost employment and incomes and the resulting human suffering. This situation cries out for innovative policy solutions that can restore global growth on an equitable and sustainable basis.

To address all these concerns, the essays in this book have been divided into four parts: Part I, Conceptual Frameworks; Part II, Issues in U.S. Trade Policy; Part III, Macroeconomic Perspectives; and Part IV, Trade Policies in the Developing Countries.

Part I presents two challenging essays that seek to redefine the analysis of the costs and benefits of international economic relations. Chapter 1 is an edited version of Robert Kuttner's widely cited EPI report, *Managed Trade and Economic Sovereignty*, which helped to define the national debate on managed trade policies when it was first released in 1989. Although the trade policy debate has shifted since that time, the issues raised by Kuttner have not gone away. In spite of all the so-called free trade agreements (and sometimes even through them), the United States and other nations continue to manage their trade, and not always in ways that represent sensible national policies. Rather than preaching pure free trade and then tacitly giving in to special interest demands for sectoral protection, Kuttner argues, we should design better ways of explicitly managing our trade that will ensure a greater "balance of benefits" between the United States and its trading partners in those sectors in which other countries' interventions make a laissez-faire approach unviable. Kuttner's argument has become even more compelling since the collapse of the Soviet bloc, which eliminated the rationale that it was necessary for the United States to tolerate other countries' mercantilist practices and strategic interventions in order to maintain hegemony over Cold War allies. Kuttner uses examples drawn from managed trade regimes in textiles and apparel, steel, and semiconductors to show how his balance-of-benefits approach could be implemented.

In chapter 2, David P. Levine provides a comprehensive new conceptualization of the international economy that does not rely on the traditional paradigm of "comparative advantage." The author suggests a new analytical framework that includes three kinds of advantages from international trade: gains in productivity, gains in income and employment, and gains from lower-cost consumer goods. Levine argues for replacing the traditional notion of an international "division of labor" with the concept of an international "division of markets"; such a model would highlight the potential for conflict among competing national firms. He suggests that free trade is not always equally beneficial to all nations, but rather may produce concentrated benefits for more competitive nations and lesser benefits or even harmful outcomes for other nations. Public policies inevitably affect trade relations, regardless of whether governments explicitly intervene in trade or not, and the use of trade policies to influence a nation's economic development process can sometimes (although not always) be beneficial. Levine also analyzes the problem of low-wage competition in an environment of mobile capital and technology and the dilemma that this poses for high-wage nations like the United States.

Part II includes three essays on current issues in U.S. trade policy. Chapter 3 is Dale Belman and Thea M. Lee's survey of recent research on the relationship between international trade and the wages and employment of U.S. workers. The authors show that popular fears that trade liberalization eliminates jobs and puts downward pressure on wages do in fact have solid support in most recent empirical studies, in spite of efforts by some economists to dismiss those concerns. While some studies claim to prove that technological change alone accounts for the negative trends in U.S. wages and manufacturing employment (especially for less skilled workers), Belman and Lee argue that the methods of these studies are flawed and their conclusions unreliable. While acknowledging that more research needs to be done in this area, the authors find clear evidence that trade is a contributing factor (increasingly so in recent years) in the deterioration of labor market performance and the worsening of income inequality in the United States.

Chapter 4, by Robert E. Scott and Thea M. Lee, summarizes the results of the authors' EPI-sponsored research into the costs and benefits of protection in three important U.S. industries: steel, textiles, and apparel. Scott and Lee argue that the costs of protection (and the benefits of trade liberalization) in these industries have been exaggerated by economists who have failed to examine the specific structures of the industries involved as well as the relevant policy alternatives. In steel especially, trade protection has enabled workers to keep jobs with higher wages than they could otherwise obtain, due to the presence of "labor rents." In both steel and textiles, trade protection has encouraged firms to invest more in new technologies that have improved productivity. In women's apparel, the rise of highly concentrated distribution channels with significant market power and high profit margins means that most of the benefits of trade liberalization would probably not be passed on to consumers. In all these cases, the sometimes high costs of the actual forms of protection (especially market-sharing arrangements or voluntary export restraints) need to be compared with the costs of alternative types of trade protection (such as tariffs or auction quotas) as well as domestic industrial policies and the free trade option. When all these factors are taken into account, the benefits of trade liberalization are far less certain, and in some cases trade protection can even be shown to bring net national benefits.

In chapter 5, Robert A. Blecker revisits the NAFTA debate and provides a critical evaluation of the multitude of studies that tried to forecast the "likely effects" of this agreement. The author argues that the emphasis in the political debate over the net employment impact of NAFTA was misplaced, and that the most significant effect of this agreement is likely to be in contributing to downward pressures on U.S. wages. The investment liberalization provisions of NAFTA are even more significant than the pure trade liberalization provisions, and could lead to significant amounts of job displacement even if the total number of employed workers is little affected. Overall, NAFTA is seen as creating a trading bloc that manages U.S. trade in the interest of U.S. multinational corporations, which can use export platforms in Mexico to strengthen their international competitive positions at the expense of domestic workers in the United States. Blecker also argues that NAFTA is unlikely to bring the huge growth gains that the Mexican government hoped to achieve, especially if the Mexican government keeps its commitment to restrictive monetary and fiscal policies. The devaluation of the peso in December 1994 and the resulting financial crisis in Mexico validated the author's view that the peso was overvalued and that the Mexican foreign investment boom of the early 1990s could not be expected to continue indefinitely.

Part III contains two chapters covering macroeconomic aspects of U.S. trade policy. In chapter 6, Robert A. Blecker challenges the conventional wisdom of orthodox economists that the U.S. trade deficit is only a reflection of macroeconomic problems (the budget deficit and a low saving rate). He provides evidence that the U.S. economy is suffering from a declining trend in its competitiveness, and shows how this structural trend affects macroeconomic outcomes including the trade balance and the value of the dollar. Blecker especially shows that the U.S. trade deficit has persisted at high levels in the early 1990s in spite of a falling dollar and falling wages for U.S. manufacturing workers. Blecker analyzes current U.S. trade problems, especially with Japan, China, and Taiwan, and shows how these bilateral imbalances contribute to overall trade problems. He concludes with recommendations for a combination of traditional macroeconomic and exchange rate policies with the use of trade and industrial policies to address the structural roots of the U.S. trade imbalance.

Chapter 7, by Paul Davidson, argues that the current system of flexible exchange rates contributes to global macroeconomic instability. Especially, Davidson contends that the present system puts too much of the balance-of-payments adjustment burden on the deficit countries, which have to cut back their expenditures, and too little of a burden on the surplus countries, which should be forced to increase their expenditures in order to maintain global demand growth. Davidson shows that the initial success of the Bretton Woods exchange rate regime of 1945–73 derived not only from the fact that it was a system of fixed rates but also from the fact that the leading surplus country of the postwar era (the United States) was able and willing to use expansionary demand policies to keep the global economy booming from the late 1940s to the mid-1960s. Davidson proposes a new system of fixed real exchange rates, with nominal rates adjusted to keep pace with changes in relative nominal unit labor costs, and an institutional mechanism to compel the surplus countries to share more of the adjustment burden by spending their excess monetary inflows. Davidson compares his proposal with other recent proposals for international monetary reform and shows that these other proposals lack a similar mechanism to prevent deflationary adjustments. This shortcoming, he argues, could imperil global growth.

Part IV extends the analysis to trade policy and open-economy macroeconomic issues facing developing countries. In chapter 8, Lance Taylor presents a critique of the effects of the orthodox macroeconomic stabilization policies and structural adjustment programs promoted by the IMF, the World Bank, and the U.S. government in the developing countries since the 1980s. The analysis is based on eighteen country studies that were done under the author's direction through the United Nations World Institute for Development Economics Research (WIDER), as well as on Taylor's own innovative theoretical work on growth and income distribution in developing countries. Taylor shows that these orthodox policies have often failed to achieve their objectives, or have achieved the objectives at an excessive social cost, because the policies were not designed with the specific structural characteristics of the affected countries in mind. Taylor also demonstrates that much of the poor growth performance of the developing countries in the 1980s was due to external financial constraints imposed as a result of the cutoff of foreign lending after the 1982 debt crisis. While Taylor acknowledges that developing countries need to have realistic macroeconomic policies and to promote exports, he argues that pure trade liberalization per se has not generally worked well, while more interventionist export-promotion policies have often achieved better results. Taylor concludes that the prospects for reviving the development process in the Third World depend heavily on reversing the net outflow of resources from those countries and obtaining new net inflows of capital.

Finally, chapter 9, by Stephen C. Smith, focuses more specifically on the trade and industrial policies actually used in the most successful newly industrializing countries (NICs), especially South Korea and Taiwan. Smith shows that the export-led growth of these nations has been supported by active forms of government intervention and sectoral targeting, including all kinds of subsidies and protectionist devices. Thus, the view that these countries succeeded simply by liberalizing trade and letting markets work is simply wrong. Smith does not deny the usefulness of an export orientation in the development process, but he argues that it should not be equated with free trade policies. Rather, Smith shows that the most successful NICs have had government policies that deliberately encouraged manufacturing exports and that stimulated domestic producers to improve their technology, skills, and product quality over time. Smith also argues that it is only exporters of manufactures that have grown rapidly in recent years, and documents why exporters of primary products have done relatively poorly. He concludes by recommending that the IMF, the World Bank, and the U.S. government stop promoting indiscriminate trade liberalization and export-promotion policies in developing countries and instead study and apply the real lessons of the East Asian "miracles."

All the chapters in this book address controversial topics and take strong positions. It is not expected that every reader will come away agreeing with everything that is written here. If these essays encourage critical thinking about the real costs and benefits of pure free trade policies as well as about potential policy alternatives, then this volume will have succeeded. In the end, the gains from trade cannot be measured only in terms of the value of the goods traded or how much they contribute to total national income; they must also reflect how trade affects the distribution of income, the security of employment, the standard of living, and the stability of the social fabric both at home and abroad. It is hoped that this book will stimulate more research and thought on how to make international trade serve these objectives, rather than how to subordinate all other social and economic goals to the imperatives of corporate interests in opening up markets to corporations' movements of goods and capital.

Robert A. Blecker
Washington, DC
January 1995

ACKNOWLEDGMENTS

A book like this could not be produced without a great deal of support and assistance. I would like to thank, first and foremost, the research director of the Economic Policy Institute (EPI), Larry Mishel, and the associate research director, Eileen Applebaum, for their constant support and encouragement. It is a tribute to the work they have done in building up the Research Department of EPI that so many of the chapters in this book were written by EPI staff economists or research associates. I would particularly like to thank my friends and colleagues on the EPI "trade team," Dean Baker, Dale Belman, Thea Lee, Rob Scott, and Bill Spriggs, for valuable discussions and suggestions too numerous to be mentioned individually. I have also benefited from my many discussions with EPI President Jeff Faux on the political economy of trade issues.

I would also like to thank the Institute for the organizational and financial support that made this volume possible. EPI Communications Director Nan Gibson oversaw the contracting of the book with M. E. Sharpe, Inc. Ruth Polk and Patrick Watson did superb copyediting. Stephanie Scott capably did the lion's share of the (seemingly endless) word processing for this book, with the able assistance of Jessica Burton and Miranda Martin. David Webster produced the graphics in record time, and Terrell Hale provided valuable library assistance. To all of them I owe a large debt of gratitude.

Thanks are also due to Cambridge University Press for permission to reprint material included in chapter 2 by David P. Levine. Last but not least, I would like to thank the entire staff of M. E. Sharpe, Inc., and especially economics editor Richard D. Bartel, for their help in bringing this book into print.

Robert A. Blecker

PART I
Conceptual Frameworks

CHAPTER ONE

Managed Trade and Economic Sovereignty

ROBERT KUTTNER

> International trade remains a political act whether it takes place under a system of free trade or protection, of state trading or private enterprise, of most-favored nation clause, or of discriminating treatments.
> — Albert O. Hirschman (1945, p. 78)

Introduction

The contemporary problem of global political economy is that nations are losing sovereignty to private economic actors, yet the very turmoil of an unregulated market intensifies the pressure on nations to secure acceptable outcomes for their citizens. Despite the impetus toward an integrated global private economy, the nation-state remains the instrument of political mediation. The state, not private corporations or banks, remains accountable to its citizens for their economic welfare. The state bears the ultimate fiscal responsibility. The polity remains the arena in which social contracts are negotiated. Yet the growing imbalance between an integrated, unregulated global economy and a weakened set of national and supranational instruments for its governance deprives individual nations of the machinery to deal constructively with those dislocations. The Keynesian nation-state has lost most of its economic rudder—not to supranational public authority but to internationalized private capital.

The confusion about the appropriate role for the state and the market is at its most muddled in the thinking about the desirable norms for the trading system that governs cross-border commerce, where the reach of the state is weakest and that of private capital strongest. The confusion is perhaps most severe in the United States, because the United States, as guarantor of the global system and purveyor of the ideal of liberal trade, is increasingly unsure how to reconcile

This chapter is an edited version of the author's previous Economic Policy Institute report by the same title (Kuttner 1989). The author would like to acknowledge comments and suggestions from Mark Anderson, Steve Beckman, Ron Blackwell, Robert Blecker, Jeff Faux, Larry Mishel, Clyde Prestowitz, Lee Price, Dominick Salvatore, David Smith, Dan Tarullo, Brian Turner, Laura D'Andrea Tyson, and Alan Wolff.

these twin goals with its own national interest as an economy. For the most part, official opinion seems to think that the remedy for the dislocations of laissez-faire is more laissez-faire.

The United States, as the hegemonic power and as the nation most ideologically committed to economic liberalism, also experiences these dilemmas most acutely because it has the least consciousness of them. By the lights of orthodox economics and the ideology of the Reagan and Bush administrations, the remedy for the range of international economic problems is the perfection of free trade. Other trading nations, lacking the effortless commercial dominance that postwar America once enjoyed, feel far less guilty about using the economic instruments of the state. Long accustomed to higher levels of both exports and imports as a share of gross national product (GNP), and lacking the American sense of special responsibility for the system as a whole, these nations developed the survival skills and institutions of economic adjustment and development that the United States lacks (Katzenstein 1985; Gourevitch 1986).

In some countries, such as Japan, Korea, France, and Brazil, these strategies have been overtly mercantilist. These nations have been willing to use the economic power of the state to promote industrial development, to shelter home markets, and to seek trade surpluses. Other successful small trading nations, such as Sweden and Austria, while supporting a generally open trading system, have devised their own mechanisms of adaptation and indirect subsidy that violate the norms of liberal trade in more subtle ways. Still other nations, of the Pacific basin, most of them small, have achieved rapid growth by combining entrepreneurial dynamism with very low wages and state support, turning themselves into export powerhouses by letting their domestic consumption lag their production for world markets. Though this is ostensibly a subsidy, it is better understood as a different form of free riding on the trading system, since it depresses demand nationally and hence globally, and creates lopsided trade surpluses that are the reciprocal of other nations' trade deficits.

In general, it is the United States that has been the advocate of the purest version of free trade. Most other nations have loyally given lip service to these U.S.-inspired norms, while devising pragmatic measures necessary for their survival in a global economy. At the same time, the United States' own practice has been far from the paragon of economic liberalism that is often professed. Yet because of the United States' fierce ideological commitment to laissez-faire, U.S. departures from it have typically been poorly thought out, lacking in long-term industrial goals, and generally not helpful either to the trading system or to America's own economic self-interest.

There is thus a grave dilemma, both for the global trading system and for the United States as its chief architect and sponsor. Many other nations have demonstrated, by their actions if not their words, that they are not interested in a system of pure free trade. By some calculations, more than half the cross-border trade that takes place today operates by some standard other than the norms of classical free trade (Choate and Linger 1988, p. 91). Yet, curiously enough, the volume of trade continues to increase substantially faster than the growth of total world GNP. The sins against liberal trade vary from economic development initiatives undertaken by poor countries that might be justified as variations on the traditional "infant-industry" loophole, to de facto industrial policies cloaked in national defense, to covert market-closing measures undertaken by the world's richest and most successful trade-surplus nations.

A different order of problem is the institutional disjuncture between trade negotiations, debt negotiations, and the other policy-making machinery that establishes rules for the global economy. One set of diplomats, at the General Agreement on Trade and Tariffs (GATT) in Geneva, is hectoring Third World nations to open their markets to U.S., European, and Japanese manufactured goods. A different set of bureaucrats, associated with the World Bank, the International Monetary Fund (IMF), and the private creditor banks, is pressing debtor nations to reduce their imports and increase export earnings. Finally, the most pressing, overarching trade questions, such as the problem of chronic Japanese and West German surpluses and the problem of U.S. deficits in manufactured goods, are widely acknowledged, but these issues are not part of the GATT portfolio; they seem to be on the diplomatic agenda everywhere but at the trade talks. Once again, the assumption of liberal economics is that if "barriers" are removed, then the "correct" pattern of trade will naturally ensue. For example, Japan's chronic surplus, or balance in the trading system, is not an issue per se, except to the extent that illegitimate trading practices can be demonstrated. Desperation remedies such as the Gephardt amendment (which seeks to legislate reductions in U.S. trade deficits with specific countries) are then branded as illegitimate because they flout the stated norms of the trading system that the United States champions.

The GATT system, which will be discussed in more detail below, has only limited criteria for differentiating "good" violations of laissez-faire from bad ones. Aside from giving nations the right to countervail, and being somewhat indulgent of statist policies in developing nations, the GATT does not effectively parse out departures from free trade; it has no mechanism for assuring rough balance in the total calculus of mercantilism. The basic GATT norm is nondiscrimination, and the basic GATT goal is ever freer universal market access. All "trade-distorting" subsidies are presumed to be bad. All departures from the principle of multilateral nondiscrimination are deemed regrettable. Economic development schemes, viewed through the GATT lens, are generally damned as merely protectionist, and it is never conceded that they might have positive-sum benefits in the form of technological gains or redistributions of production.

Advocates of liberal trade tend to see themselves as possessors of special virtue, maintaining the dikes against tides of self-serving protectionism. It is presumed that more laissez-faire is invariably better than less, even though economic theory says this is not necessarily true in an imperfect world. There is no taxonomy for sorting out a world of necessary second bests in practice, and there is little recognition of the necessity of economic management, except through the reluctant toleration of escape clause relief and other "safeguards," in GATT jargon, which are supposed to be temporary and used sparingly.

If this is a problem for the GATT system, it is a special problem for the United States, which tends to see its own self-interest as identical to the liberalism of the trading system as a whole. The United States seems to view it as its special mission to bring laissez-faire to the world, rather than to hammer out with its trading partners a sustainable mixed system, which tolerates some state involvement in the economy, but with rough overall balance, and in which the United States has an equitable share of benefits and costs.

The prevailing U.S. ideology of economic liberalism eschews industrial goals for the United States. In principle, it is none of the government's business where steel, or automobiles, or semiconductors, or videocassette recorders (VCRs), or civilian aircraft are produced. If production migrates, this must be the market speaking. If the invisible hand operates through the guiding hands of foreign industrial policies, this is deemed to make no significant difference. Classical trade theory holds that if other nations are stupid enough to subsidize their export industries, American consumers ought to welcome the gift. These presumptions have four consequences, all of them negative for the U.S. national self-interest and confusing to the trading system.

First, the lack of a set of U.S. industrial goals means that it is impossible to have any trade goals for U.S. policy, other than to exhort other nations to practice laissez-faire in the American image. In practice, this makes America's industrial fate partly the captive of other nations' industrial policies. Second, because the United States continues to view itself as the political leader of the western world, it is reluctant to play tactical hardball on trade issues, lest it alienate key geopolitical allies. Third, when exhortation fails to achieve equitable results, or to open markets, the United States is reluctant to resort to explicit market-sharing remedies, because this of course would be a version of the managed trade it claims to disdain and would violate the very ideology it is promoting. Finally, and perhaps most seriously, U.S. devotion to the ideal of laissez-faire means that the U.S. departures from liberal trade that do intermittently occur are undertaken guiltily and without strategic purpose, and are seen by U.S. officials as unfortunate concessions to domestic politics rather than as economic development initiatives.

The cases are legion. For example, the United States disingenuously imposed a quota regime on autos, disguised as voluntary export restraints (VERs). This allowed the Japanese to determine just what was exported to the United States and to capture the quota rents; it also exposed the United States as a perfect hypocrite. The United States backed into an "industrial policy"—for motorcycles (!)—via a trade relief case, but disdained an industrial policy for the far more consequential machine tool industry. It has long had a highly protectionist regime for agriculture, which it does not know how to dismantle except by having everyone else forswear all price regulation for farm products, which other nations regard as unrealistic and probably cynical. It has had an extensive and unacknowledged industrial policy for aircraft, via the Pentagon. Because national defense is the one available loophole in the otherwise seamless ideology of laissez-faire, we recently witnessed the Pentagon sponsoring an industrial (and trade) policy for semiconductors, and another for high-definition television (HDTV). We have even seen an advisory body to the Secretary of Defense drawing the seemingly logical conclusion that the Pentagon should widen that sole loophole and simply take over the task of modernizing all American industry (Defense Science Board Report 1988).

In the prevailing ideology, perfect laissez-faire is presumed to be not only the first best but the only defensible goal. As even most orthodox economists will admit when pressed hard enough, it is neither. Because the United States has no criteria or taxonomy for sorting out second bests in a necessarily mixed world economy that can never attain pure free trade, this self-defeating pattern keeps recurring. It is the purpose of this chapter to help us understand and evaluate the available second bests. Contrary to the standard assumptions of free traders, the case for managed trade is not simply a set of special pleadings on behalf of retrograde industries; it also reflects a dissenting analysis of political economy, of the dynamics of trade, and of the interconnections between trade and geopolitics.

History

To understand the deep confusion in American thinking about trade, it is helpful to recall the remarkable period of the late 1940s when the present global trading regime was conceived. In the revisionist memory of the 1940s, the western nations under U.S. leadership set the postwar economy on its present course of economic liberalism, gradually dismantling wartime controls and looking toward ever freer movements of capital and goods. "The Bretton Woods conference, held in 1944," wrote influential economist Jagdish Bhagwati, "had designed an institutional infrastructure that embodied the principles of a liberal international order" (1988, p. 1).

But postwar reconstruction did nothing of the sort. The statesmen of the 1940s who devised the Bretton Woods regime, the IMF, the World Bank, the stillborn International Trade Organization (ITO), the GATT, and the first European common market in coal and steel were mindful of avoiding two extremes that had been burned into their consciousness by recent experience—the extreme instability of laissez-faire capitalism in the 1920s, and the destructive failure of global economic cooperation and retreat into currency blocs and autarky that followed in the 1930s—which together led to mass unemployment, popular revolt against liberal democratic rule, extreme nationalism, and world war.

Postwar reconstruction aimed at a compromise between the anarchy of laissez-faire capitalism and the autarky of state planning. This blend of opposite impulses often seemed contradictory. President Franklin Delano Roosevelt, early in his first term, called American representatives home from the world economic conference of 1933 (which aimed to restore a stable international monetary regime) because he had no intention of holding his domestic recovery policies hostage to the deflationary constraints of an international gold standard. Yet, a year later, his secretary of state, the free trader Cordell Hull, successfully promoted the Reciprocal Trade Agreements Act, which enshrined the principles of nondiscrimination and multilateral most favored nation (MFN) policy as American trade objectives. These of course took on new life after the war. The Roosevelt administration simultaneously sought freer trade and a freer hand in pursuing domestic stabilization policies unfettered by the constraints of global finance. This seeming contradiction required a new set of public multilateral institutions, which relieved the dependency on self-serving private banks and opened up fiscal space, allowing nations to resist the turbulence and inequity of pure laissez-faire at home.

In the aftermath of World War II, most of the western nations were governed by people who believed deeply in a mixed economy, in which the state assumed responsibility for full employment, trade unions were important counterweights to private capital, and a welfare state was an economic extension of political citizenship in a democratic society. The far right had been discredited by fascism; the far left was outside this consensus. Even the nationalist conservatives of the day—Charles de Gaulle, Winston Churchill, and the members of moderately conservative Christian Democratic movement of Konrad Adenauer, Robert Schuman, and Alcide de Gasperi—believed strongly in this brand of mixed economy.

Moreover, in the immediate postwar period, the issue of protectionism was largely moot. From the perspective of war-ravaged Europe, the question would have been: Protection of what? For the United States, the question would have been: Protection from what? With global undercapacity rather than overcapacity as the problem of the day, the politics of liberalization were easy. Rather than pressing its advantage to obliterate its competitors, the United States, as protector of the trading system, moved to reduce its own trade surplus from about 4.5 percent of GNP in 1947 to about 1 percent during the early 1950s (U.S. Council of Economic Advisors 1988, table B–96).

Taken as a whole, the initiatives of the 1944–49 period sought to restore international commerce, but within a framework that left substantial room for policies of social welfare and domestic economic reconstruction and stabilization. A bitter lesson of the interwar period was that a pure gold standard was deflationary; nations were constrained to balance their external accounts at the cost of economic contraction at home. In the nineteenth century this system more or less worked because the Bank of England played the role of flywheel by furnishing credit and anchoring a regime of fixed exchange rates based on the price of gold. In the interwar period, however, with nobody playing the role of central banker, the result was a beggar-thy-neighbor game of competitive deflation, which added up to worldwide depression. In response to depression, many countries cut loose from the world economy, or negotiated bilateral trade and monetary deals, which reduced the overall flow of commerce and added up to a drag on global economic growth. This did, however, provide room for relatively autarkic strategies of reflation and internal growth. These ranged from democratic in New Deal America and socialist Sweden, to authoritarian in Imperial Japan and Nazi Germany. The architects of the postwar system wanted to restore multilateral commerce, but with room for domestic stabilization. John Ruggie, in his classic essay on international regimes, summed up: "This was the essence of the [postwar] compromise: unlike the economic nationalism of the 1930s, it would be multilateral in character; unlike the liberalism of the gold standard and free trade, its multilateralism would be predicated upon domestic interventionism" (1983, p. 209).

As John Maynard Keynes and Harry Dexter White conceived the Bretton Woods arrangements, the central objective was to decouple domestic economic policy from the deflationary influence of a simple global gold standard, yet still maintain some discipline and encourage the restoration and expansion of world commerce. A related goal was to replace the traditional deflationary bias of external discipline with an expansionary one. Traditionally, a gold standard compelled debtor nations to contract, because shipments of gold overseas to balance accounts reduced the domestic supply of money and credit. In an open global economy yoked by a gold standard, the contraction imposed on debtor nations exported deflationary pressures to the entire system.

Under the proposed Bretton Woods arrangements, Keynes's alternative was to compel creditor nations to expand. Exchange rates were fixed; central banks were to intervene to help maintain those rates, which could be revised in extreme circumstances. New reserves were to be created through the IMF, and these reserves were to be advanced to correct short-term imbalances; exchange rates could be adjusted when imbalances proved chronic. The machinery invented at Bretton Woods included the IMF—Keynes wanted an overdraft facility with $25 billion to $30 billion in new liquidity—and the World Bank, which was to provide development capital. Both Keynes and White imagined that nations would cede a significant degree of sovereignty to these two institutions. These departures from the traditional world monetary system were radical both in their expansionary (Keynesian) bias and in their public character, since the power of private banks and national treasuries was substantially ceded to new supranational and public institutions.

In practice, however, neither the IMF nor the World Bank attained the influence anticipated, mainly because the United States was momentarily preeminent both economically and politically, and influential U.S. politicians saw no reason to cede that degree of economic sovereignty. Instead, under pressure of the emerging Cold War, the dollar rather than Keynes's imagined "bancor" became the de facto global currency, and the Marshall Plan rather than the World Bank became the principal engine of recovery. Keynes's "scarce currency clause," permitting member nations to discriminate against the exports of nations with chronic surpluses, was included, but it conflicted with free trade norms and never worked as envisioned. The proposed International Trade Organization, which was conceived as far broader than the GATT, was never ratified, for much the same reason. (The Havana Conference of 1948 was conceived as the "International Conference on Trade and Employment," and one of the notions was that liberal trade had to be subordinated to domestic full employment.) In the truncated GATT, which emerged as the locus of the trade regime by default, such ITO issues as antitrust, international investment, and of course full employment, were excluded; but the twin, somewhat contradictory goals of promoting multilateralist principles and expanded trade while also safeguarding domestic stabilization policies were maintained, though within a narrowed domain.

Though the GATT is popularly regarded as the citadel of free trade, paradoxically it was predicated on rather mercantilist assumptions. The pure free traders of mid-nineteenth-century Britain insisted that countries that practiced protectionism were only hurting themselves, and that reciprocal trade liberalization was both impolitic and unnecessary. Richard Cobden, the crusader for free trade, argued, "We should abolish Protection for our own selves, and leave other countries to take whatever course they liked" (in Bhagwati 1988, p. 29). For that reason, the initial British tariff reductions of the 1830s and 1840s were unilateral. Free trade of the Cordell Hull variety, which became the GATT norm, viewed tariff reductions as "concessions"—limitations on a nation's economic sovereignty—which required reciprocal concessions by trading partners. It presumed that nations started out as mercantilists, for which a reduction in a tariff meant giving something up. The GATT dealt with the world as it was; it realistically assumed a world of multiple barriers to liberal trade, which could be reduced only by mutual negotiation, since in practice nations preferred exports to imports. For a variety of reasons, mostly expedient rather than theoretical, much trade remained outside the GATT regime.

The global political economy that emerged after 1945 was thus in many respects contradictory and misleading. It was intended to be a necessary compromise between the one ideal of multilateral, free commerce among nations, and the other imperative of domestic interventionism. It was further complicated by the Cold War, which required further departures from liberal trade in the form of export controls and which seemed to require the United States, as hegemon, to tolerate substantial lapses in nations that were mercantilist but Cold War allies. In practice, despite the presumption that the domestic economics of John Maynard Keynes coexisted with the international economics of Adam Smith and David Ricardo, in reality capital controls and high tariffs provided substantial insulation against international free movement of goods and money as well. So did the fact that the new instruments of monetary governance were accountable to public rather than private agencies.

This, however, also involved a paradox. Nominally, a degree of authority had been conceded to supranational institutions. In practice, much of the political power in these institutions was tightly held by the then preeminent United States, which retained the voting power to control the IMF and the World Bank, as well as the political power to set agendas for other nominally supranational institutions. That Europe was also dependent on American military force to restrain an expansionist Soviet Union intensified the U.S. influence. So, although the postwar period was a uniquely successful era of multilateral institutions, in reality, as John Ruggie (1983) observed, the forms of multilateralism could flourish because they were extensions of the power of the United States.

One further paradox: though the global economic order devised in the 1940s was emphatically a mixed regime with Keynesian and social democratic stabilizers, rather than a classically liberal one, the nation that was the essential guarantor of the entire system, the United States, had the least appetite for departures from economic liberalism and the least enthusiasm for genuinely supranational authority. These twin concerns reinforced each other, for ceding sovereignty was not only objectionable per se to American nationalists at the very moment of American preeminence; it was doubly objectionable since it meant ceding power to a bunch of collectivists.

Thus the very departures from laissez-faire that helped anchor a mixed system were not entirely acknowledged by the system's prime sponsor. Conservative Americans accepted nominally transnational public institutions only because they were surrogates for American power. They accepted restrictions on the free flow of private capital as temporary leftovers from the war. They tolerated the Keynesian welfare states of Western Europe as suboptimal economic arrangements that had to be endured tactically for the sake of a common anticommunism. When laissez-faire again became fashionable and private capital again became mobile, it was in the United States that the resurgence of economic liberalism was greeted with particular glee.

Yet, as the ethic of laissez-faire capitalism has gained new ground in recent years at the expense of the social democratic/Keynesian ethic of a mixed economy, it has done so precisely in parallel with the decline in the influence of the United States. The United States is the most fervent booster of laissez-faire, yet its economic and political influence within the trading system has waned. So its effort to inject its own preferred norms into the policies of other nations, while retaining its cherished role as system leader, comes at escalating cost to America's own (poorly grasped) economic national interest.

As America becomes relatively less dominant economically, the cost of hegemony increases. This has been conventionally understood primarily in military terms, as the increasingly unsustainable cost of maintaining the American empire. The more serious and subtle costs have to do with the stresses between America's national economic interest and its hegemonic role in the trading system.

Hegemony and Ideology

The relationship between American geopolitical dominance, the norms of the trading system, and the American ideological devotion to liberal trade is central to the current American impasse on trade policy, and is not well appreciated. Charles Kindleberger's classic work on the 1930s, *The World in Depression* (1973), has spawned a whole genre of scholarly writing on what is now generally known as the theory of hegemonic stability (see Keohane 1984, Krasner 1983, and Gilpin 1987). According to this view, an international trading system with relatively liberal norms tends to be unstable in the absence of a dominant power, or hegemon.

The reason, according to Kindleberger, has to do with the essential anarchy of global capitalism and the destabilizing tendencies that result when national capitalisms freely compete without a set of rules that reconcile open commerce with monetary stability, trading norms, macroeconomic balance, and growth. The functions of the hegemonic nation include guaranteeing the peace, maintaining relatively open markets for imports (and encouraging other nations to do likewise), providing the dominant currency and surplus investment capital, and serving as lender of last resort. The hegemon therefore functions as the ballast of the global economy, giving it a quasi-Keynesian stability that would otherwise not operate at the level of the global economy where no general political authority and hence no macroeconomic policy functions. In Kindleberger's conception, the leadership of the hegemon must be relatively light-handed and benign. By definition, a Kindleberger-style hegemon has to believe in economic liberalism; otherwise membership in the hegemon's system is coerced on the basis of sheer military or economic power rather than invited on the basis of shared benefits.

To oversimplify, it is generally held that Britain played the role of hegemon in the nineteenth century in three respects: through the role the Bank of England played in anchoring the classical gold standard, freely buying and selling gold and manipulating domestic interest rates in order to maintain exchange rates and price stability; through Britain's willingness to provide generally open markets for other nations' exports; and through the Royal Navy's guarantee of freedom of the seas. A roughly similar hegemonic role has been played by the United States during the postwar era. In the interwar period, much of the instability resulted because no nation was both able and willing to play the hegemonic role, no supranational scheme functioned as an effective substitute, and the world economy degenerated into self-serving national polices that together destroyed the global economic order.

Much of the recent scholarship in this vein has assessed the dilemmas of the United States as "hegemon in decline." These dilemmas include the military costs of what Paul Kennedy (1986) called "imperial overstretch"; the inevitable failure of the dollar to maintain its role as provider of global liquidity without compromising its stability as a national currency (known as the Triffin dilemma)[1]; and the instability and unpredictability resulting from the monetary gyrations of the post–Bretton Woods floating exchange regime. Another symptom of hegemonic decline is the anomalous and ultimately unsustainable position of the United States as simultaneously economic hegemon and major debtor. Not only has the United States ceded relative influence to other nations, but nation-states generally have ceded influence to private market institutions, such as multinational corporations and banks, and have lost a degree of control over liquidity creation, as well as policy control over such issues as the Third World debt. The resurrection of laissez-faire ideology has welcomed the creation of relatively unregulated multinationals, while new technology has facilitated the worldwide dispersion of technology and private capital.

The political science literature on this dilemma (see Keohane 1984, Krasner 1983, and Gilpin 1987) has focused on such issues as whether the benefits of America's hegemonic role still outweigh the costs, and whether pluralist alternatives to a hegemonic regime are sustainable. What is briefly noted in this literature, but has received somewhat less attention, is the logical connection between the role of geopolitical hegemon and the norms of free trade. That connection is central to this discussion. The logic of hegemony requires that the hegemon be a devout free trader; otherwise other nations have far less reason to defer to the hegemon's leadership. Being a member in good standing of the U.S.-sponsored trading system brings with it the important perquisite of access to the U.S. domestic market. Moreover, it is logical for the hegemon to see the system that it sponsors as an extension of itself, and to subordinate the narrow nationalist goals that lesser nations pursue to systemwide goals. Free trade as an overriding virtue and desideratum thus becomes burned into the consciousness of the hegemon's governing elite.

Postwar America followed this pattern. While it was establishing itself as hegemon of the new trading system in the late 1940s, many of the "carrots" offered by the United States were economic. Given the overriding economic supremacy of the U.S. economy at the time, this offer seemed to be a relatively costless form of enlightened self-interest. The economic carrots included the Marshall Plan, other foreign aid, footing the lion's share of the bill for the Atlantic alliance and other regional alliances, paying a disproportionate share of the costs of multilateral organizations, making lopsided tariff concessions in the early GATT rounds, and providing dollars to create international liquidity through sustained U.S. balance-of-payments deficits.

More subtly, with respect to the trading system, American hegemony meant that the United States tolerated a good deal of free riding on the part of its geopolitical allies by keeping its own market open to the exports of trading partners whose economic practices were rather more mercantilistic than our own. It meant that in order to promote industrial recovery in Europe and Japan, and in order to reduce the enormous dollar surpluses of the early postwar era (which were dollar shortages overseas), the U.S. government encouraged American industry to set up production facilities overseas rather than export goods. All this seemed to serve the broader American foreign policy interest in a strong western political-economic system, by cementing the loyalties of trading partners to that system. It was assumed that America's national economic self-interest would take care of itself. But these hegemonic habits—providing open markets while tolerating mercantilism in allies; exporting capital rather than goods; seeing a laissez-faire system as necessarily identical to American national self-interest; placing geopolitical objectives ahead of geoeconomic ones—hardened into habits that were difficult to shake as the global economic realities changed.

The openness of the U.S. market and the free flow of capital and merchandise came to be two of the bedrock principles of American foreign economic policy, not just out of ideological conviction but because they were two key policy instruments that linked U.S. allies to the U.S. economic orbit during the first three postwar decades. They also seemed consistent with steady global economic growth. Given that membership in the U.S.-sponsored system was essentially voluntary rather than coerced, and given American commercial supremacy, the United States refrained from demanding full reciprocity in market access overseas and resisted wielding economic weapons lest it alienate key allies.

These habits, of course, have outlived the economic underpinnings of American hegemony. Though the United States is no longer as economically preeminent as it was in the immediate postwar period, its role of hegemon requires that it still provide the world's most open market. In fact, the weaker the U.S. economy becomes relative to its trading partners, the more desperately the United States clings to the hegemonic role, which provides a number of benefits useful to a hegemon in decline, including the unique ability to incur (and devalue) foreign debt in its own currency. The more the United States behaves as if it had the surplus economic wealth to function as hegemon—exporting private investment capital without regard to industrial consequences, incurring foreign debt, weakening its currency as a substitute for strengthening its underlying competitiveness, and tolerating free riding by its allies—the more it weakens its domestic economy.

Moreover, the hegemonic habits of the postwar era created a now deeply ingrained set of attitudes among American diplomats and economic officials. To be a member of the American foreign policy elite is to be a devout believer in free trade as an intrinsic good the logic of which is beyond question. To raise questions about the reality of free trade is to be suspect as an incipient mercantilist. The assumed virtue of a selfless double standard on liberal trade vis-à-vis American allies ("you mercantilist, me liberal"), which initially reflected a conception of U.S. self-interest that fit the economic and geopolitical realities of 1955, has hardened into a dogma that no longer fits the world balance of economic and financial power.

Fundamentally, the doctrine of free trade rests on the classical economic theory of comparative advantage, originally promulgated in the work of David

Ricardo in 1817 (see Ricardo 1951). This theory assumes that there are certain commodities that each nation can produce relatively more efficiently, given its natural resources, its labor force, and its technological capabilities. If all countries specialize in the commodities in which they have comparative advantages, exporting these goods and importing all others, an optimal allocation of world resources will result. The welfare of each individual country, as well as of the world as a whole, is maximized with perfectly free trade. It follows that any effort to protect a domestic industry necessarily involves a sacrifice of aggregate national welfare, although it is admitted that some classes within society (e.g., English landlords in Ricardo's time) may benefit at the expense of others.

The Ricardian approach to international trade originated as a liberal critique of aristocratic privilege in early nineteenth-century England, where the landed gentry wanted to protect English agriculture and the industrial capitalists wanted free trade. This doctrine served Britain well in the mid-nineteenth century, at the height of British hegemony. In America, however, the industrial interests were more protectionist from the beginning, as early American manufacturers realized that they could not initially compete with cheaper British imports (the famous infant-industry argument). Paradoxically, the United States industrialized largely behind tariff walls in the nineteenth and early twentieth centuries. When the United States achieved a dominant position in the world economy in the 1940s, the Ricardian doctrine of comparative advantage was invoked to justify this country's conversion to a free trade stance.

In reality, of course, free trade has coexisted with various forms of managed trade ever since the dawn of organized commerce. Yet in the American diplomatic corps today, as well as among economists with policy influence, what is found is an almost universal devotion to the theory of comparative advantage as both politically and scientifically essential. This view is taken to require not only that the United States reject industrial policies at home but also that it wink at them abroad. Just as Britain maintained free trade even with mercantilist trading partners in the late nineteenth century, so the United States clings to this position (at least in principle, if not in practice) at the end of the twentieth.

The free trade view has been internalized and treated as gospel by American diplomats precisely *because it is so congruent with the logic of American hegemony*. The idiom of free trade theory is one in which all departures from free trade are protectionist, opportunistic, politically motivated, and self-defeating. Protectionism, in this view, does not merely alienate the United States' friends and allies, but also sacrifices economic efficiency, harms domestic consumers, and causes the protected industries to stagnate.

Moreover, the rhetoric of free trade is littered with misleading metaphors. It is said, after an aphorism first attributed to the nineteenth-century French philosopher Frédéric Bastiat, that even if other nations are stupid enough to "throw rocks into their harbors" (apparently meaning barricading themselves against commerce), this does not mean we should do likewise (paraphrased in Krugman and Obstfeld 1988, p. 258). But what if other nations dredge their harbors and build port facilities, the better to export? It is also said that free trade is "like a bicycle"—you have to keep pedaling ever faster or you tip over. Whoever thinks that is true never rode a bicycle!

Good free traders are supposed to be constantly vigilant against "backsliding." They must persuade trading partners (who are even more subject to protectionist pressures than is the United States) to strive for free trade, by constantly setting a good example. Protectionist pressures are seen by free traders as an unfortunate and shortsighted result of misguided macroeconomic policies, never as the result of structural imbalances or other nations' mercantilism. For example, the "Statement on Trade Policy" issued by thirty-eight prominent economists on April 10, 1989, warns that U.S. trade policy is "at a perilous turning point," that sector-by-sector managed trade targets are in the offing, and that the real sources of the U.S. trade imbalance that need to be addressed are the budget deficit and inadequate rates of savings and investment. This view is arrived at deductively, from the premise that trade policies ultimately do not matter because by definition they cannot matter.

In fact, U.S. rates of (gross) investment during the 1980s have been at about historic norms. The national savings rate has declined during the 1980s, primarily because the public deficit has consumed private savings and also because the personal saving rate has fallen. The gap has been made up by borrowing from abroad and by net sales of U.S. assets. However, if other nations are pursuing sectoral and trade policies that capture advantage for their own industries at the expense of U.S. industries, it is entirely possible that the United States suffers both from macroeconomic imbalance and from imbalance in the trading system.

Moreover, the cause-and-effect relationship in the way macroeconomic and trade measures are used to ameliorate the current imbalances can run in either direction. Macroeconomic shifts (smaller public deficit, higher domestic savings, lower interest rates, cheaper dollar) can indeed produce benefits for the trade balance. But an improvement in the competitive position of U.S. industry (whether for structural reasons or as a result of different trade policies) can also produce macroeconomic benefits (more U.S. exports, more jobs, higher growth, higher incomes, more private savings and tax revenue, higher profits and more investment, lower real interest rates, external balance with a stronger currency) at a lower cost to American well-being. The strategy of cheapening the dollar has produced only modest trade benefits but has put U.S. assets on sale and has generated inflationary pressures.

In the orthodox view, any form of national economic planning is seen as a departure from the free market's chosen allocation of capital, and is hence both an inefficient economic distortion and a political threat to the logic of the GATT. As the eight rounds of multilateral negotiation have progressed, American support for purer and purer laissez-faire has grown more intense. By the Kennedy

Round of trade liberalization, most tariffs had been lowered to relatively moderate levels. By the Tokyo Round (1973–79), the United States had begun pursuing "nontariff barriers" (NTBs), such as government subsidies, technical standards, and preferential procurement. Although the Tokyo Round did produce a minimalist subsidies code, it did not produce clear criteria on what was a "trade-distorting subsidy," nor a remedy other than the traditional right to countervail. Since the 1970s, free traders have lamented that as tariff barriers have fallen, nontariff interventionism has increased, in the form of national industrial policies abroad—subsidies, market closings, recession cartels, preferential capital allocation schemes—as well as subterfuges such as orderly marketing agreements and VERs demanded of trading partners by the United States.

In the Uruguay Round, the United States proposed a grandiose series of objectives intended to extirpate NTBs; to strengthen the dispute settlement machinery of the GATT; and to bring the GATT norms of liberal trade to areas currently outside the GATT, such as trade in services and agriculture. The administration convinced itself that a natural U.S. comparative advantage in a garbage-can category called services (which includes repatriation of profits from sunk investments as well as banking, insurance, and construction) might offset the escalating trade deficit in visible exports. Politically, the Reagan administration sought to build a constituency for trade liberalization and a counterweight for the forces of "protection" by organizing those segments of American capital with a self-interest in liberalized markets, most notably multinational corporations, financial service businesses, and industries looking toward expanded opportunities for export and/or direct foreign investment.

Concurrent with this intensified rush toward ever freer trade was a series of halting and rather guilt-ridden measures undertaken by the free market Reagan administration that were, by its own definition, protectionist. Agricultural legislation gave the administration enhanced ability to subsidize farm exports. The 1986 semiconductor agreement with Japan, after a series of failed earlier agreements, resorted to a market-share target for U.S. exports to Japan (which has not been reached), as well as a domestic industrial policy to maintain U.S. competitiveness in chips. After the failed efforts of previous administrations to stabilize the steel industry, the Reagan administration imposed quantitative restraints—VERs—on steel imports. Textiles continued to be subject to a managed trade regime, under the Multi-Fiber Arrangement (MFA). The VER on automobiles with Japan was continued. Despite its railing against bilateral trading blocs as an affront to the fundamental multilateral logic of the GATT, the Reagan administration pointedly negotiated bilateral free trade agreements with Israel and Canada, as well as a regional Caribbean basin trade pact, while promoting initiatives that eventually led to the North American Free Trade Agreement (NAFTA) with Mexico and Canada.

The administration was never clear, either with itself or with its allies, about which of these measures were temporary adjustment expedients, which were merely tactical maneuvers intended to be bargained away for reciprocal liberal-izations, which were adjuncts of domestic industrial policies, which were craven capitulations to domestic pressure groups, and which were necessary long-term regimes in industries that simply don't lend themselves to comparative advan-tage trade. As this creeping protectionism burgeoned, the administration, like an intermittent alcoholic, intensified its crusade to persuade its trading partners to abandon all forms of mercantilism in one grand pledge of mutual temperance.

Viewed casually, these opposite thrusts seem hypocritical if not incoherent. Understood in terms of the logic of the hegemonic role, they make a certain amount of sense. Quotas are an instructive case in point. As neoclassical econo-mists constantly point out, an allocated quota is probably the most inefficient form of protection. It gives the foreign exporting nation the power to rig the market—and if that nation is a mercantilist country like Japan, this is a formida-ble power indeed. It raises prices for a country's own consumers, while deliver-ing the quota rents to the trading partner. Unless it is coupled with a careful domestic program to restructure the protected industry (which is ideologically anathema to conservatives), the domestic industry is very likely to take a free ride on the import restraint, raising its own prices but not its productivity. If the quota is a quantity of units rather than a sum of dollars, the quota also encour-ages the exporting nation to move upscale and capture a richer segment of the protected market.

Economists urge that, if a spell of protection is necessary, tariffs (which are at least transparent and marketlike) are always preferable to quotas; and that, if quotas must be resorted to, they should be auctioned—so that the low-cost for-eign producer gets them, while the United States captures the quota rents. This is all clear enough and the logic is seemingly irrefutable. Why, then, would a nation devoted to a free trade system and to free market principles resort to, of all things, allocated quotas? The answer, once again, lies in the logic of geopolit-ical hegemony.

As a form of protection, a multilateral tariff or an auctioned quota leaves a nation with nothing to selectively bestow on its friends; but an allocated quota is a form of geopolitical currency, because it is discretionary. Whenever the United States departs from the principle of multilateral MFN, its stated norm for the trading system, the United States as hegemon prefers departures that provide some bargaining counters. This has been the case with oil, where import quotas were bargained and allocated; with steel; with textiles; and with farm products. If steel quotas were auctioned rather than allocated, this would enrage the country's high-cost producer friends, which include debtor nations like Brazil. Allocating import quotas is a long-standing hegemonic habit. When Fidel Castro became an intolerable thorn in the side of the United States, what did the United States withdraw? Cuba's sugar *quota*. Moreover, a quota disguised as a "voluntary" restraint on the part of the exporting nation also complies with the letter of the GATT, even though it is in reality an overt form of bilateralism as well as a departure from free trade that fools no one. Yet the hegemonic nation, because of its systemic responsibilities, cannot be in the position of breaking the rules. In each of these instances, a political objective drowns out competing economic objectives and makes the United States appear foolish and disingenuous.

The National Interest

Much of the debate about free trade, managed trade, industrial policy, and so forth, is confused by implied conceptions of the "national interest." From the perspective of traditional economic liberalism, questions of national interest are limited to narrow military and geopolitical security. There is also a supposed abstract and generalized "consumer" interest in free trade, which is treated in isolation from the influence of trade on domestic productive employment. To the extent that an open trading system wins friends for the United States, liberal trade complements traditional national security goals. In this conception, there is no room for an economic national interest defined in terms of industrial objectives, nor are there geopolitical economic goals beyond those that supposedly flow naturally from free markets. By definition, the freest possible market yields results that are "natural" and hence optimal. Even if other trading nations violate those norms, the United States still allegedly gains both economic and geopolitical advantage by practicing liberal trade. The possibility of a national interest colliding with free trade norms is thus neatly excluded by definition.

This perspective, however, begs several questions. In practice, it is possible to identify several concrete goals for the U.S. economy, which do not necessarily result from a conventional free trade environment—particularly when that environment is lopsided. These goals include full employment at decent wages, rapid productivity growth, rising levels of real income distributed equitably, retention of technological leadership in a broad spectrum of major industries, and maintenance of a skilled workforce.

While it is conventional to argue that "we" must do this or that for the economy to thrive, it is not always clear who "we" refers to. For example, the interests of American-based banks and multinational corporations (MNCs), which are key advocates of liberal trade, are not always identical to the goals of high and rising living standards for American citizens and the maintenance of technological leadership within the United States. The relative merits of different approaches to trade policy need to be weighed against true national objectives (rather than narrow corporate ones); they also need to be assessed in the context of other U.S. foreign policy objectives, with which trade objectives sometimes compete.

The New View

Interestingly enough, American policy has embraced a purer and purer devotion to free trade principles at precisely a moment when some orthodox economists are having serious second thoughts about whether the traditional theory of comparative advantage is reliable, either as a description of how trade really works or as a norm for optimal policy. The new view has emerged in the work of Paul Krugman, an economics professor formerly at the Massachusetts Institute of Technology and now at Stanford University, and in related work by Avinash Dixit, James Brander, Barbara Spencer, and numerous others.[2]

In order to understand the significance of the new view, it is important to recall some of the implications of the old view. According to the old view, countries have inherent comparative advantages in particular products due to some intrinsic national characteristics. In the original formulation of comparative advantage theory, Ricardo assumed that international differences in resources and technology would give each country a comparative advantage in certain goods that it could produce with relatively lower labor costs. Later, the Swedish economists Eli Heckscher (1919) and Bertil Ohlin (1933) argued that comparative advantages were due to differences in "factor proportions": the relative abundance of land, labor, and capital in each country, compared with the relative intensities with which these factors are used in producing various commodities. As formalized by Paul Samuelson in 1949 (see Samuelson 1987), this theory required the assumptions of identical technology in all countries as well as perfect competition in all markets. Under these and other, more technical, conditions, each country will export those goods which incorporate relatively more of its relatively abundant factor or factors.

Whether in the traditional Ricardian view or the more modern Heckscher-Ohlin-Samuelson (HOS) variant, the old view had the powerful implication that *there is a naturally ordained pattern of trade.* The location of industries is not arbitrary: with free trade, industries will automatically be located where they can be most efficiently operated. There are some subtle differences between the two variants. The Ricardian emphasis on different technological capabilities of nations implicitly admits that social institutions and public policies can potentially affect a nation's "inherent" comparative advantages. The HOS view, on the other hand, implies a more extreme bias against intervention, since this theory holds technology constant and assumes that only natural and immutable "endowments" of productive factors matter to trade. Both theories imply that there is a unique allocation of industries among countries that is economically efficient at any point in time, and that this allocation can be achieved only through free trade.

The new view rejects this conclusion of the old view. The new view asserts that the location of manufacturing production in the world is not a reflection of any inherent comparative advantages in the traditionally understood sense but is essentially the result of historical accidents. The indeterminacy of industrial location reflects several characteristics of the advanced global economy. These include increasing returns to scale and the ability of firms to "slide down the learning curve." In essence, innovators compete on the basis of entrepreneurial and technological prowess rather than factor endowments. Technological leadership can sometimes flow from such arguably "natural" endowments as a skilled labor force (which itself reflects the policy influence of education and training interventions), but it can also be the deliberate result or fortuitous by-product of a more explicit national policy to promote technology.

The significance of the new view is borne out by, among other indicators, the large amount of intra-industry trade, in which trading partners both export and import similar products—a phenomenon that is not predicted by the standard theory of specialization based on comparative advantage. As Klaus Stegemann has observed in studying intra-industry specialization in the context of European integration,

> Which country makes which products within any manufacturing industry . . . cannot be explained exclusively on the basis of differences in natural ability or factor proportions. Variables such as entrepreneurial initiative, investment in human capital, research and development, product design, economies of scale, and learning by doing were recognized to be crucial for the expansion of intra-industry trade. (1989, pp. 75–76)

These, in turn, are subject to policy intervention. Such intervention, if it leads to technological breakthroughs, may even produce positive-sum benefits.

A somewhat narrower strand of the new view holds that much international trade can be understood as a form of imperfect competition, in which some producers enjoy supernormal profits, or "rents." Contrary to standard theory, such rents are not instantly competed away but persist as innovators enjoy an array of niche positions. Given that these rents are widespread, a nation that captures them gains an advantage over its competitors, both in the form of profits and in the continuation of technological dominance. Particular trade policies (tariffs, subsidies, export taxes, etc.) can, under certain circumstances, be shown to raise national income by extracting more of these rents at the expense of foreigners. The deliberate use of such instruments is referred to as "strategic trade policy." These insights embellish an older literature on imperfect competition in international trade, dating back to the early 1900s. However, it is not necessary to demonstrate the presence of oligopolistic rents in order to show that the capture of leading industries can produce beneficial externalities, or that the location of industries may be historically contingent. These points are logically separate.

If the location of production, especially in advanced industries, is fundamentally arbitrary, then it is arguably subject to manipulation by national policy interventions, whether microeconomic policies aimed at capturing positions in emerging industries, human capital policies aimed at improving the quality of the workforce, or macroeconomic policies intended to influence savings rates, capital costs, and so on. However, the more orthodox version of the new view, while it has blown a big hole in the traditional theory of comparative advantage, has stopped well short of advocating industrial policies for two reasons, one ideological and the other technical.

First, ideologically, most orthodox economists remain sufficiently steadfast neoclassicists to harbor grave doubts about the competence of collective action, particularly on the part of politicians who are responsive to interest groups, to undertake economically optimal policies that could improve on decisions of the market. This enterprise is deemed particularly perilous for the United States, whose political system is said to be uniquely vulnerable to special interest groups. ("The trouble with picking winners," Senator William Roth [1989] declared, "is that each Congressman would want one for his District.") Second, the technical economics demonstrating the possibility of welfare-enhancing strategic trade policy are dependent on the assumptions of the particular model. Changing an assumption can change whether a particular policy instrument (e.g., tariff or subsidy) ought to be used. Since there are potentially grave informational difficulties in knowing which model can be applied to any given industry, it may be safer to do nothing than to risk using the wrong instrument.

Typical new view papers, especially those written by economists who wish to keep their neoclassical union cards, take care to include the disclaimer that even if profit shifting or interventions aimed at generating positive externalities are possible in theory, they are implausible in practice. According to Krugman, most economists who subscribe to the new view are very uneasy about giving aid and comfort to mercantilists. Krugman concluded a rueful essay entitled "Is Free Trade Passé?" by threading his way between contradictory positions: "To abandon the free trade principle in pursuit of the gains from sophisticated intervention could . . . open the door to adverse political consequences that would outweigh the potential gains. It is possible, then, both to believe that comparative advantage is an incomplete model of trade and to believe that free trade is the right policy" (1987, p. 143).

Nonetheless, the new view radically alters the context of debate, for it removes the premise that nations such as Japan that practice strategic trade could not, by definition, be improving their welfare. It means that orthodox economists now concede that advocates of industrial policy are not, by definition, economic illiterates. And it invites a far more subtle policy debate on the instruments and the purposes of departures from free trade, which is no longer optimal by definition, after all.

Toward a Mixed System

Let me recapitulate the argument thus far and summarize why I am uneasy with pure free trade either as a description of a systemic norm or as a strategy that serves the interest of the United States and the world. Trade theory now holds that the location of production in manufactures is not necessarily dictated by inherent comparative advantages. In an imperfect world, national policies can and do capture or create advantages. Substantial trade in which cheap labor, climate, or the presence of natural resources significantly affects relative production costs still proceeds along Ricardian lines. But semiconductors, for example, can and will be produced most efficiently wherever the best technology has been developed and applied. This is not only true for high-tech products; German firms have successfully applied advanced production technology to the textile industry, and they remain competitive in global markets on the basis of efficient capital rather than cheap labor.

⌐Politically, the United States has pursued free trade, not because it is necessarily economically optimal either for the United States or for the world economy (though, as mentioned above, U.S. politicians have convinced themselves that it is) but because liberal trade is a logical imperative for a nation that cares to play the role of hegemon. This made sense in the early postwar period, when, as the leading nation, the United States gained from free trade because its industry was dominant and its products were superior. But America's system goals as hegemon and its national goals as an economy are no longer identical. In order to maintain its hegemonic role, the United States has tolerated asymmetries in the trading system and has contorted its domestic responses to the pressures of trade, in a fashion that has done serious harm to the U.S. domestic economy, as well as to the sustainability of the global trading system.⌐

Laissez-faire fails, either as an empirical description of what is or as a normative ideal for what should be, on several grounds. Contrary to classical economics, economies are not self-regulating. History shows that purely private economic forces, left to their own devices, wreak social havoc, distributive injustice, and economic instability, which in turn produce political consequences that are far worse than a preventive dose of economic management. It is not even clear that free markets "optimize" outcomes in the narrow sense of allocative efficiency.

However, to acknowledge that laissez-faire is a false lodestar, and that the costs of a hegemonic role have become economically unsustainable for the United States, is not to know precisely what a mixed system ought to look like. It is tricky enough to design a mixed system within national borders, where sovereignty is a settled question. A mixed system is far more difficult to fashion across national frontiers, in a realm where political sovereignty is widely dispersed. Clearly, a mixed system is far messier than a system of perfectly free trade—though the fairer comparison is with the existing system, which is also highly messy. Even if an ideal system could be designed to regulate a global mixed economy, there remains the political problem of negotiating the way from here to there.

In the U.S. trade debate, there has been a remarkable confusion of ends with means, and of goals with tactics. Advocates of tactical hardball aimed at opening closed markets overseas find themselves accused, incredibly, of sabotaging "free trade"—as if enforcing fair play among all trading partners were a betrayal of the principle. Thus, in discussing managed alternatives to free trade, it is necessary to clarify when these are merely tactical responses to other nations' refusal to honor free trade norms, as the "Super-301" provision of the 1988 Trade Act is held to be, versus economic development initiatives that make sense in their own terms. Because of the widespread support among American conservatives for laissez-faire, domestically as well as globally, departures from free trade are usually defended only in tactical terms, and seldom as necessary measures of domestic industrial development.

The presumption of this chapter is that departures from free trade policies in most countries are seldom merely tactical. Moreover, there are sectors in which managed trade makes sense, first, for the sake of stabilization and to enhance productive innovation, and, second, in order to get nations to operate according to rules that are at least universal and reciprocal. The United States should not manage trade in, say, semiconductors, merely as a lever to win concessions that move the entire system toward freer semiconductor trade. For the moment, retaining and restoring U.S. capacity in that crucial sector takes priority over "liberalization" of markets as a trade system goal, especially if the country's major trading partners insist that they wish to develop and maintain their own semiconductor capacity. It is not helpful to disguise that goal as merely a tactic aimed to make Japan "play fair" and open its market—to products that the United States may no longer make, thanks to earlier Japanese mercantilism.

On the other hand, in certain industries and at certain moments, nations may conclude that the sum total of interventionist subsidies and other market manipulations is imposing total costs that exceed benefits, and may wish to negotiate reciprocal limits on such subsidies and greater mutual market access. Agriculture—in which trade does take place more nearly according to comparative advantages—is a case in point. It is also necessary to be clear about whether allowing room for industrial policy and complementary managed trade is to be understood as a unilateral attempt to capture advantage at the expense of other nations, or whether managed trade can have positive-sum benefits for the system as a whole in the form of technological innovation, stabilization, and diffusion of productive wealth. To the extent that the United States wishes to remain an influential and well-behaved citizen of the trading system (though perhaps not its hegemon), it does not wish to revert to Japan-like unilateralism. Therefore, let us briefly consider three examples of managed trade, their costs and benefits, and the rationales for their pursuit.

Market Allocation in a Growing Industry: The MFA

The Multi-Fiber Arrangement (MFA) provides a good contemporary example of a reasonably successful managed trade regime. This regime sought to regulate trade in natural fibers and apparel, and subsequently synthetics as well, not by allocating rigid quotas per se, but by limiting the rate of growth of imports and engaging in bargaining about shares of that increase. While the growth of imports was supposed to be held to an annual rate of 6 percent, the actual growth rate reached 17 percent in the 1980s. Under this flexible form of protection, the rate of inflation in textiles and apparel lagged the general inflation rate by 7.8 percent during the MFA's first decade, and by 27.5 percent during its second. Productivity gains in textiles were the second greatest of any U.S. industry; only microelectronics had greater gains (Cline 1987, p. 46).

Textiles and apparel are a case in which the doctrine of comparative advantage would argue that the wealthier producer nations in Europe and North America should have simply "let go." Moreover, unlike, say, semiconductors, it is not self-evident that textiles and apparel are key industries with important linkages or broader dynamic technological benefits that would justify a departure from free trade on either national security or "learning-curve" grounds. In addition, textiles (and more precisely apparel) are seen as examples of labor-intensive, relatively low-technology industries that give newly industrializing nations important experience in the organization of production and entrepreneurship for world markets. Therefore, the presumptive case against managed trade in textiles and apparel is strong indeed.

The systemic, as opposed to the self-interested, arguments in favor of the MFA boil down to two: First, although protection is popularly held to result in stagnation and excessive wage levels in the protected industry, in fact productivity growth in American and European textile production has been about double the industrial average. Textile products may be low-tech, but the textile *production process* can be high-tech. Wages in textiles have remained among the lowest of all manufacturing wages, although this is more true in the United States than in Europe because the United States has lower minimum wages and generally tolerates much greater wage dispersion.

Domestic producers responded by automating because the MFA regime struck a good balance between providing a partially protected market (which made it rational to invest) and allowing some import penetration (which maintained competitive pressure to invest). The import growth occurred both via the MFA and through various leakages, including the proliferation of substitute materials not initially covered by the MFA, and the entry of new producer nations not party to the MFA. In effect, domestic producers were able to calculate that they remained under pressure from imports but were not at risk of being obliterated by them. This climate dictated a strategy of investing in productivity-enhancing automation.

Second, there is more than a little evidence that many of the new producing nations were not entirely unhappy with the MFA, because it offered predictability in an otherwise chronically unstable market. It gave their producers some ability to forecast market share and hence needed capacity, and therefore some basis for making costly investments. It would also be hard to argue that the MFA has seriously impeded enterprise, since Third World textile and apparel production are hotbeds of entrepreneurship. In this sense, though it is a regime that "regulates" markets, the MFA stops well short of "cartelization." There is widespread competition, and much of it is price competition. Despite a good deal of spuriously precise calculation by neoclassical economists of the cost of textile protection to American consumers[3]—William Cline (1987) puts it at exactly $135,000 per job—and of the markets lost to Third World producers, it is all but impossible to predict what would have ensued in the absence of the MFA or something like it.

It is reasonable to argue that a free trade regime in textiles and apparel is improbable, and that the MFA regime has brought benefits in the form of relative price and earnings stability and hence greater productivity-enhancing capital investment. This conclusion of course does not tell us whether the present MFA is more or less "fair" or economically "efficient" than some other theoretically possible system. What it does suggest is that regimes such as the MFA take into account a factor that is often left out of conventional static economic analysis, namely time. Substantial shifting of the world's textile and apparel production to lower-wage developing countries has indeed occurred under the auspices of the MFA, but it has occurred at a sufficiently slow rate to permit industrialized nations to retain a share of world textile production and to invest in advanced production technology (which itself is soon diffused to the Third World).

National Subsidy, Cartels, and Glut: The Case of Steel

Depending on the choice of lenses, the steel industry can be seen either as a case of a bungled managed trade regime or as an industry that cries out for more managed trade. Rightly or wrongly, most of the world's major nations (and many minor ones, too) have decided that a domestic steel industry provides positive externalities. These may include everything from import substitution benefits, to the prospect of sliding down the learning curve in advanced metallurgy, to capturing "labor rents" (high-wage jobs), to the status benefits of having one's own steel mills. If completely free markets left to their own devices produce excess capacity, falling profits, competitive overproduction, and a pressure for cartelization, unorganized nation-by-nation mercantilism produces an even more extreme case of the same. What is important to realize is that the present trade regime in steel, such as it is, is the cumulative result of individual national mercantilist strategies, and not a deliberate global system.

As recently as 1975, world steel production and consumption were roughly in balance. In the 1970s, new industrial powers such as Japan, South Korea, and Brazil made massive investments in steel capacity. Established steel-producing nations in Western Europe defensively invested in the modernization of their plants, in order to meet the competition of the more productive newer entrants. Virtually all this new steel capacity, with the exception of that in the United States, Canada, and West Germany, was the result of national market-distorting subsidy programs, which included cheap loans, grants, wage subsidies, import restraints, recession cartels, and every other known form of mercantilism. Just about the time that some 40 million metric tons of new capacity were coming on line, the twin oil price shocks of the 1970s and the recessions of 1975 and 1980–82 sharply reduced the demand for steel. By the early 1980s, worldwide capacity was nearly double worldwide output (Howell, Noellert, Kreier, and Wolff 1988, p. 51).

Within Western Europe, which has had a common market regime in steel since 1952, the European Community (EC) pursued a common program of plant modernization, rationalization, and politically negotiated closings of outmoded facilities, attempting to spread around the painful costs of making the industry more efficient and reducing capacity. However, this politically allocated sharing of the burden meant that while EC steelmaking grew generally more productive, the industry did not necessarily migrate to the most efficient producers within Europe. The EC also used price controls, allocation of market shares, and import controls. Between 1980 and 1985, steel subsidies in the EC exceeded $35 billion (Howell et al. 1988). The immense subsidy also left the industry in an artificially competitive position, since capital costs that had to be amortized by U.S. producers playing by market rules were often written off in advance, embedding subsidy in ostensible European production costs for years to come.

Most other steelmaking nations, such as Japan, Korea, and Brazil, solved the problem of worldwide excess capacity simply by excluding imports and regulating their domestic prices. The flip side of this story of domestic overcapacity and cartelization is a tremendous pressure to dump excess production, since the per-unit cost of steel falls sharply when capacity is more fully utilized. Unlike textiles, steel production has important economies of scale, while steel demand is price-inelastic. If one producer lowers its price, that mainly shifts market shares rather than increasing the overall demand for steel. Steel, unlike textiles, involves extremely expensive and long-lived plant and equipment. As a result, the market for steel is slow to equilibrate shifts in supply and demand—that old devil time, again—and it adjusts even more slowly when governments contribute subsidies. (Purists might reflect on the fact that U.S. investment tax credits, pension bailouts, bankruptcy reorganizations with payoffs at so many cents on the dollar, and even employee stock ownership plans [ESOPs] and worker retraining schemes are also subsidies, however nonstrategically they may be deployed.)

In the 1970s and 1980s, the only major steelmaking nation substantially open to imports was, of course, the United States. This position was perfectly consistent with the hegemonic imperative to confer the benefits of open import markets on your trading partners, however mercantilist their own practices. It also comported with the prevailing American ideology of free trade. In the accounts of the growing uncompetitive position of American steel, what got the attention of economists and editorial writers was the relatively high wages paid to steelworkers and the poor capital investment decisions of American managers. The reality of foreign mercantilism and the risks of losing an industry as basic as steel were seen as minor details. Most editorialists accepted the old view of orthodox trade theory—that if foreign nations were dumb enough to subsidize their shipments to us, we should gratefully accept the gift, regardless of the long-term consequences and costs. (The Trojan horse is not a metaphor known to free trade enthusiasts.)

Moreover, the remedy sanctioned by both GATT law and domestic trade law—antidumping suits—tends to make American administrations very uneasy since it leads to actions perceived as unfriendly but directed against geopolitical allies. This is another aspect of the burdens of hegemony (uneasy is the head that wears the hegemonic crown). If membership in the U.S.-sponsored GATT system is cajoled rather than coerced, then American administrations will go to great lengths to avoid resorting to remedies that engender intra-alliance conflict. The EC, abjuring both hegemonic perquisites and responsibilities, is far more willing to let antidumping complaints go the route.

Constrained by its geopolitical objectives, the United States embarked on a series of halfhearted measures attempting to reconcile a degree of import restraint with marketlike principles and respect for the formal norms of the GATT. The first of these was the ill-starred trigger price mechanism of the Carter administration, which regulated imports according to a pricing formula supposedly based on the unsubsidized Japanese cost of production. This, however, let European steelmakers dump steel at the Japanese price, which was below European costs; created a glut on U.S. markets; and failed to slow the accelerating rate of import penetration. Eventually, after several false starts, it fell to the free market Reagan administration to impose a quota regime, characteristically disguised as VERs. Giving up the hegemonic concession of totally open access to the U.S. market, the U.S. government nonetheless retained something of diplomatic value: the ability to allocate quota shares.

VERs have worked rather well in steel, in spite of the quota rents lost to foreign producers. Prodded by Congress, the administration insisted that the profits earned from the protection of domestic steel production must go into steel modernization. The domestic industry, after being underpriced for a decade by subsidized foreign steel, turned profitable in 1987 and became even more profitable in 1988. Steel capacity was reduced from about 144 million metric tons in 1977 to about 73 million metric tons in 1987 (Howell et al. 1988, p. 496). The remaining capacity is now among the world's most productive. At current exchange rates, America can produce cheaper steel than Japan. Yet, characteristically, this managed-trade-regime-cum-minimalist-industrial-policy was widely depicted not as something economically sensible in its own right, nor even as a necessary adjustment to the cartelization of the world steel industry, but as a scandalous and GATT-defying capitulation to a domestic special interest group.

The implicit industrial goal in the advocacy of unilateral free trade in steel is the ultimate disappearance of much of America's steel industry. The missing policy debate here is not so much free trade versus managed trade (since managed trade is what most of the world has) as whether or not the United States should maintain and develop the capacity to make basic steel at state-of-the-art productivity. Why, if other nations almost unanimously have chosen to operate mercantilist policies for steel, should it fall to the United States to purify the world and to begin by giving up much of its own steel industry? Why should the United States expend scarce diplomatic capital—and in this case real capital as well—to sell laissez-faire steelmaking to a skeptical world?

The problem with the current regime for steel is that, unlike the MFA, it is not really a regime at all. Most countries subsidize, protect, and dump the excess where they can, with no common set of norms or rules. Logically, if most nations wish to retain domestic steelmaking capacity, one possible regime would require all participants to concede a share of their domestic markets to open import competition, and to agree to a common program for the gradual reduction of levels of subsidy and excess capacity. If the import penetration level were set at, say, 25 percent, those quotas could be auctioned by the importing nation, and the quota receipts could be used to subsidize a program of capacity phase-out and worker retraining. A worldwide goal might be to restore steel capacity to its historic level of about 125 percent of average production.

In order to have access to the available (unprotected) domestic import markets of member nations, all such participating nations would have to agree to the common program of 25 percent market opening and the gradual phase-out of subsidies and excess capacity. This program, of course, would not be "free trade," but it would be a far more viable, efficient, and balanced system than the current one. It would also reflect what seems to be the clear preference of most major trading nations—near self-sufficiency in steel—and would give major nations the ability to pursue variations in their domestic strategies for steel. It would relieve the United States of its current Atlas-like burden, of attempting to shoulder the entire burden of the world's gap between stated ideology and reality in steel.

The steel case suggests one problem with the way that most Americans view the trading system. We believe in our hegemonic soul that agreeing to a stated set of norms that falls short of pure free trade is simply sinful. Paradoxically, the proposed regime in steel, though a form of managed trade, would be substantially more marketlike than the present one. Presumably it would leave plenty of room for domestic competition, as long as a given nation chose to enforce its antitrust laws. Moreover, it would benefit the U.S. industry, since this country is the only major industrial nation that is now a net importer of steel. American steel mills are now among the world's most productive, and we could presumably compete for a share of newly opened foreign markets. The facts that advanced production technology is portable and that most trade does not reflect pure comparative advantage mean that allocative efficiency does not in truth require all nations to import their steel from the "most efficient nation"; what may matter more is that nations keep their seats at the steelmakers' table.

Bargaining Chips: The Case of Semiconductors

The semiconductor industry offers yet another case—a dynamic industry with a rapidly evolving technology and only a few producer nations. It also suggests some important lessons about the relationship between the issues of free trade versus managed trade and bilateralism versus multilateralism. Compare the problems of the bilateral U.S.-Japan semiconductor accord with some hypothetical multilateral semiconductor arrangement. U.S. semiconductor manufacturers complained that Japanese semiconductor firms were simply playing by different rules. The Japanese goals were long-term growth, technological supremacy, and a gradual increase in the market share. Although there was not much identifiable government subsidy in the traditional sense, this was clearly a coordinated strategy between government and industry. The fact that Japanese electronics and semiconductor manufacturers are largely integrated gave Japanese firms market power not available to their U.S. competitors. U.S. firms argued that Japan was dumping—selling below cost—both in the United States and in third markets. But dumping is another of those economic phenomena that requires the injection of a time factor. Looked at over a twenty-year time horizon, the Japanese semiconductor strategy was profitable. Japan might be selling below its cost this month or this year, but over time as market share and technological prowess increased, the overall strategy was profitable indeed.

When earlier approaches failed, and the U.S. semiconductor industry suffered to the point where militarily defined national security concerns emerged, the United States at last put aside its ideological qualms about managed trade and negotiated a quasi cartelization of semiconductor trade. The Japanese pledged to cease selling below cost in the United States and third markets, and promised to set a 20 percent market-share target for U.S. semiconductor exports to Japan. While Japan did stop dumping steel in the United States, it continued to dump in third markets until threatened with sanctions in 1987, and it never kept its promise of buying U.S. semiconductors. In the summer of 1989, the United States and Japan announced yet another agreement to fulfill previously broken promises.

In any event, this attempted regime was also a clear violation of the GATT. Europe, the world's number three producer, loudly and justifiably complained that it had been left out of the negotiations, and that its semiconductor market was likely to become a virtual prisoner of Japanese industrial policy. Depending on market conditions, semiconductors exported from Japan to Europe would sometimes be "too cheap," which would undercut Europe's fledgling attempt to develop its own semiconductor market, and would sometimes be "too expensive," which would disadvantage the users—European electronics manufacturers—by pricing their end products out of the market. Europe then defensively negotiated its own semiconductor deal with Japan.

Seemingly, there is a case for a managed trade arrangement in semiconductors, assuring nations that wish to develop semiconductor industries dominance in their own markets, while allowing residual competition domestically and in third markets. However, the semiconductor case presents yet another problem. Unlike steel and textiles, which are produced worldwide, there are at present only two major semiconductor producers—the United States and Japan—though there is an emerging third one in the EC. Therefore, most third-country markets would be 100 percent open to exports, even under a managed trade regime. However, if Japan has a fundamentally different long-term strategy than that of the United States—relentless price cutting in order to gain market share—then the Japanese will gradually capture the lion's share of these third-country markets in ways the United States and perhaps the EC consider illegitimate. This gives the United States and the EC an effective choice of either ceding markets or fighting fire with fire, leading to the familiar pattern of subsidy wars, excess capacity, widespread dumping, and staggering losses.

As the frustrations of the U.S.-Japan semiconductor deal illustrate, this is a problem whether the rules of the trading system are ostensibly liberal or managed; in fact, though the present "management" of semiconductor trade is incoherent and asymmetrical, the current semiconductor regime is plainly something other than liberal. Again, the problems are surely more soluble if the management is explicit rather than covert and guilt-ridden, since it is easier to enforce accountability with a system of explicit rules and in a multilateral context. A multilateral semiconductor accord would have to embody common rules for fair and unfair pricing and subsidy—something akin to a shared understanding of the principles of antitrust, by which nations party to the semiconductor arrangement would have to abide. The alternative is to cartelize semiconductor markets worldwide, which is surely a third best, if that. A managed trade regime in semiconductors, as in steel, might assure each major producing nation a share of its domestic market, allow free competition for the remainder, and require a common understanding of antitrust principles and of predatory pricing.

Some Common Principles

This review of three industries suggests that if nations wish to retain domestic production capacity and not cede their entire markets to foreign suppliers, it is possible to design relatively liberal and balanced managed trade regimes: not free trade, but freer trade. However, several caveats are in order.

Note first that there is no one template that fits all industries. In textiles and apparel, the "threat" to established producers is from low-wage countries; the problem of emerging worldwide excess capacity is tempered by the fact that "capacity" is rather less expensive and long-lived than in steel. Moreover, there is plenty of competition among advanced nations (enough to maintain competitive pressure), and there is no reason to cartelize that sphere of the industry. A regime based on limiting the total rate of increase of imports has been moderately successful, though it produces far more leakage than the domestic industry wants. In steel, on the other hand, the problem is worldwide subsidy and over-capacity, coupled with a nearly universal desire among nations to retain steel-making facilities. In the steel case, the present nonregime is a series of purely tactical expedients. The necessary remedy may be a more explicit managed regime based on market shares. In semiconductors, though a reciprocal import share regime would solve the problem in the home economies of producer nations, it would require an entirely new set of negotiated common principles to establish norms of behavior in third-country markets.

Second, the suitability of managed trade regimes in some products—steel, textiles, semiconductors, some farm products, among others—does not mean that a generic system of managed trade is needed. Ideally, the norm should be roughly that of the GATT: relatively liberal trade, based on the familiar principles of multilateral MFN nondiscrimination; national treatment, with limited tolerance for market-distorting subsidies; quotas; and market-closing devices. The reason that a GATT-like system should be the residual is that it is relatively simpler and cleaner (though, as the long, complex history of dumping disputes attests, it is not nearly as simple and clean as its defenders claim).

How to choose which products are candidates for a managed trade regime? The most logical place to look is at the products for which nations are currently restraining trade and, for one reason or another, wish to retain or develop technological and production capacity. In that case, if there is widespread reluctance to observe the norms of liberal trade, a frankly acknowledged managed trade regime, with a balance of benefits as the core principle, is vastly preferable to the current patchwork of subterfuges and imbalanced concessions. If, at some point, the members of the GATT wish to shift their managed trade regime, say in wheat, toward freer and freer trade, that is of course their prerogative.

A balance-of-benefits approach is also a better way of reconciling the reality of widespread domestic economic interventions with equity and comity in the trading system as a whole. Simply countervailing against other nations' subsidies or market-closing policies is no solution. In an emerging industry, such as high-definition television, in which each major region wishes to develop production capacity, a balance-of-benefits approach could attempt to calculate and negotiate limits on the total amount of subsidy. Nations that wanted their products to be freely traded would have to abide by those limits. Alternatively, a sector in which major nations had fairly mercantilist goals could follow the formula outlined above for steel, in which a portion of each nation's domestic market could be reserved for domestic suppliers, and the rest could be available for imports, perhaps with auctioned quotas. If trading nations eventually grew weary of ruinous subsidy wars as the industry matured, reciprocal reductions in subsidies could be negotiated.

Though this chapter has not treated agriculture, the recent U.S. position on farm trade is a splendid illustration of the best being the enemy of the good when it comes to reciprocal reduction of subsidy and oversupply. In the Montreal midterm review of the GATT Round, the EC urged the United States to pursue a medium-term program of reciprocal reduction of subsidies, with some tolerance for supply and price management and a mutual respect for historic regional export markets. The United States took the position that it would agree to this interim approach only if Europe joined the United States in a grandiose commitment to absolutely free trade in agriculture by the year 2000. The Europeans rightly saw this as a cynical maneuver that the U.S. delegation contrived in order to seem absolutely devoted to the freest possible trade while winking to assure domestic farm interests that no capitulation was genuinely contemplated. The diplomatic result, predictably, was impasse. Even the nations that were the lowest-cost producers and the most committed to liberal trade in agriculture, such as Canada and Australia, shared the EC view that partially managed trade in farm products was the only conceivable route toward freer trade.

The point that free traders need to comprehend is that a regime of partially managed trade can be the route to relatively freer and more sustainable trade, as well as to a more balanced and sustainable role for the United States in the system. They should also note that this approach would inject a greater degree of multilateralism into the trading system. At present, in the mind of free traders, the ideal of "multilateralism" is irrevocably yoked to the ideal of "liberal," for both historical and ideological reasons. But these two ideals are logically separable. It is possible to have a trading regime that is slightly less liberal, in that it tolerates some explicitly managed trade, but that is also more genuinely multilateral than the present system, in which various subterfuges invariably involve bilateral side deals that do real harm both to the multilateral norms and to the flow of commerce.

This chapter has necessarily treated the subject partly from a systemic perspective—how a managed trade system could work, while still providing the benefits of relatively open commerce and competition. It is also worth dwelling on the U.S. national interest in such a system. Because of its devotion to the GATT, the United States typically regards all departures from liberal trade as short-term tactical expedients, to be unilaterally given up as soon as possible. By recognizing that managed trade is sometimes the best available option, the United States would be more able to differentiate short-term tactical maneuvers from long-term strategic economic goals.

If managed trade in key industries is legitimate, the United States becomes much freer to press its trading partners—not simply to practice laissez-faire in their own economies (the traditional U.S. diplomatic goal) but to bring a balance of obligations and benefits to the trading system. The United States is also freed to define industrial goals for its own domestic economy, as well as strategies for carrying out these goals. Such strategies might or might not require targeted industrial policies in any given sector. Under a managed trade regime for semiconductors, the United States might choose to subsidize semiconductor research and development (R&D) via a Sematech consortium. In the case of steel, the

United States might decide that holding foreign-subsidized steel to a 25 percent market share would be sufficient to allow a renaissance in American steel through free market principles, with only a reinvestment quid pro quo and some retraining aid as minimalist industrial policies.[4]

Pluralism and the American National Interest

We have now come full circle to the aspirations of the early postwar regime: the ceding of some national economic sovereignty to supranational public authority, the better to permit individual nations to operate mixed economies at home. In the late 1940s, this vision stalled, because the real supranational authority was the hegemonic supremacy of the United States. In the 1970s and 1980s, as national sovereignty had been ceded to global private capital and the hegemonic position of the United States had weakened, the American protectorate was in many respects no longer viable. That the two emerging rival centers of economic power—the EC and Japan—are both more comfortable with a mix of mercantilism and liberalism makes it that much more likely that a mixed trading system is the only durable alternative and that the rules should acknowledge the reality. I have suggested in this chapter that, by adjusting its hegemonic ambitions to its economic capacity, and by modifying its concomitant devotion to laissez-faire as a standard for itself and others, the United States will be in a better position both to work toward a sustainable, multilateral trading regime and to define and advance its own national interests. Obviously, ceasing to play the hegemonic role will involve not only a change of habits; it will involve a loss of perquisites.

Readers should not mistake this observation for the wish that the United States play a less influential global role. There was a time when the United States loomed so large that it could play the role of hegemon and serve its national economic interests as well as its goals for the trading system and for the western alliance. For the most part, the United States threw its economic weight around in a remarkably enlightened fashion. The issue is not whether it would be nice to maintain that role; the relative shrinkage of the U.S. economy makes such a role unsustainable. The issue is how best to adjust to the new realities.

The scholars who investigate the logic of hegemony and global economic stability are divided on the question of whether a stable global order is possible in the absence of a hegemonic nation. The interwar period is a chilling precedent. Clinging to the illusion of American hegemony in a laissez-faire world will only weaken the U.S. economy and the global economic order. The United States is no longer preeminent, and most other nations favor a mixed form of capitalism rather than laissez-faire. We had better work toward the goal of a stable, pluralist system, because all the economic indicators suggest that a pluralist world is what we now have.

Notes

1. After Robert Triffin (1960).
2. See Krugman (1984, 1986, 1987); Dixit (1988); and Dixit and Grossman (1984). A nontechnical summary of the new view is given in the textbook by Krugman and Obstfeld (1988, chapter 6).
3. See chapter 4, by Robert E. Scott and Thea M. Lee, for a more detailed critique of cost-of-protection studies in textiles and other industries.
4. Some Americans willing to embrace a modest dose of planning but skeptical of mercantilism have posed the choice as "protectionism" versus "adjustment" (e.g., Reich 1983; Hufbauer and Rosen 1986). Supposedly, protection means keeping other people's products out, while adjustment means temporary restraints while labor and capital are redirected to "higher value-added" sectors, using the policy tools of reskilling workers and perhaps discreetly allocating some capital or subsidizing research. The trouble with this high-sounding middle ground is twofold. First, it doesn't tell us what to do when other nations' mercantilism pushes the United States out of industries in which it would like to maintain some self-sufficiency (steel happens to be a very high value-added industry) and in which U.S. industry is actually or potentially very competitive. Second, while professing to reject laissez-faire purism, in fact it embraces most of the Ricardian shibboleths about trade.

Bibliography

Bhagwati, Jagdish. 1988. *Protectionism.* Cambridge, MA: MIT Press.
Choate, Pat, and Juyne Linger. 1988. "Tailored Trade: Dealing with the World as It Is." *Harvard Business Review,* Vol. 66 (January–February), pp. 86–93.
Cline, William. 1987. *The Future of World Trade in Textiles and Apparel.* Washington, DC: Institute for International Economics.
Defense Science Board Report to the Secretary of Defense ("Fuhrman Report"). 1988. Washington, DC (October).
Dixit, Avinash. 1988. "International Research and Development Competition and Policy." In A. M. Spence and H. Hazard, eds., *International Competitiveness.* Cambridge, MA: Ballinger Press.
Dixit, Avinash, and Gene M. Grossman. 1984. "Targeted Export Promotion with Several Oligopolistic Industries." Discussion Paper No. 71. Princeton, NJ: Princeton University, Woodrow Wilson School.
Gilpin, Robert. 1987. *The Political Economy of International Relations.* Princeton, NJ: Princeton University Press.
Gourevitch, Peter. 1986. *Politics in Hard Times.* Ithaca, NY: Cornell University Press.
Heckscher, Eli. 1950. "The Effect of Foreign Trade on the Distribution of Income." In H. S. Ellis and Lloyd A. Metzler, eds. *Readings in the Theory of International Trade.* Philadelphia, PA: Blackiston. Originally published in *Ekonomisk Tidskrift,* Vol. 21, 1919, pp. 497–512.
Hirschman, Albert. 1945. *National Power and the Structure of Foreign Trade.* Berkeley: University of California Press.
Howell, T. R., W. A. Noellert, J. G. Kreier, and A. W. Wolff. 1988. *Steel and the State.* Boulder, CO: Westview Press.
Hufbauer, Gary Clyde, and Howard F. Rosen. 1986. *Trade Policies for Troubled Industries.* Washington, DC: Institute for International Economics.
Katzenstein, Peter. 1985. *Small States in World Markets.* Ithaca, NY: Cornell University Press.

Kennedy, Paul. 1986. *The Rise and Fall of the Great Powers.* New York: Random House.

Keohane, Robert O. 1984. *After Hegemony.* Princeton, NJ: Princeton University Press.

Kindleberger, Charles P. 1973. *The World in Depression.* Berkeley: University of California Press.

Krasner, Stephen D., ed. 1983. *International Regimes.* Ithaca, NY: Cornell University Press.

Krugman, Paul. 1984. "The U.S. Response to Foreign Industrial Targeting." *Brookings Papers on Economic Activity,* No. 1. Washington, DC: Brookings Institution.

————. 1987. "Is Free Trade Passé?" *Journal of Economic Perspectives,* Vol. 1 (Fall), pp. 131–44.

Krugman, Paul, ed. 1986. *Strategic Trade Policy and the New International Economics.* Cambridge, MA: MIT Press.

Krugman, Paul, and Maurice Obstfeld. 1988. *International Economics: Theory and Policy.* Boston, MA: Scott, Foresman and Little-Brown.

Kuttner, Robert. 1989. *Managed Trade and Economic Sovereignty.* Washington, DC: Economic Policy Institute.

Ohlin, Bertil. 1933. *Interregional and International Trade.* Cambridge, MA: Harvard University Press.

Reich, Robert B. 1983. "Beyond Free Trade." *Foreign Affairs,* Vol. 61 (Spring), pp. 773–804.

Ricardo, David. 1951. *Principles of Political Economy and Taxation.* London: 1817; 3d ed., 1821. Reprinted, Cambridge, England: Cambridge University Press.

Roth, Senator William. 1989. Speech to Chicago Council on Foreign Relations, Chicago, IL, April 11.

Ruggie, John Gerard. 1983. "International Regimes, Transactions and Change: Embedded Liberalism in the Postwar Economic Order." In Stephen D. Krasner, ed., *International Regimes.* Ithaca, NY: Cornell University Press.

Samuelson, Paul A. 1987. "International Factor-Price Equalisation Once Again." In Jagdish Bhagwati, ed., *International Trade Selected Readings,* 2d ed. Cambridge, MA: MIT Press. Originally published in *Economic Journal,* June 1949, pp. 181–97.

Stegemann, Klaus. 1989. "Policy Rivalry among Industrial States: What Can We Learn from Models of Strategic Trade Policy?" *International Organization,* Vol. 43 (Winter), pp. 73–100.

Triffin, Robert. 1960. *Gold and the Dollar Crisis.* New Haven, CT: Yale University Press.

U.S. Council of Economic Advisors. 1988. *Economic Report of the President.* Washington, DC: U.S. Government Printing Office.

CHAPTER TWO

Global Interdependence and National Prosperity

David P. Levine

Introduction

The question of the appropriate attitude of the nation toward the opportunities and hazards posed by international trade was one of the original concerns of political economy. Perhaps the first great debate in economics, between the classical economists and the mercantilists, was a debate over the appropriate policy of the state vis-à-vis trade with other countries. In simple terms, this debate concerned the wisdom of free trade as opposed to restrictions on the movement of goods across borders. For example, when the United States opens its economy to free trade, does it lose markets to others and thus diminish its citizens' welfare, or does the scope of its buying and selling activities expand, improving efficiency and raising the level of welfare of the population? Does opening the U.S. economy to trade facilitate or retard the process of economic growth and development? If we envision a world without political restrictions on trade across national boundaries, will all (or most) nations benefit, or will only a few benefit while others lose out? Do the nations that make up the global economy have a harmony of interests best served by free trade, or do economic interests conflict so that political guidance and restrictive policies are needed to secure the national interest?

In evaluating the free trade debate, an important difficulty arises because of an ambiguity in the meaning of the term "free trade." This meaning might be clear enough if the only government policies affecting trade were those specifically intended to do so. Then "free trade" would refer simply to the absence of government policy influencing the movement of goods across national borders. Yet, government policies not directed at regulating trade between nations can also have significant effects on the international flow of goods.

This essay is an adaptation of two chapters from *Wealth and Freedom* (Levine 1995). Substantial material from that book is reproduced here by permission of Cambridge University Press. I would like to thank Harry Bloch, Robert Blecker, Dean Baker, and Nawfal Umari for comments on an earlier draft.

Any policy that affects the cost of goods, or otherwise differentiates goods produced at home from those produced abroad, can affect the nation's trading position. Discussions of so-called nontariff barriers (NTBs) to trade emphasize ways in which government can influence trade without directly regulating (or intending to regulate) imports or exports. Examples include regulations aimed at protecting consumers by controlling the quality of products, environmental protections that regulate the way goods are produced, legislation aimed at protecting workers that affects labor costs, and specification of units of weight and measure that differ from nation to nation. In all these areas, government activity affects trade.

In fact, no trade is possible without government regulation, which defines the nature and limits of enforceable contracts, protects property rights, maintains an infrastructure of collective life adequate for the sorts of intercourse demanded by trade, and determines when costs will be borne socially and when privately. Differences between nations in the attitude, orientation, and policy of government toward the economy affect their international positions. Thus, if free trade means absence of government influence on trade, then free trade means no trade.

In light of this difficulty, we might opt for a narrower definition, one that makes the term "free trade" refer to the absence of government policy specifically aimed at affecting the levels of imports and exports of goods and services. Thus, under free trade, the (no doubt significant) influence of government on trade is an unintended consequence of the pursuit of other objectives.

How, then, do we link free trade in this sense with international interdependence and economic development? This chapter explores this question, and suggests why free trade can potentially become a significant impediment to economic well-being.

To support this suggestion is to dispute some common wisdom. This chapter argues that the classically inspired approach to understanding international economic relations (linked to the idea of comparative advantage) is not convincing, and that division of markets linked to competition is a more powerful concept than division of labor and specialization for understanding global economic processes and outcomes. It follows that the global system of free trade is unlikely to enhance the welfare of all parties, but likely to produce winners and losers. This happens because economic development is an uneven process that tends to concentrate production and markets, thus benefiting some while harming, or at least excluding, others. Because of this, government has an important role in determining the way a nation relates to an uncertain global system and in taking responsibility for the welfare of citizens adversely affected by the vicissitudes of that system.

International Interdependence

Two senses of economic interdependence between nations have special significance. The first focuses on the division of labor or degree of mutual dependence in production, the second on the location of markets.

Economic interdependence in the first sense refers to the dependence of production in one region or nation upon inputs from another. Two regions can be economically interdependent when most production processes in one require a single vital input from the other. Thus, Japan's economy may be considered interdependent with that of the Middle Eastern oil-producing nations even if Japan requires only one input (oil) from those nations. It happens that this one input is used in the production of most goods produced in Japan and is therefore vital to the whole Japanese economy.

Interdependence in production also exists when the goods produced and consumed in each country employ a wide set of inputs from the other. In this case, it is not one vital input that links the two, but a whole set of inputs. Productive interdependence in this second sense suggests that, although the two nations are politically separate, in important respects they share one economy.

Rather than defining interdependence as mutual dependence in production, we can define it in terms of markets and demand. This is the second sense of interdependence. If a country, such as Japan, sells a significant proportion of its output to another country (say, the United States), then the level of economic activity in Japan will depend on the level of demand for goods in the United States. A recession in the United States will depress demand for imports from Japan. Indeed, on the assumption that the proportion of income spent on imports is more or less fixed, imports will fall in proportion to the fall in the level of economic activity in the United States.

The nature and degree of interdependence between countries varies over time and from country to country. Up to a point, it also varies with national economic policies—whether governments encourage free trade or restrict imports. Restrictive policies can reduce interdependence. It is generally thought that the degree of economic interdependence has increased notably during the post–World War II period (see Cooper 1972). This has been especially important in the United States, where the implications of interdependence are now being felt in ways that are novel and disturbing.

Interdependence may be more or less symmetrical. That is, one country may be dependent on another, while the other is more or less autonomous. The Japanese are dependent on the market for their goods in the United States to a degree far exceeding the dependence of U.S. corporations on sales in Japan. Many less developed countries (LDCs) are dependent on imports of oil from petroleum-exporting countries, while the latter are not similarly dependent on the LDCs for necessary inputs.

Asymmetries in interdependence are important both economically and politically. Economically, they make one country or group of countries sensitive to economic policies and economic cycles in other countries that are not so dependent themselves. Politically, asymmetries create power relations between countries and vulnerabilities open to political exploitation. They give countries that are less dependent leverage over countries that are more dependent (see Keohane and Nye 1977).

If, by accident or policy, a country remains self-sufficient, we speak of its economy as autarchic. Economic autarchy refers to the absence of interdependence. Domestic production processes are not significantly dependent on inputs from abroad, and the level of domestic economic activity is not significantly affected by the state of markets abroad.

Autarchy has advantages and disadvantages paralleling those of interdependence. The main advantage of autarchy is domestic control over the nation's economic destiny. Interdependence seriously limits the nation's ability to chart its own course. Rather, its course is charted by the world economy as a whole, or by powerful nations and international organizations (such as the International Monetary Fund [IMF]). The main disadvantage of autarchy is that it excludes the nation from the benefits of trade, from markets in which to sell its produce, and from access to goods produced in other countries.

The advantages of interdependence arise from an expansion of markets and market opportunities. Expansion of markets yields three potential gains: (1) gains in productivity, (2) gains in income and employment, and (3) gains in welfare stemming from access to lower-cost consumer goods.

The first type of gain was originally suggested by Adam Smith (1937), who linked the productivity of labor to the extent of the market. Growth in income follows increasing labor productivity. Productivity depends on the division of labor. Since the division of labor increases productivity, it increases the level of output corresponding to any level of employment. Thus, growth in productivity demands growth in markets to absorb the increasing levels of output. In one of his most famous formulations, Adam Smith stated that "the division of labor is limited by the extent of the market" (1937, p. 17).

We can put the same idea in more general language. Adam Smith's vision tied economic growth to what economists refer to as increasing returns to scale. Increasing returns to scale means that as the amount produced increases, unit costs fall. For example, it is much cheaper per car for General Motors to produce 200,000 cars annually than it is to produce only 200. One of the reasons for this is that larger-scale production affords opportunities for extending the division of labor, but there are other reasons as well. One of the most important has to do with plant and equipment. When purchase of the most advanced technology requires a large investment in plant and equipment, this will be feasible only if production can be maintained on a comparatively large scale. To utilize the investment profitably, the market must be large enough to absorb output in quantities much greater than those needed for smaller investments. The extent of the market helps to define the kind of capital stock it will prove profitable to acquire, and thus to determine the unit costs of production.

When the more costly capital stock has a greater productive capacity and yields lower unit costs, the extent of the market becomes a major determinant of the productivity of labor. Increasing returns to scale means that the productivity of labor is limited by the extent of the market.

Finding new markets therefore facilitates productivity growth. Because economic interdependence means access to new markets (in other countries), it provides an opportunity for market expansion. If the size of the home market impedes productivity growth, involvement in international trade can mean access to higher levels of productivity. Access to larger markets enables domestic producers to reap the benefits of economies of scale. Doing so yields lower production costs that can lead to lower prices. Benefits of a widening market attendant on expanded participation in the world economy may accrue to consumers as cheaper domestic goods. Whether or not those benefits accrue will depend on aspects of market structure (such as concentration and product differentiation).

In addition to productivity gains, interdependence can lead to a second type of gain in output and employment. For an economy operating at less than full capacity, the opportunity to sell abroad is an opportunity to expand domestic levels of production and employment. Doing so increases domestic incomes and thus domestic consumption. Export markets can also stimulate new investment in plant and equipment. This new investment, if it takes place at home, will further stimulate demand and employment. The multiplier implies that the net impact of investment on demand and employment may be considerably greater than its original level.

The circular flow of economic life magnifies the effect of exports (and associated investment) on income and employment. The degree of magnification (the multiplier) depends in part on the proportion of export revenue spent on imports. If part of the revenue generated by production for exports is spent on imports, then its impact on income and employment will be felt abroad rather than at home. To this extent, exports stimulate imports that lessen their potential impact on the domestic level of economic activity.

The conclusion to draw is that, for open economies operating at less than full employment of labor and capital, the magnitude of exports and the proportion of revenue spent on imports play a vital part in determining the level of economic activity (see Thirwall 1979).

A given level of domestic investment will generate a level of output depending on the multiplier. The level of employment that corresponds to this level of output is that level of employment needed to produce the output stimulated by investment. This may or may not be full employment. If domestic investment is inadequate to maintain full employment, exports can further stimulate output and employment.

Thus, if domestic markets are inadequate to maintain full utilization of domestic capital and labor, exploitation of world markets can fill in the gap. In a world of unemployed resources, a balance of exports and imports has limited appeal as the goal of economic policy since expansion of exports can increase the level of utilization of domestic labor and capital (see Robinson 1966).

Economic interdependence has the potential for enhancing the domestic level of economic activity. Those countries that succeed in capturing world markets for their domestic products employ workers and generate incomes by selling to consumers and producers abroad. Such countries garner to (some of) their citizens a greater share of global income and wealth.

Matters appear different for the country at the receiving end of the exports. Imports displace domestic products when they meet a need that can be and has been met in the past by domestic producers. The income formerly used to buy a domestically produced good is now spent on a good produced abroad. Rather than enhancing the levels of economic activity and employment domestically, it enhances those levels abroad. If this happens, trade moves income and employment from one country to another and the gain for one is at the expense of, and in proportion to the loss of, another.

This assumes that the goods in question are or have been produced in both countries. A more difficult question arises when this assumption does not hold. Could the good imported from abroad be produced at home instead, and could home production be reasonably efficient so that the consumer would not be overly penalized by the price of a domestically produced good?

Under conditions of high unemployment, domestic production of goods currently imported might enhance employment and incomes, thus raising the level of economic activity and yielding the benefits associated with higher levels of output and demand. Governments, then, may wish to protect domestic producers from foreign competition in order to gain the benefits of a growing domestic market. Economists term this strategy for economic growth "import substitution."

We can learn something important about the likely success of this strategy by referring to the notion of increasing returns to scale. If productivity increases with the scale of production, and therefore with the scale of the market, the larger the market in which the producer sells (assuming an adequate degree of competition among sellers), the greater the benefit for the consumer. If the home country has a small domestic market and limited prospects for market growth, then import substitution that limits either access to, or orientation of production toward, foreign markets will likely assure higher cost to consumers over the long run, while also causing inefficient domestic production (inefficient because it is limited to producing for a restricted domestic market). By contrast, if the home country has a large and potentially expanding domestic market, that market can be made a basis for economic development.

If, on the other hand, import restrictions enhance the home market for domestic producers (by lowering the propensity to import) without adversely affecting exports, they can increase the scale of the market for domestic producers. Historically, restricting foreign access to the home market has not always resulted in restricted access on the part of domestic producers to the world market. It all depends on the relation of the country to its trading partners. Thus, an import-substitution policy does not rule out the use of foreign markets to solve the problem posed by a restricted internal market (see Krugman 1990).

Given the importance of market size, the virtues of an export-oriented development strategy loom large, especially for countries with small home markets. In such cases, the advantage goes to the countries that are able to create incentives for domestic producers to produce for export markets while also encouraging import substitution (see Amsden 1989).

One economist notes that import substitution can work well when the home market is expanding and the policy of restricting imports secures an expanding market for domestic producers (see Krugman 1991, pp. 91–92). He suggests that the Canadian experience provides a good example of trade restrictions forcing consumers of manufactured goods (especially Canadian agricultural producers) to purchase domestic products. This Canadian strategy increased domestic employment in manufacturing. Job expansion in Canada absorbed immigration while stemming the tide of migration of Canadian workers to the United States. The result was expansion of the domestic market. Thus, in thinking about trade restrictions aimed at forcing substitution of domestic for imported goods, the growth of the home market must be given primary consideration.

The Canadian experience is by no means an isolated example of the successful use of trade restrictions in the service of economic development. During the nineteenth century the United States successfully industrialized behind protectionist barriers that helped to secure a growing internal market for domestic manufacturers.

The import-substitution strategy poses a dilemma for some developing countries. Participation in world trade can endanger domestic levels of demand and employment. It can channel incomes abroad and impair local economic activity. At the same time, the strategy of replacing imports with domestic products encounters a problem in the restricted scale of the domestic market. A stagnant domestic market is likely to undermine any strategy for economic development.

The third type of gain from interdependence accrues to buyers of imported goods. Producers can gain from access to cheaper inputs available from abroad, while consumers gain from access to cheaper consumer goods produced abroad. In the classical theory, this advantage stems from productivity differences across countries (or regions). Each country supplies others with the goods it is relatively more efficient at producing.

If we consider productivity differences between nations to be given, we can imagine a global division of labor that takes advantage of these differences. Global specialization allows buyers to acquire goods from those best situated to produce them. This conclusion focuses our attention on efficient use of labor and other resources. It does not take into account the impact of trade on the level of output and employment, as that reflects the global distribution of market shares, or the impact of trade on productivity differences themselves.

Each of the advantages of interdependence carries some risks: (1) just as exports expand our markets, imports reduce them; (2) the opportunity to sell abroad may or may not mean expansion of domestic production; and (3) interdependence weakens autonomy and lowers the possibility of domestic economic self-determination.

If greater interdependence means a higher propensity to import, then it means a lower level of economic activity for any given rate of investment and level of exports. The impact of investment on domestic demand is dampened by the leakage of demand into purchases of foreign goods. Similarly, the full potential of government budget deficits to expand domestic income is reduced since part of the income generated is spent on goods produced abroad. An open economy can be a larger economy or a smaller economy, depending on the competitiveness of domestically produced goods.

The question of competitiveness carries particular weight for latecomers to modern industrial technology. Because costs tend to fall as the scale of production increases, those producers that, because of a longer history in a particular market, have larger markets also have a competitive advantage. If producers in countries at early stages of industrial development are disadvantaged, they may benefit from government protection aimed at giving them the opportunity to catch up both in technology and in scale of production.[1]

Even if goods produced by domestic firms are competitive and openness expands markets, those producers may not expand their domestic capital investments to meet the expanding market. They can meet the expanding markets by investing in productive capacity abroad. If they do so, the income and employment benefits of trade accrue to other countries. The question of who gains from interdependence, then, is not a question simply about the competitiveness of goods produced by domestic firms but also about where those firms choose to produce those goods. General Motors (GM) can produce for the U.S. market in the United States or in Mexico. If it produces more cheaply in Mexico, GM benefits; but the U.S. economy does not benefit and indeed may suffer a loss of employment and income.

The fact that U.S. firms make decisions concerning where to produce based not on the benefits or harms to the U.S. economy but on the likely impact of the decision on the firm's profitability should caution us against identifying the corporate interest with the national interest. What is good for GM may not be good for America. The health of "our" corporations bears a complex relationship to the health of "our" economy. National economic policy should target the domestic economy. By so doing, it may very well conflict with the interests of firms legally domiciled within the nation's borders or historically identified with domestic economic activities.

Finally, openness to world trade reduces domestic control over the economy. When we depend on exports, we make ourselves vulnerable to the effects of recession abroad. When we import goods, we risk importing inflation along with those goods. Not only are we affected by economic affairs outside our borders and thus less under our own control, but our government's capacity to guide our economy diminishes.

In a closed economy, when government stimulates economic activity, it affects domestic income and employment. In an open economy, part of the impact drains off in purchases abroad. If we spend a proportion of our income on imports, government deficit spending, by stimulating an increase in domestic incomes, stimulates an increase in imports. Since government spending does not stimulate exports, the balance of trade deteriorates. Thus, in an open economy, government economic policy encounters a difficulty not present in a closed economy. The impact of policy on domestic employment is less because incomes are used to buy goods produced abroad.

If we value our ability to control our economic destiny, openness of our economy can be harmful. This harm is felt in limitations of government control. It is also felt in the vulnerability attendant upon interdependence. If we require oil imports to sustain domestic production of goods and services, then our destiny depends on decisions made by oil exporters and circumstances in oil producing regions. The same holds true for dependence on markets abroad. In an export-oriented economy, domestic income and employment (and therefore welfare) are inextricably linked with the world market. This makes the nation vulnerable, especially to those foreign countries whose nationals purchase a large part of the goods exported.

The more widespread our interdependence, the greater our vulnerability to events in other parts of the world. Economic interdependence poses political challenges since we are dependent on forces we may not control. We no longer rule our own destiny.

Growing economic interdependence carries with it a challenge to national sovereignty insofar as sovereignty is tied up with national self-determination. National self-determination, on a political level, involves such matters as the security of national borders and the autonomy of domestic political decision making.

Political sovereignty means more than the security of borders and protection against the subversion of domestic political process. It also means a capacity for the nation to determine its direction: to pursue economic development as a national goal, to pursue welfare state economic policies should it choose to do so, to define its own forms of political economy (e.g., which lean more or less in the direction of free markets). Economic interdependence can reduce the ability of governments to accomplish these goals. It can place their accomplishments in the hands of the impersonal forces of the global market and the not so impersonal forces of other national interests.

The North American Free Trade Agreement (NAFTA) encountered opposition for reasons connected to these problems. Under a free trade regime, U.S. firms can evade environmental or occupational health and safety regulations by moving production south of the border. If this happens, we face the dilemma that job safety and a clean environment have to be sacrificed in order to maintain income and employment. To this extent, interdependence and openness can erode sovereignty and with it the nation's capacity to define itself and pursue its ends.

Comparative Advantage

The classical economists analyzed international relations assuming that nations were interdependent, but only to a limited degree. David Ricardo developed one of the most influential arguments for free trade assuming limited interdependence (Ricardo 1951). He argued that free trade would lead to a global division of labor, allocating production of different goods to the nations capable of producing them relatively more efficiently. His theory is termed the theory of "comparative advantage."

The theory begins by making a distinction between *absolute* and *comparative* advantage. A nation has an *absolute advantage* over another nation in the production of a good when it can produce that good using fewer inputs per unit of output. The classical economists focused on labor cost, so absolute advantage meant lower unit labor requirements (or higher labor productivity). Nations might specialize according to their absolute advantage, producing the goods for which they are more efficient than their trading partners. Of course, some nations might not be more efficient in any goods and would, by the criterion of absolute advantage, have nothing to sell internationally.

By contrast, *comparative advantage* refers to differences between nations in the relation between labor productivity in the production of different goods. A country has a comparative advantage, say in the production of cheese, when the ratio between its labor productivities in cheese and wine exceeds that ratio in another country. The country specializing in cheese is relatively, rather than absolutely, more productive in that good.

The theory of comparative advantage suggests that these two countries can engage in mutually beneficial trade with the first specializing in cheese and the second in wine. It also suggests that such mutual benefits exist even if the second country has an absolute advantage in both cheese and wine. Indeed, a nation may be less efficient in production of all goods and still have a comparative advantage in some. Each country would specialize in production of those goods for which it had a *relative* advantage in productivity.

The theory of comparative advantage is a *theory* about the benefits of trade and specialization. It is important to bear this in mind because the term "comparative advantage" is sometimes used not to refer to a theory of global specialization and trade, but simply to describe situations in which nations specialize in and trade different goods. The existence of specialization does not imply the workings of the forces summarized in the theory of comparative advantage. The latter carries a set of special assumptions, such as the assumption of full employment of labor and other resources and the assumption that relative productivities are given independently of trade, which may or may not hold. It explains trade in a special way that may or may not be illuminating for particular cases, even those in which nations specialize in ways the theory might predict.

The theory of comparative advantage focuses our attention on differences in productivity within and across nations. Ricardo did not much specify what factors were responsible for differences in labor productivity in different countries (and thus what accounts for the greater efficiency of certain global distributions of production over others). It makes a difference whether we emphasize the level of technical know-how and capital investment or the abundance of resources and natural fertility of the earth. The former is a product of history and shaped by social institutions, possibly influenced by economic and social policies. The latter is often assumed to be given, a force that shapes but is not shaped by the historical process. This assumption may not be entirely accurate since both what we recognize as a "resource" and the amount of it available vary with history and technology.

In the classical comparative advantage conception, different countries would produce different goods, each specializing in what it did best. If the world economy conformed to this image, imports would not displace domestic production but would enhance the welfare of domestic consumers by making production more efficient. Domestic incomes would vary with the qualities and quantities of domestic resources. Some countries would fare better, but this would be primarily because they happened to be better endowed with resources and capabilities. Countries would not fare better because their producers were more competitive and thus were able to displace producers elsewhere. In this vision, the world economy would be a harmonious place. Gains in welfare for one country would not be at the expense of another. Rather, such gains would reflect the accidents of endowments in different countries.

The implied argument for free trade runs into difficulty when the trading partners compete over markets for the same goods rather than specializing in the different products in which each has its relative advantage. When nations sell the same sorts of goods to each other, they are said to engage in *intra*-industry trade. Such trade challenges the image of the global economy fostered by the theory of comparative advantage.[2]

Specialization may follow competition over market shares when the less competitive are driven from the market. It is less clear, however, that such specialization implies an efficient use of geographically distributed resources.[3] From the standpoint of the geographic distribution of resource endowments, the pattern of trade seems more and more arbitrary. Viewed, of course, within a context of the process of global competition and uneven development, that pattern will not appear arbitrary at all. Indeed, moving away from an emphasis on the older issues of geographic location of inputs will help to highlight the forces governing the uneven growth and development of nations and regions.

This does not necessarily make trade a bad idea, but it does make the virtues of free trade problematic. We need, then, to look more closely at the circumstances in different nations to evaluate the benefits and costs of openness to trade.

The vision of world production organized by prior location of inputs clearly fits poorly when the primary inputs are not location-specific. We can speak of certain countries having an advantage in production of certain goods when it matters where those goods are produced. Clearly it matters for many primary products: oranges, bananas, coffee. It also matters for minerals such as gold and cobalt. But why should it matter where cars, computers, and shirts are produced? For these products, the capital investment can be located wherever an appropriate labor supply, transportation system, and perhaps political environment exist. It is the location of the capital investment that determines who gets the employment and associated incomes. In such cases, the problem of the location of investment, with its profound implications for national economic life, cannot be resolved by asking where resource endowments make it (relatively) more efficient to produce. The increasing importance of trade in manufactured goods rather than primary products significantly alters the terms of the classical debate over free trade.

The Benefits and Harms of Openness

Economic development has brought about important changes in the structure of trade and interdependence. With development, costs of transportation decline, reducing or eliminating the advantage of producing in close proximity to markets. Increasing size and scale of production, together with an emerging global perspective, reduce the firm's orientation toward production in its home country. Adam Smith and David Ricardo both believed that producers would naturally invest their profits at home, in part for patriotic reasons, in part because they felt more secure doing so. In the world of commerce, however, patriotism is no match for the calculation of cost and profitability. Producers produce where it is most profitable to do so.

Natural advantage plays less of a role in the geographic location of manufacturing. Because of this, geographic considerations per se do not explain the location of industry. This means, in brief, that firms, whatever their country of origin, strive to produce where production is least costly and to sell where they can find the best markets.

When firms from different countries produce the same or similar goods, they compete for global markets. U.S.- and Canadian-based firms sell both in Canada and in the United States; they treat the market as a single unit, and the same goods flow across the border in both directions.

As economic development enhances the weight of manufactured goods in trade, the image of a global division of labor recedes. Instead of exporting and importing different kinds of goods, we export and import groups of goods that are broadly similar. We can still wonder whether doing so brings prosperity. The answer closely follows the vicissitudes of domestic producers in a world of international competition.

The benefits and costs of participation in the global economy depend on factors affecting the competitive position of domestic producers. We can judge competitive position by the trend over time in global market shares for relevant industries. Contraction (expansion) of market shares suggests declining (increasing) competitiveness.[4] A strong competitive position in world markets brings with it higher levels of domestic output and investment. What kinds of factors determine a country's competitive position in the world economy?

Economists continue to debate this question. The factors claimed to explain failure range broadly: labor costs are too high, the workforce is poorly educated, capital stock is outdated, corporate strategies are too shortsighted, government is too heavily involved in the economy, government is not involved enough, and so on.

In much of this literature, one point stands out. The competitive position of domestic industry in the world economy depends on the quality of productive inputs as compared with those available to competitors. The quality of productive inputs has a number of dimensions: cost, productivity, reliability, and skill, to name a few. An industry will do better if it has newer and better equipment, equally skilled or better-skilled but less costly labor, and more competent management.

Since where firms sell does not determine where they produce, the home market becomes less important than the ability to exploit a global market. Because of this, the interests of firms can diverge from those of the nation. It becomes vital, then, for the nation to make its economic policies independent, to a significant degree, of corporate interests.

The process of global competition parallels the process of competition between domestic producers. One affects regional development within a nation while the other affects development across nations. Within the United States, different regions fare differently at different times. Industry moves from the Northeast and the Upper Midwest to the South and the Southwest, where the investment climate is more favorable, in part because labor is less expensive and less well organized. In the same way, industry moves from the United States to Mexico, where labor is even less expensive. In this sort of world economy, international trade is a part of the broader problem of the location of industry and the competition between producers within and across industries.

If labor productivity in relevant U.S. industries is not significantly higher than in China, South Korea, or Mexico (for example), and if wages in these countries are significantly lower than in the United States, producers located in the United States will have difficulty competing (see Mead 1990). Obviously, higher productivity abroad compounds the problem. Wages in South Korea challenge standards of living in the United States when producers in South Korea increase their market shares at the expense of U.S. producers. As a result, the United States' competitive position in the world economy deteriorates. To maintain living standards in the United States, or in any high-wage economy, means accomplishing one or more of the following goals:

1. *Increase productivity relative to competitors.* This requires higher levels of investment in new capital stock embodying more productive technology, higher levels of expenditure on research and development (R&D), higher-quality labor, and improved organization and management of industry. Of course, even if a nation succeeds in raising levels of investment and R&D expenditures, this may or may not improve its productivity *relative to* that of its competitors, which are already investing at a higher rate than it is. High rates of investment tend to follow high rates of market expansion. It is difficult to build new capital when the old is underutilized. Nonetheless, government policies aimed at encouraging investment in plant and equipment and in research expenditures speak directly to the problem of competitive failure.

2. *Specialize in production of goods for which wage differentials do not matter.* The lower the proportion of costs made up of wages (the higher the proportion made up of capital and materials), the less disadvantageous are higher wages in the competitive struggle.[5]

3. *Protect domestic producers from foreign competition by erecting barriers to imports.*

4. *Accept the decline of competitiveness and the stagnation of incomes, focusing attention on ameliorating effects rather than on attacking the causes.* This entails redistributing a given (or slowly growing) output to protect living standards of those affected by loss of markets by expanding the government sector, providing income supports and more fairly apportioning the burden of waning competitiveness, and/or focusing on a socially acceptable living standard rather than on continual improvement in real incomes.

Politically, the third solution often gains ground during hard times. It takes us back to Adam Smith's argument with the mercantilists and deserves closer consideration. It raises, once again, the question of the benefits and dangers of trade.

If a nation's competitive position is strong, then it may oppose restraints on trade since they can only impede the growth of its markets and the expansion of domestic income and employment.[6] If its competitive position is weak, domestic interests favor restraints on imports. These interests hope that forcing consumers to buy domestically produced goods will secure markets for home industry. Doing so, it is hoped, will also secure incomes and employment.

Posed in this way, the problem of restraint on trade looms as a political one that pits the nation as consumer against the nation as producer. As producers and workers we favor restraints, but as consumers we favor open markets so that we can buy what we want (sometimes imported goods) at the best price we can get. Of course consumers must also work, and their interests will depend on what sort of work they do and how vulnerable their work is to imports of goods from abroad.

If a struggle between interest groups determines our trade policy, we should have little reason to expect that policy to benefit the nation as a whole or to serve the national interest. On the contrary, policy will likely serve the interests of the more powerful groups. These interests may be in trade restrictions that protect poorly organized and poorly run industry at the expense of the consumer. The national interest in economic growth and development will be served only by accident, through policies put in place at the behest of groups influential with government officials and elected representatives.

Questions remain concerning how trade policy might be tailored to serve a nation's broader interest in the welfare of the people. Ideology looms large here, since it often plays a crucial role in defining the national interest (see Krasner 1978). In the United States, government typically adheres (ideologically) to the doctrine of free trade, accepting the classical argument that all will benefit from open markets. This belief encourages free trade policies, yet often runs up against vested domestic interests that expect to lose out if not protected from foreign competition. Trade policy, then, follows not only a struggle between domestic interest groups, but a struggle between interests and ideology.

If we attempt to stand above private interest, we need to know the national interest in the area of trade, and the policy most likely to advance that interest. For many, such a policy is one that would revive competitiveness and thus strengthen the national economy.

It is an open question whether such a policy exists. Economists who favor free trade consider it hard medicine but the medicine most likely to make domestic producers more productive and more efficient, since they will have to be more efficient to survive. Restraints on trade allow domestic producers to remain inefficient by international standards. Advocates of free trade consider trade restraints an encouragement to slovenliness. They argue that limiting competition reduces the pressure to produce efficiently, improve productivity, and enhance product quality. Even if this is true, however, it does not follow that free trade will assure that domestic producers will become more efficient and more competitive. They might just go out of business.

It is always important to bear in mind that a capitalist world economy is a competitive world economy. It is a world of winners and losers. Domestic growth depends on the exploitation of international markets. If each nation could develop within a particular sector, and could trade its output to other nations that had specialized differently, the world economy would be one of mutual or reciprocal advantage. This would be, once again, the world economy of a global division of labor.[7]

In the modern world economy, however, competitive success for a country does not mean success in marketing a single product or a limited group of products. It may start out that way (e.g., with cheap textiles), but the characteristics of the domestic economy that made it so competitive in a restricted area are soon found to apply more broadly. High-quality inputs can be used to produce any (manufactured) good more efficiently than the competition. Because of this, the more competitive countries or regions produce for and sell to the world. They become wealthy by appropriating the markets in other countries. International competition brings with it a concentration rather than a dispersion of production and investment. It implies that economic development will be an uneven process, favoring some and injuring others.

Instead of being advantageous to all, international competition is advantageous to the regions and nations whose industries are the most competitive. Their success in international competition means that their markets are wider and expand more rapidly than the markets of their less successful competitors. The rapid expansion of their markets means rapid accumulation at home and rapid growth in domestic incomes, but it also means contraction and slower growth of markets for their competitors. The world economy grows unequally; global growth concentrates rather than diffuses.

This observation suggests a dilemma for countries (such as the United States) whose competitive position is waning. Protection of industry through trade restrictions can sustain rather than cure the disease. It may allow us to live with our failings rather than doing something about them. Protecting the domestic market secures demand, but may throw an obstacle in the path of growth.

Whether protection has adverse consequences for development depends on the size of the domestic market and the likely dynamism of industry in a protected environment. Closing off a large domestic market for domestic producers enables them to enjoy the benefits of economies of scale. These benefits may be lost in an open economy, since the growth of domestic producers will be limited, and even curtailed, by competition from more efficient foreign producers. When foreign competition is kept out, the gains in productivity that come from exploiting a large domestic market accrue to domestic producers. These domestic producers may, in time, become sufficiently productive to compete successfully in the world market.

Protection makes this possible but provides no guarantee. For the trick to work, the domestic producers must use the home market as the basis for new capital investment embodying more efficient production methods. They must face strong incentives to modernize and produce efficiently even though they are protected from foreign competition. Domestic competition may play an important role here, which brings us back to the problem of the size of the domestic market. A large home market can sustain a number of competing producers in an industry, keeping that industry competitive even when it is protected from foreign competition. In a small market this must prove difficult. Thus, a smaller country may need to protect its home market without losing access to the world market if it is to become competitive. It needs to combine import restrictions with an export-oriented growth strategy.

A large enough country may not be so dependent on the world market. If domestic market growth can provide adequate opportunity for industry to exploit economies of scale, protection of markets can be a part of a viable policy of economic growth and development.

The policy of free trade subjects the economy to the vicissitudes of international competition and the unequal growth implied in the competitive process. No international law assures success to participants. Only some can succeed, since their success comes at least partly at the expense of their competitors. Contrary to what we are sometimes told, no nation has a special claim to be number one. If a nation competes, it is at least as likely to come in tenth as first, to lose markets to other nations as to win over theirs.

This is the dilemma faced by countries whose competitive position is weak. Withdrawal from the world economy protects domestic producers and the incomes they generate. But, by limiting access to global markets, protection of the home market protects domestic producers at a potential cost in the potential gains in productivity available to producers in rapidly growing markets. Yet participation in the world economy provides no assurance that a nation will become more efficient, and can mean a continuing loss of markets, incomes, and employment.

The Global Division of Markets

As we have seen, political economy sometimes employs the concept of a "global division of labor" to characterize the organization of the world economy. The concept suggests a system of specialization and mutual dependence. It encourages us to think of the global economy as one large production process divided up among nations, with each region or nation taking on responsibility for one or more of the elements (goods and services) necessary to keep the whole in operation.

With this image in mind, economists since David Ricardo have argued that the market organizes the division of tasks in such a way as to take advantage of differences across regions in skills, endowments, and other capacities. Trade between regions and nations enhances overall efficiency.

This image might work well if specialization followed natural endowment. But, while consideration of natural capabilities is obviously relevant for some goods, the fundamental contours of international specialization and of global wealth and poverty are poorly explained by trying to apply this rule.

Much more important has been the rule of market size and market shares. Specialization follows competitive success. Regions specialize in manufactured goods, in high-technology products, and in financial services, not because of their endowments of resources, but because of their historic success in competition over market shares in those industries. Such success has much to do with their institutional framework, past access to markets, and past accumulations of capital. What appears to be a global division of labor is, on closer inspection, a global division of markets. The division of labor follows the division of markets, rather than vice versa.

The idea of a global division of markets makes more sense, the more the global economy consists of an integrated market system rather than a series of quasi-autonomous markets linked by a limited group of traded goods. The more we can speak of one global market, the more we must be concerned with the way shares of that market are divided among competing producers and among producers in different nations. The emergence of a more integrated market system goes hand in hand with a movement away from differentiation in economic structure across nations and regions and toward economic systems organized along similar lines and moving toward similar levels of development.

The "Competitive Price of Labor"

When we buy the products of low-wage countries at a cost lower than we would pay if we produced the goods ourselves, we benefit from the low wages paid in those countries.[8] If we can sell what we produce at a high price (i.e., under favorable terms of trade), we can benefit from our own high wages. When we buy goods under these conditions, in effect, we buy foreign labor cheap and sell our own at a high price.

Eventually, however, the high price of our own labor can become a competitive disadvantage for us. It does so when countries that pay lower wages develop the ability to produce some of the same goods that we produce at home at a higher cost. We can still buy the (products of the) cheaper labor abroad, but when we do so we forfeit the chance to sell our more expensive goods both at home and abroad. As measured by standards of the world market, our labor is too expensive.

We can think of the cost of the cheapest labor available in the world market for producing a particular commodity as the "competitive price of labor." If we pay our workers more than this without an offsetting advantage in productivity, our products become expensive and eventually uncompetitive. When our goods become uncompetitive, the workers who were hired at the price that exceeded the competitive price of labor lose their jobs. This job loss is the way the free market goes about adjusting wage costs to the competitive price of labor. The free market will do this automatically. In a world of free trade, we can continue to buy (the products of) cheap labor, but we cannot sustain the level of income associated with selling (the products of) our own expensive labor.

This creates a dilemma a free market economy cannot resolve for us. We must choose between (1) cheapening our own labor by adjusting its price toward the competitive world price and (2) imposing limits on the way we participate in the world market. Because different nations are at different levels of economic development, and because their peoples expect different living standards, the world market is always one in which products of labor bought at different prices confront one another. This confrontation does not always work to our advantage; we cannot always sell dear and buy cheap. When it works against us, the economic problem cannot help becoming a political one. In a real sense, the market fails to sustain our living standards. It threatens, instead, to adjust them to the competitive price of labor.

The problem is to bring our cost of labor into line with a cost determined by a lower standard of living in another country. To do so, we can: (1) import cheap laborers willing to work for a wage allowing a standard of living closer to that of our competitors; (2) drive down the living standards of our own workers; or (3) create a distinction between the wage we pay our workers (and therefore their cost to producers) and their standard of living. The first two solutions pose significant social problems. They both challenge historically achieved levels of living. This leaves the third alternative.

The third solution requires us to socialize part of the costs of labor. When private industry must foot the bill for medical insurance for its employees, rising costs of medical care mean rising labor costs. If government subsidizes health care, the cost of labor to the firm diminishes (or rises more slowly).

Clearly, attempting to maintain living standards by socializing labor costs leads to a significant expansion of the government budget. Financing this solution to the problems of a maturing economy means a shift in the way we divide our incomes between the parts devoted to private and public ends (i.e., that part spent by the government rather than by the private citizen). This shift also shifts our standard of living by changing the mix of consumption in the direction of social expenditures.

Economic maturity raises an issue concerning the appropriate mix between private and public activities. Debate over this issue has been significantly hampered (especially in the United States) by the so-called tax revolt, which has been aimed at preventing exactly that shift demanded by a changing relationship with the global political economy.

The prospect of socializing a set of basic expenses that are currently the responsibility of the individual (e.g., health care) challenges a basic premise of the private enterprise economy: that livelihood should depend on exchange (see Lindblom 1977). It does so by explicitly acknowledging that the wage serves two potentially conflicting functions: it is both a cost of production and a determinant of livelihood. When conflict arises between these functions, we need to reconsider the institutions of the wage system and possible modifications that redefine the link between the cost of labor and the standard of living of the laborer.

The government must, insofar as possible, assure living standards where the market fails to do so. The global market does not know the appropriate standard of life for the citizen of a particular nation. The market can adjust cost and price so as to assure that full advantage accrues to the buyer from the lowest-cost production available. But the buyer must also sell something. Circumstances arise, the world economy being one, in which the circle that connects buyer and seller favors the buyer at the expense of the seller, when they are both in fact the same person.

Conclusion

Only with difficulty can the problem of global interdependence be separated from the question of free trade. Free trade policy encourages expansion of interdependence, realizing the benefits and harms discussed above. The significance of the idea of free trade stems from the way it embodies the nation's commitment to make its economy more fully a part of a global system. Logically, this commitment entails more than free trade in the narrow sense. It includes broad integration of national policy and practice with policy and practice of other nations. Consideration of the benefits and harms of such a policy of integration cannot be restricted to matters of economic growth and prosperity, for these benefits and harms involve the entire range of issues centering on the role of the state in economic and social development.

The policy of free trade is ultimately a policy of abdication. It is part of an ideal of the state-economy relationship that minimizes the role of the state. When the state abdicates its responsibility and sacrifices its power to direct economic development, it places the nation at risk.

Not only do free trade and global integration express a policy of abdication; they also create a situation that reduces the capacity of the state to act on the national interest in the area of economic development. The greater the integration of the national economy into the global system, the less effective is state economic policy domestically. Thus the policy of free trade means not only that the state does not want to play a role; it means also that, to an increasing degree, the state becomes unable to play a role.

The question of free trade must be answered, then, in a larger context. It must be understood as a question about the state, about its capacities and its responsibilities. Given some of the considerations advanced in this chapter, we must judge the policy of free trade a risky one for the United States, primarily because it weakens our will to affect our national destiny and takes out of our hands the ability to do so.

Notes

1. Economists schooled in the theory of comparative advantage tend to dismiss arguments centering on competitiveness because such arguments emphasize absolute rather than relative advantages in productivity. See, for example, Krugman and Obstfeld (1991, chapter 2). But absolute advantage—i.e., the higher productivity of one nation in the production of a single good—is important so long as productivity differences depend on market scale, and therefore market share, and so long as we do not base our arguments on the assumption of a tendency toward full employment. I explore the notion of comparative advantage at greater length below.

2. Note that product differentiation means that goods sold are similar, serving in a broad sense the same purpose but not necessarily exactly the same. Personal computers produced in the United States and abroad are broadly the same goods but will not exhibit all the same features.

3. Krugman (1991) suggests that the geographic distribution of production might be arbitrary in important respects.

4. For a fuller discussion of competitiveness and trade, see Blecker (1992).

5. This strategy refers us back to product life-cycle arguments concerning the global distribution of productive activities; see Vernon (1966).

6. We might not. Why give up advantages unless you are compelled to do so? If a country can maintain domestic monopolies or near-monopolies for its own producers and yet sell extensively abroad, little in the way of economic argument stands in its way.

7. The global division of labor carries its own risks. It matters how countries specialize, particularly whether they specialize in agriculture or manufacturing (see Lewis 1978).

8. This is a low cost in goods we produce and exchange for imports, and thus it depends on the terms of trade.

Bibliography

Amsden, Alice. 1989. *Asia's Next Giant: South Korea and Late Industrialization.* Oxford, England: Oxford University Press.

Blecker, Robert A. 1992. *Beyond the Twin Deficits: A Trade Strategy for the 1990s.* Economic Policy Institute Series. Armonk, NY: M. E. Sharpe.

Cooper, Richard N. 1972. "Economic Interdependence and Foreign Policy in the Seventies." *World Politics,* Vol. 24, No. 2 (January), pp. 159–81.

Keohane, Robert O., and Joseph Nye, Jr. 1977. *Power and Interdependence: World Politics in Transition.* Boston, MA: Little, Brown.

Krasner, Stephen D. 1978. *Defending the National Interest: Raw Materials Investments and U.S. Foreign Policy.* Princeton, NJ: Princeton University Press.

Krugman, Paul. 1990. "Import Protection as Export Promotion: International Competition in the Presence of Oligopoly and Economies of Scale." In Paul Krugman, ed., *Rethinking International Trade.* Cambridge, MA: MIT Press.

———. 1991. *Geography and Trade.* Cambridge, MA: MIT Press.

Krugman, Paul, and Maurice Obstfeld. 1991. *International Economics: Theory and Practice,* 2d ed. New York: HarperCollins.

Levine, David P. 1995. *Wealth and Freedom: An Introduction to Political Economy.* New York: Cambridge University Press.

Lewis, W. Arthur. 1978. *The Evolution of the International Economic Order.* Princeton, NJ: Princeton University Press.

Lindblom, Charles E. 1977. *Politics and Markets: The World's Political-Economic Systems.* New York: Basic Books.

Mead, Walter Russell. 1990. *The Low-Wage Challenge to Global Growth.* Washington, DC: Economic Policy Institute.

Ricardo, David. 1951. *The Principles of Political Economy and Taxation.* In Piero Sraffa, ed., *The Works and Correspondence of David Ricardo.* Cambridge, England: Cambridge University Press.

Robinson, Joan. 1966. *The New Mercantilism.* Cambridge, England: Cambridge University Press.

Smith, Adam. 1937. *The Wealth of Nations.* New York: Modern Library.

Thirwall, A. P. 1979. "The Balance of Payments Constraint as an Explanation of International Growth Rate Differences." *Banco Nazionale del Lavoro Quarterly Review,* No. 128 (March), pp. 45–53.

Vernon, Raymond. 1966. "International Investment and International Trade in the Product Cycle." *Quarterly Journal of Economics,* Vol. 80, No. 2 (May), pp. 190–207.

PART II
Issues in U.S. Trade Policy

CHAPTER THREE

International Trade and the Performance of U.S. Labor Markets

DALE BELMAN AND THEA M. LEE

Introduction

The U.S. economy has become progressively more open to international trade during the last several decades, with successive rounds of tariff reductions through the General Agreement on Tariffs and Trade (GATT) and the implementation of various regional trade agreements (with Israel, Canada, and Mexico). Since 1973 average real wages in the United States have stagnated or fallen, and since 1980 the gap between the wages of college-educated and non-college-educated workers has widened dramatically. What, if any, connection is there between these two trends?

The economics profession has attempted to answer various versions of this question in recent years. What impact does freer trade have on wages and employment in the United States? To be more precise, have lower trade barriers (or the growing trade deficit or growing trade with developing countries) been responsible for some portion of the decline in wages for non-college-educated American workers? Has trade exacerbated growing inequality in the distribution of income between the highest- and the lowest-paid workers? Has increased trade been a cause of declining employment in manufacturing? What impact does increasing the volume of balanced trade (i.e., increasing exports and imports by equivalent amounts) have on the quality of jobs available? In other words, are export jobs superior to import jobs on average? What will be the consequences for U.S. workers of increased trade with less developed countries (LDCs) that have large and rapidly growing labor forces?

To many Americans—especially those living in the communities hardest hit by import competition—it seems intuitively true that an influx of cheap imports from countries where wages are a small fraction of U.S. wages puts downward pressure on domestic wages and leads to a loss of domestic jobs. Certainly, many workers have been laid off from plants unable to compete with imports, while

The authors would like to thank Robert Blecker, Steve Beckman, Larry Mishel, and Robert Scott for comments on earlier drafts.

others have been confronted with a choice between deep pay cuts and plant relocation abroad. Furthermore, the trend of rising wage inequality in the United States roughly coincides with the rapid growth in the trade deficit and the expansion of trade with developing countries (see Batra 1993). Nor has the recent growth in U.S. exports brought clear gains in jobs and wages (see, for example, University of Illinois at Chicago 1994).

As Harvard University economists Jeffrey D. Sachs and Howard J. Shatz have acknowledged,

> both the Heckscher-Ohlin-Samuelson . . . model [of trade] and standard models of international capital mobility predict that internationalization will narrow the gap between U.S. and rest-of-world wages and widen the gap between wages of skilled and unskilled workers within the United States. Moreover, these standard theories predict that U.S. manufacturing sectors that are intensive in low-skilled workers will shrink in the face of increased integration with developing countries abundant in low-skilled workers. (1994, pp. 2–3)

Yet many international trade economists have resisted accepting these conclusions, apparently because their political implications appear to imperil the free trade agenda. Jagdish Bhagwati, a prominent trade theorist at Columbia University, writes that "the fear that has grown in the United States and in Western Europe that the freeing of trade with the poor countries of the South will hurt the real wages of the unskilled" is one of two great threats to free trade today—along with demands for a "level playing field" (Bhagwati and Dehejia 1994, pp. 36–37). These economists point to other theoretical possibilities, such as economies of scale or dynamic gains in productivity, that could more than compensate for the wage-reducing effects of trade liberalization predicted in the standard models.

A few influential articles have appeared in the last few years claiming to resolve this issue by exonerating trade (see especially Lawrence and Slaughter 1993; Krugman and Lawrence 1993; Bound and Johnson 1992). International trade is not responsible for the increasingly unequal distribution of wages, these authors argue. Rather, the true culprit is alleged to be technological change, which has increased demand for skilled workers, thus bidding up their wages relative to the wages of less skilled workers. Moreover, international trade is argued to be too small relative to the aggregate economy to possibly account for any dramatic changes in employment, wages, or income distribution (Krugman 1994a).

The mainstream business press responded to these claims with evident relief, immediately seizing upon these (still preliminary) results. "The Victim Has a Blue Collar, but Free Trade Has an Alibi," proclaimed a *New York Times* headline (Passell 1992). *Business Week* joined in, concluding that "technological advances—not a flood of cheap goods from abroad—led to an increase in manufacturing productivity and resulted in a decline in manufacturing employment" (Ullmann 1993).

This chapter will assess the current body of economic literature on the topic of trade, employment, and wages, critically reviewing the most important articles. The conclusions that emerge from this review are fairly strong: most of the research, using a range of empirical methods and theoretical assumptions, has found that increased trade (or import competition) is associated to some extent with reduced domestic employment and/or wages, with the employment effect usually estimated to be several times larger than the direct wage impact. Some of these studies focus on specific industries or the manufacturing sector; others attempt to measure the aggregate impact of trade. Trade appears to have a more significant effect on the distribution of wages than on the average wage, although there is some disagreement about what portion of the widening wage gap between college-educated and non-college-educated workers is accounted for by trade. There is also evidence that the negative connection between increased imports and employment tends to be stronger than the positive connection between exports and employment.

In our judgment, it is inappropriate to conclude at present—on the basis of current research—that trade "has an alibi" or that the debate is closed. As will be argued below, the research that supports the view that only technology is to blame is both conceptually and technically flawed. If anything, the preponderance of evidence indicates that increased trade has had a negative effect on wages in manufacturing and has accelerated the decline in employment in this sector. The consequent movement of jobs out of manufacturing and into lower-wage service sectors has also contributed to the declining average real wage in the U.S. economy as a whole. By eliminating high-quality jobs for non-college-educated workers, this process has also exacerbated wage inequality between the most and least educated workers during the last decade. Trade is by no means the only factor that has contributed to these trends; technology may also have played a role. It is difficult to distinguish the effects of trade and technology because they are not necessarily independent of each other (especially if new technologies are adopted partly in response to international competitive pressures).

Given the accelerated entrance into world markets of large, labor-abundant developing countries like China and India, as well as the Eastern European economies, increased trade flows can be expected to exert even more influence in the near future than they have in the past. Increasing flows of direct foreign investment to developing countries, reinforced by liberalized investment rules under the North American Free Trade Agreement (NAFTA) and the Uruguay Round of GATT, will also magnify the effects of international trade on wages and employment. Thus, the issues addressed in this chapter are of critical importance for assessing the current direction of U.S. trade policy and global economic trends.

Trade, Wages, and Inequality: Some Descriptive Statistics

It is useful to begin with a brief description of the circumstances that have led to so much interest in the possible linkages between increased trade and worsened labor market performance. In 1960, merchandise exports and imports combined represented 6.7 percent of U.S. gross domestic product (GDP); by 1993, this trade share had more than doubled to 16.5 percent.[1] Imports have grown far more dramatically than exports, particularly since the early 1980s. By 1993, the United States had a $132.5 billion merchandise trade deficit. The current account, which takes into account income from abroad and the trade surplus in services, registered a deficit of $103.9 billion in the same year. In contrast, in 1980 the United States had a merchandise trade deficit of only $25.5 billion and a $2.3 billion surplus on the current account.[2]

Since 1980, U.S. trade with fast-growing developing countries has also risen rapidly, again with import growth outstripping exports by a wide margin. While trade with Japan still accounts for over half of the U.S. overall trade deficit, the newly industrializing countries (NICs), along with the next tier of developing countries, are increasingly competing in a broad range of industries. Imports from the Asian NICs, plus China, Brazil, and Mexico, grew 121 percent from 1980 to 1992, while U.S. exports to these countries grew by only 52 percent.[3] Consequently, the U.S. merchandise trade balance with this group swung from a $7 billion surplus in 1980 to a deficit of $23 billion in 1992 (measured in 1992 dollars). Compared to both Europe and Japan, the United States imports a significantly larger share of manufactured goods (relative to GDP). This is especially true with respect to low-wage countries: manufacturing imports from low-wage countries made up 2.6 percent of U.S. GDP in 1991, compared to 1.7 percent for the European Community (EC) and 1.2 percent for Japan (Howes and Markusen 1993, p. 26).

Growth in international trade has been both complemented and spurred by a rapid rise in direct foreign investment and a growing role for multinational enterprises (MNEs). The stock of worldwide direct foreign investment approximately doubled between 1987 and 1992, to almost $2 trillion, according to United Nations Conference on Trade and Development (UNCTAD) data (cited in Sengenberger 1994, p. 398). Sengenberger points out:

> Overseas investment by multinationals has become a bigger force in the world economy than world trade. In 1992, sales generated by multinationals outside their country of origin totalled $5.5 trillion, compared with total world exports of $4 trillion. MNEs control one-third of the world's private sector assets . . . [and account] for about 20 per cent of paid employment in non-agricultural activities in OECD countries. (1994, pp. 397–98)

During the recent period of steadily increasing trade volume, gradual (although uneven) reduction in trade barriers, and rising direct foreign investment, the employment prospects and earnings of the majority of Americans have deteriorated.[4] Real hourly compensation has been stagnant since 1973 and falling since 1977. Growth in median family income also slowed over this period. While real family income (in 1991 dollars) rose by $5,000 between 1967 and

1973, it rose by only $1,530 between 1973 and 1989, and all this increase was a result of increasing hours of work. The same period has seen an increase in the rate of unemployment, from 3.8 percent in 1973 to 5.3 percent in 1989; a decline in the rate of employment growth, from 3.6 percent in the 1970–73 expansion to 3.0 percent in the 1982–90 expansion; decreases in coverage of health and pension benefits in the private sector; increased earnings inequality; and an increased proportion of the population living in poverty, from 11.1 percent in 1973 to 12.8 percent in 1989.

There are many indicators of rising inequality among workers as well.[5] The proportion of the labor force earning between 125 and 300 percent of the poverty wage fell from 54.5 to 48.3 percent between 1973 and 1993. The only two income categories that expanded were those earning over 300 percent of the poverty wage, which rose from 9.2 to 10.3 percent, and those earning between 100 and 125 percent of that wage, which expanded from 12.5 to 14.5 percent of the labor force. Between 1979 and 1989, pension coverage of the labor force declined from 50 to 42.9 percent, and health insurance coverage declined from 68.5 to 61.1 percent. Even the upgrading of employees into better occupations does not have the beneficial effects of past decades. Occupational upgrading produced a 0.18 percent annual increase in wages between 1972 and 1979, a 0.23 percent annual increase between 1979 and 1989, but only a 0.09 percent annual increase between 1989 and 1993. Trends such as these have led to concern about the disappearance of the middle of the income distribution.

The manufacturing sector in particular suffered severe loss of both jobs and output during this period, regaining only some of the lost ground when the trade deficit fell in the late 1980s and early 1990s. Although not the highest-paying sector in the economy (that distinction goes to construction), manufacturing pays better than the service sectors, such as retail trade, that have experienced the most rapid employment growth over the past few decades.[6] In 1979, prior to the large increase in trade deficits, the average wage in manufacturing was $6.70, 32 percent more than retail trade ($4.53), 21 percent more than finance ($5.27), 20 percent more than services ($5.36), and 5 percent more than wholesale trade ($6.39). Even after a decade of buffeting by trade, production and nonsupervisory employees in manufacturing, who on average earned $11.74 an hour in wages in 1993, earned 38 percent more than those in retail trade ($7.29), 3.3 percent more than those in finance ($11.35) and 8 percent more than those in services ($10.79). Wholesale trade paid the same hourly wage as manufacturing in 1993. In 1993 the three lowest-paid industries in the manufacturing sector— apparel at $7.06, leather and leather products at $7.62, and textile mill products at $8.88—paid wages similar to or better than the average wage in the retail trade sector.

While the wage performance of the manufacturing sector has been modest over the past decade, its employment performance has been far worse. Private sector employment increased by 99 percent between 1960 and 1993, but manufacturing employment grew by only 6 percent over this period. Even this impression is too favorable; manufacturing employment peaked at 21 million in 1979, contracted by 1.6 million by 1982, recovered to a level of 19.4 million in 1988, and then declined to 17.8 million employees in 1993.

In the manufacturing sector, wages and employment are sensitive to an industry's place in trade patterns. In 1983 the typical worker in an exporting industry earned $9.55 per hour, while the typical worker in an import-competing industry earned $8.28 per hour. After adjusting for individual characteristics affecting wages, Katz and Summers (1989) found that wages in export-intensive industries were 11 percent above the average manufacturing wage, while wages in import-intensive industries were 15 percent below the manufacturing average. If attention is restricted to the ten industries with the largest volume of exports and an equal-sized set of import-exposed industries, the exporting industries pay a premium of 16 percent more than the average manufacturing wage, while the importing industries pay 27 percent less (Katz and Summers 1989, p. 262).

In terms of employment, however, imports appear to have a negative impact not offset by exports. Examining data on employment by manufacturing establishments for the period 1972 to 1988, Davis, Haltiwanger, and Schuh (1994) find that manufacturing plants in industries faced with high levels of import penetration[7] have heightened rates of job loss. The 20 percent of establishments (plants) in industries with the highest levels of import penetration had annual employment losses averaging 2.8 percent, while the other 80 percent of establishments had average employment losses of only 0.9 percent annually.

The poor jobs performance of import-exposed industries is not balanced by the superior performance of exporting industries. Rearranging establishments into quintiles according to export performance, the 20 percent of plants in industries with the largest export share perform only marginally better than the remaining 80 percent of establishments. Average job losses were 1.0 percent in establishments in the top exporting industries, only slightly better than the 1.2 percent annual losses recorded for the remainder of establishments. The effects of trade on employment thus seem to be asymmetrical: imports appear to accelerate employment decline in manufacturing and to increase instability in employment, while exports do little to ameliorate these problems. The sources of these differences are not readily apparent from descriptive statistics and will be discussed at length below.

Trade Theory and Possible Causal Channels

The coincidence of the aforementioned trends in trade, wages, and employment does not, of course, prove the existence of causal relationships among them. In order to understand how increasing trade could be related to changing labor market conditions, it is useful to review the potential causal mechanisms of how trade can affect income distribution and job creation. Over the years, economic theorists have developed a number of models of trade-distribution linkages. This section will review some of the most important theories of trade and distribution in order to lay the ground for the review of empirical studies in the following section. While theories of trade and employment are less well developed (especially since most trade theories tend to assume full employment), we will also comment on employment issues here; they will receive a fuller treatment in the review of the empirical literature later in this chapter.

The most widely accepted trade theory is based on the Heckscher-Ohlin-Samuelson (HOS) model, which was originally intended to illuminate the effects of trade on the distribution of income between owners of different "factors of production" (such as labor, land, and capital).[8] The standard "2 × 2 × 2" version of the HOS model portrays a world consisting of two countries, each capable of producing the same two commodities using inputs of the same two factors of production (usually capital and labor or land and labor).[9] Product and factor markets are assumed to be perfectly competitive, with prices automatically adjusting so that supply equals demand. This rules out market "imperfections," such as monopolistic pricing, long-term trade imbalances, and chronic unemployment. Since the model assumes full employment, all the effects of trade on the demand for labor are reflected in wage changes.

Within the context of the HOS model, trade arises because countries differ in their "endowments" (supplies) of factors and thus are relatively better suited to the production of different goods. For example, if country A has an abundance of capital and a scarcity of labor (relative to country B), then, as long as there are some barriers to trade, capital will be cheap relative to labor in A. (Essentially, A will be a "high-wage" country.) As a result, country A can produce the more capital-intensive good at lower relative cost, and therefore has a "comparative advantage" in that product. The labor-intensive good will be more expensive in A, however. The opposite applies to country B. If the two nations specialize according to their respective comparative advantages, they can both benefit from trade in the sense that their total consumption will be greater in the absence of trade barriers than in the presence of trade barriers. Free trade benefits both countries because it allows all resources to be used in their most productive capacities.

However, this theory neither promises nor predicts that every individual in both countries will find himself or herself better off under free trade. The owners of the two factors of production (in this case, capital and labor) will be affected in opposite directions. In the HOS model, the owners of the relatively scarce factor will be made worse off by a reduction in trade barriers, while the owners of the abundant factor will be made better off. Intuitively, the scarce factor is seen to become less scarce in a more open global economy, so its price (the wage rate) adjusts downward accordingly. This result is known as the Stolper-Samuelson (SS) theorem (after Stolper and Samuelson 1941).

For example, if country A lowers a tariff on its labor-intensive good, then the domestic price of that good falls. Consequently, the wage of labor, which is used relatively intensively in the production of that good, also falls, while the return to the other factor, capital, rises. The loss to labor is more than offset by the gains to capital, leading to the net national gains from trade.

Trade theorists often gloss over these distributional difficulties by arguing that it is *possible* to redistribute income after trade liberalization so that every individual is better off under free trade than with trade barriers. Although theoretically possible, such redistribution of the gains from trade has never been part of the standard policy package accompanying trade liberalization.[10] Certainly, there is no automatic mechanism that compels the winners to compensate the losers.

In applying the simple, two-factor theorem to the United States, we would assume that this country is relatively abundant in capital and scarce in labor, compared to the rest of the world. In this case, trade liberalization in the United States causes the domestic price of capital-intensive goods to rise relative to the price of labor-intensive goods. As a result, we would expect to see returns to capital rise and workers' wages to fall. Expanding on the basic model, it is also possible to designate the two factors of production as skilled and less skilled labor (as in Wood 1994), or to expand the model to encompass three factors (e.g., capital, professional and technical labor, and "other labor," as in Leamer 1993). In these cases, the model would predict increased wage inequality as a consequence of liberalized trade, with the wage of the more skilled labor (the abundant factor) rising (possibly along with returns to capital) and the wage of the less skilled labor (the scarce factor) falling. In empirical terms, these two categories are typically translated into college graduates and workers without college degrees, approximately one-quarter and three-quarters of the U.S. labor force, respectively.

A second theorem that also bears on the distributional impact of trade is factor price equalization (FPE). FPE predicts that, in the absence of any trade barriers (including transportation costs, tariffs, quotas, and any other impediments), perfectly free trade that equalizes commodity prices will result in the equalization of factor prices as well. In other words, if goods are allowed to cross national borders freely, then eventually the returns to factors of production (in the trading countries) will be equalized, even if the factors themselves are not allowed to move internationally. This would imply, for example, that wages in the United States, Mexico, and China would be completely equalized if trade barriers were completely removed.

The conditions under which the FPE theorem holds are more stringent than those required for the SS theorem. In a two-country model, it is also necessary that both countries produce both goods (neither may completely specialize), that there be "constant returns to scale" (no economies or diseconomies of scale), and that both countries employ identical technology. The factors must be able to move freely between sectors within each country, and the quality of the factors must be identical in the two countries.

How relevant is FPE today? Obviously, not all factor prices are actually equalized internationally, especially wages. This is not surprising theoretically, since the stringent conditions required for the FPE theorem are generally violated in practice. The relevant question, then, is whether there is a tendency for factor prices (particularly the wages of "unskilled" workers) to converge internationally as the world moves closer to fulfilling the conditions for FPE (for example, through reductions in trade barriers and the diffusion of modern technology to LDCs). If so, this could have potentially serious implications for the United States and other high-wage nations, if their wages have to fall for convergence to take place.

Laying out the basic model and accompanying assumptions makes it quite clear that neither of these theorems should be accepted literally. Most of the necessary assumptions for the whole HOS model of trade are frequently violated: there is not always full employment and balanced trade (so markets are not adjusting as smoothly as assumed); there are often economies of scale, especially in manufacturing; technology does differ between countries; factor endowments are not fixed, but are constantly changing; countries do sometimes specialize completely (e.g., the United States produces no bananas, while Honduras produces no airplanes); capital is increasingly mobile between countries, and even labor mobility seems to be on the rise; and prices of both commodities and factors tend to reflect institutional and market-structure factors as well as pure supply-and-demand forces.

Explicitly taking some of these factors into account could dampen or reverse the standard predictions of both SS and FPE. There may be positive effects of trade liberalization beyond those incorporated in the standard model (see the discussion in Bhagwati and Dehejia 1994). These are sometimes called "lifting-all-boats" effects. For example, if production is characterized by economies of scale (advantages of large-scale production) rather than constant returns, as the standard model assumes, then freer trade can reduce per-unit costs by expanding the size of the market. This will increase the gains from trade over the standard efficiency gains. If this effect is large enough, it could result in rising returns for both factors of production, eliminating the SS prediction of falling wages in response to a reduction in the tariff on the labor-intensive good.[11] A similar effect can arise if, as is sometimes argued, international competition compels companies to improve their productivity and the productivity gains are passed on to workers (these are often referred to as dynamic gains from trade, since the requisite technological and organizational improvements take time to be implemented).

Although most of the recent theoretical writing has focused on these forces that tend to offset SS and FPE effects, other sometimes neglected forces could actually strengthen their predictions. Factor mobility in particular can achieve the same distributional outcome as FPE even if there are still some barriers to trade. Labor migration tends to relieve downward pressures on wages in the low-wage countries from which workers emigrate and to contribute to downward pressures on wages in the high-wage countries into which they immigrate. Capital mobility has a similar effect, by lowering the demand for labor and thus tending to reduce wages in capital-exporting (high-wage) countries, and by doing the opposite in capital-importing (low-wage) countries.

There are other trade models in which the predictions about wage effects are more ambiguous. When some factors of production are not mobile between sectors within a country (contrary to the HOS assumption), then their incomes depend only on the relative price of the good they help to produce. This is called a *specific factors model*. For example, in a model in which capital and land are specific to particular sectors (manufacturing and agriculture, respectively), but labor can be used in both industries, trade liberalization has an ambiguous effect on the real wage, depending on the relative importance of the two goods in workers' budgets and other parameters of the model (see Deardorff and Hakura 1994; Caves, Frankel, and Jones 1993). Alternatively, there could be a model in which different types of labor would be specific to particular industries (e.g., textile and aerospace workers would not be interchangeable). In these situations, trade would benefit workers in whichever industry produced for export, and would injure workers in whichever industry competed with imports. However, to the extent that these two groups of workers roughly correspond to the skilled/ unskilled distinction, then the distributional predictions of such a model are similar to the predictions of an HOS model with two types of labor.

Trade can also affect wages through a variety of channels that are not readily captured by any conventional trade models. First, trade may slow wage growth or reduce wages through an implicit (or sometimes explicit) threat effect: workers may be threatened with outsourcing or runaway shops if they do not accept pay cuts. This can occur in the absence of actual changes in international trade or investment, although certainly experience with some import competition or foreign investment helps to make the threat "credible." Basically, this mechanism assumes that wages are determined by labor-management bargaining in which the relative strength of employees and employers affects the outcome of the negotiations, rather than in the perfectly competitive "auction" markets of standard trade theory. Import competition or a threat of job relocation can reduce workers' bargaining strength and therefore reduce wages. We might think that export success would put a parallel and offsetting upward pressure on wage rates in export sectors, and there is some evidence that workers in export industries do better than average on this score (Galbraith and Calmon 1994). Exports may not be symmetrical to imports in this respect; employers in export industries may try to keep the lid on wages in order to remain competitive in global markets—or they may relocate production abroad in order to lessen the bargaining strength of labor at home.

Second, the movement of capital to low-wage countries may be motivated in part by lower trade barriers (i.e., companies may move plants in order to take advantage of lower wages and continue selling in the domestic market). Often, this outflow of capital goes hand in hand with transfers of technology that raise productivity in the export sectors of the low-wage countries to competitive levels. The resulting outflow of capital lowers the domestic capital stock, thus reducing the demand for labor and putting downward pressure on wages at home. Although the outcome is similar to that induced by capital mobility in an HOS-type model, the motivation is different. While, in an HOS model, capital mobility substitutes for commodity trade (because either one tends to eliminate differences in factor prices), the mechanism alluded to here suggests that capital mobility and commodity trade can be complements (and hence that trade liberalization can encourage rather than discourage capital mobility).

Third, standard trade models often do not take account of the fact that large parts of domestic economies consist of nontradable goods and services (e.g., goods that do not meet international quality standards, personal and government services, etc.).[12] When workers are displaced from tradable goods industries by import competition, they may get jobs in nontradable sectors such as services rather than in higher-wage export sectors. If the service jobs pay lower wages, then economywide average wages can be lowered by trade even if wages of those who remain in the traded goods sectors do not fall.

This type of concern arises especially in light of the evidence for the existence of "labor rents" in many manufacturing activities: wage premiums that are received by workers who are lucky enough to have jobs in these industries, regardless of their individual characteristics (see Dickens and Lang 1988; Katz and Summers 1989; Dickens 1994). While the sources of labor rents are still debated by economists, one of the most likely reasons is the prevalence of oligopolistic market structures in some branches of industry that enable firms to reap above-normal profits (called "oligopoly rents")—and the potential for workers in these industries to win a share of these rents through wage bargaining (Borjas and Ramey 1994). This line of reasoning suggests that import competition that displaces workers from oligopolistic, rent-paying industries is likely to lower average wages as the displaced workers are reemployed (if at all) in lower-wage competitive industries or in the service sector.

Finally, standard trade models assume balanced trade and full employment overall, which is why their predictions center on changes in commodity and factor prices (which have to be flexible in order for markets to "clear" and thus maintain full employment with balanced trade). In reality, prices and wages are not so flexible, and imbalanced trade and unemployment frequently coexist. Under these circumstances, trade can have a variety of effects not contemplated in conventional models. For example, the impact of trade can be felt more on employment than on wages. Trade deficits, especially if concentrated in high-wage sectors such as manufacturing, can have an especially depressing effect on both employment and the average wages of those employed. As we shall see below, the empirical studies thus far have found more evidence for negative employment effects of trade than for wage effects, although there may be some statistical biases in the currently used methods that make it hard to measure the latter accurately.

As the preceding discussion illustrates, small alterations in the analytical framework used can cause considerable variations in the predicted effects of trade on income distribution. Wages may rise or fall, or become more or less unequal, depending on the sizes of the various offsetting effects. We cannot look to theory to provide definitive answers to the questions we are examining. Instead, we must turn to the empirical research that tries to measure the impact of these offsetting changes.

Empirical Studies of Trade and Labor Market Performance

The literature on international trade and labor market performance is large and growing. This section organizes the literature into five topics. The first deals with studies of the effects of increasing trade on wages and employment in the manufacturing sector. The second topic is the effect of growth in international trade on the quality of jobs, both within the manufacturing sector and in the economy as a whole. The third topic is whether and how trade has influenced the average wage level throughout the economy. The fourth topic is whether trade is a source of increased wage inequality among different groups of workers, especially those with different levels of skill or training. The fifth and last topic is studies that have explicitly tested the relevance of the Stolper-Samuelson and factor price equalization theorems from trade theory.

The Effects of Trade in the Manufacturing Sector

The impact of trade is likely to be felt first and most strongly in the manufacturing sector. Although manufacturing accounted for only 18.5 percent of U.S. GDP in 1991, manufactured goods accounted for 63 percent of the value of trade in goods and services. Duchin and Lange (1988) found that the trade deficit of 1987 was associated with the loss of 5.1 million job opportunities, of which 3.1 million were lost in the manufacturing sector. More recently, Sachs and Shatz (1994) have found that the increase in the trade deficit in manufactured goods between 1978 and 1990 reduced employment of production workers in manufacturing by 6.5 percent, compared with a reduction of 2.7 percent in nonproduction employment.

Befitting the importance of trade in goods, the literature on international trade in manufacturing industries is extensive and varied. Industry-level studies of the effects of international trade in manufacturing vary considerably in how trade is measured, the period under study, the specification of models, and estimation techniques. Table 3.1 (pages 74–75) summarizes the most important recent studies.

Using measures of import and export quantities for 428 manufacturing industries for the period 1958 to 1984, Freeman and Katz (1991) find that a 10 percent increase in imports reduces wages within an industry by 0.0 to 0.64 percent and employment by 5 to 6 percent. Equivalent increases in exports raise wages by 0.0 to 0.76 percent and employment by about 7 percent.[13] Using the same data set as Freeman and Katz, Brauer (1990) examines both the within-industry and the between-industry effects of imports and exports on wages. Between industries, an industry with a 10 percent greater volume of imports would have a 3 percent lower wage; a similar difference in the volume of exports would cause the wage to be 1.3 percent higher. Within an industry, a 10 percent increase in the volume of imports would reduce the wage by 1.0 to 1.8 percent. Exports do not have a statistically significant within-industry effect on wages.

Some studies have looked only at the import side. Grossman (1987) estimated the wage and employment consequences of trade within nine import-sensitive industries for 1967–79. He found that declining import prices reduce hours of employment in eight of the nine industries (the exception was photographic equipment). A 10 percent decline in real import prices was found to cause hours of work to fall by 30 percent in radio and TV equipment, 6 percent in the pottery industry, 7 percent in hardwood veneers, and 5 percent in leather tanning. Smaller effects were found for footwear (2.6 percent) and ball bearings (3.2 percent). Estimated wage elasticities also varied considerably between industries, but all were much smaller than the employment effects. Grossman's estimates show that wages declined by between 0.07 and 1.3 percent in response to a 10 percent decrease in the price of imports, depending on the industry.[14]

Based on these figures, Grossman concluded that imports have not had a major effect on hourly wages and, excepting radios and televisions, have not cost the United States a significant number of jobs. However, given the import price decreases actually experienced during Grossman's sample period, imports had negative employment effects in the range of 10 to 23 percent for four of the nine industries covered, and 71 percent in the radio and television industry. These are not negligible employment effects.

In later research that focused on the effect of import volume on the wages of individuals between 1981 and 1986, Heywood (1991) and Heywood and Broehm (1991) found that a 10 percent increase in imports was associated with a 1 percent lower wage.[15] Revenga's (1992) study of thirty-eight importing industries for the period 1977 to 1987 estimates that a 10 percent decline in the real import prices faced by an industry is associated with a 2.4 to 3.9 percent decline in employment and a 0.6 to 0.9 percent decline in wages in the industry. This study is especially noteworthy for the careful attention paid by the author to some of the statistical problems that are inherent in the estimation of the trade-jobs and trade-wages relationships.[16]

That imports reduce both wages and employment is not surprising; what may be surprising is that the employment effects are consistently larger than the wage effects. In all the studies that consider both employment and wage effects, esti-

Table 3.1

Studies of Wage and Employment Effects of Trade in U.S. Manufacturing

Study	Issues and Methods	Estimated Effects
Grossman (1987)	Employment and wages in nine import-sensitive industries from 1967 to 1979. Limited numbers of observations and large numbers of variables make estimates subject to substantial variation.	A 10% decline in the price of imports causes a 2.6–30% decline in employment and a 0.07–1.3% decline in wages, depending on the industry.
Freeman and Katz (1991)	Use data on 428 four-digit SIC[a] industries to calculate changes between 1958 and 1984. Regressions include controls for unionization, percentage of production workers in the labor force, and two-digit industry. Some models include controls for value added.	A 10% increase in imports causes wages to fall 0.0–0.6% and employment to fall 5–6%. A 10% increase in exports causes wages to increase 0.0–0.76% and employment to increase 7%. Imports have a negative effect on within-industry earnings during 1958–70 and 1980–84. Exports have a positive effect on wages before 1970, but no effect after that.
Freeman and Katz (1991)	Part of the previous study using CPS data for 1974 and 1984.	A 10% increase in imports reduces wages 2.3%. Exports do not have a positive effect on wages.
Brauer (1990)	Extends Freeman and Katz (1991) by using more flexible forms to allow for time effects.	Effect of imports on reducing wages increases steadily during the 1970s. By the end of the decade, a 10% increase in imports reduces wages 2.3%. Effects of exports on wages show no trend through the decade and are unstable.
Heywood (1991), and Heywood and Broehm (1991)	Use Panel Study of Income Dynamics to look at the effect of individuals shifting between industries affected by different levels of imports.	An industry with 10% higher imports has wages that are 1% lower.

Table 3.1 *(continued)*

Revenga (1992)	Instrumental variables estimates using panel data for 38 industries for 1977–87. Import prices are instrumented exchange rates.	A 10% decline in the price of imports causes a 2.4–3.9% decline in employment and a 0.6–0.9% decrease in wages.
Martines (1993)	Analyzes how market structures and product differentiation affect the relationship between international trade and wages. Uses data on 22 industries in 12 OECD[b] countries for 1970–90 to estimate country-specific, within-industry wage equations.	Imports reduce wages in industries with little product differentiation and competitive market structures; exports have some tendency to increase wages under these conditions. Results with other market and product structures are too mixed to support any theory.
Gaston and Trefler (1994)	Uses 1984 CPS data with appended industry trade data to measure between-industry effects on wages.	Imports do not reduce wages, but a 10% difference in export shares between industries will raise wages 44%. A 10% higher rate of growth of imports reduces wages 13.7%. A 1 standard deviation increase in tariff rates would reduce wages 3.4%.
Davis, Haltiwanger, and Schuh (1994)	Effect of imports and exports on job loss and job stability.	The 20% of establishments in industries most affected by imports have 3 times the rate of job loss as the remaining 80% of establishments, but the 20% of establishments with the largest exports do not have lower rates of job loss than the remaining 80% of establishments.
Sachs and Shatz (1994)	Consider how trade, particularly with developing countries, has affected employment and the employment of skilled and unskilled workers.	In manufacturing, 5.2% of employment was lost due to trade between 1978 and 1990. Of this, 4.2% was lost due to trade with developing countries. All loss of nonproduction employment during this period is ascribed to trade with developing countries.

[a]Standard Industrial Classification.
[b]Organization for Economic Cooperation and Development.

mated employment effects are considerably larger than wage effects regardless of whether imports are measured by prices or volumes. If these results are reliable, then, at least in manufacturing labor markets, responses to changing trade conditions are dominated by shifts in quantity (employment) rather than price (wage).

If the employment shifts consequent to international trade are not realized mainly as shifts in the level of unemployment or labor force participation, there is an additional implication that increased trade will reallocate employment between industries. "Taken together with the findings of Murphy and Welch [1991] among others, these results suggest that workers are highly mobile across industries . . ." (Revenga 1992, p. 277). By shifting the labor supply of industries outside the traded goods sector, international trade will affect wages and workers throughout the economy. Measurement of the full impact of international trade on labor markets will involve accounting for such shifts in employment and wages.

However, it is also possible that the small estimated effects of imports on industry-level wages in all the existing studies reflect a statistical difficulty in estimating this type of effect. It should be recalled that the jobs in any given industry offer a range (or "distribution") of wages, not a single wage rate. Brauer and Hickok (1994) and Wood (1994) suggest that increases in trade, particularly with low-wage countries, are likely to have their largest effects on low-productivity, low-wage U.S. producers and will drive some of these producers from the market. Under such a scenario, if the wages of the surviving employees remained unchanged, then increases in imports would lead to an *increase* in the industry-average wage, since many of the lowest-wage jobs would be eliminated. It may be that the small measured effects of imports on average wages are a consequence of this "selection effect," counterbalancing import-induced wage declines for the remaining workers.[17]

There is also some evidence that the negative effects of imports on wages at the industry level have increased over time. Exploring an unexpected lack of relationship between trade and wages in a particular data set, Freeman and Katz (1991) reestimated their model over the three subperiods 1958–70, 1970–80, and 1980–84.[18] Import shares have the expected negative effect on within-industry earnings for the periods before 1970 and after 1980, but no effect during the middle period. The estimate for 1980–84, that a 10 percent increase in import volume would cause a 0.7 percent decline in industry wages, is comparable to estimates for 1958–84, reported earlier. In contrast, exports had a positive wage effect prior to 1970 and no statistically measurable effect after that. Analysis of Current Population Survey (CPS) data confirms these patterns. Aggregating wages by two-digit industry, Freeman and Katz find that between 1974 and 1984 a 10 percent increase in imports was associated with a 2.3 percent decline in wages, but that there was no statistically detectable relationship between exports or domestic demand and wages.[19]

Brauer (1990) confirms and extends these estimates. Brauer finds that imports had no measurable effect on wages prior to 1970. The effect increases steadily in the 1970s until, by the end of the decade, an industry with a 10 percent higher volume of imports would have 2 to 3 percent lower wages. The effect of exports has no trend, but there is considerable annual variation. Depending on the year, an industry with a 10 percent higher volume of exports would have wages that were 1.5 to 8.5 percent higher than those of an otherwise comparable industry. Brauer also compares the effect of imports and exports in two periods: 1983–85 and 1975–77. His estimates indicate that exports did not have a statistically significant effect on wages in either period, but that the effect of imports increased between the two periods. While a 10 percent increase in imports reduced wages by 1.1 percent in the mid-1970s, a similar increase in imports reduced wages by 1.8 percent in the mid-1980s.

Such findings, which suggest that trade is undergoing structural changes unfavorable to American workers, is consistent with the work of Sachs and Shatz (1994) on trade with developing countries. This research finds that increased trade with developing countries has been the source of most trade-related employment loss over the last decade. Thus, it appears that research from the 1960s and the 1970s no longer accurately represents the effects of trade.

As noted earlier, contemporary theory explains how economies of scale and imperfect competition may limit or reverse the wage and employment consequences of the SS and FPE mechanisms. An implication of these theories is that industry and product market structures mediate the effects of trade. In particular, industries in which producers have control over price and in which there are high levels of product differentiation will perform better in export markets and in markets in which they face competition from imports.

Martines (1993) investigates the role of industry and product-market structure in mediating the effect of imports on wages. Using industry data on twenty-two consistently defined industries for twelve industrialized countries between 1970 and 1990, he finds a negative effect of imports on wages in industries with competitive market structures and little product differentiation. There is a strong negative relationship between imports and within-industry wages for competitive industries selling undifferentiated products. For the United States, a 10 percent increase in imports would cause a 2.4 percent decline in industry wages. The effect of exports under this market structure is less certain; there is a positive relationship in half the countries, but there is no statistically significant relationship in the other half. For the United States, a 10 percent increase in exports would cause U.S. wages to rise by 3.5 percent in competitive industries with undifferentiated products. Martines's results for other industry and market structures (competitive with differentiated products, oligopolistic with undifferentiated products, and oligopolistic with differentiated products) are less certain, however.[20] To the degree that any general conclusion may be reached from Martines's study, it is that imports depress wages in competitive industries.

As noted earlier, some trade theories predict that increased trade with developing countries, which have large endowments of low-skilled workers, will have negative effects on less skilled workers in American manufacturing, particularly in industries with a large proportion of low-skilled employees. This is confirmed by Sachs and Shatz (1994). They find that, from 1978 to 1990, trade with developing countries was concentrated in industries that required lower levels of worker skill and paid relatively low wages. Trade deficits with the developing countries were largest in the industries with the highest proportion of low-skilled employees.[21]

Industries with the smallest proportion of low-skilled workers frequently have trade surpluses. Industry trade deficits are particularly large where industry skill requirements are low and the wages of trading partners are low relative to the wages paid by the U.S. industry. Job loss is also closely associated with trade with developing countries. Almost all of the manufacturing employment lost to trade between 1978 and 1990 (5.7 percent out of 5.9 percent) is associated with trade with developing countries. Virtually all trade-associated loss of non-production-worker employment is due to trade with developing countries.

What conclusions may be drawn from this literature? First, there is evidence that international trade affects both wages and employment in the manufacturing sector and that the employment effects are several times the size of the wage effects. Although the estimated effects of trade on wages have been moderate, increased trade has reduced employment in manufacturing by about 6 percent, or about 1 million jobs, since 1978 (Sachs and Shatz 1994). Second, the negative consequences of imports for wages seem to have been increasing through the 1970s and the 1980s. Third, the relatively large employment effects of trade suggest considerable mobility of workers between jobs, which in turn implies that the problems of manufacturing are unlikely to remain within that sector. By displacing labor from manufacturing, international trade increases the supply of labor to other sectors that generally pay lower wages, and also places downward pressure on wages in those sectors.

Loss of wage leadership from the manufacturing sector may also be a source of poor wage performance throughout the economy. As recently as the early 1980s, pattern bargaining, wage contours, and wage emulation linked national wage trends to the negotiated wages and benefits of autoworkers, steelworkers, and others in the manufacturing sector. The continued existence of wage linkages between manufacturing and other industries is confirmed in the work of Galbraith and Calmon (1994), who find that wage movements in men's and women's clothing, department stores, and shoe stores are similar to those in the textile industry; wage movements in grocery stores are similar to those in bakeries and breweries; and wage movements in auto dealerships are similar to those of autoworkers. Given such linkages, slackening job and wage growth in manufacturing might well have disproportionate influence on wages throughout the economy.

Trade and Job Quality

One aspect of the poor performance of the U.S. labor market has been its flagging capacity to create "good" jobs, as reflected in the slippage in income and benefits over the last twenty years, documented above. Also as discussed previously, jobs in export industries tend to pay higher wages than those in import-competing industries. Some economists have therefore suggested that balanced expansion of international trade could play an important role in improving the quality of jobs by shifting workers from lower- to higher-wage industries. Historic evidence cited by Katz and Summers favors this argument:

> Between 1960 and 1980 the number of jobs displaced by imports was approximately equal to the number of jobs created by exports. Particularly during the 1970s increased imports led to a reallocation of labor out of the lowest-wage jobs in the manufacturing sector, and increased U.S. exports led to a rise in employment in high-wage sectors of the economy. (1989, p. 266)

The dynamic by which increased imports eliminate the lowest-wage jobs in the manufacturing sector is also apparent even through the early 1980s:

> During the 1980s the fraction of workers employed in producing tradable goods declined as the trade deficit increased. Between 1980 and 1984, . . . the increase in the trade deficit was associated with a reduction of 1.4 million workers producing traded manufacturing goods. More than 600,000, or 45 percent, of these workers had been employed in the quartile of industries that paid the lowest wages. This reflects the substantial increase in import penetration in industries like apparel during the early 1980s. (Katz and Summers 1989, p. 266)

Katz and Summers estimate that if the $150 billion manufacturing trade deficit were reduced through increased exports, rather than a reduction of imports, labor income would increase by $13 billion.

This favorable view of export jobs is, in part, an artifact of a focus on manufacturing, but international trade also involves industries and jobs outside manufacturing. Export growth has been an important source of employment growth in several low-wage industries, particularly agriculture and wholesale warehousing. Allowing for employment outside manufacturing in the calculation of trade-associated wage premiums reduces the wage difference between importing and exporting industries to five cents per hour, less than one-twentieth of Katz and Summers's estimate (Dickens and Lang 1988, pp. 100–105). As noted previously, the shift of some workers out of manufacturing and into services as a result of trade further weakens the case for job improvement via trade expansion, since even import-competing manufacturing jobs tend to pay better than nonmanufacturing jobs.

The work of Katz and Summers (1989) and of Dickens and Lange (1988),

which considers the average consequences of trade, implicitly compares a manufacturing sector with trade to one without trade. An alternative approach, more
relevant to foreseeable policy decisions, is to examine the consequences of moderate (marginal) changes in the amount of imports and exports. The econometric
studies reviewed previously in this chapter find that, even within manufacturing,
there is little evidence for a favorable trade-off between export-producing and
import-competing jobs at the margin. The only study clearly favorable to exports
is Gaston and Trefler (1994), which finds the positive effects of exports to be
substantially larger than the negative effect of imports and import growth. However, this study seems to suffer from a number of econometric flaws, especially
in regard to a problem of omitted variables.[22] In contrast, Freeman and Katz
(1991), Brauer (1990), and Martines (1993) find that parallel expansion of imports and exports would have largely offsetting wage effects. Freeman and Katz
and Brauer also find that the detrimental effects of imports on wages have been
rising over the last two decades, while the effects of exports have been stable or
declining.

The literature is not united in demonstrating that balanced growth in trade will
lead to job upgrading either in the economy as a whole or within manufacturing.
The evidence on the effect of moderate increases in trade finds that balanced
increases in exports and imports would, at best, have slightly positive effects on
wages, but this may differ for trade with different groups of countries. Even here,
the long-run trend toward larger trade deficits in the manufacturing sector makes
gains from exporting moot, unless this trend is turned around.

Trade and the Performance of Average Wages

Of all the topics covered by this review, the effect of international trade on
average wages in the U.S. economy is the least researched. Most economists now
agree that average real wages stagnated, the real wages of the majority of employees declined, and wage inequality rose during the last decade. However,
there is no consensus on whether factors related to international trade, such as
increased import penetration, foreign productivity growth, or the rising trade
deficit could account for any part of these trends in average wages. Robert Z.
Lawrence and two coauthors (in Lawrence and Slaughter 1993; Lawrence 1994;
Krugman and Lawrence 1993) have argued strenuously that trade cannot be part
of the explanation because real wages, properly measured, have closely tracked
labor productivity. The slow growth in wages observed over the last decade is
therefore caused by sluggish growth in productivity rather than by forces such as
international trade, which would have caused divergence between wages and
productivity, according to these authors.[23]

The crux of this argument is that real wages have not been measured in a
correct fashion for comparisons with productivity. Lawrence and his coauthors
argue that the usual measure of real wages underestimates growth of total labor

compensation because it does not include benefit costs, because the survey of wages on which it is based excludes 20 percent of the workforce, and because it is deflated by consumer rather than product prices. According to these economists, there is no gap between wage and productivity growth when total compensation is deflated by product prices, and hence there is no "puzzle" to be explained by international competitive forces.

This argument is illustrated in Table 3.2, which shows how Lawrence, Slaughter, and Krugman move from a standard measure of the real wage to their preferred measure. Between 1979 and 1991, labor productivity as measured by the Bureau of Labor Statistics (BLS) rose by a total of 10.4 percent. The standard measure of the real wage, which is the ratio of the wage rate for production and nonsupervisory workers in the BLS *Employment, Hours, and Earnings* series to the BLS consumer price index (CPI), fell by 11.0 percent. This leaves a productivity-wage gap of 21.4 percent, which is the apparent excess of the increase in productivity over the increase in the real wage (and this number is larger than the productivity increase since the real wage as conventionally measured actually fell).

Lawrence and his coauthors claim that this entire gap is illusory. If the standard wage measure is replaced by a measure of total compensation that includes benefit costs and covers both wage and salary workers (along with sole proprietors),[24] total compensation per hour actually rose by 1.5 percent between 1979 and 1991. Half of this increase is attributable to inclusion of benefit costs, the other half to inclusion of employees outside the production and nonsupervisory classification. The second correction is to shift from deflating wages by consumer prices to deflation by a measure of producer prices. Although consumer prices are appropriate for the evaluation of consumer welfare, producer prices are the appropriate deflator in an evaluation of how closely wages have tracked output per worker-hour (labor productivity). The shift from the CPI to the GDP output deflator causes the increase in total real compensation per hour to rise from 1.5 to 9.5 percent. Since labor productivity rose by 10.4 percent between 1979 and 1991, there is only a negligible productivity-wage gap of 0.9 percent over a twelve-year period. In other words, by this calculation there is virtually no productivity-wage gap to explain, and hence there is no reason to believe that trade has depressed wage (compensation) growth.

We could certainly challenge the inclusion of the salaries of managers, executives, and other "overhead" employees, as well as the income of self-employed proprietors, in the "total compensation" to be attributed to U.S. "workers." The self-employed are not employees by definition, and managers, executives, and other professional employees certainly do not fit commonly accepted notions of who "workers" are. Moreover, the "salaries" of many managers and executives contain elements that mimic returns to ownership rather than to labor effort. Even leaving this issue aside, other problems of measurement remain.

The appropriateness of the GDP deflator used by Lawrence and his coauthors has been questioned by Hall (1993), who argues that it is better to use the *final*

Table 3.2

Alternative Measures of Real Wage Change and the Productivity-Wage Gap, 1979–91 (except as indicated)

Measure	Real Wage Change	Productivity-Wage Gap
Standard measure (ratio of EHE[a] wages to the CPI)	−11.0%	21.5%
Replace EHE wages with BEA/BLS measure of total compensation	1.5	8.9
Replace CPI with GDP deflator	9.5	0.9
Replace GDP deflator with final output deflator	5.1	5.3
Replace BEA/BLS measure of total compensation with current-weighted ECI (1977–89, private sector only)	−7.4	17.1

Sources: Lawrence and Slaughter (1993) for the first four measures. The last measure was constructed by the authors from data reported in Mishel and Bernstein (1993, table 3.2, p. 132) after converting from a CPI deflator to the NIPA final output deflator.

Notes: All numbers in the table are total percentage changes for the years indicated. The productivity-wage gap is the difference between the productivity growth rate of 10.4% from 1979 to 1991 and the growth rate of the real wage for the same period (according to each definition shown in the table), except in the last row, where the years are different. All CPIs referred to in this table are for all urban consumers.
[a]Employment, hours, and earnings.

product deflator (excluding investment goods) from the BLS National Income and Product Accounts (NIPAs), rather than the total GDP deflator (from the same accounts), which includes investment goods that are properly regarded as a type of intermediate good.[25] With this correction, the increase in real compensation is reduced to 5.1 percent,[26] and a small wage-productivity gap (of 5.3 percent over 12 years) is opened up.

There are also measurement issues with the total compensation index used by Lawrence and Slaughter, which we call the BEA/BLS index.[27] Lawrence suggests that rapid growth of this index reflects the faster growth of benefit payments relative to wages. The data underlying the BEA/BLS index show nominal, per capita benefit costs growing about 20 percent faster than nominal wages (91.9 versus 71.1 percent) between 1979 and 1991. However, this large gap is not consistent with other indexes of wages and benefits. The methodologically superior fixed-weight Employment Cost Index (ECI)[28] of the BLS indicates that the difference between growth in wages and total compensation was only 9 percent.

An alternative measure of total compensation from the NIPAs indicates that benefit costs rose only 3 percent faster than wages. Movements in both the fixed-weight ECI and the NIPA compensation series are consonant with the finding of Bosworth and Perry (1994) that, as rapid increases in some components of total benefit costs (medical care) have been offset by declining costs in other areas (notably pension costs), total benefit costs have risen only slightly more rapidly than wages.[29] Further confirmation is found in Bound and Johnson (1992, p. 372), who report that benefit increases accounted for only one-eighth of the change in total compensation between 1979 and 1988. Benefits are unlikely to explain a substantial portion of the gap between wages and productivity.

Thus, it appears that the BEA/BLS index of total compensation overestimates increases in total compensation.[30] This suspicion is confirmed by comparison of the BEA/BLS index to a current-weighted version of the ECI, which adjusts for changes in the distribution of employment between occupations and industries. Using this variant of the ECI for the period 1977–89[31] and deflating by the NIPA final output deflator, real compensation per hour *fell* by 7.4 percent. This contrasts with the 6.6 percent rise in total real private sector compensation found by the similarly deflated BEA/BLS measure, and opens up a wage-productivity gap of 17.1 percent between 1977 and 1989. In other words, an accurately measured wage-productivity gap is nearly as large as the gap implied by the standard measure of real wages rejected by Lawrence and his coauthors.

Apart from all these measurement issues, there are two conceptual problems with the argument of Lawrence and his coauthors. First, in their view, trade can affect wages only if it opens up a wedge between growth in productivity and in the real product wage. Another way of stating the same point is that trade-induced wage reductions must be associated with a decline in labor's share of national income. These authors therefore take the apparent stability of labor's share between 1979 and 1991 as further evidence that trade has not influenced wages.

However, stability of the wage share does not necessarily mean that wages are not being affected by trade. Consider once again the Lawrence argument against the use of CPI-deflated real wages. This argument hinges on the (correct) presumption that the prices of consumer goods and services (as measured by the CPI) have risen relative to the average price of total output (whether measured by the GDP deflator or the final output deflator, although more so with the former). Why has this relative price change occurred? The CPI includes many nontradable goods and services, such as housing and health care, as well as food products that have prices linked to agricultural supply and demand conditions. But national output as a whole includes many manufactured goods that are traded in highly competitive global markets (including investment goods, if we use a GDP measure as Lawrence does). This could be one reason why, as Clarida and Hickok report,

> A rebound in manufacturing productivity [in the 1980s] did not translate into a significant rise in real manufacturing wages—or profits, but instead resulted in a substantial fall in the relative price of manufactured goods. (1993, p. 175)

If international competitive pressures restrain or reduce the prices at which domestic producers can sell these products, this could help to explain why their prices have fallen relative to a typical "basket" of consumer goods and services. Firms whose ability to set prices is thus constrained may, in turn, pressure their workers to agree to lower nominal wages than they would otherwise accept. In this case, both labor and capital income (real wages and profits) could be reduced by trade, and as a result the wage share of total income would remain fairly stable.

A second point is that, even if real wage increases have closely tracked productivity increases, trade could have affected the slowdown in productivity growth and thus impacted on real wages as well. Indeed, the average annual rate of productivity growth for the nonfarm business sector fell from 2.8 percent in 1960–69 to 1.4 percent in 1970–79 and 1.0 percent in 1980–89.[32] If the shift of manufacturing overseas (part of which is attributable to U.S. companies' investing abroad rather than at home) has contributed in any way to the productivity growth slowdown at home, then this could be causing real wage growth to falter even without workers getting a lower share of total income. Both of these points are speculative at present and cannot be decided without further empirical research. These points are raised here merely to show that the type of argument put forward by Lawrence and his coauthors is not sufficient to rule out possible negative effects of trade on average wages without additional types of evidence beyond what these provide.

International Trade and Relative Wages

International trade can affect the wages of large parts of the working population without affecting the average wage. If trade simultaneously reduces wages for some groups of employees and induces counterbalancing increases for other groups, then the average wage may be unchanged while the economic condition of large parts of the population shifts dramatically. Such shifts in the structure of wages will be reflected in movement in income inequality. In fact, the body of research on the effect of trade on wage inequality is much more extensive and better developed than the research on how trade affects average wages. The existing research focuses in particular on how trade may have served to worsen the economic position of less skilled workers.[33] Table 3.3 (pages 86–87) provides a summary of the most important studies in this category.

One approach to the issue of wage inequality is to calculate, first, the effect of trade on the effective supply of labor for various parts of the population and, second, how changes in their labor supply have affected wages. Borjas, Freeman, and Katz (1991) use data for the period 1964–88 from the Current Population Survey (CPS) to estimate worker-hours, employment, and wages for sixty-four skill groups defined by gender, education, and experience. These figures are then combined with data on imports and exports from the Annual Survey of Manufactures (ASM) to determine the labor supply needed to produce exports and the implicit increase in the supply of labor associated with the import of goods from abroad.

The results indicate that international trade had different effects on aggregate labor markets before and after 1983. Before 1983, trade had little effect on implicit labor supplies. With some exceptions, labor supply was either unaffected or reduced by the net effect of imports and exports. This changed beginning in 1983, when increased imports added 0.5 percent to the domestic supply of labor. By 1984 the increase in the trade deficit increased labor supply by 1.3 percent; in 1985 this figure rose to 1.6 percent. Although these numbers may appear to be small, they represent 7.0 percent of hours in the manufacturing sector,[34] which is where most of the increased trade deficit occurred. Results are not altered if labor supply is measured in efficiency units, a skill-adjusted measure of labor supply.[35]

The effects of trade were not spread evenly by education or gender. For male high school dropouts, the trade deficit of the 1980s increased the implicit supply of labor by between 4 and 8 percent; for female high school dropouts, the increase was 8 to 13 percent. The implicit supply of high school graduates rose by 2 to 3 percent for males and by 2 percent for females. Depending on the period under consideration, trade either did not affect or reduced the supply of college-educated workers. Effects within the manufacturing sector were larger, with trade increasing the supply of employees without high school diplomas by 14 to 27 percent for men and by 24 to 40 percent for women. Overall, increases in the trade deficit increased the relative supply of non-college-educated labor.

How did this affect relative wages? Drawing on outside estimates of the elasticity of the wage with respect to labor supply, Borjas, Freeman, and Katz (1991) calculate that increased relative labor supply associated with trade and immigration explains between 14 and 27 percent of the increase in inequality between high school and college graduates for the period 1980–85 and between 8 and 15 percent for the period 1980–88. How are these effects divided between trade and immigration? For both years the increase in the supply of high school–equivalent employees relative to college-degreed employees is entirely attributable to trade; immigration did not contribute to the increase in the supply of labor.

The effects of trade and immigration on the wages of employees without high school educations are larger, accounting for about 40 percent of the relative wage decline suffered by this group between 1980 and 1988. Between 1980 and 1985, trade and immigration together caused an increase in wage inequality of 28 to 68 percent between those with less than a high school education and the remainder of the labor force. Trade contributed one-third of the increase in the supply of non-high-school-educated labor relative to all other employees, with immigration accounting for the remaining two-thirds. Thus, from 9 to 23 percent of the increase in wage inequality between U.S. dropouts and all other employ-

Table 3.3

Studies of International Trade and Relative Wages

Study	Issues and Methods	Estimated Effects
Borjas, Freeman, and Katz (1991)	How international trade and immigration have affected the supply of labor of various skill levels.	International trade shifted from decreasing to increasing the effective supply of labor in the United States in the early 1980s. By 1985, trade added 1.5% to the labor supply. For male high school dropouts, trade increased the labor supply by 4–8%; for high school graduates, the figure was 2–3%. Trade did not affect or reduce the effective supply of college-educated labor during this period. Effects within manufacturing were much greater. The ratio of the wages of high school graduates to college graduates fell 8–15% due to trade. The wages of those who had failed to complete high school declined 9–23% relative to the rest of the population because of trade.
Murphy and Welch (1991)	CPS data for 1979–86 are aggregated into four industry groupings: nontraded goods, durable goods, nondurable goods, and traded services. Data on trade patterns are then used to calculate the effects of trade on labor demand.	Trade accounts for 0.80–1.36% of the 3.43% decline in male wages, and 1.35–2.31% of the 5.81% increase in women's wages between 1979 and 1986. By level of education, 1.55–3.14% of the 7.33% fall in the wages of those with less than a high school education is accounted for by trade. Trade caused 0.36–0.45% of the 3% decline in wages of those with high school educations.

Table 3.3 *(continued)*

Katz and Murphy (1992)	Similar to Murphy and Welch but uses less aggregate data. Estimates allow only for the immediate effects of trade and do not allow for input-output linkages.	Measured effects of trade are smaller than the earlier article. For males with less than a high school education, trade reduced employment by 0.63–1.48% from 1979 to 1985; for women in this group, the trade-induced reduction in employment was 2.2–4.0%. For male high school graduates, the reduction was 0.28–0.71%; for female high school graduates, it was 0.16–0.27%. Trade increased demand for those with at least some college education.
Wood (1994)	Factor content analysis modified to allow for trade-induced changes in factor utilization and induced technological change.	International trade has reduced demand for manufacturing labor in developed countries by 12% and increased demand for skilled labor by about 5.5%. Induced technological change has doubled these effects.
Borjas and Ramey (1994)	Uses cointegration to measure the relation between a variety of factors, including the trade balance in durable goods and the ratio of high school to college wages.	The trade balance in durable manufacturing is the only cointegrating factor related to wage inequality. Imports have a large effect on increasing wage inequality, while exports reduce inequality in a less pronounced fashion.

ees in the period 1980–85 can be attributed to changes in the trade deficit.

An alternative to the labor-supply approach of Borjas, Freeman, and Katz is to model the effects of trade on the demand for labor of different types. This approach, developed by Murphy and Welch (1991), recognizes the fact that there are substantial interindustry variations in worker characteristics such as the level of education and racial and gender composition.[36] Given such differences, trade that is concentrated in certain industries will have a large effect on groups of workers disproportionately employed in those industries. Dividing industries into those producing traded durable goods, traded nondurable goods, traded services, and nontraded goods, Murphy and Welch calculate the effect of trade on the product demand for each sector and then translate that shift into demand for labor in that industry.

Using this method, Murphy and Welch find that the increase in the trade deficit between 1979 and 1986 and the consequent decline in employment in manufacturing reduced the demand for and depressed the wages of the employees with less than a college degree but had little effect on the college educated. The authors estimate that the trade deficit caused employment to decline by 14.7 percent in durable goods manufacturing and by 1.8 percent in nondurable goods manufacturing; it increased employment slightly in traded services and by 4.1 percent in nontraded services. Translating these sectoral changes into changes in demand for different qualities of labor, international trade decreased employment for men with less than a high school education by between 2 and 3.5 percent. Men with high school diplomas saw a 1.25 to 2.3 percent decrease in labor demand, while trade increased demand for college-educated males by 0.7 to 1.5 percent. For women with less than a high school education, trade decreased demand by 0.6 to 2.2 percent. Women with high school education had a 1.0 to 2.2 percent increase in demand, while demand for women with college degrees increased by 3.3 to 4.3 percent.[37]

Murphy and Welch do not explicitly link labor demand and wages, but they report that the changes in demand comport with the changes in wages observed between 1979 and 1988. The wages of men with less than a high school education declined 10 percent between 1979 and 1986; for women the decline was 7.3 percent. In contrast, men with a college education saw their wages increase by 7.8 percent, and college-educated women saw a 9.4 percent increase. Those who faced declining demand due to trade also faced declining wages; those whose demand was buoyed by trade saw increasing real wages. The pattern of wage change on groups within the working population parallels the impact of trade.

The strongest statistical linkage between trade deficits and wage inequality is found by Borjas and Ramey (1994). They use the ratios of the wages of (1) college graduates to high school graduates and (2) college graduates to people with less than a high school education as measures of wage inequality. In their statistical analysis, the trade deficit in durable goods manufacturing is the only variable that is significantly correlated with these measures of wage inequality for the period 1963–88. Further estimates find asymmetries in the magnitude of the effects of imports and exports: imports increase wage inequality while exports decrease inequality in a less pronounced fashion.[38]

The durable goods manufacturing sector emphasized by Borjas and Ramey includes many industries that have historically operated in oligopolistic markets and earned "monopoly" rents. As discussed earlier, when compelled by unions to share these rents with workers, firms in these industries have paid high wages and provided generous benefits. Increased competition from imports reduced the rents and decreased both employment and wages. Production employees were displaced into lower-wage sectors of the economy, thus reducing both average wages and the relative wages of workers with less than college degrees and the less skilled.

This explanation is incomplete, as it addresses only durable goods and, within that sector, firms with market power. Some of the industries most affected by trade, such as apparel and auto parts, produce under relatively competitive conditions.[39] While not including monopoly rents, wages in these industries are higher than the wages available to workers outside manufacturing. Increased import competition based on lower wages and labor standards has displaced employment from these industries into other sectors with lower productivity and wages. This movement would have its largest effect on the wages of non-college-educated American workers.

Tests of the Factor Price Equalization and Stolper-Samuelson Effects

As discussed earlier, standard international trade theory implies that trade liberalization with developing countries that are abundant in (less skilled) labor can depress real wages in a more capital- and skill-abundant country like the United States. The FPE theorem predicts that wages of unskilled workers in rich and poor countries will tend to converge as trade barriers fall. The SS theorem also predicts that reducing tariffs on labor-intensive products will tend to reduce the wages of less skilled labor. As the earlier theoretical survey also showed, these propositions have been challenged by newer theories in which trade "lifts all boats" and raises wages. The magnitude of FPE and SS effects relative to other, offsetting effects is therefore an empirical question. This section reviews the studies that have explicitly sought to measure or test the importance of FPE and SS effects.

Lawrence and Slaughter (1993) and Lawrence (1994) have argued that the evidence is not consistent with SS effects in the U.S. economy. They argue that, in order for the SS theorem to hold, increased relative wages for more skilled workers must be associated with both a decline in the ratio of skilled to unskilled workers within each industry and an increase in the international price of skilled-labor–intensive products. Using scatter plots of disaggregated manufacturing industries, the authors argue that there is no relationship between relative wages and relative employment. Similarly, they conclude that the prices of skilled-labor–intensive goods fell, rather than rose, in the 1980s. In their view, some greater force such as technological change (which increases the demand for skilled labor) must have overshadowed the effects of trade on wage inequality predicted by SS.

This line of argument has been criticized by Leamer (1994) and by Sachs and Shatz (1994). Among other things, Lawrence and Slaughter do not control for the general increase in skill levels in the economy over the period under study.[40]

In addition, the import and export price indexes used by Lawrence and Slaughter are not consistent, since the indexes for different industries cover different time periods (Sachs and Shatz 1994, pp. 36–37). Using more carefully constructed price indexes and controlling for the trend toward higher levels of skill, Sachs and Shatz find that the predicted inverse relationship between the proportion of unskilled employees in the labor force and changes in product prices holds for the 1980s.

More explicit research on factor price convergence comes to varying conclusions, but all studies find some evidence of wage convergence. Tovias (1982) found convergence in wages associated with the formation of the EC but divergence in the period 1969–77. Extension of this work by Gremmen (1985) indicated that greater economic integration reduced the tendencies toward factor price convergence. Mokhtari and Rassekh (1989) found convergence in wages in sixteen countries of the Organization for Economic Cooperation and Development (OECD) during the period of increasing trade openness, 1961–84.

In some of the most recent research on this topic, Burgman and Geppert (1993) examine wage convergence between the United States, Canada, Germany, France, Japan, and the United Kingdom between 1950 and 1989 by testing for long-run equilibrium relationships and the speed of the convergence toward that equilibrium. Using a new econometric technique based on the cointegration of time-series data, the authors conclude that the economic linkages among these six countries are sufficiently strong that their wages are tied to one another and move in tandem. Further, if some event causes wages of one of these countries to diverge from this international equilibrium, they will reequalize over time. Germany, which has the most rapid rate of adjustment, would eliminate 29 percent of any deviation from the long-run equilibrium in the first year. Canada, with a much slower speed of adjustment, would offset only 8 percent.

Further evidence for relative wage convergence is reported by Davis (1992). He finds common, if not universal, trends in wage inequality, returns to education, and experience in the United States, Japan, the United Kingdom, France, Canada, Sweden, West Germany, Brazil, South Korea, Venezuela, and Colombia. Evidence for convergence is particularly strong in returns to education. In the 1980s, lower trade barriers were associated with reduced gains to education in middle-income countries and increased gains in more advanced countries where there was a higher proportion of educated workers in the labor force. However, the decrease in returns to education in the advanced countries in the 1970s does not comport with convergence in factor returns.

Davis's results show that increased trade openness decreases the deviation of wages around the world mean. While his estimates vary among different models, on average a 10 percent increase in net trade as a percentage of gross national product (GNP) decreases the standard deviation of the wage residuals by 2 to 3 percent. Convergence occurs only in high-income countries; trade does not have an effect on relative wages in middle-income countries. The effects of imports and exports are asymmetrical: imports produce a large and statistically significant convergence toward average wage structure, while exports induce a divergence from world wages that is smaller in absolute value than that of imports. Although the results are generally consistent with the FPE, the effect of exports is unexpected.

Leamer (1993) produced measures of SS effects in a study of the prospective distributional effects of NAFTA.[41] According to Leamer's calculations, a falling relative price of labor-intensive goods causes a small increase in the return to capital, a large increase in the earnings of professional and technical labor, and a substantial decline in the real wages of "other workers." While acknowledging that his specific estimates were subject to considerable uncertainty, Leamer concluded that:

> the numbers are in the right ballpark, and at least they serve to focus attention on the important fact that everyone need not benefit from increased international commerce. Indeed, if the reason for the expansion of international commerce is increased access to low-wage unskilled foreign labor, it is virtually certain that our low-skilled workers will have their earnings reduced. Reductions in annual earnings over the next decade on the order of $1000 seem very plausible. (1993, p. 122)

Challenges to the Trade and Wages Connection

While the evidence linking trade to declines in manufacturing employment and increases in wage inequality has been mounting, the studies pointing in this direction have not gone without challenge. We have already discussed some of the challenges here, but two major points have been asserted so widely that they require a more detailed discussion. The first, already alluded to above, is the argument that rising wage inequality is caused entirely by changes in technology rather than by increases in trade. The second is the contention that, even if some of these negative effects have been identified, they are "too small" to matter.

The Role of Technology

Some economists have asserted that technology, rather than trade, is responsible for rising wage inequality. The first Clinton administration *Economic Report of the President* endorses this technological determinist view:

> Since the use of more-educated labor has increased in all industries, a logical explanation of this trend is technical change. For example, one study shows that people who work with personal computers earn a substantial wage premium over those who do not, and that this can account for half of the increasing gap between the wages of college and high school graduates. (U.S. Council of Economic Advisors 1994, p. 119)

Table 3.4 summarizes the few studies that actually support this position, along with some contrary studies of the same issue.

Table 3.4

Studies of Technology and Wage Inequality

Study	Issues and Methods	Estimated Effects
Bound and Johnson (1992)	Uses 1973–74, 1979, and 1988 CPS data to examine the effects of structural shifts in labor demand, structural shifts in employment between industries, and specific and general technological change on wage inequality. General technological change is measured as a residual, and specific technology is interpreted as occurring in manufacturing, mining, transportation, and utilities.	General technological change accounted for 120% of the change in gross wages between high school and college graduates in 1979–88, and industry-specific technological change accounted for 11.7%. The increase in the supply of college men decreased wage inequality by 61%. Without offsetting factors, technological change would have increased gross wage inequality by an additional 31%.
Berman, Bound, and Griliches (1993)	Data on 450 industries for the period 1979 to 1987 are used to determine the sources of change in the ratio of production to nonproduction wages and employment.	10% of the increase in the ratio of nonproduction employees in manufacturing is associated with imports and exports. Only 3.3% of the decline in the earnings of production employees relative to nonproduction employees is accounted for by imports and exports.
Borjas and Ramey (1994)	Uses cointegration to measure the relation between a variety of factors, including the trade balance in durable goods and the high-school/college wages ratio.	There is no cointegrating relation between per capita R&D expenditures and the high-school/college wage ratio or the less-than-high-school/college wage ratio for the period 1963–88.
Mishel and Bernstein (1994)	Uses ASM data for 1973–79 and 1979–89 for 34 two-digit industries and regressive measures of wage inequality on capital investment, investment in computers, and the proportion of employment in scientific and engineering positions.	There is no evidence that investment in technology was related to the acceleration of inequality in the 1980s or that investment in computers had a different effect from investment in other capital goods.

Table 3.4 *(continued)*

Howell (1994)	Investigates whether the shift away from production employment in manufacturing came after investment in new technologies, particularly computers.	The decline in production employment was completed by the early 1980s and preceded the rapid increase in investment in computer technologies (as in most industries.

The most frequently cited study in support of this view is by Bound and Johnson (1992). They consider various explanations of changes in the structure of relative wages, including changes in industry wage structure and unionization, changes in the structure of labor demand, shifts in employment between industries, industry-specific technological change, and general technological change. These authors find that adverse changes in wage inequality in the 1980s were almost entirely associated with what they call general technological change. By their calculations, general technological change accounted for 120.0 percent of the gross increase in the ratio of wages of college-educated to high school–educated men; industry-specific technological change accounted for another 11.7 percent. Thus, without offsetting factors, the technology factor alone would have caused wage inequality to increase 31.7 percent more than actually occurred between 1979 and 1988. By these calculations, technological change is the predominant source of increased wage inequality.

The biggest problem with Bound and Johnson's study, and it is a serious one, is their method of measuring technological change. In fact, these authors do not have an actual variable that measures general technological change; instead, they rely on a method that uses the "residuals" from a regression model, which they try to control for all relevant factors except technology, as the measure of technology.[42] In other words, whatever part of the variation in relative wages is not explained by the factors actually included in Bound and Johnson's model is assumed to be explained by general technological change.[43] In this method, any factor that is omitted will be reflected in the residuals of the model. Building a statistical model in which the only factor of consequence that is omitted is technology would be a difficult if not impossible undertaking. It is unlikely to be achieved by any specification, no matter how sophisticated. Despite the effort to remove the effects of changing patterns in industrial wage structure and product demand, factors such as unionization and trade likely remain part of the residual. That the estimated 120 percent residual effect includes technology is not in question; the issue is whether it also includes other factors such as trade. The authors are aware of this limitation in their method, as they admit here:

> The major difficulty with this explanation, unlike the explanations involving industry wage effects, supply, and product demand, is (as in the analysis of

the sources of economic growth) that it involves the residuals of the intra-factor demand function rather than directly observable phenomena. (Bound and Johnson 1992, p. 383)

Unfortunately, the journalists and politicians who have cited Bound and Johnson's study as proving that trade is a small or an irrelevant factor contributing to wage inequality have failed to note this important qualification.

Berman, Bound, and Griliches (1993) also find that technology, rather than trade, has been the preeminent force increasing both employment of nonproduction workers and wage inequality between production and nonproduction employees in manufacturing. The first step in their analysis is to distinguish the effects of international trade on wages and employment from those originating from domestic sources including technological change. Analyzing data on 450 industries, Berman and his coauthors find that trade accounted for only 18.0 percent of the increase in the proportion of nonproduction employees (i.e., skilled workers) in the labor force between 1979 and 1987, while changes in domestic, nonmilitary consumption account for 73.4 percent of that increase. Parallel results are obtained for the relative wages of nonproduction employees. These authors find that only 2.4 percent of the improvement in the relative wage position of nonproduction employees is attributable to trade, while 83.5 percent is attributable to domestic nonmilitary consumption. Given this weighty role for domestic conditions, technological change is a prime candidate for explaining increasing inequality.

Like Bound and Johnson (1992), Berman, Bound, and Griliches (1993) use a method that tends to minimize the estimated impact of trade. Basically, Berman and his coauthors *assume* that the causes of changes in the average ratios (the proportion of nonproduction workers in the labor force and the relative wage of nonproduction workers) are fundamentally domestic, and that only the *differences* between changes in this ratio in a given industry and the average change for all industries are due to foreign trade or defense spending.[44] This is not an innocent assumption, and it strongly biases the results toward finding that the effects of trade are minimal.

An example may help to clarify this problem. Suppose there are two industries, one of which (industry A) only exports and one of which (industry B) only produces for domestic consumption. Each industry employs half of the labor force. Suppose in the first period the nonproduction wage ratio is equal to 1 in both industries, and in the second period the wage ratio triples in industry A but only doubles in industry B. The nonproduction ratio for the country increases from 1 to 2.5 between the first and second periods. What proportion of the change is attributed to trade? This depends on the method used to calculate the answer. Using the method adopted by Berman and his coauthors, one-third is attributed to industry A, the traded goods industry. Using the method that does not subtract out the average shift in the domestic consumption sector, two-thirds of the change in the wage ratio is attributed to the traded goods industry.[45]

Sachs and Shatz (1994) provide more explicit evidence for the view that technology has been a key factor in reducing production employment. Explaining changes in employment at the industry level between 1978 and 1990, Sachs and Shatz find that a 1 percent increase in R&D expenditures is associated with a 4 percent reduction in the employment of production workers. According to their findings, R&D expenditures have no measurable association with total or nonproduction employment. Their model also finds that the loss of production employment is highest in industries with large capital shares and a high proportion of production employees in their labor force. As no trade variables are included, it is not possible to compare the effects of trade and technology in this part of Sachs and Shatz's study, but at least they used actual measures of technology instead of econometric residuals.

In contrast, some new research (also using explicit measures of technology) suggests that technology has not contributed to increasing wage inequality. Borjas and Ramey (1994) find that per capita R&D expenditures have no meaningful statistical relationship to either the high-school/college wage ratio or the less-than-high-school/college wage ratio. Mishel and Bernstein (1994) find that, although measures of technology are related to increased wage inequality in a sample of thirty-four industries over the 1973–89 period, there is no evidence that technology is related to the *acceleration* of inequality experienced in the 1980s compared with the 1970s. Similarly, they find no evidence that computer equipment had a different effect on wage inequality compared to other forms of capital investment (Mishel and Bernstein, 1994, pp. 28–30).[46]

In what he calls a "very preliminary" study, Leamer (1994) finds that capital-using technological change (i.e., increases in the capital/output ratio) actually *increased* the wages of production workers between 1976 and 1986. Building on a theoretical model in which wages of skilled and unskilled workers are determined by technology, factor input requirements, and product prices, Leamer develops an econometric model that estimates the determinants of payroll savings (reductions in labor costs) across a sample of 450 industries.[47] Using payroll savings for the entire labor force (production and nonproduction workers), increases in capital/output ratios caused wages of production workers to rise by 19.5 to 22.4 percent, depending on the specification. Using payroll savings for production workers only, Leamer finds that increases in capital/output ratios caused wages of production workers to rise by 18.5 to 43.5 percent, also depending on the specification. Although he expresses reservations about using the data on production and nonproduction workers as a proxy for the unskilled/skilled distinction, Leamer concludes that "*technology has led to a larger increase in wages for production (unskilled?)* [workers] *than for the nonproduction (skilled?)* [workers], *completely the opposite of the conclusions of Lawrence and Slaughter (1993) and Krugman and Lawrence (1993)*" (1994, p. 20, italics in original).

The timing of the introduction of new technologies also argues against technology-determinist theories. The technology explanation is premised on new technologies in manufacturing, particularly computers, displacing low-skilled employees into lower-wage positions outside manufacturing. For this to be sensible, investment in new technologies must accelerate prior to the decline in non-production labor in manufacturing. The timing was, however, reversed (Howell 1994). The increase in the ratio of nonproduction to total employment in manufacturing was completed by 1981; the rapid increases in investment in office, accounting, and computing machinery began no earlier than 1980 and, in many industries, occurred in the mid-1980s. Given such a pattern, there must be a strong presumption against the technology explanation.[48]

A deeper problem in the whole dichotomy of technology versus trade explanations of wage inequality is that technological innovation is not necessarily independent of international trade relations and competitive pressures. This is an especially serious problem if trade accelerates the adoption of labor-saving technologies.[49] Imports of goods from low-wage countries compel producers in developed countries to reduce unit labor costs. This reduction can be achieved by increasing labor productivity, typically by investing in new capital and new technologies, as well as by trying to cut workers' wages (or limit their wage increases). Such improvements will result in reduced demand for labor, and yet, by many of the empirical methodologies discussed above, the ensuing decrease in employment will be attributed to "technology" rather than to trade. While there are other possible connections between trade and technology as well, it is at least likely that part of what has been ascribed to technology is, at the least, trade-induced.[50]

That technological advance has affected wages and may have had an effect on wage inequality is not controversial. What is in dispute is whether technological change is the sole source of increases in wage inequality over the past decade, as well as whether technology itself is independent of trade. The empirical evidence supporting the monocausal position is weak; the evidence that technology has not increased wage inequality (and may even have reduced it) is as strong or stronger. Central questions about the timing and acceleration of new investment remain to be addressed by the advocates of the technological explanation. Certainly, the ascription of growth in wage inequality to technology alone has been premature.

Are Trade Effects "Small"?

Some economists have argued that even if trade may have a negative impact on wages, the effect is so tiny as to be irrelevant. For example, Paul Krugman (1994a) has recently argued that trade could not induce large-scale wage changes. Basing his calculations on the 30 percent differential between average wages in manufacturing and services and noting that 1 million employees account for less than 1 percent of the U.S. labor force, he finds that trade-induced displacement of 1 million manufacturing workers would reduce economywide wages by 0.3 percent. Krugman comments:

This is too small to explain the 6 percent real wage decline by a factor of 20. Or to look at it another way, the annual wage loss from deficit induced de-industrialization, which [Lester] Thurow clearly implies is at the heart of U.S. economic difficulties, is on the basis of his own numbers roughly equal to what the U.S. spends on health care every week. (1994a, p. 36)

Such calculations do not take account of the dynamics of the labor market or of the role of manufacturing in establishing employee expectations for wage increases throughout the economy. Trade effects that induce this scale of displacement do more than reduce the wages of displaced workers. An increase of 1 million persons in the supply of labor to nonmanufacturing industries will place downward pressures on wages in those sectors. Weak wage leadership from the manufacturing sector may also reduce wage growth throughout the economy. All these factors argue that the effect of trade on wages is likely to be substantially larger than estimated by Krugman.

It is not difficult to label fractions "small" if we choose a large enough denominator. For example, by comparing manufactured imports from newly industrializing countries to the combined gross domestic products (GDPs) of all the OECD nations, Krugman (1994b, p. 116) can argue that trade with low-wage countries comes to "only" 1.2 percent.[51] However, U.S. imports from developing countries made up 36 percent of U.S. manufacturing imports in 1990, up from only 29 percent in 1978 (Sachs and Shatz 1994, table 4, p. 12). The rate of growth of certain types of trade, as well as its concentration in certain sectors or regions, can magnify its impact significantly. If one of our tasks is to explain increasing inequality in the wage distribution, in addition to changes in the average wage level, then the concentrated impact of trade on a few sectors within manufacturing may be quite relevant.

In the regression analyses used to identify the various factors affecting the wage distribution, trade is usually found to account for between about 10 and 20 percent of the increase in wage inequality during the 1980s. Borjas, Freeman, and Katz (1991) find that trade increased the gap between the wages of workers with high school and college educations by 8 to 15 percent; trade also accounted for between 9 and 23 percent of the decline in wages of those with less than a high school education. Testing a number of theories of wage inequality, Borjas and Ramey (1994) find that the trade deficit in durable manufacturing is the only statistically significant correlate of measures of wage inequality for the period 1963–88. Whether this is "large" or "small" depends on the other factors included and the total variation explained by the regression.

Wood (1994) suggests that measurement of trade with developing countries involves conceptual and measurement problems that, because of the approach typically adopted, generate systematic understatement of the volume of trade. In Wood's view, trade between developed and developing countries is motivated by differences in the costs of skilled and unskilled labor. As predicted in the HO theory of trade, developed countries import labor-intensive manufactures built with less skilled labor and export capital- and skilled-labor–intensive products. Over time, trade will cause developed countries to specialize in capital- and skill-intensive production. Even if the developed and developing countries produce related goods, developed countries will produce variants that are amenable to capital- and skill-intensive production, products that will not compete directly with those from developing countries.

Studies such as those of Borjas, Freeman, and Katz (1991) use factor input coefficients (ratios of labor to output) to calculate the implicit labor supply associated with trade. However, due to trade with developing countries, currently produced goods use more capital and less unskilled labor than did the goods replaced by imports. For example, imports of low-cost shoes from abroad will compel American manufacturers to specialize in high-quality shoes manufactured by highly trained workers using up-to-date capital. The new capital and the high level of training will increase output per employee. The contemporary ratio of labor to output will not be representative of the ratio that existed in the shoe industry prior to the extension of trade. Thus, using factor content coefficients based on developed countries' current production practices will systematically underestimate the labor content of trade. Wood (1994) argues that appropriate factor content coefficients can be developed by adjusting factor content coefficients to reflect the relative prices faced by developed countries.

Finally, it is worth noting the asymmetry inherent in the "too-small-to-matter" line of argument. When trade economists argue that our present tariffs cost consumers tens of billions of dollars, these costs are never described as "small," even if they are only 1 percent of GDP or less. When the business press discusses international competition, there is never any doubt that international differences in labor costs are big enough to matter for U.S., European, and Japanese companies. For example, a recent *Washington Post* article stated that:

> Faced with escalating competition as global barriers to capital have fallen, European employers are pleading for a rollback in obligatory benefits . . . that have pushed wage costs up to a level 80 percent above those in the United States or Japan. In Third World nations such as India and Vietnam, labor costs as little as one-tenth the level in Europe. (Drozdiak 1994, p. A1)

Losses to workers that are proportionally as large as (or larger than) the aggregate gains from trade cannot be dismissed as insignificant if the losses are the flip side of the coin of the gains. It seems doubtful that competitive pressures, which seem obvious to business leaders and journalists, to reduce labor costs by cutting wages or benefits could not be having appreciable real effects.

Conclusion

This chapter has found significant support in the literature for the proposition that greater openness to trade may be one of the sources of the poor U.S. labor market performance for many workers over the last decade. Although the evidence is yet incomplete and more research remains to be done, there is a body of evidence on hand to demonstrate that international trade has caused wages and employment to decline in U.S. manufacturing; that international trade accounts for about 10 to 20 percent of the increase in wage inequality in the United States in the last decade; that increased international trade with labor-abundant developing countries has a particularly negative effect on U.S. employment and possibly on wages as well; that balanced growth of exports and imports will not automatically improve the wages or quality of jobs available to American workers; that unemployment and wage problems in the United States are not solely a consequence of new technology; that these deleterious consequences do not affect just some small minority but, using the standard definitions of "unskilled" labor, could touch 70 to 80 percent of American wage earners. The balance of research supports the view that the consequences of trade are real, they are not negligible, and they affect far more than a few.

Notes

1. Authors' calculations, based on export and import data taken from the international transactions accounts and GDP figures taken from the national income and product accounts, as reported in U.S. Council of Economic Advisors (1994) and U.S. Congress, Joint Economic Committee (1994). All data in this paragraph are from these sources.

2. For further discussion of the U.S. trade deficit, see chapter 6 in this volume.

3. Hong Kong, Singapore, and South Korea are included here; data for Taiwan were not available for the earlier period. Statistics were calculated by the authors using data from International Monetary Fund (1987, 1993).

4. Data in this paragraph are from Mishel and Bernstein (1993, pp. 33, 132, 224, 274).

5. Data on wages relative to the poverty level and pension coverage in this paragraph are from Mishel and Bernstein (1993, pp. 124, 133).

6. Data on sectoral wages and employment in this paragraph and the next are from U.S. Department of Labor, Bureau of Labor Statistics (1989, tables 68, 80, and 81), plus updates from the U.S. Department of Labor, Bureau of Labor Statistics, *Monthly Labor Review* (various issues), and the authors' calculations.

7. Import penetration in this study is measured by the ratio of imports to total sales at the industry level. Individual establishments (plants) are classified into quintiles according to the import penetration ratios of the industries to which they belong. The quintile of establishments with the highest import penetration ratios accounts for 17.7 percent of employment in the whole sample.

8. For some of the original sources of this theory, see chapter 1 in this book.

9. For modern textbook presentations of this type of model see, for example, Caves, Frankel, and Jones (1993); Krugman and Obstfeld (1994); or Appleyard and Field (1995). In more complex models with more than two goods, factors, and countries, it is not a simple matter to categorize countries or goods in terms of their factor proportions. Multiple factors of production such as different skill grades of labor, different types of natural resources, and the degree to which the "services" of these factors are incorporated in net trade flows must be taken into account in determining countries' comparative advantages. See Leamer (1984) for a comprehensive theoretical and empirical treatment of a multidimensional HO model.

10. Adjustment assistance for displaced workers is a transitional measure designed to help workers who lose their jobs in the short run, not a permanent compensation paid to losers by winners—and even adjustment assistance is often incomplete or nonexistent.

11. See Krugman and Obstfeld (1994, chapter 6) for a presentation of models of trade with scale economies. For examples of how models emphasizing scale economies were used in the analysis of the effects of NAFTA on U.S. wages, see chapter 5 in this book.

12. Models with nontradables sectors abound in the open-economy macroeconomics literature but are less commonly used for microeconomic analysis of the effects of trade on income distribution.

13. The estimating equations are based on a model of labor supply, labor demand, product demand, the relation of wages to product price, and wage determination. Employment and wages are determined by the three determinants of sales: total domestic demand, exports, and the import share of domestic demand. Controls for unionization, the proportion of production workers in the industry labor force, and for year and industry effects are included in all models, as is a measure of the ratio of immigrants in the industry labor force. Control for value added per employee is incorporated into some models. Models are estimated in the log of rates of change rather than levels, although some controls are incorporated as both changes and levels. Inclusion of a value-added measure may be a source of simultaneity as employment, the dependent variable in some equations, is incorporated into the denominator of this measure.

14. Grossman's work (1987) has some unusual results, and many estimates are not statistically significant. This is a consequence of an elaborate specification and extensive lag structure, which leave the regression equations with very limited degrees of freedom for hypothesis tests. More statistically significant results were later obtained by Revenga (1992), who corrected many of the purely statistical flaws in Grossman's study.

15. These studies, which use the Panel Study on Income Dynamics, follow individuals over time. The coefficients may be interpreted as indicating the wage change that occurs when individuals are subject to changing levels of imports over time or because of a change in industries. Omission of controls for occupation may be a source of bias in estimates.

16. Revenga's work regresses measures of the change in the average production wage; the average weekly volume of worker-hours; or the average weekly employment, on an industry-specific weighted average of production prices of major exporting countries, an index of materials prices, the reservation wage, a measure of the business cycle, and two-digit industry dummies. The regression equation is estimated as a reduced form with corrections for autocorrelation and the use of instrumental variables to correct for correlation between the import price index and the error term. In particular, Revenga used exchange rates as an instrument for actual import prices due to the endogeneity of the latter.

17. This type of issue, one of sample selection, is common to many areas of economic research. No current research on trade attempts to correct for the nonrandom loss of employment in import-affected industries.

18. The results reported for Freeman and Katz (1991) are for a model comparing wages and employment in 1984 with wages and employment in 1958. The unexpected results were found in panel data for annual data for the period 1958–84.

19. A related analysis indicates that wages of union members are more sensitive to changes in imports than are wages of employees who are not members of a union.

20. Each industry or product market categorization contains a mix of positive, negative, and nonsignificant wage effects of both imports and exports.

21. Skill was proxied by the proportion of production employees in the industry labor force.

22. These authors estimate an equation using data on individuals from the 1984 Current Population Survey and appending data on tariffs, nontariff barriers (NTBs), exports,

imports, import growth, and intra-industry trade. Although this approach is potentially interesting, omission of other dimensions of industry structure such as unionization, capital/labor ratios, and market concentration can cause substantial bias in the equation (see Belman 1988 for a discussion of the specification of industry variables for this type of model). Such omissions are sufficiently important to raise serious concerns about the bias of the coefficients on the trade variables. The authors acknowledge that addition of other industry variables to a restricted data set, covering fifty-four rather than eighty-two industries, produced unusual results. The consequences were not further specified.

23. Implicitly, this argument assumes that trade can affect wages only if it changes the wage share of total output. The possibility that trade could affect the growth of total output (including the returns to capital as well as the wages of labor) is thus dismissed by these authors.

24. This measure is produced by the BLS productivity division using data on employee compensation taken from the Bureau of Economic Analysis (BEA). The BLS adjusts the data in various ways, such as by adding an imputation for the labor income of proprietors. See U.S. Department of Labor, Bureau of Labor Statistics (1988, p. 72) for details. The actual data series can be found in U.S. Council of Economic Advisors (1994, table B-47).

25. The prices of intermediate products, which are not purchased by final consumers but are used in the further production of other goods, are not directly incorporated into any of the output deflators for the national income accounts (either GDP or final output). Of course, any effects of changes in their prices are incorporated as they affect the prices of final goods.

26. Lawrence and Slaughter (1993) include an index that deflates wages by the GDP deflator less investment, but they do not discuss it. Lawrence (1994) presents this index and omits the index that incorporates investment goods.

27. See note 24 for details on this index.

28. The ECI uses data collected directly from employers and does not include any imputations as the BEA/BLS measure does. However, the fixed-weight ECI may overestimate wages and benefit costs in the 1980s, since it does not adjust for shifts in the distribution of employment between industries and occupations. See below for a discussion of a new, alternative ECI that is current-weighted.

29. Inclusion of self-employment income and problems in the measurement of the hours of employees not included in the production and nonsupervisory classification may also impart an upward bias to the BEA/BLS total compensation index.

30. Taking the period 1987–93, the BEA/BLS index indicates that total compensation increased by 3.1 percent. In contrast, the current-weighted ECI index, which adjusts for changes in the distribution of employment by industry and occupation, shows costs declining by 2.9 percent. The fixed-weight ECI index, which is more commonly used, uses constant industry and occupation distributions. The current-weighted version that allows for changes in industrial and occupational composition of the labor force has been available only since 1987.

31. The shift in years is necessary because estimates of current-weighted compensation are only available for selected years in the 1970s (when the current-weighted ECI was not calculated).

32. Authors' calculations based on data from U.S. Council of Economic Advisors (1994, table B-47).

33. Categorization of employees by skill is central to all of these studies. Those using the CPS categorize employees according to educational attainment, typically whether employees have less than a high school education, a high school diploma, some college, a college degree, or education beyond college. Other studies, which employ the Census of

Manufactures (CM) or the ASM, proxy the skilled/unskilled distinction with that between production and nonproduction employees. Leamer (1994) questions the accuracy of this categorization as a proxy for skill, but Berman, Bound, and Griliches (1993) find rough correspondence between this classification. Sachs and Shatz (1994) find the production/nonproduction division generally corresponds to a white-collar/blue-collar division and correlates with more sophisticated indexes of skill. Under any scheme the majority of the U.S. labor force is classified as "low-skilled": 80 percent of the U.S. labor force are production workers; 75 percent have less than a four-year college degree.

34. Authors' calculation based on data from U.S. Council of Economic Advisors (1994, tables B-44, B-45).

35. Efficiency units are measures of labor supply that are weighted by wages to adjust for differences in productivity for different groups within the population. Prior to 1982, trade decreased the supply of labor efficiency units as exports increased demand for the products of skilled workers. After 1983 this reversed, with net imports adding about 1 percent to labor efficiency units in 1984 and 1.3 percent in 1985.

36. For example, according to the data cited by Murphy and Welch, 28 percent of men with less than a high school diploma were employed in the traded durable goods sector, but only 15.2 percent of men with a college degree were employed in this sector between 1967 and 1988. Among women, 18.3 percent of those with less than a high school education were located in traded durable goods, but only 3.3 percent of women with college degrees were in this industry. The traded nondurable goods industry employed 24 percent of women with less than a high school diploma but only 3.8 percent of women with high school educations.

37. Similar, if somewhat smaller, estimates are found in Katz and Murphy (1992). In the period 1979–85, Katz and Murphy find that trade in manufactured goods caused a 0.63 percent decrease in the demand for male dropouts, a 0.3 percent decline in the demand for male high school graduates, and an increase in the demand for males with some college and college degrees. Among women, demand fell by 2.2 percent for dropouts and by 0.1 percent for high school graduates, while demand for college graduates increased by 1.3 percent. If trade in manufactures is assumed to have its main effect on production workers, demand for male dropouts fell by 1.5 percent, demand for male high school graduates fell by 0.7 percent, and trade caused an increase in the demand for men with some college or with college degrees. Under this same assumption, demand declined by 4 percent for female dropouts and by 0.3 percent for women with a high school education; it rose for the remaining education classes. One explanation for these relatively small effects is that the measures include only direct effects; upstream effects on supplier industries are not incorporated into the calculations.

38. These results appear to be at odds with the prior conclusion that wages in importing and exporting industries are similar. However, if the effect of trade is to displace workers from the traded goods sector into other parts of the economy, then the Borjas and Ramey finding is compatible with the rough equality of wages in importing and exporting industries. Likewise, it is possible that increased trade deficits increase within-industry wage inequality rather than the between-industry measures that are studied by Katz and Summers (1989) and by Dickens and Lang (1988).

39. Auto parts producers who were not part of the big three operated in oligopsonistic rather than competitive markets. Workers in auto parts, including workers employed by General Motors (GM), Ford, and Chrysler, earned 87 percent of main auto wages in 1983. Workers in truck bodies earned 67 percent of main auto wages.

40. The SS theorem assumes that technology and factor endowments are fixed; accurate measurement of SS effects requires control for this and other conditions that violate the assumptions of the theorem.

41. See chapter 5 in this book for further discussion of Leamer's study and other analyses of the distributional effects of increased U.S.-Mexican trade under NAFTA.

42. Bound and Johnson's analysis of wage inequality compares the change in real average hourly wages of thirty-two demographic groups defined by education, potential labor market experience, and gender. The groups were defined by four education groupings (dropouts, high school diploma, some college, and college or more), potential labor market experience (0–9 years, 10–19 years, 20–29 years, 30+ years), and two genders. The effect of generalized technological change is modeled by changes in the annualized proportionate change in the wage of these thirty-two groups as the outcome of the annual proportionate change in their labor supply, industry-specific technology, change in industry-average wage effects, and shifts in product demand. The residual from this model is used as the measure of general technological change, and it is this residual that underlies the statement that 120 percent of the increase in wages is attributable to general technological change. Bound and Johnson conclude that:

> It is apparent from inspection of the estimated values of GEN (the general technology variable) for the 1980's that our major conclusion, which will be discussed more completely below, is that the principal cause of the significant wage-structure changes of the past decade was a shift in the structure of the b_i's (the technology effect) that were extremely favorable to certain groups, especially women and the highly educated. (1992, p. 386)

They note, however, that these results might also be the result of increasing hours of work by women, declining effectiveness of education for younger workers, or competition from undocumented immigrants.

43. The measure of industry-specific technology suffers a related problem of interpretation. Lacking a measure of sector-specific technological change, Bound and Johnson (1992) interpret the large changes in the relative wages in "four of the five traditional blue collar industries (durable/mining, nondurables, transportation, and public utilities)" as the consequence of industry-specific technological change. As in the case of general technological change, this measure may include the effects of technology, but cannot be distinguished from any other factor, such as trade, that had a particularly large effect in these sectors. The authors' approach is also problematic because they use their data on relative wage change to define the group of industries most affected by technological change.

44. The analysis by Berman, Bound, and Griliches (1993) begins with a shift-share decomposition of the ratio of the change in the ratio of nonproduction employee wages to average wages in manufacturing. The change in the nonproduction wage ratio is decomposed into the change that occurs because industries have altered their use of nonproduction employment (e.g., aerospace increases its employment of engineers) and the change that occurs because employment has shifted toward industries that use more nonproduction employees (e.g., employment falls in apparel but rises in aerospace). These two components of change are then further decomposed into four sources: exports, imports, defense, and domestic consumption (to simplify, imports and exports will be referred to as trade). The resulting equations answer the question: What proportion of the change in the nonproduction wage ratio is explained by changes in trade (or defense or domestic consumption)?

Unfortunately, Berman et al. take an additional step and, in doing so, alter the question they address. In the equation for the change in the within-industries wage ratio, they calculate the change in this ratio for domestic consumption for all manufacturing and then subtract this average from each of the four components of demand. The "average" change is then added back into the domestic consumption effect. The between-industries equation is transformed in a similar manner. With this step, that part of the change in the wage ratio in trade or defense that is similar to the change in the wage ratio for domestic consumption for all manufacturing is attributed to the domestic sector. The equations now answer the question, What is the additional effect of trade and defense, the effect beyond the average change in manufacturing in the domestic production sector, on the nonproduction wage ratio? The consequence of this transformation is to increase the proportion of change in the wage ratio attributed to domestic consumption and, conversely, to decrease the proportion attributed to trade or defense.

45. Using the method of Berman et al., the equation for calculating the change in the wage ratio is

$1.5 = 0.5(2-1) + 0.5(1-1) + 1$

and the ratio of the change in the traded goods industry to the total change is $0.5(2-1)/1.5$ = 1/3. If we use the equation that does not subtract out the mean of the change in the domestic goods industry, the equation is

$1.5 = 0.5(2) + 0.5(1)$

and the ratio of change in traded goods to total change is $0.5(2)/1.5 = 2/3$.

46. Growth in technology was proxied by the annual growth in equipment per full-time employee, in computer equipment per full-time employee, and in the employment share of scientists and engineers.

47. The independent variables in this model include the utilization of production labor, nonproduction labor, and capital stock at the beginning of the period (1976) and the change in the capital stock from 1976 to 1989.

48. The issue of timing could not be addressed by Bound and Johnson (1992) or Berman et al. (1993), since their measures span the period from 1979 to the late 1980s.

49. Considering all developing and developed countries, Wood (1994) estimates that international trade has reduced the demand for manufacturing labor in the developed countries by 12 percent and increased demand for skilled labor by about 5.5 percent. The effects of induced technological change are not computed precisely, but Wood speculates that it has doubled the impact of trade on the demand for skilled and unskilled labor in the developed countries.

50. Contrary to Wood (1994), Deardorff and Hakura (1994) argue that the consequences of trade-induced technological change should not be counted as trade effects. In their view, trade merely serves as a conduit in this case for technological effects that would eventually occur anyway. Thus, technology is the true source of the declining demand for less skilled labor. However, with the sole exception of Wood, none of the researchers to date have included technological effects in their estimates of trade effects.

51. Since many OECD countries restrict imports of manufactured goods to a greater extent than the United States, aggregate import figures for the OECD are not a good representation of the import of manufactured goods into the United States.

Bibliography

Appleyard, Dennis R., and Alfred J. Field, Jr. 1995. *International Economics,* 2d ed. Chicago: Richard D. Irwin.

Batra, Ravi. 1993. *The Myth of Free Trade.* New York: Charles Scribner's Sons.

Belman, Dale. 1988. "Concentration, Unionism, and Labor Earnings: A Sample Selection Approach." *Review of Economics and Statistics,* Vol. 70, No. 3, pp. 391–97.

Berman, Eli, John Bound, and Zvi Griliches. 1993. "Changes in the Demand for Skilled Labor within U.S. Manufacturing Industries: Evidence from the Annual Survey of Manufacturing." Working Paper No. 4255. Cambridge, MA: National Bureau of Economic Research.

Bhagwati, Jagdish, and Vivek H. Dehejia. 1994. "Freer Trade and Wages of the Unskilled—Is Marx Striking Again?" In Jagdish Bhagwati and Marvin H. Kosters, eds., *Trade and Wages: Leveling Wages Down?* Washington, DC: American Enterprise Institute.

Borjas, George J., Richard B. Freeman, and Lawrence F. Katz. 1991. "On the Labor Market Effects of Immigration and Trade." Working Paper No. 3761. Cambridge, MA: National Bureau of Economic Research.

Borjas, George J., and Valerie A. Ramey. 1994. "Time-Series Evidence on the Sources of Trends in Wage Inequality." *American Economic Review: Papers and Proceedings,* Vol. 84, No. 2, pp. 10–16.

Bosworth, Barry, and George L. Perry. 1994. "Productivity and Real Wages: Is There a Puzzle?" *Brookings Papers on Economic Activity,* No. 1, pp. 317–35.

Bound, John, and George Johnson. 1992. "Changes in the Structure of Wages in the 1980's: An Evaluation of Alternative Explanations." *American Economic Review,* Vol. 82, No. 3, pp. 371–92.

Brauer, David A. 1990. "The Effect of Import Competition on Manufacturing Wages." Research Paper No. 9030. New York: Federal Reserve Bank of New York.

Brauer, David, A., and Susan Hickok. 1994. "Explaining the Growing Gap between Low-Skilled and High-Skilled Wages." Research Paper No. 9418. New York: Federal Reserve Bank of New York.

Burgman, Todd A., and John M. Geppert. 1993. "Factor Price Equalization: A Cointegration Approach." *Weltwirtschaftliches Archiv,* Vol. 129, No. 3, pp. 472–87.

Caves, Richard E., Jeffrey A. Frankel, and Ronald W. Jones. 1993. *World Trade and Payments: An Introduction,* 6th ed. New York: HarperCollins.

Clarida, Richard H., and Susan Hickok. 1993. "US Manufacturing and the Deindustrialization Debate." *World Economy,* Vol. 16, No. 2, pp. 173–92.

Davis, Steven J. 1992. "Cross-Country Patterns of Change in Relative Wages." *NBER Macroeconomics Annual, 1992.* Cambridge, MA: National Bureau of Economic Research.

Davis, Steven J., John C. Haltiwanger, and Scott Schuh. 1994. *Gross Job Flows in U.S. Manufacturing.* Washington, DC: U.S. Bureau of the Census.

Deardorff, Alan V., and Dalia S. Hakura. 1994. "Trade and Wages: What Are the Questions?" In Jagdish Bhagwati and Marvin H. Kosters, eds., *Trade and Wages: Leveling Wages Down?* Washington, DC: American Enterprise Institute.

Dickens, William T. 1988. "The Effects of Trade on Employment." In Laura D. Tyson, William T. Dickens, and John Zysman, eds., *The Dynamics of Trade and Employment.* Cambridge, MA: Ballinger Press.

———. 1994. "Good Jobs: Increasing Worker Productivity with Trade and Industrial Policy." Mimeo. Berkeley: University of California, and Cambridge, MA: National Bureau of Economic Research.

Dickens, William T., and Kevin Lang. 1988. "Why It Matters What We Trade: A Case for Active Policy." In Laura D. Tyson, William T. Dickens, and John Zysman, eds., *The Dynamics of Trade and Employment.* Cambridge, MA: Ballinger Press.

Drozdiak, William. 1994. "New Global Markets Mean Grim Trade-Offs; Europe's Welfare Benefits Hang in Balance." *Washington Post* (August 8), p. A1.

Duchin, Faye, and Glenn-Marie Lange. 1988. *Trading Away Jobs: The Effects of the U.S. Merchandise Trade Deficit on Employment.* Working Paper No. 102. Washington, DC: Economic Policy Institute.

Freeman, Richard, and Lawrence Katz. 1991. "Industrial Wage and Employment Determination in an Open Economy." In John Abowd and Richard Freeman, eds., *Immigration, Trade, and the Labor Market.* Chicago: University of Chicago Press.

Galbraith, James K., and Paulo Du Pin Calmon. 1994. "Industries, Trade, and Wages." In

Michael A. Bernstein and David E. Adler, eds., *Understanding American Economic Decline*. Cambridge, England: Cambridge University Press.

Gaston, Noel, and Daniel Trefler. 1994. "Protection, Trade, and Wages: Evidence from U.S. Manufacturing." *Industrial and Labor Relations Review*, Vol. 47, No. 4, pp. 574–93.

Gremmen, Hans. 1985. "Testing the Factor Price Equalization Theorem in the E.C.: An Alternative Approach." *Journal of Common Market Studies*, Vol. 23, pp. 277–86.

Grossman, Gene M. 1987. "The Employment and Wage Effects of Import Competition in the United States." *Journal of International Economic Integration*, Vol. 2, No. 1, pp. 1–27.

Hall, Robert. 1993. "Comment." *Brookings Papers on Economic Activity: Microeconomics*, No. 2, pp. 211–14.

Heywood, John. 1991. "Imports and Domestic Wages: Is the Relationship Consistent with Expense Preference Behavior?" *Journal of Law, Economics, and Organization*, Vol. 7, No. 2, pp. 355–72.

Heywood, John, and Romkaew Broehm. 1991. "Imports, Domestic Wages and Unions: Panel Data Estimates." Mimeo. Milwaukee: University of Wisconsin.

Howell, David R. 1994. "The Collapse of Low-Skilled Male Earnings in the 1980's: Skill Mismatch or Shifting Wage Norms?" Mimeo. New York: New School for Social Research.

Howes, Candace, and Ann R. Markusen. 1993. "Trade, Industry, and Economic Development." In Helzi Noponen, Julie Graham, and Ann R. Markusen, eds., *Trading Industries, Trading Regions: International Trade, American Industry, and Regional Economic Development*. New York: Guilford Press.

International Monetary Fund. 1987, 1993. *Direction of Trade Statistics Yearbook*. Washington, DC: IMF.

Katz, Lawrence F., and Kevin M. Murphy. 1992. "Changes in Relative Wages, 1963–1987: Supply and Demand Factors." *Quarterly Journal of Economics*, Vol. 107 (February), pp. 35–78.

Katz, Lawrence F., and Lawrence H. Summers. 1989. "Industry Rents: Evidence and Implications." *Brookings Papers on Economic Activity: Microeconomics*, pp. 209–75.

Krugman, Paul. 1994a. "Competitiveness: A Dangerous Obsession." *Foreign Affairs*, Vol. 73, No. 2 (March–April), pp. 28–44.

———. 1994b. "Does Third World Growth Hurt First World Prosperity?" *Harvard Business Review* (July–August), pp. 113–21.

Krugman, Paul, and Robert Z. Lawrence. 1993. "Trade, Jobs, and Wages." Working Paper No. 4478. Cambridge, MA: National Bureau of Economic Research.

Krugman, Paul, and Maurice Obstfeld. 1994. *International Economics: Theory and Policy*, 3d ed. New York: HarperCollins.

Lawrence, Robert Z. 1994. *The Impact of Trade on OECD Labor Markets*. Washington, DC: Group of Thirty.

Lawrence, Robert Z., and Matthew J. Slaughter. 1993. "International Trade and American Wages in the 1980s: Giant Sucking Sound or Small Hiccup?" *Brookings Papers on Economic Activity: Microeconomics*, No. 2, pp. 161–210.

Leamer, Edward E. 1984. *Sources of International Comparative Advantage*. Cambridge, MA: MIT Press.

———. 1993. "Wage Effects of a U.S.-Mexican Free Trade Agreement." In Peter M. Garber, ed., *The U.S.-Mexico Free Trade Agreement*. Cambridge, MA: MIT Press.

———. 1994. "Trade, Wages, and Revolving Door Ideas." Working Paper No. 4716. Cambridge, MA: National Bureau of Economic Research.

Martines, Joaquim Oliveira. 1993. "Market Structure, International Trade, and Relative Wages." Working Paper No. 134. Paris: Organization for Economic Cooperation and Development, Economics Department.

Mishel, Lawrence, and Jared Bernstein. 1993. *The State of Working America, 1992–93.* Armonk, NY: M. E. Sharpe.

———. 1994. "Is the Technology Black Box Empty? An Empirical Examination of the Impact of Technology on Wage Inequality and Employment Structure." Mimeo. Washington, DC: Economic Policy Institute.

Mokhtari, Manouchehr, and Farhad Rassekh. 1989. "The Tendency towards Factor Price Equalization among OECD Countries." *Review of Economics and Statistics,* Vol. 71, No. 4, pp. 636–42.

Murphy, Kevin, and Finis Welch. 1991. "The Role of International Trade in Wage Differentials." In Marvin Kosters, ed., *Workers and Their Wages.* Washington, DC: American Enterprise Institute.

Passell, Peter. 1992. "The Victim Has a Blue Collar, but Free Trade Has an Alibi." *New York Times* (August 16), section 4, p. 4.

Revenga, Ana L. 1992. "Exporting Jobs? The Impact of Import Competition on Employment and Wages in U.S. Manufacturing." *Quarterly Journal of Economics,* Vol. 107 (February), pp. 255–84.

Sachs, Jeffrey D., and Howard J. Shatz. 1994. "Trade and Jobs in U.S. Manufacturing." *Brookings Papers on Economic Activity,* No. 1, pp. 1–69.

Sengenberger, Werner. 1994. "Restructuring at the Global Level: The Role of International Labour Standards." In Werner Sengenberger and Duncan Campbell, eds., *Creating Economic Opportunities: The Role of Labour Standards in Industrial Restructuring.* Geneva: International Labour Organization.

Stolper, Wolfgang F., and Paul A. Samuelson. 1941. "Protection and Real Wages." *Review of Economic Studies,* Vol. 9 (November), pp. 58–73.

Tovias, Alfred. 1982. "Testing Factor Price Equalization in the EEC." *Journal of Common Market Studies,* Vol. 20, pp. 375–88.

Ullmann, Owen. 1993. "Economic Trends: U.S. Economic Woes." *Business Week* (November 15), p. 22.

University of Illinois at Chicago. 1994. *Monitoring Manufacturing Employment Trends in Chicago and Illinois: Implications for NAFTA Impacts.* Chicago: Center for Urban Economic Development.

U.S. Congress, Joint Economic Committee. 1994. *Economic Indicators* (November). Washington, DC: U.S. Government Printing Office.

U.S. Council of Economic Advisors. 1994. *Economic Report of the President.* Washington, DC: U.S. Government Printing Office.

U.S. Department of Labor, Bureau of Labor Statistics. Various years. *Employment, Hours, and Earnings.* Washington, DC: U.S. Government Printing Office.

———. 1988. *Handbook of Methods,* Bulletin 2285. Washington, DC: U.S. Government Printing Office.

———. 1989. *Handbook of Labor Statistics,* Bulletin 2340. Washington, DC: U.S. Government Printing Office.

———. Various years. *Monthly Labor Review.* Washington, DC: U.S. Government Printing Office.

Wood, Adrian. 1994. *North-South Trade, Employment, and Inequality: Changing Fortunes in a Skill Driven World.* Oxford, England: Oxford University Press.

CHAPTER FOUR

The Costs of Trade Protection Reconsidered: U.S. Steel, Textiles, and Apparel

ROBERT E. SCOTT AND THEA M. LEE

Introduction

Since Adam Smith and David Ricardo, most economists have subscribed to the belief that trade liberalization benefits both trading partners because it lowers the cost of imports and competing domestic products; expands markets for exports, allowing producers to take advantage of scale economies; and allows workers to move from low-productivity industries to high-productivity export sectors. Based on these sorts of considerations, many studies have shown that the elimination of trade restraints has great benefits for home consumers and for overall national welfare. However, these studies have emphasized the beneficial impact of trade policy on consumers and ignored or neglected its effects on producers (especially workers and owners in import-competing industries). While lower prices for consumers are equated with the "national interest," the goal of maintaining production and jobs in particular industries is disdained as catering to special interests.

This consumer-oriented framework for evaluating trade restrictions is based on a static model of perfectly functioning competitive markets, both for goods and for labor. Within this model, any intervention by the government in the economy, including the imposition of tariffs or other trade barriers, will necessarily distort an otherwise ideal outcome. But this view gives little or no weight to the possible long-term benefits for a nation of developing its productive capacity in certain directions. It assumes that unregulated trade will automatically create an optimal industrial structure for each nation, based on that nation's initial endowment of resources.

This chapter includes research previously released by the Economic Policy Institute in Blecker, Lee, and Scott (1993) and Scott and Lee (1991), as well as unpublished research reported in Scott and Blecker (1993).

This traditional approach has several weaknesses. First, by assuming that freely functioning markets will generate full employment of all resources, it eliminates one of the key political issues in any trade debate—namely, whether eliminating existing trade protection will cost jobs. In a full-employment framework, each job lost in an import-competing industry is quickly replaced by a new job in an export industry.

Second, by focusing on productive resources at a single moment in time, this methodology ignores all the factors that might affect the development of productive capacity (i.e., the capital stock, the infrastructure, or the quantity of skilled labor) over time. It also ignores the interactions between one country's trade and industrial policies and another's prospects for producing or marketing in a particular industry. For example, in industries such as aircraft, in which there are significant economies of scale and a limited number of global producers, one country's decision to subsidize or protect its aircraft industry could affect its trading partners' subsequent decisions. Cost-of-protection studies based purely on consumer impacts in domestic markets fail to capture these interactions.

This chapter emphasizes the effects of protection on producers as well as consumers on the premise that a country's industrial structure does matter and that trade affects how it develops. The nation's industrial structure is continuously evolving and requires an optimal balance between competition and protection in order to be innovative, keep improving, and provide the highest level of wages and economywide productivity growth. In the next section we will briefly review the two approaches to trade theory. The following sections will then explain how the implications of the new trade theory are tested in our case studies.

The Old and New Views

Neoclassical trade theory (the "old view" of trade) assumes that trade patterns are determined by relative supplies of factors of production (e.g., skilled and unskilled labor, capital, and natural resources) and/or by exogenously given differences in tastes and technology. Models that assume perfect competition and constant returns to scale form the basis of the theory of comparative advantage, which assumes that the location of industries and patterns of trade is determined by national resource "endowments," consumer tastes, and technical capabilities, all of which are given in each nation independently of its trade relations.

Neoclassical theory explains why the United States exports corn and wheat and imports oil—patterns of *interindustry* trade that are clearly related to our endowments of natural resources. In the theory of comparative advantage, countries specialize in products that they can produce *relatively* more efficiently than their trading partners.

The theory of comparative advantage cannot, however, explain *intra-industry trade,* in which one country both imports and exports similar products or products *in the same industry.* The United States engages in such two-way trade in most manufacturing industries. It exports and imports memory chips, machinery, autos, computers, aircraft, steel, furniture, and many other industrial and consumer goods. Over half of all U.S. trade was of the intra-industry variety in the 1970s and the 1980s. The intra-industry share of total trade has increased substantially since the 1950s and the 1960s. Over the past fifteen years, 63 percent of U.S. merchandise exports and 59 percent of U.S. imports, on average, have been exchanged with other industrialized countries, most of which possess resources and patterns of comparative advantage that are roughly similar to those of the United States (Lincoln 1990).

Neoclassical trade theory is also unable to explain why firms engage in direct foreign investment or why multinational corporations (MNCs) exist. There is no reason for firms to invest abroad, in the traditional theory. However, the growth of MNCs and of direct foreign investment is one of the most important recent developments in the world economy. Between 1970 and 1989, world output, measured in current dollars, increased by 400 percent. Total world exports grew twice as fast as total output, and direct foreign investment increased by over 1,400 percent, or 3.5 times as rapidly as world output (Preston and Windsor 1992, p. 270).

In 1987, MNCs (both domestic- and foreign-based) and their affiliates generated 90.7 percent of all U.S. exports and 75.6 percent of all U.S. imports.[1] Almost half of all trade took place *entirely within* MNCs and their affiliates (intrafirm trade). The growth of direct foreign investment and the dominant role of MNCs are two of the most important features of the international economic landscape of the late twentieth century, and yet the theory of comparative advantage is unable to explain why they exist or how they affect trade patterns.

In contrast, the new trade theory provides explanations for both intra-industry trade and direct foreign investment. The new view analyzes the effects of market "imperfections" on trade patterns. These imperfections include the following:

1. *Scale economies,* which can leave room for only a few firms in the global industry (such as aircraft production), and which may reflect large fixed costs for research and development, as well as traditional scale factors.
2. *Learning curves,* which generate sustained cost reductions as output expands (common in the production of innovative products such as transistors, computer chips, and photovoltaic cells).
3. *Knowledge spillovers,* which benefit consumers of new products, as well as producers, and are common in high-technology industries such as biotechnology (green revolution plants), computers, and machine tools.
4. *High risks in producing and marketing new products,* which, combined with capital market barriers facing small firms, limit investments in fields such as pharmaceuticals and biotechnology.

The new view of trade helps us to understand why countries engage in intra-industry trade and why firms engage in direct foreign investment. Firms can take advantage of scale economies and proprietary technology by seeking out global markets for their products. Firms based in one country may be able to dominate niches for their products, while firms in other countries will have advantages in other market niches.

One of the most important contributions of the new trade theory is to our understanding of the positive effects that government policy can have on trade and incomes, by taking advantage of market imperfections. These insights are not new to governments in many of the industrial or developing countries with which the United States trades and competes, nor is the general principle that trade restrictions are needed in some circumstances to correct market failures. The infant-industry theory of economic development is an old example. How-ever, the new trade theory provides a broader theoretical foundation for a posi-tive government role in regulating trade and industrial institutions.

Trade Policy and Producer Interests

Cost-of-protection studies overstate the benefits of trade liberalization because they tend to ignore issues of industrial structure and problems caused by market failures. Careful study of particular cases and industries shows that, at least for the United States, some types of trade protection can potentially generate net benefits for the economy as a whole.

There are at least four problems with traditional cost-of-protection estimates. First, when trade is liberalized, workers who lose their jobs in import-competing industries usually end up with lower incomes as a result. When we examine the earnings records of displaced workers, we discover that they usually experience both temporary *and permanent* reductions in incomes and wages. This conflicts with the assumption of many free trade advocates that workers will move into higher-productivity occupations after trade liberalization. These wage losses occur because workers are often forced to move from higher-paying (high-pro-ductivity) jobs in manufacturing to lower-paying (low-productivity) jobs in ser-vice industries.[2] Recent research shows that some jobs are endowed with large, persistent rents or wage premiums, and that these jobs predominate in the manu-facturing sectors of the U.S. economy (Katz and Summers 1989).[3] Even the studies that do consider the effects of trade liberalization on wages and labor income tend to underestimate the size of the wage effect.[4] The existence of market failures, such as those considered in the new trade theory, is one reason for the persistence of wage premiums.

The second problem is that cost-of-protection studies ignore the potential beneficial effects of trade restraints on domestic productivity and prices. These studies assume that technological change and investment are independent of trade protection. This is not always the case. In both the textile industry and the steel industry, as we will discuss below, the trade protection of the 1980s coincided with high rates of investment and with productivity growth well above the manufacturing average.

Trade restrictions can increase business confidence in domestic markets and thereby encourage investment that would not otherwise have taken place. This can actually reduce prices to consumers in the long run, offsetting the effect of higher import prices. This effect should be taken into account by studies attempting to measure the costs of trade protection. Since the effect is likely to vary by industry, it should be assessed on a case-by-case basis.

The third problem is that most comprehensive cost-of-protection studies assume that all industries are perfectly competitive, and that identical general models can be used to estimate the effects of trade liberalization on import and domestic prices and on trade flows in every sector (see, for example, Hufbauer and Elliott 1994; Cline 1990). The existence of extensive concentration in some industries and significant barriers to entry in some segments of the production and marketing process suggests that it is important to consider industry-specific market failures in analyzing the costs of protection and when designing optimal trade policies.

The final problem is that cost-of-protection studies often fail to consider the costs of alternative trade restraints that could improve the welfare of consumers and producers in the home country.[5] The United States often implements forms of protection that are known to be highly inefficient, such as quota-type restraints, for political reasons and because of our obligations under the General Agreement on Trade and Tariffs (GATT), the multilateral agreement governing most postwar trade. In some cases, such as that of the steel industry, as discussed below, the government's choice to employ quantitative restraints rather than tariffs increased the net national welfare costs of protection severalfold, according to several recent studies.[6] Thus, most of the national costs of protection in this industry result from a political decision to use an inefficient form of trade restriction. This implication is rarely emphasized.

The costs and benefits of trade liberalization depend heavily on the particular industry involved. Labor rents and opportunities for productivity gain or welfare-enhancing trade and industrial policy arrangements can differ substantially across sectors. The remainder of this chapter will illustrate these points by reviewing and synthesizing the results of three case studies of the cost of protection. The effects of trade liberalization on the wages of (potentially) displaced workers are illustrated in the cases of the steel and apparel industries. The beneficial effects of protection on productivity and prices are illustrated with respect to steel and textiles. The problems raised by barriers to entry are examined in the case of the apparel sector, in which market concentration in apparel distribution and marketing suggests that importers and retailing may capture most of the benefits of trade liberalization. As a result, the consumer benefits of trade liberalization in this sector may be vastly overstated by models that fail to take this into account. Finally, the benefits of tariffs and other revenue-generating forms of trade restraint, as compared to quotas, are illustrated in the steel and apparel cases.

Review of these cases will show that trade liberalization does not necessarily generate unambiguously positive contributions to national welfare at all times, for all industries. These cases suggest that although trade restrictions do tend to raise direct costs to consumers, in some cases there may be offsetting benefits that should be weighed in policy decisions. Our results also suggest that the process and timing of trade liberalization—when and how trade barriers are lowered—will have important effects on the costs and benefits of such policies. The costs of wage adjustment depend on the general level of unemployment in society and are large when unemployment is high and smaller when unemployment is low.[7] For this reason, trade policy must take into account business-cycle timing and the effects of structural changes on wage and income levels.

The optimal trade policy thus depends on sectoral characteristics such as market structure, the potential for productivity improvement and economies of scale, the size of wage losses relative to consumer costs, and thoughtful design of the policy itself. We ignore information about the needs and performance of individual industries at our own peril, in both economic analysis and policy-making arenas.

The Steel Industry: Labor Displacement and Inefficient Quotas

In this section, we present new estimates of the costs (and benefits) of protection in the U.S. steel industry in the 1980s. In the early 1980s, the U.S. steel industry was hit hard by several factors: the 1982 recession; the overvalued dollar; and a surge of imports, some of which had been heavily subsidized by foreign governments. Capacity utilization fell to less than 50 percent, and employment plummeted. Rather than allow the resulting trade petitions from the steel industry to be decided on a case-by-case basis, the Reagan administration negotiated a series of voluntary restraint agreements (VRAs), to limit the total volume of steel imports to about 20 percent of the U.S. market.

The U.S. steel industry has made enormous strides toward greater efficiency and competitiveness since the VRAs were implemented. A New York Times article concluded that, "the American steel industry . . . has undergone a transformation in the last decade that has drastically sharpened the industry's competitive position" (Hicks 1992, p. A1). The U.S. International Trade Commission (USITC) similarly found that, "in terms of price, quality, and service, U.S. producers are better able to meet the needs of their domestic and (increasingly) foreign customers [than before the 1980s]. The rationalization of facilities, continued capital investment, and the implementation of new technologies have contributed to the improvement" (1991, p. i). During this period, productivity growth has accelerated, compared to both the past history of the steel industry and the average for all manufacturing. We argue here that the combination of competitive pressure from the low-cost electric furnace producers (the minimills), and some imports, along with the stability provided by the VRAs, worked to foster higher levels of investment and the resulting productivity growth.

Between 1984 and 1990, output per production worker in the steel industry (Standard Industrial Classification [SIC] Sector 331) grew at an annual average rate of 4.5 percent a year, compared to 2.4 percent a year from 1960 to 1972 and 1.2 percent a year from 1972 to 1983. U.S. labor productivity in steel is now the best in the world: it takes 5.3 worker-hours to produce a metric ton of cold-rolled steel in the United States, compared to 5.6 worker-hours per ton in Japan and Canada, and 11.2 worker-hours per ton in Brazil.[8] (In the early 1980s, it took about 10 worker-hours to produce the same ton of steel in the United States.) The real price of steel (deflated by the aggregate producers' price index) rose in the 1960s and the 1970s and then fell between 1984 and 1990. The competitiveness of U.S. steel producers, as reflected by changes in the real price of steel, thus increased during this period.

The picture of the steel VRAs that emerges from the analysis in this chapter is different from the conventional view that they were utterly misguided and that any form of trade protection for steel was unwarranted. The VRAs did *not* inhibit the steel industry from making the structural adjustments that were necessary for it to become more efficient and competitive. On the contrary, to the extent that the VRAs encouraged investment and increased capacity utilization, they helped to reduce costs, leading to lower steel prices for domestic consumers in the long run. Thus, the VRAs helped to ameliorate the short-run social costs of industry shrinkage, without preventing necessary adjustments from taking place. Furthermore, the impact of the VRAs on the domestic price of steel must be viewed in the context of the windfall gains that steel consumers were reaping during the early part of this period from the overvaluation of the dollar and global excess supply of steel. When these factors are taken into account, consumers were still *better off* during this period than they would have been under a scenario in which the dollar had not been overvalued and the VRAs had not been implemented.[9] However, less costly alternatives were available and should be used in the future if the industry is damaged by unfair foreign competition.

We use a partial equilibrium model of the steel industry to estimate the supply and demand for imported and domestic products, which we assume to be imperfect substitutes for each other.10 We then calculate the impact of the VRAs on the prices of both domestic and imported steel. Since there has been little "market power" in the steel industry since the 1960s, we use a model appropriate for a competitive industry (see Blecker 1989). We supplement these figures with estimates of the losses in wage income for workers whose jobs would have been lost if the VRAs had been eliminated. This allows us to compare the total costs of protection to its benefits.[11]

Several different, but closely related, definitions of the cost of protection are used by economists, as follows: (1) the consumer cost of protection; (2) the net national welfare cost of existing protection; (3) the net national welfare cost of alternative forms of protection (e.g., tariff or auction quota equivalents); and (4) the adjusted net national welfare cost, which takes into account gains in worker income. Consumer cost includes the total increase in prices of both domestic and imported steel accounted for by trade restrictions. The net national welfare cost deducts gains to producers that result from higher prices from the consumer losses to estimate the net impact on national welfare. Estimates of the net national welfare costs are therefore much smaller than the consumer cost. These represent true efficiency losses to the nation, rather than redistribution of income from one group to another. Even these efficiency losses do not take account of the gains to workers who keep jobs that pay above-average wages.

In the case of the steel VRA, it was not trade protection per se that imposed the bulk of the net national cost of protection, but rather the particular form of protection that was implemented. If an equivalent degree of protection had been achieved using a tariff or an auction quota instead of the VRA, the net national cost of protection would have been quite minimal.[12] Moreover, using an adjusted measure of net national cost that takes into account the social benefits of increased wage incomes to workers whose jobs were saved, we will show below that tariff-equivalent trade protection would have yielded *net benefits* to the nation as a whole because the gains in labor income exceed the net national costs of such protection.[13]

The method for obtaining estimates of each of these cost measures is explained in the appendix to this chapter. The estimates for the steel case are summarized in Table 4.1, which shows the average effects of the VRA between 1984 and 1989. The VRA increased the price of imported steel by an average of 9.5 percent over this period. As a result, consumers paid $868 million per year more for imported steel than they would have in the absence of the VRA. There was an additional consumption efficiency loss on imports that would have been purchased at the unprotected price—a loss that averaged $89 million per year. Domestic steel prices increased by about 2.3 percent as a result of the VRA, resulting in increased consumer costs of $1,046 million. Thus, the total consumer costs of the VRA amounted to an average of about $2 billion per year, according to our model.

The great bulk of the consumer costs of the steel VRA was composed of transfers to domestic and foreign producers. The net national costs of the VRA to the United States, which included producer efficiency losses of $27 million but excluded transfers to domestic producers of $1,046 million, averaged $984 million per year, less than half the consumer costs. If tariffs had been used to limit

Table 4.1

Estimated Cost of Protection in Steel, Annual Average for 1984–89
(in millions of dollars)

Cost Element	Amount
A Higher import costs (quota rents)	868
B Loss of consumption efficiency	89
C Higher price of domestic steel (transfer to producers)	1,046
W_C Consumer cost of VRA $(A + B + C)$	2,004
D Loss of production efficiency	27
W Net national welfare cost of VRA $(A + B + D)$	984
W′ Net national cost of tariff-equivalent protection $(B + D)$	116
L Gains in labor income	246
W* Adjusted net national cost of tariff-equivalent protection $(B + D - L)$	−130

Source: Authors' calculations, as explained in the appendix to this chapter.

Note: A negative net cost indicates a net benefit. Letters *A*, *B*, etc., refer to areas in Figure 4.1 in the appendix to this chapter.

imports, instead of the VRA, then the increase in the cost of imports of $868 million would have been captured by the U.S. government. In that case, the national welfare cost of tariff-equivalent protection would have averaged only $116 million per year—barely one-twentieth of the consumer cost. This includes only the losses of efficiency in consumption and production, which are an order of magnitude smaller than the transfers to foreign and domestic producers that resulted from the VRA.

The labor gains that resulted from the VRA reflect the additional wages earned by workers who would otherwise have been unemployed, compared with what they would have received in lower-paying jobs or if they had dropped out of the labor force altogether. We estimate that the VRA saved an average of about 7,500 jobs per year in the steel industry and about 13,700 jobs per year in related supplier industries during the period 1984–89. Retention of these positions resulted in direct wage gains of $129 million per year in the steel industry and $117 million per year in other related (indirect) manufacturing industries, for a total labor gain of $246 million.

When these labor gains are included, we see that a tariff equivalent to the VRA would have resulted in a net benefit to the domestic economy of $130 million per year between 1984 and 1989. This surprising result is explained by three factors. First, the efficiency losses associated with trade protection are relatively small. Second, these are more than offset by the wage losses that would have resulted in the absence of protection, because wages in the steel industry in particular, and the manufacturing sector in general, are much higher than in the rest of the United States economy, and because many of the unemployed steelworkers would have remained either temporarily or permanently unemployed. Third, most of the consumer costs of protection are transfers to foreign and domestic producers, which do not affect net national welfare if a tariff is used to capture the increased payments for imported steel.

This analysis shows that the great majority of the net national costs of the steel VRA consisted of benefits to foreign producers: that is, restricting imports allowed their price to rise, and those gains were reaped by foreign producers. A more cost-effective form of trade protection would have allowed the U.S. government to capture those benefits, so that a given level of trade restriction could have been implemented at a lower cost (or even a net gain) to the nation as a whole. Two such options are a global auction quota, in which the U.S. government sells the quota rights to foreign producers, and a tariff on imports. In either case, the U.S. government would collect revenues.

The Textile Industry: Estimating the Benefits of Induced Innovation

Since 1961, the United States has enacted a series of import-restrictive measures concerning the textile industry—which produces fabric for apparel and other uses—and for the apparel-making sectors that convert the fabric into finished garments. This section is concerned with the textile industry. Trade protection in textile and apparels includes both the Multi-Fiber Arrangement (MFA), which limits the growth in the volume of imports from most developing countries, and tariffs. The Uruguay Round GATT agreement calls for the MFA to be phased out over a ten-year period and for current tariffs to be reduced significantly.

While the textile industry has been called one of the most heavily protected U.S. industries, it has also experienced rapid and sustained productivity growth during the period of trade protection. We argue here that in the textile industry, past protection—in the form of both tariffs and quotas—was a significant contributing factor that made possible the industry's rapid productivity gains during the 1960s, 1970s, and 1980s. If this is the case, then protection would have two opposing price effects: induced innovation would reduce prices to consumers, while limited access to cheaper foreign goods would raise consumer prices.

These two separate—and contradictory—effects on technological innovation are both compatible with economic theory. On the one hand, by reducing competition, protection could reduce incentives to innovate. This is especially relevant where a domestic industry is oligopolistic or monopolistic, since in that case restrictions on foreign competition would lessen pressures to cut costs and improve quality. On the other hand, by shielding the domestic industry from severe price-based competition, protection could also provide the extra profit margin or liquidity necessary to finance investment in new machinery. This implies that there is an optimal amount of protection for each industry—one that will ensure that competition is adequate, but not excessive.

There have been three stages of technological change in the modern U.S. textile industry. The first started in the 1930s and accelerated in the 1960s. U.S.-based technologies were used to produce rapidly growing amounts of synthetic and blended-fiber textiles during this stage.[14] The second stage of modernization was dominated by European and Japanese innovations in textile machinery. This stage began in the mid-1960s and has continued to the present. Despite the fact that the U.S. textile machinery industry lost tremendous ground during this period, U.S. textile manufacturers nevertheless invested heavily in new machinery. The result is that "many industry experts still consider the U.S. textile industry the most productive and cost efficient in the world" (Toyne, Arpan, Barnett, Ricks, and Shimp 1984, p. 44).

The third stage of technological change is still in process. Starting approximately in the mid-1980s, this stage involves the entire textile-fiber-apparel-retail chain of production and distribution. Called "quick response," the system uses an electronic network that connects textile and apparel producers to retailers. Bob Frazier, a director at New York–based consulting firm Kurt Salmon Associates, says quick response was born when U.S. fabric and garment producers realized they could not best their foreign competitors strictly on price.[15] "By cutting production time and linking production more closely to sales patterns," one analyst writes, "U.S. firms gain an edge over importers because they can supply retailers with small, fast-moving inventories better tailored to the changing winds of fashion" (Jerome 1989, p. 171).

The evidence of a causal relationship between protection and technical change in the U.S. textile industry is mixed. On the one hand, some of the improvements in textile productivity appear to result from factors not related to trade or trade policy, such as the development of new machinery imported from abroad or tighter workplace health and safety regulations that spurred additional automation.[16] On the other hand, the stability and predictability in import growth imposed by the MFA also encouraged investment by the domestic industry. By allowing a steady, but controlled, growth in imports, the MFA struck a balance between providing a protected and thus profitable market and allowing enough import penetration to maintain competitive pressure.[17]

Protection can increase national welfare when it stimulates research and development and investment that might not otherwise occur. In order to estimate the magnitude of this effect, we modify William Cline's (1990) model of the costs and benefits of protection by allowing for the possibility that protection, by spurring productivity improvements and thus lowering costs, would shift the domestic supply curve down and to the right.[18] Our estimates suggest that downward shifts in the supply curve could push the protected domestic textile price below the unprotected 1986 price in as few as four years (see Table 4.2).

The cost-of-protection analysis in Table 4.2 uses the same basic framework applied in the steel case, which is explained in the appendix to this chapter. The consumer cost of protection is augmented in this case to include the consumer

Table 4.2

Cost of Protection in the Textile Industry with Induced Innovation Effects, 1993 (in millions of dollars)

		Induced Innovation Effect	
Cost Element		Low (0.81 Percent)	High (1.37 Percent)
A	Higher import costs (quota rents)	1,072	1,072
B	Loss of consumption efficiency	203	203
E	Benefits of induced price change	179	1,302
W_c	Consumer cost of protection $(A + B - E)$	1,096	−27
D	Loss of production efficiency	24	24
A_1	Tariff revenue gain	488	488
W	Net national welfare cost of protection $(A + B + D - A_1 - E)$	632	−491
W'	Net national cost of tariff-equivalent protection $(B + D - E)$	48	−1,075

Sources: Cline (1990, p. 191) and Scott (1990).

Note: A negative net cost indicates a net benefit. Letters A, B, etc., refer to areas in Figure 4.1 in the appendix to this chapter.

benefits of price reductions resulting from induced productivity growth. In order to estimate the effects of productivity growth, we begin by noting that, according to Cline's calculations, productivity growth in the textile sector exceeded the manufacturing average by 1.37 percentage points in the 1961–72 period and by 0.81 percentage points from 1973 to 1985. We then assume that the above-average part of the increase in productivity growth (relative to the manufacturing average) shifts the supply curve outward at the same rate. Using the assumptions of Cline's model, we find that the supply shifts would cause domestic prices to fall by 0.5 to 0.85 percent per year. The line in Table 4.2 for the "benefits of induced price change" is our estimate of net consumer benefits in 1993 (the seventh year of production, relative to the cost of protection in 1986), assuming that productivity growth continues at the rate shown at the top of each column and that the rate of price reduction discussed here is maintained.

Cline estimates that protection increased domestic textile prices by 3.1 percent, on average, in 1986. This price effect would be more than offset by the supply curve shifts assumed here, in a minimum of seven years. By the seventh year, falling prices would generate net benefits for consumers of domestic textiles, as shown in Table 4.2.

In the case of the highest productivity effect (1.37 percent per year, last column of Table 4.2), consumers experience a net benefit from protection (negative consumer costs) in 1993. Even using the lower estimate of 0.81

(assuming that productivity growth in textiles continues to exceed the manufac-turing average by this amount), Cline's estimated consumer cost of protection of $2.778 billion may be well over twice the actual cost.

The MFA system consists of both tariffs and quotas on textile products. Tariffs on imported textiles averaged 12 percent in 1986. Cline estimated that the tariff-equivalent protection of the MFA quotas equaled 16 percent in 1986, for a total level of tariff-equivalent protection of 28 percent (Cline 1990, p. 191). Elimination of the tariff would result in a loss of government tariff revenues, so the net national cost of protection is reduced by the amount of the tariff revenues. Thus, in the high-productivity effect case, the net benefits of protection are increased by this amount. Finally, the net benefits of productivity growth would exceed $1 billion in 1993 if a tariff had been used to protect the industry instead of the MFA quotas, rather than the huge net national costs estimated by Cline. This finding results from the dynamic gains associated with steady technical progress and is generally ignored in the standard analysis of the effects of protec-tion (Scott 1990, p. 544).

We have evaluated the evidence and arguments about the effects of protection on productivity in the textile industry. Protection of the domestic market has apparently improved the ability of domestic manufacturers to take advantage of scale economies and learning curves, driving down production costs and thus prices below levels that would have prevailed in an unprotected market. Consid-eration of these factors suggests that in the long run (after four to seven years) the benefits of protection in textiles (through increased productivity growth) may have exceeded the short-term costs to consumers of higher prices for imported textiles because of the trade restraints.

The Apparel Industry: The Consequences of Marketing Concentration

Estimates of the cost of protection also depend critically on assumptions about the nature of competition. Recent changes in information technologies, declining shipping costs, and changes in consumer incomes and tastes have caused sub-stantial changes in the structure of retail apparel markets. Price-cost margins have been increasing in some segments of the industry, resulting in very high profit levels in some firms. Apparel retailing has become an oligopsony, an industry in which a few firms have substantial market power in the purchase of apparel from suppliers in the apparel-producing sectors. The most important implication of oligopsony power for our purposes is that it allows apparel retail-ers to price-discriminate between imported and domestic suppliers, paying them different prices for comparable products. The apparel retailing industry also appears to have increased its oligopoly power over retail customers in the 1980s. This is reflected both in increasing margins (markups) in some segments of the industry and in rapidly growing market shares for the segments of the industry that have the highest markup rates of prices over costs.

The combination of oligopsony and oligopoly power can, in turn, have substantial effects on the costs of protection. As the MFA is phased out over the next ten years, under the terms of the Uruguay Round GATT agreement, the apparel distribution industry is likely to maintain current price levels. The oligopsony can be expected to capture a substantial share of the benefits that will result from lower (wholesale) import apparel prices. The elimination of the MFA would then result in a transfer of income from the government and from those foreign producers that are currently earning quota rents to domestic distributors (wholesale and retail). Elimination of protection would also have a smaller effect on consumer apparel prices than is predicted in models assuming perfect competition. Thus, the costs of protection depend critically on the structure of the apparel market. This section will summarize the arguments regarding the effects of concentration on apparel distribution and will then estimate the consequences of distribution channel concentration for cost-of-protection estimates.

Structural Change in the Retail Apparel Market

The development of the microcomputer and the rise of the information age have revolutionized the structure of the retail apparel industry and its relationships with suppliers. Widespread adoption of the electronic cash register, connected to centralized data processing networks, has resulted in an acceleration in the pace of the production process. This has also given a productivity edge to chain stores, which are best able to take advantage of these new technologies (Friedman 1988, p. 19).

At the same time, these computer technologies, combined with the development of international data communications networks and declining transportation costs, have allowed offshore producers to participate in this revolution in the production process. Relatively new firms such as Benetton, The Limited, and Liz Claiborne experienced very high rates of growth in sales, profits, and rates of return in the 1980s by building direct links between specialized retail apparel stores and low-wage offshore production facilities.[19]

During this same period, changing tastes and rising levels of consumer income have resulted in an increase in the diversity of the apparel industry and an increased reliance on niche-based—as opposed to mass-based—production strategies. The increasing importance of product diversification as a marketing strategy is reflected in the rising share of clothing sold through specialized family and women's clothing stores.

While some segments of the industry have been specializing in high-margin niches, the off-price distribution channel also grew rapidly in the 1980s. This evolution reflects the increasing disparity in income distribution that characterized U.S. income patterns in the 1980s. Sales in the off-price market increased at a rate of 20 percent per year in the early 1980s. Some analysts have suggested that the growth of off-price retailers reflects an increase in competition in the retail industry. However, off-price stores have sales volumes twice as high per square foot as conventional department and discount stores. Their average gross margin return on investment is 360 percent ($2.60 per dollar invested).[20]

The increasing diversification and specialization of retail distribution channels may also have contributed to the creation of market power at the retail level. This imbalance of power between the retail and wholesale stages makes it difficult for foreign apparel manufacturers that are not fully integrated into U.S. apparel distribution markets to receive full wholesale value for their products.

There are significant and growing barriers to entry into the retail business. Development of a distribution channel requires large amounts of managerial expertise and capital for retail and warehouse space, advertising, and market research. As shopping malls continue to replace central business districts, developers are increasingly looking to nationally known store names to attract customers. This places small and independent retailers at a disadvantage relative to large department stores and national retail chains. These barriers to entry are reflected in recent reports that small retailers in all fields have experienced an increased rate of bankruptcies in the last year. "Large retailers now use technology to tailor their merchandise to individual markets," a recent *Wall Street Journal* article reported, "thereby undercutting the small retailer" (Marsh 1991). As a result, department store chains have experienced a growth resurgence in the 1990s.

Concentration has been increasing in most segments of apparel distribution. As a result, retail prices have grown faster than wholesale prices since 1982. In addition, margins (markups) are increasing in the segments of the industry that have benefited from the technological revolution in apparel design and distribution. Furthermore, market shares for the segments of the industry that have the highest markup rates of prices over costs grew rapidly in the 1980s.

As a result of these changes, rates of return have been very high, especially in the women's apparel specialty store segments. Furthermore, while the cost of a selected group of apparel imports was found to be only 58 percent of the wholesale cost of domestically produced substitutes according to data cited in Scott and Lee (1991, pp. 15–16), the market prices of imported apparel were only about 12 percent lower than the corresponding domestically produced apparel, according to another survey (Cline 1979, pp. 3–24). All these data outline a pattern of structure and performance in apparel retailing that is indicative of the exercise of substantial degrees of monopsony power. This analysis suggests that distributors are capturing a large share of the profits (including quota rents) in apparel distribution. In the next section we investigate the ways in which prices and profits in this industry will change if protection is eliminated. Our analysis suggests that the profits of distributors will be increased, with few benefits, in the form of lower apparel prices, flowing to retail consumers despite reductions in the costs of imported apparel.

The Effects of Retail Concentration on
Apparel Production and Trade

This subsection will first present cost-of-protection estimates developed under
the assumption that firms have oligopsony power; then contrast these estimates
with results from a model that assumes a competitive market structure; and
finally discuss the implications for consumers, workers in the apparel industries,
and national welfare. Our approach explicitly considers the implications of concentration in apparel distribution in the United States. The standard trade model,
as applied to the apparel industry, implicitly assumes that wholesaling and retailing are costless activities and that any cost savings (such as lower import prices)
will be automatically passed on to consumers.

Cline (1990) assumes that both product and distribution markets are competi-
tively structured. We assume instead that a small number of apparel distribution
firms are the only buyers of imported clothing (oligopsonists), and that they also
possess market power over consumers. This structure allows distributors and
retailers to price-discriminate between imported and domestic suppliers of apparel (that is, they are able to pay different prices to foreign and domestic
suppliers of the same types of goods). Our model directly challenges Cline's
conclusion that the elimination of protection will lower the prices of imported
and domestic apparel by 19 to 35 percent. Our model predicts price effects of
only 3 to 10 percent.

Both models estimate the costs of protection in 1986, including both tariffs
and quotas. Tariffs on imported apparel averaged 22.5 percent in 1986. Cline
(1990, p. 191) estimated that the tariff-equivalent protection of the quotas
equaled 30.5 percent in that same year.[21] Thus, the total level of tariff-equivalent
protection for this industry was 53 percent. The quotas established under the
MFA will be phased out over a ten-year period if the Uruguay Round of GATT
is implemented, and the tariff will be reduced by about one-third. At the end of
the ten-year period the total level of tariff-equivalent protection will be approximately 15 percent, a reduction of over 70 percent from 1986 levels.

Our analysis shows that Cline overestimates the cost of protection in the
apparel industry for at least two reasons. First, if retailers have market power,
then elimination of the MFA will bring about smaller than expected increases in
imports because retailers will restrict purchases in order to keep prices at profit-
maximizing levels. As a result, the elimination of the MFA will have a smaller
than expected effect on retail prices. Second, if domestic retailers have oligopsony power, then these firms are capturing some of the quota rents that import
suppliers are assumed to earn. The elimination of the quotas will not result in a
transfer of rents from import suppliers to consumers, as assumed in the competitive model. The profits of importers (domestic retailers and distributors) will rise,
instead.

The costs of apparel tariffs and quotas under the MFA for the two studies we

Table 4.3

Cost of Protection in the Apparel Industry under Alternative Structural Assumptions, 1986 (in millions of dollars)

Cost Element		Competitive (Cline, 1990)	Oligopsony (This Study)
A	Higher import costs (tariff + quota rents)	6,421	2,332
B	Loss of consumption efficiency	3,130	97
C	Higher price of domestic apparel (transfer to producers)	8,005	1,221
W_c	Consumer cost of protection $(A + B + C)$	17,556	3,650
D	Loss of production efficiency	933	57
A_1	Tariff revenue gain	3,167	3,886
W	Net national cost of MFA $(A + B + D - A_1)$	7,317	−1,400
W'	Net national cost of tariff-equivalent protection $(B + D)$	4,063	154
L	Gains in labor income	4,203	1,912
W*	Adjusted net national cost of tariff-equivalent protection $(B + D - L)$	−140	−1,758

Sources: Cline (1990, p. 191) and authors' calculations.

Note: A negative cost indicates a net benefit. Letters *A*, *B*, etc., refer to areas in Figure 4.1 in the appendix to this chapter.

are comparing are given in Table 4.3.[22] Both studies begin with the assumption that protection increased the wholesale cost of imported apparel by 53 percent in 1986. Cline estimates that the elimination of these measures would reduce imported apparel prices by 34.6 percent. Our work suggests that the retail prices of imported apparel would decline by only 10.1 percent if distributors were able to fully exploit oligopsony and retail market power in this industry. Cline estimates that the decline in the prices of imported clothing would cause the prices of domestically produced apparel to decline by 18.9 percent. However, domestic apparel prices are projected to decline by only 2.6 percent in our oligopsony model.

The elimination of protection causes the volume of imports to increase by 56.7 percent in the Cline model, and by only 10.1 percent in our model. However, the small import volume effect in our model assumes that U.S.-made apparel is sufficiently different from imported products to withstand a 35 percent decline in the wholesale cost of imported goods. Import volume effects could be much larger under oligopsony, with few, if any effects on apparel prices. Increases in imports reduce domestic apparel production by 18.9 percent in the Cline study, but only by 8.6 percent in our model.

Apparel protection was found to add $6.4 billion to the cost of imported apparel in the Cline model, and $2.3 billion in this study. Estimates of the indirect costs of protection, in terms of increased prices for domestic apparel, are much further apart. Cline estimates that the cost of domestic apparel was increased by $8 billion, while our estimate of this cost is only $1.2 billion. Consumption efficiency losses are also much larger in the Cline model ($3.1 billion) than in the oligopsony model ($0.1 billion). These results highlight the importance of distributor behavior in determining the total consumer costs of protection. Cline estimates that the total consumer costs of protection will equal $17.6 billion, while our figure is $3.7 billion, as shown in Table 4.3.

As in the earlier cases, the great bulk of the consumer costs of protection represents transfers to domestic and foreign producers. Estimated net national costs are much smaller in both studies. However, the proportional differences between the two studies are even larger, in the range of 10:1. The difference reflects much smaller estimates of both the price and quantity effects in our model, and also the inclusion of labor income associated with protection, resulting in negative values for several measures of the net welfare cost of protection in some cases (that is, protection could provide net welfare benefits under some assumptions). The net national cost of the MFA, which includes producer efficiency losses in the United States, less tariff revenues received by the government (a benefit of protection), equals $7.3 billion in the Cline study, less than half the total consumer cost of protection. We found that the net national cost of protection was negative (that is, protection generated net benefits, from a national welfare perspective). This is because a large part of the tariff revenue ($1,533 million) and all the quota rents are captured by domestic apparel distributors when protection is eliminated.

If tariffs had been used to protect the domestic apparel producers, instead of the MFA, then all the higher cost of imports would represent transfers to producers or tariff revenue. In this case, Cline estimated the net national cost of tariff-equivalent protection to be $4.1 billion, while we found it to be $154 million (using the oligopsony model).

The labor gains that resulted from the MFA reflect the additional wages earned by apparel workers who would have to endure unemployment and then accept lower-paying jobs in other industries, or drop out of the labor force altogether. Cline's estimates for domestic production imply that the MFA saved an average of about 214,000 jobs per year in apparel production and about 167,000 jobs in related supplier industries. According to our calculations, retention of these positions resulted in direct wage gains of $1.7 billion per year in the apparel industry and $2.5 billion per year in other related manufacturing industries, for a total labor gain of $4.2 billion.[23] Our model predicts that elimination of protection has a smaller effect on domestic output than Cline's (−8.6 versus −18.9 percent), as noted above. Therefore, our estimate of the labor gains from protection is only $1.9 billion.

Adjustment costs associated with unemployment constitute 76 percent of the total labor gains from protection in both cases. Therefore, the gains from labor income should be interpreted as the labor benefit due to protection in the first year. Thereafter, the labor benefits would equal 24 percent of the total listed under L, in each case. On the other hand, much larger levels of labor displacement are possible in the United States as the MFA is phased out. One recent study has suggested that direct and indirect job loss in apparel and textiles could be as high as 1.4 million by the year 2002 if the MFA were eliminated. Complete elimination of the 1.1 million jobs in U.S. apparel production, and the associated indirect employment, would result in unemployment losses of at least $16.9 billion and permanent income losses of $5.3 billion per year for the displaced workers.[24] When labor gains are included in the welfare cost estimates, we see that a tariff equivalent to the MFA would have resulted in a net benefit to the domestic economy of $140 million per year using Cline's assumptions, and $1.8 billion using our oligopsony model.

The MFA system was designed to limit the growth in U.S. apparel imports to 6 percent per year, a goal that was achieved in the 1960s and 1970s. However, imports were allowed to grow at a much more rapid rate in the 1980s. The MFA system provided a mechanism that allowed employment in this industry to decline with natural attrition, thus limiting labor adjustment costs. The decision to phase out the MFA under the 1993 GATT agreement will result in increased labor displacement, with its associated costs.

Conclusions: Consequences for Trade Policy

Trade protection, as practiced in the United States in the three cases reviewed here, has clearly raised some prices for consumers of imported goods. However, it has also generated substantial benefits for workers (in the steel and apparel cases) and sometimes for consumers as well (in the textile case). Furthermore, protection has been unnecessarily costly for the nation as a whole because of the United States' tendency to rely on quotas to limit imports. Exclusive use of revenue-generating restraints, such as tariffs or auction quotas, would significantly improve the net national welfare effects in all three cases. Such policies could generate positive net national welfare benefits, when labor gains are included in the analysis.

An important issue for future research is the relationship between trade and industrial policies. Policies that link trade protection to limits in price increases, productivity-enhancing investments, or other performance standards could result in higher levels of domestic production and employment, with attendant gains for labor.

Finally, it is important to stress the labor market implications of these case studies. These have been virtually ignored in most other studies of the costs of protection, which tend to focus on estimates of the consumer or net national cost per job saved. Elimination of jobs through trade has permanent income as well as employment consequences that should be taken into account in designing trade and industrial policies. At a minimum, efforts should be made to ensure that trade displacement, if necessary, takes place when the economy is at the highest levels of macroeconomic output, to ease the burdens of adjustment for displaced workers. These results also suggest that trade and industrial policies can play an important role in maintaining a strong and healthy manufacturing sector, and that doing so may well be in the national interest.

Appendix: Measuring the Welfare Costs of Protection

The method used to estimate the costs of protection and the distinctions between the various measures of those costs are explained in this appendix, with the aid of Figure 4.1. This analytical framework is used in all the costs-of-protection studies in this chapter. Case-specific modifications, where necessary, are also explained here.

We assume that domestic and imported products are imperfect substitutes, which means that consumers distinguish between them, and they sell at different prices. In general, the differences that make products imperfect substitutes are mainly matters of product mix, technical quality, reliability of supplies, and delivery lead times, which may vary according to the national origins of the products. Such factors are significant in all the industries studied in this chapter. Imported products can be substituted for the domestic product, at some cost in terms of delivery time, product quality, or other relevant characteristics. This assumption of imperfect substitutability allows us to analyze the markets for these products separately. The top panel in Figure 4.1 represents the market for domestic products, while the bottom panel represents the market for imports.

Both diagrams in Figure 4.1 have prices (P_d for domestic, P_m for imports) on the vertical axis and quantities (M for imports, Q for domestic) on the horizontal axis. For all the variables in these diagrams, subscript 0 refers to a counterfactual scenario that assumes free trade, while subscript 1 refers to the actual situation with a quota in place. In the import diagram, P_{m1} and P_{m0} represent the prices of imports with and without the quota, respectively, while curve D_m represents the demand. In the domestic part of the diagram, curves D_1 and D_0 represent the demand for the domestic product with and without the quota in effect, respectively. S is the domestic supply curve.

Note that any area on these diagrams corresponds to the price times the quantity, which equals an amount of revenue in dollars. Thus, we can measure the gains and losses to producers and consumers and other interested parties (e.g., foreign suppliers or the U.S. government) by making appropriate calculations of the relevant areas on the diagram.

Conceptually, we define the *consumer surplus* as the difference between what consumers are willing to pay for a good (represented by the height of the demand curve) and the price they actually pay. Geometrically, this corresponds to the area of the three-sided figure bounded by the demand curve, the price line, and

Figure 4.1. **Components of the Cost of Protection**

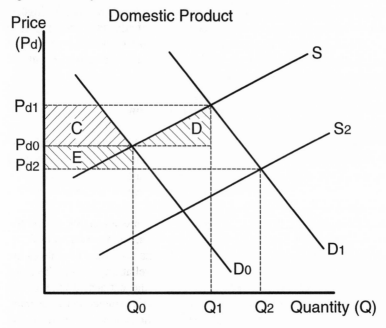

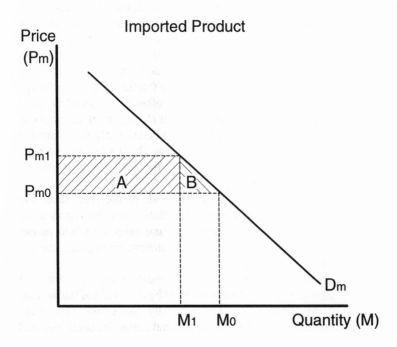

the vertical axis. The costs of protection to consumers are then measured by the reduction in this "surplus" when consumers have to pay a higher price.

In parallel fashion, the *producer surplus* is defined as the difference between the price at which firms sell the goods and their costs of production (represented by the height of the supply curve). Geometrically, this corresponds to the area of the three-sided figure bounded by the supply curve, the price line, and the vertical axis. The gains to producers from protection are measured by the increase in this "surplus" when producers get a higher price for their product. Note, however, that this definition of producers' surplus does *not* include the benefits received by workers who keep their jobs as a result of the protection (assuming that they could not get other jobs paying equal wages immediately after losing their jobs if the industry were not protected). Since wages are included in costs, they are under the supply curve and do not form part of the "surplus." Hence, any such wage gains from protection have to be calculated separately. In making all these calculations, we take the situation without the quota as the benchmark, and then compare the effects of moving toward the situation with the quota in effect.

Using this method, then, we can see how to measure the consumer costs of protection. In the import market, the quota directly limits the quantities that foreign exporters can sell from, say, M_0 to M_1. This causes the equilibrium price of imports to rise from P_{m0} to P_{m1}. A VRA would have the same effect. An equivalent tariff would also have a similar effect, but it would operate in the reverse fashion (raising the price of the imports from P_{m0} to P_{m1}, which would in turn cause the quantity demanded to shrink from M_0 to M_1). Any one of these forms of protection reduces the consumer surplus in the import market in two ways. First, since consumers must pay a higher unit price on the quantity of imports actually purchased with the protection in effect (M_1), the consumers lose the area of the rectangle labeled A in the bottom panel of Figure 4.1. Second, since the higher price induces consumers to reduce their consumption of imports from M_0 to M_1, there is an additional loss of consumer surplus on the foregone imports (quantity $M_0 - M_1$). Thus, area B in Figure 4.1, which is the near-triangle above the old import price and below the import demand curve, represents an additional loss of consumer surplus.

The textile and apparel industries are protected by a combination of tariffs and quotas. In this case, area A is divided horizontally into two components (not shown): A_1 is the tariff revenue collected by the domestic government; A_2 is the remaining tariff-equivalent effect of the quota. A is the combined effect of all trade restraints on imports.

The imposition of protection also has repercussions for consumers of domestic products. As imports become more expensive, consumers are induced to switch to domestic goods, and the domestic demand curve therefore rises from D_0 to D_1. This in turn raises the equilibrium price of domestic products from P_{d0} to P_{d1}, while the quantity of domestic goods purchased rises from Q_0 to Q_1.

Although the consumers do get more domestic products, they must pay a higher price for them, which results in an additional loss of consumer surplus. Using no-protection domestic demand curve D_0 as a benchmark,[25] the consumer surplus is reduced by area C (the four-sided figure between the two price lines P_{d0} and P_{d1}, and between the vertical axis and the demand curve D_0). Thus, the total consumer cost of protection (loss of consumer welfare) is the sum of three parts, which we call $W_C = A + B + C$.

There is an important distinction between the three parts of the loss of consumer surplus in the import market. Area B is called a "deadweight" loss because it results from the fact that consumers' purchases of cheaper imports are reduced by the trade restriction. This is a pure loss of efficiency in consumption, as consumers are forced to turn to more expensive domestic products. The other two parts of the consumers' losses—by far the largest parts in practice—are not efficiency losses per se, but rather represent transfers to other economic agents.

Area C is entirely accounted for by a gain in producer surplus[26] and thus represents a transfer from domestic consumers to domestic producers. Since it is a transfer within the country, it is not included in the net national cost of protection, as noted above. Area A is what economists call the "quota rent": the excess revenue that accrues from the fact that protection (of any kind) raises the price of the imported goods inside the home country. *Who gets area A (the quota rent) depends entirely on the type of protection adopted.* For example, when the United States protected its steel industry with the VRA in the 1980s, area A was captured by foreign exporters of steel (by charging higher prices for their product in the U.S. market), and thus it represented a net loss to the country. Had the government chosen to use a tariff instead (or to impose a quota with the quota licenses auctioned to importers), quota rent A could have been captured as revenue by the U.S. government. In that case, area A would not have been part of the net national loss. In the case of a combination of tariffs and quotas, the tariff revenue goes to the domestic government. The distribution of quota rents depends on the structure of the market.

The net national cost of protection also includes another element that is not part of the consumers' losses in this model. Since production of domestic goods is more costly than foreign production, at the margin, the higher cost of the additional domestic output (difference $Q_1 - Q_0$) represents a loss of efficiency in production. In Figure 4.1, this deadweight loss due to increased domestic production costs is area D, which is the triangle under the domestic supply curve and above the no-protection price line (P_0).

It is important to recognize that the static loss of efficiency in production (area D) may be offset over time if the domestic industry improves its productivity during the period when trade is restricted. If an industry uses the protection to invest in an increased and improved capital stock, it can cause the domestic supply curve to shift downward. Such a shift is illustrated by supply curve S_2 in Figure 4.1. In this case, domestic prices fall from P_{d1} to P_{d2}, below

P_{d0}, and domestic output rises to Q_2. These changes have two effects on consumer and national welfare. First, producer gains from protection (area C) are eliminated by the fall in domestic prices. Second, consumers enjoy a positive benefit, to the extent that domestic prices fall below the unprotected price, P_{d0}.

Using no-protection domestic demand curve D_0 as a benchmark, consumer surplus is increased by area E (the rectangle between price lines P_{d0} and P_{d2}, the vertical axis, and initial level of consumption Q_0). This gain must be subtracted from the formulas for consumer and national costs of protection. Note that area C is also eliminated from consumer costs in this case. Area E can be estimated only if information is available that links productivity growth and domestic supply behavior to protection. Estimates of these gains are developed in the textile case in this chapter.

As noted above, a large part of the consumer cost of protection (area C) is a transfer to domestic producers and thus has no effect on national welfare. In addition, the portion of area A that represents quota rents could be captured by the government if it used tariffs or other price-based forms of protection instead. Therefore, a more appropriate measure of the true economic cost to the country of protecting the industry (if we leave aside labor gains for the moment) is just the sum of the two deadweight or efficiency losses, $B + D$. This is what we call the net national welfare cost of tariff-equivalent protection ($W' = B + D$). Of course, the net national welfare cost of the VRA or the MFA ($W = A + B + D$) is much larger because it also includes the quota rents captured by foreign exporters. The greater costs of using such a quota result from the choice of the quota as the instrument of protection, rather than from the decision to protect the industry per se. Both of these measures of the net national cost of protection must also be adjusted for the gains in labor income resulting from the jobs saved, which are not reflected in the diagrams in Figure 4.1. The calculation of labor gains from protection is explained in the steel case.

Notes

1. Data on merchandise trade associated with U.S. MNCs are from Mataloni (1990, p. 42). Data on merchandise trade associated with foreign MNCs are from Howenstein (1990, p. 128). Balance-of-payments data on total merchandise imports and exports for the same years are from Compustat. The limitations of the MNC data series are discussed by Hipple (1990).

2. See Scott (1993) for a discussion of the wage effects of job destruction in the manufacturing sector.

3. Katz and Summers point out that "wages in export-intensive [manufacturing] industries are 11 percent above average, whereas wages in import-intensive industries are 15 percent below average" (1989, p. 264), and that eliminating the U.S. trade deficit by raising exports rather than reducing imports would increase labor rents substantially. Our analysis addresses a different issue, the potential losses in labor rents associated with trade displacement in individual industries.

4. For example, Takacs and Winters (1991) develop a cost-of-protection analysis that

incorporates labor adjustment costs. They use an estimate of "the wage earned by labor in its next-best alternative" to estimate the value of lost output as a result of trade-related unemployment. This measure underestimates the labor losses associated with trade liberalization because it ignores the labor rents that would have been lost if imports had captured a larger share of the domestic market. See Scott and Blecker (1993) for a detailed analysis of Takacs and Winters (1991).

5. There are several other important omissions from most studies of the costs and benefits of trade liberalization, which are not considered here. The most important among these are nonmarket costs, such as the environmental impacts of trade expansion and the effects of trade on labor standards (including labor laws and workplace safety regulations). Increases in trade between countries with different levels of labor and environmental regulation can force standards down to the lowest common denominator. While it is difficult to estimate the economic losses associated with such changes, the potential for such losses is clearly important. Leamer (1993) has estimated the potential effects of international competition on the wages of unskilled workers.

6. De Melo and Tarr (1990); Hufbauer, Berliner, and Elliott (1986); Hufbauer and Elliott (1994); Blecker, Lee, and Scott (1993). See Blecker, Lee, and Scott (1993, pp. 43–50) for a comparison of the net welfare costs of tariff-equivalent protection.

7. See tables 9 and 10, Scott and Lee (1991, p. 41). Compare earnings losses and labor force status (unemployment share) of displaced workers in 1981–85 displaced-worker surveys with those for 1983–87. These data demonstrate a consistent pattern of improvement in the 1983–87 period, when the U.S. economy was in recovery.

8. Figures are as of November 1990 (Marcus and Kirsis 1991, p. 55).

9. It should be noted that, if the dollar had not been overvalued, there would have been little political pressure to implement the VRAs.

10. The assumption of imperfect substitutes implies that the domestic and imported goods can have different prices, which is likely to occur either when the products are differentiated or when they are aggregates with different mixes of individual products. Our implementation of this model follows Cline's (1990) study of textiles and apparel. For an application of essentially the same type of model to the steel industry, see U.S. International Trade Commission (1989). Hufbauer et al. (1986) and Hufbauer and Elliott (1994) use a similar model.

11. See Blecker, Lee, and Scott (1993) for an exposition of the model used in this study, which combines reduced form with structural modeling of the domestic price equation. See Scott and Blecker (1993) for a more complete reduced-form treatment, which yields similar results on the costs of protection in this industry.

12. An auction quota is a quantitative limit on imports, in which the home government auctions the right to sell in the domestic market to the highest bidder. The effects are similar to a tariff, but the auction quota provides greater control over the volume of imports.

13. Henceforth, the phrase "tariff-equivalent protection" is meant to include an equivalent auction quota, unless otherwise indicated.

14. This section is based on the lengthy description found in Toyne, Arpan, Barnett, Ricks, and Shimp (1984, pp. 43–46).

15. As quoted in *Scientific American* (April 1990, p. 74).

16. The literature on this point is summarized by Scott and Lee (1991, pp. 49–56).

17. See also chapter 1 in this volume, by Robert Kuttner.

18. See Scott (1990) for an earlier version of this model.

19. Information in this paragraph is from interviews with Dr. Herman Starobin, director of research, International Ladies Garment Workers Union, and Art Gundershein, assistant to the president and director of international affairs, Amalgamated Clothing and

THE COSTS OF TRADE PROTECTION   133

Textile Workers Union. See also Braithwaite (1990) and Lardner (1988a, 1988b).

20. Data on off-price stores in this section are from Kirby (1985, pp. 17–18).

21. The tariff equivalent is the level of additional tariff required to achieve the same level of protection as the nontariff barrier (in this case, the MFA quotas).

22. Following Cline (1990), we assume that imported and domestic products are imperfect substitutes. In addition, retailers are assumed to possess monopsony in the retailing of imported goods but not domestically produced substitutes. This assumption allows retailers to pay import suppliers prices lower than those received by domestic manufacturers. See Scott and Lee (1991) for a complete description of the monopsony model and the data and techniques used to develop the estimates shown in Table 4.3. The components of the costs and benefits of protection are described in the appendix to this chapter.

23. Estimated labor gains include the avoidance of income losses from unemployment, from reduced wage levels after displacement from the apparel industry, and from lost wages of workers who would drop out of the labor force. Each of these factors is estimated using data from the U.S. Department of Labor's displaced-workers tapes. This estimate of L is calculated using the method described in Scott and Lee (1991, pp. 39–46) and is somewhat larger than Cline's estimate of adjustment costs, which ignores permanent income losses that would result from changing jobs and labor force dropouts.

24. These estimates are based on the adjustment cost data in Scott and Lee (1991, p. 44) and Podgursky (1991). They probably underestimate income losses for the industry as a whole, as they reflect displacement experience associated with small amounts of sector-specific job loss. Displacement of a large proportion of the workforce in this sector would probably result in more prolonged levels of unemployment; greater postdisplacement wage reductions for those reemployed; and higher rates of dropouts, because reemployment in the industry (through normal labor turnover) would be less likely.

25. We do not count the area between the two domestic demand curves as an increase in consumers' surplus, since consumers would not have been willing to buy the larger quantities of the domestic goods indicated by the curve D_1 in the absence of the import restraints.

26. In fact, the gain in producer surplus is *larger* than area C, since it also includes the near-triangle *between* C and D in Figure 4.1 (bounded by demand curve D_0); supply curve S; and the higher price, P_{d1}. In our measurement of the costs and benefits of protection, we measure the gain in producer surplus conservatively by area A only (following the procedure of Cline 1990).

Bibliography

Blecker, Robert A. 1989. "Markup Pricing, Import Competition, and the Decline of the American Steel Industry." *Journal of Post Keynesian Economics,* Vol. 12, No. 1 (Fall), pp. 70–87.

Blecker, Robert A., Thea M. Lee, and Robert E. Scott. 1993. "Trade Protection and Industrial Revitalization: American Steel in the 1980s." Working Paper No. 104. Washington, DC: Economic Policy Institute (February).

Braithwaite, Alan J. 1990. "Far East Dragons Changing Their Spots." *Bobbin* (November).

Cline, William R. 1979. "Imports and Consumer Prices: A Survey Analysis." *Journal of Retailing,* Vol. 55 (Spring), pp. 3–24.

———. 1990. *The Future of World Trade in Textiles and Apparel,* rev. ed. Washington, DC: Institute for International Economics.

De Melo, Jaime, and David Tarr. 1990. "Welfare Costs of U.S. Quotas in Textiles, Steel and Autos." *Review of Economics and Statistics,* Vol. 72 (August), pp. 489–97.

Feenstra, Robert C. 1993. "How Costly Is Protectionism?" *Journal of Economic Perspectives,* Vol. 6, No. 3, pp. 159–78.

Friedman, Brian L. 1988. "Productivity Trends in Department Stores, 1967–86." *Monthly Labor Review,* Vol. 111 (March), pp. 17–21.

Hicks, Jonathan P. 1992. "An Industrial Comeback Story: U.S. Is Competing Again in Steel." *New York Times* (March 31), pp. A1, A19.

Hipple, F. Steb. 1990. "Multinational Companies and International Trade: The Impact of Intrafirm Shipments on U.S. Foreign Trade 1977–1982." *Journal of International Business Studies* (3d quarter), pp. 495–504.

Howenstein, Ned G. 1990. "U.S. Affiliates of Foreign Companies: Operations in 1988." *Survey of Current Business,* Vol. 70, No. 7, pp. 127–44.

Hufbauer, Gary Clyde, Diane T. Berliner, and Kimberly Ann Elliott. 1986. *Trade Protection in the United States: 31 Case Studies.* Washington, DC: Institute for International Economics.

Hufbauer, Gary Clyde, and Kimberly Ann Elliott. 1994. *Measuring the Costs of Protection in the United States.* Washington, DC: Institute for International Economics.

Jerome, Marty. 1989. "Clothing Wars." *PC/Computing* (July), p. 171.

Katz, Lawrence F., and Lawrence H. Summers. 1989. "Industry Rents: Evidence and Implications." *Brookings Papers on Economic Activity: Microeconomics,* pp. 209–90.

Kirby, Gail H. 1985. "A Pricing Study of Women's Apparel in Off-Price and Department Stores." Master's thesis. College Park, MD: University of Maryland.

Lardner, James. 1988a. "Annals of Business: The Sweater Trade—1." *New Yorker* (January 11), pp. 39–40.

———. 1988b. "Annals of Business: The Sweater Trade—2." *New Yorker* (January 18), pp. 57–73.

Leamer, Edward E. 1993. "Wage Effects of a U.S.-Mexican Free Trade Agreement." In Peter M. Garber, ed., *The U.S.-Mexico Free Trade Agreement.* Cambridge, MA: MIT Press.

Lincoln, Edward J. 1990. *Japan's Unequal Trade.* Washington, DC: Brookings Institution.

Marcus, Peter F., and Karlis Kirsis. 1991. *World Steel Dynamics: Accelerating Change Threatens Traditional Producers.* New York: Paine Webber (June 18).

Marsh, Barbara. 1991. "Small Companies Lose Big in Retailing War of Attrition." *Wall Street Journal* (March 20), section B, p. 2.

Mataloni, Raymond J., Jr. 1990. "U.S. Multinational Companies: Operations in 1988." *Survey of Current Business,* Vol. 70, No. 6, pp. 31–44.

Podgursky, Michael. 1991. "Estimated Economic Losses Due to Job Displacement: Evidence from the Displaced Worker Surveys." Unpublished calculations. Washington, DC: Economic Policy Institute (April 14).

Preston, Lee E., and Duane Windsor. 1992. *The Rules of the Game in the Global Economy: Policy Regimes for International Business.* Boston: Kluwer Academic Publishers.

Scott, Robert E. 1990. "Trade Policy, Employment and the Costs and Benefits of Protection." *Industrial Relations Research Association, Proceedings of the Forty-Second Annual Meeting,* Vol. 32, pp. 536–46.

———. 1993. "Flat Earth Economics: Is There a New International Paradigm?" *Challenge* (September–October), pp. 32–39.

———. 1994. "The Effects of Protection on a Domestic Oligopoly: The Case of the U.S. Auto Market." *Journal of Policy Modeling,* Vol. 16, pp. 299–325.

Scott, Robert E., and Robert A. Blecker. 1993. "The Costs and Benefits of Trade Protection in the U.S. Steel Industry." Mimeo. College Park: University of Maryland, and Washington, DC: American University (October).

Scott, Robert E., and Thea M. Lee. 1991. "Reconsidering the Benefits and Costs of Trade Protection: The Case of Textiles and Apparel." Working Paper No. 105. Washington, DC: Economic Policy Institute (April).

Takacs, Wendy E., and L. Alan Winters. 1991. "Labour Adjustment Costs and British Footwear Protection." *Oxford Economic Papers,* Vol. 43 (July), pp. 479–501.

Toyne, Brian, Jeffrey S. Arpan, Andy H. Barnett, David A. Ricks, and Terence A. Shimp. 1984. *The Global Textile Industry.* London: George Allen & Unwin.

U.S. International Trade Commission. 1989. *The Economic Effects of Significant U.S. Import Restraints, Phase I: Manufacturing.* USITC Publication No. 2222. Washington, DC: USITC, October.

――――. 1991. *Quarterly Report on the Status of the Steel Industry.* USITC Publication No. 2465. Washington, DC: USITC, December.

CHAPTER FIVE

The Political Economy of the North American Free Trade Agreement

ROBERT A. BLECKER

Introduction

The North American Free Trade Agreement (NAFTA) between the United States, Mexico, and Canada, which went into effect on January 1, 1994, was one of the most controversial trade agreements in American history. What made NAFTA so contentious was, above all, the unprecedented effort to eliminate trade barriers between the United States and a much less developed country. Of the three NAFTA members, the United States and Canada are both rich, industrialized, high-wage nations already linked through the U.S.-Canadian Free Trade Agreement (FTA) of 1989. In contrast, Mexico is a less developed, low-wage nation, relatively poor in terms of national income but rich in human and natural resources. By opening up the three countries' markets to unfettered movements of goods, services, and capital (but not labor) by the early twenty-first century, NAFTA creates a new trading bloc that will have significant effects on the location of industries and the flow of commerce both within North America and between this continent and other regions of the world. The questions of who will benefit and who will lose as a result of this international restructuring were at the heart of the controversy over the NAFTA agreement.

Although NAFTA will greatly accelerate the process of U.S.-Mexican economic integration, the *direction* of the changes that NAFTA will induce (at least in the first several years) is already foreshadowed by recent events. The enactment of this trade agreement culminated a process of economic opening in Mexico and increased U.S. involvement in Mexico that was already under way when the agreement was first proposed in 1990. In the aftermath of the debt crisis of the early 1980s, the government of Mexico abandoned its traditional,

The author would like to thank Thea M. Lee, Robert E. Scott, and the staff of the U.S. Department of Labor, Bureau of International Labor Affairs, for helpful comments on earlier drafts. The author alone is responsible for the views expressed here and for any remaining errors.

nationalistic economic policies and welcomed foreign investment and trade. The announcement of the NAFTA proposal itself, and the subsequent expectation of its passage, greatly increased the interest of U.S. and other foreign investors in Mexico in the early 1990s. The result of these policy shifts was a boom in Mexican foreign trade *and* investment, especially with the United States.

Indeed, in spite of its billing as a "free trade agreement," NAFTA is in fact much more than a mere agreement to lower trade barriers. The central motivation of the Mexican government in proposing NAFTA was not to lower U.S. trade barriers but rather to attract more foreign investment—especially direct foreign investment in productive enterprises. Mexico had already substantially opened up its own market via the unilateral removal of trade barriers in the late 1980s, while most Mexican products already enjoyed relatively unrestricted access to the U.S. market. Indeed, by 1989 over half of U.S. imports from Mexico already received a partial or complete tariff exemption. [1]

What Mexico hoped to achieve through creating NAFTA was to stimulate the renewal of growth that all of Mexico's stabilization policies, structural adjustments, and domestic reforms (including trade liberalization) in the 1980s failed to achieve. According to the most authoritative study of Mexico's recent economic reforms,

> When foreign investment did not respond with the expected vigor to the Brady-type debt agreement and the far-reaching economic reforms, the [Mexican] government had to find new ways *to entice the capital inflows required for economic recovery and sustained growth*. Policies able to increase the expected rate of return on investment and boost private sector confidence were essential. A free trade agreement with the United States belonged to this category for two reasons in particular. An FTA would ensure future access to the U.S. market, and ensure the durability of Mexico's open economy strategy. (Lustig 1992, p. 134, italics added)

A report by the U.S. Congressional Budget Office (CBO) makes the same point:

> The key to this [development] strategy is for Mexico *to attract and productively absorb foreign capital*. In addition to making Mexico more attractive for U.S. investors (because of the investment provisions of the agreement), NAFTA reduces doubts that other foreign investors may have about the permanency of Mexico's economic reforms—that is, it helps to lock in those reforms and so reduces the risk involved in investment. (U.S. Congress, Congressional Budget Office 1993b, p. xiii, italics added)

In this light, the guarantee of permanent preferential access for Mexican exports to the United States is significant not so much for opening up the U.S. market to the products of Mexican firms, but more importantly for signaling American and other foreign firms (European, Japanese, and other Asian) that they can locate production in Mexico and still produce with virtually no restrictions for the U.S. market. Moreover, NAFTA contains numerous specific provisions designed to protect foreign investors' rights in the three signatory countries.[2] These provisions include national treatment of foreign producers, abolition of performance requirements, restrictions against expropriation, guaranteed freedom of foreign investors to move funds across borders in convertible currencies, strong protection for "intellectual property rights," and the liberalization of trade in financial and other services.[3] For these reasons, it is best to think of NAFTA as a trade *and investment* liberalization agreement.

What NAFTA does, then, is to greatly deepen and extend a process of U.S.-Mexican economic integration that is already occurring and to impose specific rules and regulations on the parties to the agreement.[4] Especially, NAFTA goes to great lengths to make sure that the rights of foreign investors in Mexico will be respected and that the continent will be even more open to flows of capital and services as well as commodities in the future. These trade and investment liberalization provisions are backed up by strong enforcement mechanisms, including specified penalties for violations. NAFTA is much more limited and circumscribed in other areas. The agreement does not, for example, open up the United States to more immigration of Mexican workers, or give any additional protection to Mexicans who have migrated to the United States (legally or illegally). The NAFTA side agreements contain vague commitments of each nation to enforce its own labor and environmental standards, but these provisions do not require any upgrading or harmonization of standards already in effect and have no effective enforcement mechanisms.[5] There are also no commitments by the NAFTA signatories to maintain democratic political systems or to respect human rights and political freedoms.

The fact that NAFTA accelerates the process of economic integration, without simultaneously seeking to promote the harmonization of social and political standards, lies at the heart of the controversy over this agreement. Although NAFTA begins a new chapter in North American integration, it is by no means the end of the story. Paradoxically, in spite of the absence of explicit or enforceable provisions on the "social dimension" of economic integration, the very enactment of NAFTA opens up the member states to increased international scrutiny of their social standards and political practices (see Pastor 1993). This irony was immediately apparent in the first month after the agreement went into effect (January 1994), when unfavorable foreign media coverage of the Mexican government's attempts to suppress a peasant uprising in Chiapas forced the government to abandon its military campaign and instead to negotiate with the rebels. Thus, in spite of the best efforts of U.S., Mexican, and Canadian negotiators to restrict the NAFTA agreement to economic relations, it is clear that the social and political issues raised in the NAFTA debate will only become more prominent now that the agreement is in effect.

This chapter focuses mainly on the likely economic effects of NAFTA, but it also seeks to place the discussion of these effects in a larger historical and social context. The chapter begins by summarizing the different positions taken in the debate over the passage of the NAFTA agreement in the United States in 1991–93. This is followed by a brief critical survey of some of the most prominent studies that tried to forecast the "likely effects" of NAFTA. This survey will try to explain how different NAFTA studies reached such opposite conclusions and will attempt to assess which studies are most credible. The chapter then discusses recent trends in U.S.-Mexican trade and investment flows, and analyzes how Mexico's conservative macroeconomic and financial policies have depressed the country's growth. The next section considers how NAFTA fits into U.S. corporations' efforts to restructure in order to meet global competition, with special emphasis on the issue of low-wage competition. The chapter concludes with a discussion of policies for rectifying the dislocations and inequities likely to be fostered by NAFTA.

The NAFTA Debate

While there were many shades of opinion on NAFTA, and numerous strange bedfellows on each side of the debate,[6] two basic positions on the economic consequences of the agreement emerged. The pro-NAFTA side generally claimed that the agreement would bring modest but positive gains to the United States in the form of jobs, exports, and investment opportunities, with minimal domestic adjustment costs. Although these gains were sometimes exaggerated, especially by the Clinton administration in its last-minute sales effort, serious NAFTA proponents always recognized that the gains to the United States would be relatively small (see, e.g., Hufbauer and Schott 1992, 1993; Lustig, Bosworth, and Lawrence 1992). In fact, the proponents frequently argued that Mexico was so economically small relative to the United States that it could not possibly have a large impact on U.S. employment or living standards one way or the other. Moreover, NAFTA advocates contended that the agreement was essential for Mexico's future growth and stability, and that the United States had a vital security interest as well as an economic interest in a prosperous and stable neighbor. While most supporters acknowledged Mexico's relatively lower wages, weaker protection of the environment, and lack of full political democracy, they argued that only the growth and prosperity that a NAFTA would bring would eventually allow Mexico to solve these problems (see, e.g., Grossman and Krueger 1993).

Anti-NAFTA arguments were focused on the closely related issues of deindustrialization, job losses, and wage reductions (see, e.g., Koechlin and Larudee 1992a; Faux and Lee 1992). NAFTA critics feared that multinational corporations would move large numbers of manufacturing operations and associated jobs from the United States or Canada to Mexico, where the wages were lower, the labor rights weaker, and the environmental and safety regulations less stringently enforced. In some circles, estimates of "jobs at risk" ran into the millions (e.g., Choate 1993), but more credible estimates of potential job losses were on the order of about half a million (e.g., Faux and Spriggs 1991; Koechlin and Larudee 1992a). Even if the actual number of jobs lost was only in the hundreds of thousands, however, opponents argued that the mere threat of job loss could weaken the bargaining position of industrial workers in the United States and Canada and thus induce them to accept lower wages and worse working conditions. Moreover, threats by businesses to move jobs to Mexico would lead to the weakening of political support for strong social regulations to protect workers, consumers, and the environment in the United States and Canada. Opponents also feared that NAFTA provisions could be used to overturn domestic health, safety, and environmental regulations as NAFTA-illegal barriers to trade.

While the public debate deteriorated into the sorry spectacle of the vice president of the United States, Al Gore, trading barbs with billionaire "populist" H. Ross Perot in a televised debate, in other quarters some progress was made in clarifying the real issues at stake. On the one side, some NAFTA supporters took seriously the arguments that the agreement could have adverse effects on jobs, wages, and income distribution in the United States (see, e.g., Leamer 1993; Chimerine and Cohen 1992). These individuals argued that we should go forward with free trade with Mexico but adopt other measures to ameliorate the possible negative side effects on American workers. On the other side, some NAFTA critics recognized that economic integration with Mexico is an inevitable trend, and they sought ways to make that integration compatible with the upward harmonization of living standards and social regulations in all three countries (see, e.g., Blecker 1993; Stanford 1993; Alliance for Responsible Trade, Citizens Trade Campaign, and Mexican Action Network on Free Trade 1993). These critics welcomed closer ties with Mexico in principle, but objected to a particular agreement that they felt was skewed toward the interests of large corporations and political elites.

A majority of professional economists supported NAFTA, although with mixed degrees of fervor and with some dissents. According to most standard economic models, free trade generally brings aggregate welfare gains to a nation.[7] These gains arise from two main sources: increases in efficiency as countries specialize in the products that they can produce relatively cheaply ("comparative advantages"), and reductions in costs as countries can increase the scale of production of the goods that they export ("scale economies"). Thus, most economists were predisposed to be favorable to any agreement that would lower trade barriers. Given these presumed gains in economic efficiency, most economists argued, any adjustment costs or social problems resulting from trade liberalization in North America should be solved by domestic measures in each country rather than by maintaining trade barriers.

Nevertheless, there were two sources of unease among many economists. First, the negotiation of NAFTA distracted attention from efforts at multilateral trade liberalization through the Uruguay Round of the General Agreement on

Tariffs and Trade (GATT). Even though a GATT agreement was reached, some worried that future multilateral efforts would take a back seat to new bilateral deals with particular countries on the NAFTA model, leaving many poorer countries out of a new world trading system based on trading blocs.[8] Pure free traders were also uncomfortable about the sometimes mercantilist arguments used to support NAFTA (e.g., that it would keep American jobs from moving to East Asia)—and the actual mercantilist provisions of the agreement in some areas (such as the strict "rules of origin," which specify the domestic content of North American products such as automobiles and apparel). These features of NAFTA, which threatened to divert trade and investment away from other parts of the world, were extremely important in the efforts of both the Bush administration and the Clinton administration to win business support for the agreement.

Second, the orthodox economic theory of international trade—the Heckscher-Ohlin (HO) model—clearly implies that trade liberalization with a relatively more labor-abundant, low-wage country like Mexico should lower the average real wages of most workers in the United States (except those with advanced professional skills or technical training). It is important to stress that, according to this theory, *all* workers who lack special professional or technical skills would have their real wages reduced by trade liberalization with a labor-abundant country like Mexico, not just workers in the particular industries that compete with imports. Thus, the potential losses in wages would be much more widespread than the possible losses of jobs due to increased imports. In fact, this theory assumes full employment, that is, that any workers who lose jobs due to increased imports succeed in getting new jobs elsewhere in the economy.

This theory makes the important point, often overlooked in discussions of NAFTA, that it is *not* necessary for the United States to experience *any* net loss of jobs in order for the vast majority of the U.S. labor force to suffer a reduction in real wages and living standards as a result of NAFTA. What is required, as emphasized by Leamer (1993), is that trade liberalization with Mexico combined with increased productivity in Mexican export industries cause a decline in the relative price of labor-intensive goods in the United States (due to competition from cheaper imports of such products). As one highly respected international trade textbook put it, in its most recent edition:

> Like the United States, Mexico is a large country, and so free trade should involve substantial adjustments in each country. With its low-skill but fairly literate labor force, Mexico's comparative advantage evidently lies in its labor-intensive activities and that of the United States in activities intensive in physical and human capital. The arrangement could thus redistribute income in both countries, *away from labor in the United States,* toward it in Mexico. The ease with which American multinational firms, already prevalent and successful in Mexico, could expand their operations speaks for the potential extent of trade creation but also underlines the possible redistribution of factor income. (Caves, Frankel, and Jones 1993, p. 294, italics added)

In spite of these concerns, the majority of professional economists still supported NAFTA. But there were dissenting voices as well, particularly among those who cared more about the distribution of the gains and losses from the agreement than about how much (or how little) it would add to the gross national product (GNP). Some economists doubted that the traditional theories of comparative advantage and scale economies could explain U.S.-Mexican trade; rather, they believed that industries would relocate production in Mexico based on absolute competitive advantages due to low unit labor costs (wages adjusted for productivity) in export industries (see Daly 1993; Blecker and Spriggs 1992). These arguments will be explored in more depth below, after a survey of the economic studies of the likely effects of NAFTA.

Studies of the Employment and Wage Effects of NAFTA

In the course of the NAFTA debate, there was an outpouring of economic studies that used models of the U.S., Mexican, and (in some cases) Canadian economies to project the impact of NAFTA on the employment and wages of U.S. workers.[9] This section will review a selection of these studies, with particular emphasis on some of the most influential and widely cited studies that used different methodologies and reached opposite conclusions. As will be seen, the studies vary greatly in their perspectives and even their objectivity. For the most part, the authors constructed models that reflect their own preferred views and that basically tried to quantify what the authors thought was likely to happen. By revealing the assumptions that underlie the conflicting results, we can help to identify the most likely scenarios for the impact of NAFTA in the United States.

Employment Effects

There is a widespread consensus that NAFTA will have a small to negligible impact on the total number of jobs in the U.S. economy, whether that impact is positive or negative. In spite of the prominence that this issue had in the public debate, there are only a handful of studies that suggest net employment effects of more than a few hundred thousand jobs *in either direction,* in an economy with roughly 120 million workers in the labor force. Job changes of these magnitudes will hardly be perceivable in aggregate statistics, compared with the much larger fluctuations due to the ups and downs of the macroeconomy.

The results of the leading studies of employment effects are summarized in Table 5.1. Perhaps the best-known positive job forecast was that of Hufbauer and Schott (1992, 1993). Hufbauer and Schott originally estimated a net gain of 130,500 jobs in their 1992 book, and then revised this estimate up to 171,400 in their 1993 update. Basically, what Hufbauer and Schott do is project changes in U.S.-Mexican trade flows due to "NAFTA and related reforms" from a base of 1990 to the "foreseeable future" (specified as 1995 in the earlier book),

Table 5.1

Selected Estimates of Aggregate Employment Effects of NAFTA

Study	Base Year	Year(s) of Forecast	Predicted Job Change (in 1,000s)
Hufbauer and Schott (1993)	1990	1995[a]	171.4[b]
Hufbauer (1993)	1990	"Very long term"	−5.4
Koechlin and Larudee (1992a)	1990	1992–2000	−29 to −53 per year −260 to −490 cumulative
Chimerine and Cohen (1992)	—	1994 1998 2002	70 to 137.5 70 to 220 −32.5 to −220
INFORUM (Interindustry Economic Research Fund, Inc., 1990)[c]	1990	1995	(1) 29.3 (2) 44.5
Roland-Holst, Reinert, and Shiells (1992)[d]	1988	—	(1) 92 (2) 2,161 (3) 2,058 (4) 2,840
Faux and Spriggs (1991)	1992	2000	−550[e]

Sources: See the bibliography for references and the text for descriptions of studies.

[a]Called the "foreseeable future" in Hufbauer and Schott (1993), but reported as 1995 in Hufbauer and Schott (1992).

[b]Reported as 130,000 in Hufbauer and Schott (1992), based on the same assumptions about changes in U.S. net exports to Mexico, but using a different method of computing the jobs created.

[c]Taken from the summary by Shiells and Shelburne (1992) of study by the Interindustry Economic Research Fund, Inc., with Clopper Almon as principal investigator; covers U.S.-Mexican trade only. The sceanarios are (1) tariff elimination only and (2) tariff and NTB removal together.

[d]Results were given in percentage terms but have been converted to thousands of jobs (for comparison with the other studies), using actual U.S. civilian employment in 1988 of 114,968,000. The four "experiments" are (1) constant returns to scale, tariffs only; (2) constant returns to scale, tariffs and NTBs; (3) increasing returns to scale with Cournot competition, tariffs, and NTBs; (4) increasing returns to scale with contestable markets, tariffs, and NTBs.

[e]This figure represents a shift of workers from high-wage to low-wage sectors, not a net employment change. See the text for more details.

and then infer net employment effects from the projected changes in the bilateral trade balance.

While many elements go into Hufbauer and Schott's estimates, the key to the prediction of net job gains in the United States is the assumption that the bilateral U.S.-Mexican trade surplus rises by $9.0 billion.[10] The $9.0 billion figure comes simply from assuming that there will be "excess" net capital inflows into Mexico of $12.0 billion as a result of NAFTA, and that three-quarters of these inflows will be used to finance increased Mexican imports from the United States (U.S. exports to Mexico).[11] The $12.0 billion figure is asserted to be "reasonable" in light of past experiences with capital market liberalization, but it is not based on any hard evidence. These authors also implicitly assume that none of the increased capital inflows into Mexico will come at the expense of U.S. domestic investment.

Hufbauer and Schott's work makes an important point: to the extent that NAFTA causes increased net outflows of capital from the United States to Mexico, holding all other factors constant, the U.S. trade surplus with Mexico will increase, and this should have a positive (albeit small) effect on total U.S. employment. However, this is not the end of the issue. To begin with, this is at best only a short-run effect of NAFTA (and it actually incorporates the effects of pre-NAFTA reforms as well). One of the authors (Hufbauer 1993) has separately released "long-run" projections in which bilateral trade is approximately balanced, and there is a tiny net U.S. job loss (5,400). More important, this study focuses only on bilateral U.S.-Mexican trade and ignores the potential trade diversion effects of NAFTA on U.S. trade with other countries as well as potential domestic repercussions (such as possible diversion of U.S. domestic investment).

At the other end of the spectrum is the work of Koechlin and Larudee (1992a). These authors also emphasize the outflow of U.S. capital to Mexico, but they view it from a totally different perspective from that of Hufbauer and Schott. Koechlin and Larudee do not consider the consequences of this capital outflow for the U.S. trade balance; rather, they assume that all the increased U.S. foreign investment in Mexico comes at the expense of domestic investment in the United States. Then they estimate the employment losses that would be associated with the predicted reduction in U.S. domestic investment—ignoring possible offsets such as increased exports to Mexico.

Koechlin and Larudee obtain a range of estimates by using two alternative methods to estimate the outflow of direct foreign investment and two alternative methods for translating investment reductions into job losses.[12] These alternative methods result in a range of estimates of between 260,000 and 490,000 jobs lost *over a nine-year period* (1992–2000). The estimated annual losses are much smaller, of course, ranging from a low of about 29,000 to a high of about 53,000. Even taking the long-run, cumulative effects, Koechlin and Larudee's estimates of job losses are all under 500,000.

Koechlin and Larudee do not consider the balance-of-payments impact of the capital outflows that they predict, and they simply assume that all the predicted investment outflows come at the expense of domestic investment in the United States.[13] The Koechlin-Larudee estimates do provide a reasonable range for the maximum likely number of jobs displaced by outflows of capital to Mexico in the first decade of the agreement, but these are not necessarily net job losses since other impacts of NAFTA on employment are not taken into account.

Like Hufbauer and Schott, Chimerine and Cohen (1992) focus only on the direct trade effects of NAFTA and do not consider possible repercussions for U.S. domestic investment. However, there are several distinguishing features of the Chimerine and Cohen analysis. First, they rely on detailed industry case studies to make projections of trade changes and then aggregate these industry trade changes together. Second, they use information on current strategies of U.S. companies trading with and investing in Mexico rather than relying on analogies to other historical experiences. Third, they consider the impact of NAFTA on the overall U.S. trade balance (not just the bilateral U.S.-Mexican balance) by correcting for the diversion of U.S. imports from other countries to Mexico; this correction lessens the negative impact of increased imports from Mexico on the U.S. economy.[14] Fourth, these authors give a range of estimates of the net trade and employment effects of NAFTA for three different time frames (short-, medium-, and long-run, identified as the years 1994, 1998, and 2002, respectively). Perhaps most notably, Chimerine and Cohen do not portray a one-sided picture of NAFTA but rather show possible gains *and* losses.

For the short run (1994), Chimerine and Cohen agree with Hufbauer and Schott that the U.S. trade surplus will increase as a result of NAFTA, resulting in net job gains (compared with a 1990 base) of between 70,000 and 137,500.[15] By 1998, as U.S. export growth to Mexico could accelerate, the range of net job gains extends from 70,000 to 220,000; but by 2002, when most of NAFTA's provisions would be fully in effect, Chimerine and Cohen foresee a very different outcome. By the early 2000s, they project U.S. export growth to Mexico to slacken, as Mexican industries will be able to source more parts and equipment domestically. At the same time, "the new plants created by new investment in Mexico will all be fully on stream and exporting much of their production back to the United States" (Chimerine and Cohen 1992, p. 23). As a result of these two factors, the U.S. trade balance with Mexico will turn into a deficit large enough to outweigh any continued gains from trade diversion, resulting in net job losses in the range of 32,500 to 220,000.

Some economists have used "linked" macroeconomic models of the U.S. and Mexican economies to predict the employment effects of NAFTA. The first effort in this direction was INFORUM, the work of the Interindustry Economic Research Fund, Inc. (1990), under the direction of Clopper Almon.[16] This exercise combined input-output (I-O) models with considerable sectoral detail (seventy-eight sectors for the United States) and macroeconometric models of the U.S. and Mexican economies with trade linkages. Almon ran two simulations of the

INFORUM model, one with tariff removal only and one with tariff removal plus elimination of nontariff barriers (NTBs). International investment effects were not considered. Both simulations show very small but positive employment gains for the United States after five years: 29,300 with only tariffs removed and 44,500 with tariffs and NTBs (both after ten years).

Many NAFTA models do not allow for any net employment effects due to the assumption of full employment. This assumption is especially common in the computable general equilibrium (CGE) models, but it is not a necessary assumption in a CGE framework.[17] The CGE model of Roland-Holst, Reinert, and Shiells (1992), which allows for employment changes (by assuming a fixed real wage), actually obtains the largest estimates of net employment gains due to NAFTA, as large as 2.8 million jobs in their scenario 4, as shown in Table 5.1.[18] However, this extreme result appears to be due primarily to an exaggerated measure of the effects of reducing Mexican NTBs[19] and is not replicated in any other study.

To summarize, all the credible estimates of the net employment effects of NAFTA are quite small, although they do not all agree as to the direction of the effects. Taking into account all the offsetting effects (including gains from increased exports, as well as losses from increased imports and investment diversion), a range of about 200,000 probably represents the maximum net effects of NAFTA on total employment. Even 200,000 workers represent less than 0.2 percent of the U.S. labor force. There is no evidence that NAFTA will have a large net impact on the total amount of employment in the U.S. economy.

Nevertheless, the total number of jobs that could be affected by NAFTA is undoubtedly larger than the net employment changes. We can define "gross job displacement" as the reduction in employment due to increased imports from Mexico (net of any imports that are diverted from other countries to Mexico). This is an important indicator of the labor market effects of NAFTA, since many of the workers who lose jobs will not be the same people who get the new jobs that are created, or will get other jobs only by accepting lower wages than they currently earn (and only after a period of some transitional unemployment). However, care is essential in interpreting the phrase "gross job dislocation." Some of the jobs "displaced" by imports will be potential future jobs that do not get created; thus, gross job displacement in this sense does not necessarily measure the *number of workers* who actually lose jobs that they already have.

The credible estimates of gross dislocation range from fairly negligible amounts up to nearly 1 million workers.[20] At the low end, Hufbauer and Schott (1993, table 2.1, p. 16) estimate gross displacement of 145,000 in the short run, based on their predicted increase in U.S. imports from Mexico of $7.7 billion due to "NAFTA and related reforms."[21] However, this prediction is based on an analogy to other countries' experiences of trade liberalization in the past; it may not be relevant to the case of Mexico joining a free trade area with the much larger and richer United States.[22] Since NAFTA guarantees preferential access to the U.S. market for Mexican exports, Mexico may be able to achieve rates of export growth far greater than what other developing countries have achieved simply by removing their own trade restrictions but without gaining free access to developed country markets in return. Hufbauer's long-run estimates, in which trade is assumed to be roughly balanced, imply long-run gross dislocation of 324,000 workers (see Hufbauer 1993, p. 4, n. 4).

At the high end, the work of Chimerine and Cohen (1992) implies quite large gross displacement, especially in the long run. After adjustments for trade diversion from non-NAFTA countries to Mexico, Chimerine and Cohen estimate that the net increase in total U.S. manufactured imports as a result of NAFTA will be between $33.5 billion and $36.5 billion by 2002. Using their employment multiplier of 25,000 jobs per $1 billion of trade, a range of 837,500 to 912,500 workers dislocated is implied.

An intermediate figure for gross displacement was obtained in the study by Faux and Spriggs (1991). Faux and Spriggs used a variant of the model later published by Hinojosa-Ojeda and McCleery (1992) to investigate the effects of capital outflows from the United States to Mexico in a CGE framework. Assuming that the risk premium on capital invested in Mexico will fall by 10 percent as a result of NAFTA, the model predicted a cumulative $44 billion shift of capital from the United States to Mexico between 1992 and 2000. Since the model assumes full employment, there is no effect on the total number of U.S. workers employed, but 550,000 high-wage jobs are lost and replaced by an equal number of low-wage jobs in the simulation with the capital outflow by the final year of the simulation (compared with the baseline simulation of the model).[23]

The estimates of the long-run gross job dislocation attributable to NAFTA cited here thus range from a low of about 300,000 to a high of about 900,000, with two intermediate studies (Koechlin and Larudee 1992a, 1992b; and Faux and Spriggs 1991) suggesting displacement roughly on the order of half a million jobs. All these estimates suggest that gross dislocation effects are likely to be considerably larger than the net employment effects. Although even the highest estimates of the former are still under 1 percent of the total U.S. labor force, they are much larger (as much as 5 percent) in relation to manufacturing employment.[24]

Wage Effects and Income Distribution

The main studies that have predicted wage effects of NAFTA are summarized in Table 5.2 (on pages 150–51). Perhaps the most widely cited estimates are those of Leamer (1993). Leamer's study is the only one that directly applies the logic of the traditional HO theory of international trade and income distribution to the U.S.-Mexican case. A part of this theory, called the Stolper-Samuelson (SS) theorem, predicts that the scarce factor of production (which is nonprofessional, nontechnical labor in the United States)[25] will suffer a real income loss as a result of trade liberalization. Specifically, Leamer estimates how much the average wages of nonprofessional, nontechnical workers could fall[26] as a result of trade liberalization with low-wage countries like Mexico, on the assumption that such liberalization will lower the relative price of labor-intensive goods in the United States. Leamer's estimates are based on the experiences of a sample of thirteen industrialized countries that liberalized their restrictions on imports of labor-intensive goods in the period 1972–85.[27] As shown in Table 5.2, Leamer's estimates range from losses of about $500 to $9,000 annually, depending on whether the relative price decline for labor-intensive goods is one or five times the 1972–85 average and on whether the petroleum industry is included in the sample. Although Leamer admits that his estimates are "highly uncertain," he concludes that "[r]eductions in annual earnings over the next decade on the order of $1,000 seem very plausible" (1993, pp. 121–22).

Leamer's estimates are not based directly on specific quantitative measures of how liberalized trade with Mexico will affect the U.S. labor market. Rather, his estimates pertain to a generalized process of trade liberalization with labor-abundant, low-wage countries, not just Mexico. Nevertheless, Leamer clearly views the formation of NAFTA as signaling the end of a protectionist strategy for keeping U.S. wages from falling, because NAFTA will transform Mexico into an export platform for reaching the U.S. market. In his own words,

> *preferential access to the U.S. marketplace encourages the Mexicans to export all of their product to the protected U.S. market and to import for consumption from third* [country] *sources.* This trade diversion effect by itself is enough to allow Mexico today to play a major role in the U.S. markets for some commodities. . . .
>
> If the Mexico of the future is as big as I argue, the NAFTA means that the United States will not be able to impose trade barriers to maintain the wages of our low-skilled workers. (Leamer 1993, pp. 58–59, italics in original)

This is a subtle argument, to be sure, but one that effectively implies a negative effect of NAFTA on U.S. wages.

In contrast to Leamer, there are several major studies that have found overall wage gains from NAFTA. Three frequently cited representatives of these studies are the CGE models of Brown, Deardorff, and Stern (1992a) and Bachrach and Mizrahi (1992),[28] and the linked macro/I-O model of the INFORUM (Interindustry Economic Research Fund, Inc. 1990), which are summarized in Table 5.2. There are several features of these studies that deserve comment. First, the wage gains they imply are all very small; all are under 0.3 percent, and most are much smaller.[29] The results obtained by Brown and her coauthors are especially interesting because they report scenarios for the United States and Mexico alone, separately from scenarios for the United States, Mexico, and Canada combined. The wage gains are notably larger in the latter case, presumably because liberalized trade with Canada (which has a larger GNP than Mexico, in spite of a much

smaller population) offers greater prospects for scale economies for U.S. producers (and Brown and her coauthors assume that most U.S. industries have scale
economies with monopolistic competition).[30]

Second, these models incorporate numerous theoretical assumptions that have
an important impact on the predicted distributional outcomes. Essentially, these
models assume specifications that are more likely to imply wage increases rather
than decreases. As Brown and her coauthors acknowledge, "Model features that
overwhelm Stolper-Samuelson mechanics are fairly straightforward to implement, and *most modelers choose to do so*" (1992b, p. 1511, italics added). There
are two such features that are mainly employed. One is to assume that, by
forming a free trade area with Canada and Mexico, and thus diverting trade away
from other nations, the United States gets a terms-of-trade gain with the rest of
the world (since reduced U.S. demand for non-NAFTA imports lowers the relative price of other countries' exports). If this terms-of-trade gain is large enough,
it can more than offset the fall in the real wages that would otherwise occur due
to SS effects, and this is what usually occurs in the NAFTA simulations.[31] The
other feature is to assume the form of monopolistic competition originally modeled by Krugman (1979), in which workers gain from lower prices of goods
produced for wider markets with trade liberalization, assuming that there are
decreasing average costs of production (scale economies) and that free entry
keeps prices equal to average costs.

Third, the treatment of foreign investment in these models deserves special
attention. Although both Brown and her coauthors (1992a) and Bachrach and
Mizrahi (1992) allow for increased foreign investment in Mexico as a result of
NAFTA, they both make the incredible assumption that *none of the additional
foreign investment comes from the United States or Canada.*[32] Given that the
main purpose of NAFTA from the Mexican viewpoint (as well as from that of
American business) is to open up Mexico to more foreign investment—and that
surely the United States, which is by far Mexico's largest trading partner, would
account for the lion's share of that investment—the assumption by these model
builders that *none* of the extra investment in Mexico would come from the
United States strains credulity, and raises some evident questions about the objectivity of their studies.[33]

In contrast with these studies, the "structuralist" CGE model of Stanford
(1993) makes capital flows between the United States, Canada, and Mexico
endogenous and assumes that U.S. and Canadian domestic investment are reduced by capital outflows for direct foreign investment in Mexico.[34] However,
instead of simply presenting the results of his own preferred specification, Stanford also shows the effects of dropping some of his own assumptions and replacing them with more standard ones. These sensitivity tests effectively demonstrate
how assumptions such as exogenous capital flows into Mexico (not from the
United States), low substitution elasticities for nationally differentiated products,
investment determined by available savings, and full employment with market-

150

Table 5.2

Alternative Predicted Effects of NAFTA on Average U.S. Wages

Study	Scenario	Wage Effect
Learner (1993)[a]	Including petroleum	
	Low relative price change	−$1,862
	High relative price change	−$9,312
	Excluding petroleum	
	Low relative price change	−$465
	High relative price change	−$2,323
Brown, Deardorff, and Stern (1992a)[b]	A. Tariffs and NTBs, United States, Mexico, and Canada	0.2%
	B. Tariffs, NTBs, and DFI, United States, Mexico, and Canada	0.2%
	C. Tariffs and NTBs, United States and Mexico	0.0%
	D. Tariffs, NTBs, and DFI, United States and Mexico	0.1%
Bachrach and Mizrahi (1992)[c]	Tariffs and NTBs	0.02%
	Tariffs, NTBs, and DFI	0.03%
Interindustry Economic Research Fund, Inc. (INFORUM, 1990)[d]	Tariffs only (after 10 years)	0.19%
	Tariffs and NTBs (after 10 years)	0.28%
Stanford (1993)[e]	NAFTA base case	−0.41%
	Maximum dislocation	−1.08%
	Social NAFTA	0.53%
	Neoclassical scenario	0.12%

Robinson, Burfisher, Hinojosa-Ojeda, and Thierfelder (1993)[f]	
Rural workers	-3.4%
Urban unskilled workers	-4.2%
Urban skilled workers	0.3%
Professional workers	0.3%

Sources: See the bibliography for references, and the text for further discussion.

[a]Effects reported are for "other workers" (nonprofessional, nontechnical) at annual rates. These calculations assume that trade liberalization lowers the relative price of labor-intensive goods. The degree of relative price change for labor-intensive goods is compared with the average changes observed in thirteen OECD (Organization for Economic Cooperation and Development) countries between 1972 and 1985: low is the same as the actual changes for those years; high is five times as large.

[b]NTBs are nontariff barriers; DFI is direct foreign investment, which is assumed (in scenarios B and D) to increase in Mexico by 10% but to come entirely from thirty-one other countries (non-NAFTA members). Canada is excluded from scenarios C and D.

[c]The model of U.S.-Mexican trade is developed only for the KPMG Peat Marwick consulting group. Additional U.S. DFI in Mexico is assumed to come entirely out of U.S. DFI in other (non-NAFTA) countries, not out of U.S. domestic investment. Results are essentially the same as reported in KPMG Peak Marwick (1991).

[d]Study by the Interindustry Economic Research Fund, Inc., Clopper Almon, principal investigator; covers U.S.-Mexican trade only. Results were taken from the summary by Shiells and Shelburne (1992).

[e]A three-country (United States, Canada, and Mexico) model. The first three scenarios make "structuralist" assumptions described in the text. The NAFTA base case assumes tariff removal and an endogenous increase in U.S. and Canadian DFI in Mexico. Maximum dislocation assumes the base case plus improved Mexican technology, displaced labor from Mexican agriculture, and higher elasticities of substitution. The social NAFTA assumes the base case plus debt relief for Mexico (50% write-off), higher Mexican labor standards, and an investment stimulus (lower interest rates) in the United States and Canada. The neoclassical scenario, described in the text, includes tariff removal with additional investment in Mexico not financed by capital flows from the United States or Canada.

[f]Results shown here are for the scenario with complete agricultural liberalization in Mexico. See the text for discussion of some other scenarios.

clearing wages lead to the types of results found in most of the other CGE models.[35]

In Stanford's "NAFTA base case" (see Table 5.2), a combination of tariff elimination and a 10 percent reduction in the risk premium on capital invested in Mexico results in capital outflows from the United States and Canada to Mexico, causing the U.S. real wage to fall by 0.41 percent while output and employment are virtually unchanged.[36] However, the same scenario generates very large benefits for Mexico, including real increases of 13 percent in GDP and 29 percent in wages.[37] In the "maximum dislocation" scenario, Stanford assumes that NAFTA results in improved Mexican productivity and causes displacement of labor from Mexican agriculture; this scenario also assumes higher elasticities of substitution between Mexican, Canadian, and U.S. products. The result is larger losses for workers in the United States and Canada, with American wages falling by 1.08 percent. However, Mexico gets an even larger inflow of foreign investment in this case, and even greater gains (29 percent in GDP and 32 percent in wages).

Then Stanford considers what he calls a "social NAFTA," which starts with the base case but adds a 50 percent write-off of Mexican foreign debt, an increase in Mexican labor standards, additional public infrastructure spending by the Mexican government, and lower interest rates to stimulate private investment in the United States and Canada in order to offset capital outflows. In this case, U.S. wages increase by 0.53 percent. While Mexico gets smaller capital inflows in this scenario, it nevertheless gets very large gains of 30 percent in GDP and 90 percent in real wages—even larger than in the "maximum dislocation" scenario.

Stanford's model is not beyond criticism. For one thing, his model's lack of a rest-of-world sector forces all the increased direct foreign investment into Mexico to come from the United States and Canada; at least some would probably come from other countries. The very large wage increases that Stanford's model predicts for Mexico also raise some questions about his specification of the Mexican labor market.[38] Stanford also does not include the liberalization of NTBs, which could produce additional gains for U.S. exporters. In spite of these problems, Stanford offers a much wider range of assumptions and results than most of the other NAFTA modelers, and shows specifically which assumptions imply that U.S. wages will rise and which assumptions imply that they will fall.

Some studies have disaggregated the U.S. labor force, and Table 5.2 gives an example of one such study (Robinson, Burfisher, Hinojosa-Ojeda, and Thierfelder 1993).[39] This study focuses on the consequences of agricultural liberalization (elimination of trade protection and domestic agricultural subsidies in Mexico) on migration flows and trade patterns, a factor ignored by most other studies. In their scenario with complete agricultural liberalization (shown in Table 5.2), the influx of nearly 1 million Mexican migrant workers into the United States depresses wages for rural and urban unskilled American workers, while wages for other groups (urban skilled and professional) rise by much smaller amounts.

Robinson and his coauthors have contributed a valuable insight by focusing attention on the possibility of increased labor displacement in Mexico and the potential for increased rather than decreased migration of Mexican workers into the United States as a result of agricultural trade liberalization. However, the model developed by these authors seems to exaggerate the impact of the migration factor to the exclusion of other channels through which NAFTA could affect U.S. wages.[40]

Conclusions on Existing NAFTA Studies

If the preceding survey demonstrates anything, it is that the results of all the existing NAFTA studies are extremely sensitive to the assumptions made by the authors in modeling the impact of this trade agreement. As one reporter put it, "What the models do, essentially, is put numbers on theories" (Nasar 1993, p. A1). Unfortunately, the fact that the theories assumed by the authors of the studies discussed above were largely if not entirely responsible for their "estimates" was largely lost sight of in the NAFTA debate, when the results of studies based on strong and even incredible theoretical assumptions were cited as objective forecasts of the agreement's likely consequences. Yet, as one government agency conceded, "Most, though not all, of what can reliably be concluded from the [NAFTA] models merely confirms what economists already *knew* or *believed* to be very likely (U.S. Congress, Congressional Budget Office 1993a, p. 4, italics added).

These considerations suggest that the predictions of the various NAFTA models cannot be taken at face value, but need to be evaluated critically on the basis of whether their assumptions are realistic and credible for the case of U.S.-Mexican trade and investment liberalization. For example, models that rule out any possible movements of capital between the United States and Mexico, in the case of an agreement whose main purpose is to encourage foreign investment in Mexico, would seem to offer unreliable guides for estimating the effects of that agreement. In contrast, models that put the role of international capital mobility (including U.S.-Mexican capital flows) at the center of the analysis are more likely to illuminate the issues, even if these models come to opposite conclusions as a result of their other assumptions.

Also, studies that portray NAFTA as either a free lunch or an unmitigated disaster are unlikely to prove accurate. Basic economic theory teaches that trade liberalization can cause substantial losses to some segments of society while bringing potential gains to others. Moreover, it is unlikely that such strong support *and* opposition from different groups in American society would arise in the absence of some real, objective interests that are at stake. On these grounds alone, the studies by Chimerine and Cohen (1992), Leamer (1993), and Stanford (1993) stand out as exceptionally balanced and informative.

In fact, a critical reading of the existing NAFTA studies suggests some tentative conclusions about what the agreement is most likely to do. Employment effects will depend on whether the U.S. trade surplus with Mexico rises or falls and on whether the negative effects of diversion of domestic investment are large enough to offset potential gains from larger trade surpluses. Moreover, larger trade surpluses, if they occur at all, are likely to be short-lived, since the boom in capital outflows from the United States to Mexico will inevitably be transitory, while the greater export capacity installed in Mexico will be permanent. On the whole, since the net effects on domestic employment will probably be small, the emphasis in the NAFTA debate on whether the agreement would "create" or "destroy" jobs was largely misplaced. What is more important is the kinds of jobs that will be gained and lost as NAFTA reallocates employment, and particularly whether the jobs of the future will offer better or worse wages and working conditions as a result of this agreement.

On this issue, there are strong reasons to believe that greater trade and investment flows with a more labor-abundant, lower-wage neighbor will only exacerbate the downward pressures that already are causing stagnant or falling wages for U.S. workers—especially in the manufacturing sector (see Mishel and Bernstein 1993). Using methods as diverse as Leamer's SS theorem and Stanford's structuralist CGE model, the more objective studies find that NAFTA is likely to lower U.S. wages for nonprofessional, nontechnical workers in the absence of offsetting social policies. We will return to these distributional consequences of NAFTA below, after discussing the actual evolution of U.S.-Mexican trade and foreign investment flows in recent years.

Recent Trends in U.S.–Mexican Trade and Capital Flows

As discussed earlier, the NAFTA agreement builds upon and extends a process of trade liberalization and economic restructuring that has been going on in Mexico for a decade. In the late 1980s, Mexico joined the GATT and unilaterally reduced its formerly severe restrictions on imports of most industrial products as well as on direct foreign investment. Mexican tariffs were lowered from virtually prohibitive levels in many industries to an average of about 10 percent, while restrictions on foreign ownership of domestic companies were greatly relaxed (see U.S. International Trade Commission 1991, chapter 1). New incentives were given for exports, as Mexico had to earn the foreign exchange it needed to service its debt obligations. Agreements reached with the International Monetary Fund (IMF), the World Bank, and the U.S. government required Mexico to privatize former state enterprises, reduce the government budget deficit, control inflation, and generally reduce the level of government direction of the economy in order to obtain rollovers of the existing debt and eventually some modest debt relief under the U.S.-sponsored Brady Plan of 1989.[41] Since all these policies foreshadow the types of policies that Mexico is now locked into under NAFTA, the record of the last few years provides some perspective on what the actual effects of this agreement are likely to be.

Table 5.3

Mexican Merchandise Trade, Current Account Balance, and Net Private Foreign Capital Inflows, 1987–93
(in billions of U.S. dollars)

Year	Merchandise Exports	Merchandise Imports	Current Account Balance	Direct Investment[a] (net inflow)	Portfolio Investment (net inflow)
1987	$20.7	$12.2	$ 4.0	$1.8	$–0.4
1988	20.6	18.9	–2.4	0.6	–0.9
1989	22.8	23.4	–4.0	2.6	0.4
1990	26.8	31.3	–7.1	2.5	–5.4
1991	26.9	38.2	–14.9	4.7	12.1
1992	27.5	48.2	–24.8	4.4	19.2
1993	30.0	48.9	–23.4	4.9	27.9

Source: International Monetary Fund (1993, October 1994).
[a]Not including debt-equity swaps.

The evolution of Mexico's international transactions since the late 1980s is shown in the Mexican balance-of-payments data in Table 5.3. In the six years since Mexico opened up its economy, its reported exports[42] increased by 50 percent, from about $20 billion to $30 billion, while its imports *quadrupled,* from about $12 billion to over $48 billion. The Mexican current account balance, which also includes trade in services, net interest payments, and unilateral transfers not shown separately, fell from a small surplus in 1987 to deficits of over $20 billion per year by 1992–93, representing about 7 percent of Mexico's GDP in those years. These relatively enormous deficits were covered by equally huge net capital inflows as foreign investors once again flocked into Mexico. Direct investment inflows reached between $4 billion and $5 billion annually in 1992–93, while portfolio investment inflows soared to an incredible $28 billion by 1993.[43]

The widening of Mexico's trade deficit and the increased inflows of foreign capital are, of course, two sides of the same coin. But it is worthwhile to understand the precise policies that not only made imports rise faster than exports but also made portfolio investments rise so much faster than direct investments. The unilateral reductions in Mexico's import barriers in 1987 naturally led to a release of pent-up demand for imported consumer goods. At the same time, the Mexican government began serious efforts to control the country's runaway inflation. These efforts included tight monetary policies that drove up interest rates and thus made Mexican financial assets very attractive to foreign investors (especially at a time when interest rates in the United States were generally falling). As a result, a lot of "hot money" came into Mexico's "emerging financial market" in the early 1990s. While the Mexican financial markets were

Table 5.4

Growth Rates of Real Gross Domestic Product in Mexico, Selected Years, 1965–93
(average annual percentage rates)

Year(s)	Growth Rate
1965–80	6.5%
1980–86	0.4
1987	1.9
1988	1.2
1989	3.3
1990	4.4
1991	3.6
1992	2.7
1993[a]	0.4

Sources: For 1965–86, World Bank (1988); for 1987–92, author's calculations based on data in International Monetary Fund (May 1994).
[a]Preliminary figure from *Business Week*, April 11, 1994, p. 25.

booming, real economic growth was disappointing, since the same contractionary macroeconomic policies that raised interest rates so high also kept the Mexican economy from expanding at an adequate rate.

Table 5.4 provides some perspective on recent economic growth in Mexico. From 1965 to 1980, Mexican GDP grew in real terms at an average annual rate of 6.5 percent. This growth took place under the old regime of protectionist, import-substitution industrialization policies.[44] In the early 1980s, however, Mexico was buffeted by the forces that caused the international debt crisis. For Mexico in particular, falling oil prices combined with rising interest rates on short-term debt produced a squeeze on foreign exchange reserves and forced the government to suspend debt service in 1982. The years of "stabilization policies" that followed were extremely painful (see Lustig 1992), and growth fell to an average annual rate of only 0.4 percent in the years 1980–86. With population growing at a 2.2 percent annual rate at that time, this represented a real decline in the Mexican standard of living and the reversal of many years of previous development.

As Table 5.4 shows, the Mexican economy did begin to recover in the late 1980s, but the growth that has taken place since those years is disappointing by historical Mexican standards—and was slowing down in the most recent period. By 1993, on the eve of the implementation of NAFTA, the Mexican economy was again stagnating, with a growth rate of barely 0.4 percent and a loss of 612,000 jobs in the industrial sector.[45]

These disappointing growth statistics should be borne in mind in considering the real impact of the massive capital inflows that Mexico has received in the early 1990s.[46] These huge capital movements, averaging about $20 billion per year, were the source of much enthusiasm among NAFTA supporters before the agreement was approved. Yet, in fact, Mexico received relatively little real productive investment in the process, not enough even to sustain 3 percent annual growth of real GDP, nor enough to prevent an absolute decline in manufacturing employment. Most of the capital inflow consisted of portfolio investments: purchases of Mexican bonds, stocks, and other paper assets. While in theory these financial investments could help to finance additional real investment in productive capacity in Mexico, in reality they do not appear to have done so. Rather, the financial inflows themselves were largely a speculative response to the high interest rates that were also stifling Mexican economic growth. Mexico was sacrificing real growth and employment in the name of anti-inflationary policies demanded by international financial markets.

These same policies caused the Mexican peso, which had been devalued after the 1982 debt crisis and reached a record low real value in 1987, to begin appreciating again. As part of its anti-inflationary campaign, the Mexican government restricted the rate of nominal depreciation of the peso (increases in the number of pesos per dollar) to below the differential in inflation rates between Mexico and the United States. This policy kept the prices of imported goods from rising in peso terms, thus helping to contain Mexican inflation, but also made imports artificially cheap for domestic consumers. At the same time, the huge inflows of foreign capital increased demand for the peso and thus helped to sustain its high value in the foreign exchange market. The resulting real (inflation-adjusted) appreciation of the peso, shown in the first column of Table 5.5, contributed to continued rapid growth of imports and relatively slower growth of exports, putting a drag on overall Mexican growth. By 1993, the peso had appreciated by 76.2 percent over its 1987 value.

These causes of Mexico's growing trade deficit are important to bear in mind in evaluating some of the arguments in the NAFTA debate, which revolved around predictions of how NAFTA would affect the U.S.-Mexican trade balance. Some NAFTA supporters (e.g., Dornbusch 1991; Hufbauer and Schott 1992, 1993) hailed the rising U.S. trade surpluses with Mexico in 1991–92 (shown by the greater increases in U.S. exports compared with imports in Table 5.5) as evidence that the opening up of the Mexican economy would have an expansionary, job-creating effect on the U.S. economy. This argument ignored the special circumstances affecting the trade data for the early 1990s, including the appreciation of the peso discussed above. In addition, the U.S. economy went into a recession in 1990–91 and did not fully recover until 1993. As U.S. demand was weak, it is not surprising that U.S. imports from Mexico grew slowly in 1990–91 and then increased much more rapidly in 1992–93. Furthermore, Mexican economic growth was moving inversely with U.S. growth in this period. With Mexican growth peaking in 1990 and then falling through 1993 (as shown in Table 5.4, above), it is also not surprising that the growth of U.S. exports to Mexico accelerated in the early 1990s and then slowed down by 1993. In fact, by 1993

Table 5.5

Bilateral U.S.–Mexican Real Exchange Rate, Merchandise Trade, and Net Private Capital Outflows, 1987–93
(in billions of U.S. dollars, except as noted)

	Merchandise Trade			Capital Outflows[a]	
	Real Exchange Rate[b]	U.S. Exports to Mexico	U.S. Imports from Mexico	Direct Foreign Investment	Private Portfolio Investment
1987	100.0	14.6	20.3	0.3	−0.6
1988	124.9	20.6	23.3	0.6	−4.0
1989	132.0	24.7	27.1	1.4	−1.9
1990	138.9	28.1	30.5	1.9	−1.6
1991	152.2	33.1	31.5	2.3	4.9
1992	166.5	40.5	35.6	1.3	5.2
1993[c]	176.2	41.8	40.4	2.5	11.6

Sources: U.S. Department of Commerce, Bureau of Economic Analysis (various June issues of the *Survey of Current Business*); International Monetary Fund (1994); and author's calculations.

[a]Net increases in U.S. private assets in Mexico. Portfolio investment includes all assets except direct investment in productive enterprises.

[b]Index of real value of peso, 1987 = 100, measured by the nominal exchange rate (dollars per new peso) multiplied by the ratio of the Mexican to U.S. consumer price indexes.

[c]Preliminary data.

the U.S. surplus with Mexico was reduced to a mere $1.4 billion as the U.S. recovery, combined with the Mexican slowdown, led U.S. imports from Mexico nearly to catch up with U.S. exports to Mexico.

Thus, the macroeconomic and financial policies that Mexico has adopted in recent years have unduly restrained its growth, particularly by overvaluing the peso and thus preventing more rapid growth of exports. This should certainly give caution to those who expect Mexico to experience a miraculous economic boom simply as a result of joining NAFTA. If the same macroeconomic policies stay in place, it seems unlikely that the NAFTA tariff reductions and other market-opening measures by themselves will be sufficient to recharge the Mexican economy. Indeed, with U.S. tariffs on imports from Mexico averaging only about 3.4 percent in 1989 (U.S. International Trade Commission 1991, p. 2-2), Mexico could get far greater export gains from a significant depreciation of the peso than it stands to receive from the tariff reduction provisions of NAFTA[47] (although it will gain somewhat more from reductions in NTBs). Additional capital inflows will not necessarily help if they continue to be mostly of the "hot-money" variety and are not invested in increasing domestic productive capacity.

With current account deficits of 7 percent of its GDP unlikely to be sustainable in the long run, Mexico will most likely be forced to devalue the peso sometime in the late 1990s, a move that will tend to improve its trade balance and growth prospects. Moreover, whatever productive foreign investments are made in Mexico will raise its export capacity. If this happens, the reversal of U.S. trade surpluses with Mexico foreseen by Chimerine and Cohen (1992) for the early 2000s will be a likely result.

Low-Wage Competition and Corporate Restructuring

Whatever happens to the exchange rates and macroeconomic climate, the profound structural differences between the Mexican and the U.S. economies are sure to influence evolving trade patterns and investment flows. Table 5.6 gives some basic indicators of the nature and degree of the structural differences between the United States and Mexico in terms of market size, income levels, and labor supplies. Mexico is a much smaller economy in terms of its GDP, which was barely 5 percent of the U.S. level at current exchange rates in 1991. In terms of current market size, then, it would appear that trade with Mexico could not have a very large influence on the United States one way or the other. But a perspective that focuses only on the preexisting differences in the relative sizes of the Mexican and U.S. economies can be misleading. As one leading international trade economist wrote,

> The Mexico of today is not that big, but the Mexico of the future in a free trade agreement with the United States will be much larger.... Future increases in productivity, accumulation of capital, high birth rates, and concentration on those labor-intensive sectors protected by the United States will greatly increase the potential Mexican exports to the United States, enough, I argue, to greatly limit the ability of the United States to maintain wages of low-skilled workers by trade protection. (Leamer 1993, pp. 58–59)

Especially for evaluating the impact of NAFTA on labor markets and income distribution (wage levels), the relevant indicator is not the level of Mexico's market but rather the size of its labor force. As Table 5.6 shows, Mexico had a working-age population (people from 15 to 64 years old) that was 30 percent of the U.S. population in that age bracket in 1991. Although Mexico's fertility rate has recently declined,[48] the country now has a very young population, and as a result its working-age population is projected almost to double by 2025 (bringing it to nearly half of the U.S. working-age population by that time). It is this enormous and virtually inexhaustible pool of cheap labor that is the main attraction inducing corporations to relocate their production to Mexico while retaining free access to the U.S. market under NAFTA. Table 5.6 also shows that Mexico's per capita GNP was about one-seventh of the U.S. level and that its

Table 5.6

Structural Differences between the United States and Mexico

Item	United States	Mexico
GDP (in billions of 1991 U.S. dollars)	5,611	283
GNP per capita (in 1991 U.S. dollars)	22,240	3,030
Working-age population (15–64 years old), 1991 (in millions)	166	50
Projected working-age population (15–64 years old), 2025 (in millions)	197	93
Hourly compensation in manufacturing, in dollars, 1991 (index, U.S. = 100)	100	14
Share of wages in manufacturing value added (1990)	36%	20%

Sources: World Bank (1993); U.S. Department of Labor, Bureau of Labor Statistics (June 1992); and author's calculations.

real hourly compensation in manufacturing was also about one-seventh of the U.S. rate, at current exchange rates in 1991.[49] In addition, Mexico has a considerably lower share of wages (of production workers) in manufacturing value added.

These differences underlie the concern in the United States over the distributional consequences of trade and investment liberalization with its labor-abundant, low-wage neighbor to the south. With wage levels that are only one-seventh those of the United States, even at an overvalued exchange rate, Mexico is highly competitive in labor-intensive exports of manufactures. Although some East Asian countries (notably China) offer even lower wages, Mexico can easily compensate with its close proximity to the U.S. market. The overvaluation of the peso may be contributing to the extraordinary boom in Mexican imports noted earlier, and is thus contributing to Mexico's large trade deficit, but is not sufficient to eliminate the Mexican advantage in labor costs.

Traditionally, many economists have argued that low wages cannot confer an overall competitive advantage on less developed countries (LDCs) because the low wages merely compensate for low average productivity of their labor.[50] According to traditional theory, these countries can export only those goods in which they have a *comparative* advantage in labor costs, that is, in which their relative productivity exceeds their relative wage. Correspondingly, a high-wage country still enjoys comparative advantages in the sectors in which its relative productivity exceeds its relative wage. This theory rests on three crucial assumptions: that there are no transfers of technology between countries; that capital is immobile between the countries; and that there is full employment of labor in both countries. The first two assumptions together imply that firms from the high-wage country cannot relocate their capital to the low-wage country while bringing more productive technology with them; the third assumption implies that, even if firms could do this, wages in the low-wage country would rise by enough to negate any competitive advantage. None of these assumptions holds in the case of U.S.-Mexican trade.

Like most developing countries, Mexico has what is called a "dual economy": a modern, relatively efficient sector coexists alongside a technologically backward, relatively inefficient sector (sometimes called the "informal" sector). The latter sector (which includes peasant agriculture, urban handicrafts, and small-scale marketing) contains vast numbers of underemployed workers with very low productivity and meager incomes. With rapid population growth, the supply of labor in the informal sector is virtually unlimited. Wages in the modern sector are held down by the pressure of the "surplus labor," which is constantly seeking employment in the modern sector. Although part of the pressure of the surplus labor in Mexico is relieved by migration to the United States, there is still plenty of chronic slack in the Mexican labor market. This slack is increased in the present period by the elimination of jobs in formerly protected domestic manufacturing and agricultural activities, now opened to greater competition from abroad.

Thus, the traditional assumption of full employment does not hold in Mexico, implying that large numbers of additional workers could be employed without putting serious upward pressure on real wages. Moreover, with today's "global factory" model of production, it is now relatively easy to import the most up-to-date technology into a surplus-labor economy like Mexico and to combine this highly productive machinery and equipment with the cheap labor. This transfer of technology is aided by capital mobility, which allows multinational companies to invest directly in the production in Mexico and also provides financing for the acquisition of the capital goods embodying the modern technology. The result is the creation of an "export platform" in the modern sector of a dual economy that can achieve absolute competitive advantages in a wide range of labor-intensive manufacturing operations. The source of this absolute advantage in unit labor costs is the combination of cheap labor with high productivity—not cheap labor alone.[51]

The potential for creating such export platforms does not mean that a high-wage country like the United States cannot compete at all. In sectors in which labor costs are relatively unimportant, or in which transportation costs are high, or in which U.S. natural or technological advantages are overwhelming (such as corn and airplanes), the United States will continue to be competitive. There is evidently a wide range of manufacturing activities in which it is very hard for U.S.-based producers (paying wages of between $10 and $15 per hour) to compete with Mexican-located producers paying only $1 or even $2 per hour for labor, if there are no barriers to free trade and investment. Further, Mexico is only the tip of the iceberg of low-wage competition, since wages in China are only about $1 or $2 per *day*.

With wage differentials of this magnitude, the range of jobs that could be relocated to Mexico or other low-wage sites includes many jobs in relatively high-tech or high-wage industries, such as automobiles and parts, computers, and electronics. Indeed, approximately three-quarters of the jobs created in Mexico by affiliates of U.S. multinational firms in recent years have been in these industries, not in low-wage sectors like textiles and apparel (Blecker and Spriggs 1992). While the majority of the Mexican labor force currently lacks the education and training of the average American worker, Mexican workers are intrinsically no less intelligent and no less capable than American workers. With adequate training and up-to-date equipment, Mexican workers can achieve productivity levels close to those of American workers (see Shaiken 1990).

These considerations suggest a very different picture of what is really at stake in NAFTA from what appears in the rosy forecasts of some economic models. That is, NAFTA represents an important part of a strategy that U.S. corporations are using in an effort to revive their flagging profitability and to combat intensified competition from foreign rivals. In particular, U.S. companies want to use Mexico as a low-wage export platform in order to offset the advantages that Japanese companies have in combining the low wages of East Asian assembly operations with the high productivity of Japan's home economy. Of course, U.S. firms can and do invest in East Asia, and Japanese and other non-U.S. firms can and will invest in Mexico under the nondiscriminatory investment liberalization provisions of NAFTA (with some notable exceptions, such as in the auto sector, in which U.S. companies already in Mexico have advantages over newcomers, under NAFTA). This is precisely where the preferential trading aspects of NAFTA become truly important, because the elimination of tariffs on intra–North American trade gives incentives to produce in North America for North American markets. On the one side, this means gains for some U.S. producers, since they can sell capital equipment and intermediate goods in Mexico that might otherwise be sold by Japanese firms to East Asian manufacturers. On the other side, NAFTA creates definite incentives to locate the labor-intensive manufacturing or assembly operations in Mexico rather than in the United States, Asia, or anywhere else.

In reality, then, this supposed "free trade agreement" can be seen to have an implicitly mercantilist character: it is designed to divert trade away from Japan and East Asia and to strengthen U.S. corporations at the expense of their Japanese and other foreign rivals. This mercantilist thrust was made abundantly clear in some of the arguments in favor of NAFTA. In explaining his endorsement of the agreement, Prestowitz said:

> Because Mexico's barriers will only be reduced for U.S. and Canadian producers and not for Asian or European suppliers, most of the benefits of the larger market will go to U.S. companies. Japanese companies have long benefited from having a lock on the emerging markets of Asia. NAFTA will give U.S. firms a lock on a market of their own with which to fight back. (1993, p. C1)

Noting that NAFTA contains "sweetheart deals designed to help protect politically potent [U.S.] industries . . . from their competitors in Japan and Europe,"
one unusually honest business reporter even suggested that it should have been
called the "North American *Managed* Trade Agreement" (Davis 1992, p. A1,
italics in original).

The real issue, then, is in whose interest NAFTA manages trade. What is good
for General Motors—or any other U.S. corporation—is not necessarily good for
America, or for American workers. Corporations can use NAFTA to restructure
their operations in order to become more profitable by a variety of means: shifting
more labor-intensive operations to Mexico, increasing demand for capital equipment
and intermediate goods produced at their U.S. facilities, and using the *threat* of
moving jobs to Mexico to hold down wages in the United States. While U.S.
workers may face the unhappy choice of losing their jobs or accepting lower wages,
U.S. corporations win either way. This dilemma was made abundantly clear in a
recent contract negotiation at a Xerox Corporation plant in New York State. According to Swoboda (1994), the union at that plant agreed to significant concessions,
including wage cuts averaging 30 percent, out of fear that otherwise the company
would move the jobs to either Asia or Mexico. While this threat exists independently
of NAFTA, it is certainly more credible with this agreement in effect.

What is perhaps most striking in the Xerox example is the fact that Mexico
gets absolutely no gains from the U.S. workers' concessions. Not one dollar of
investment moves to Mexico, no jobs are created there, and no Mexican exports
are stimulated. The U.S. workers lose, and the gains are entirely reaped by the
corporation that employs them. Of course, the workers could lose even more if
their jobs actually did disappear; this prospect is exactly what motivated their
capitulation to the company's demands. If this is how NAFTA preserves jobs in
the U.S. economy, it is clear that it will do so only by depressing the incomes
and living standards of the workers involved.

Conclusions and Policy Options

Somewhere in between Ross Perot's rhetoric about a "giant sucking sound" of
jobs going to Mexico and the Bush and Clinton administrations' euphoria about
NAFTA's creating hundreds of thousands of jobs lies the truth about NAFTA.
Millions of jobs will not disappear overnight, but neither will huge numbers of
jobs be created. Most important, the incessant back-and-forth about whether
NAFTA would, on the whole, create or destroy jobs largely missed the point of
what this trade and investment liberalization agreement is all about.

As a starting point, it must be granted that the agreement contains definite
gains for U.S. business interests. Some important export markets in Mexico are
opened up in areas such as government procurement, financial services, the oil
industry, and finished automobiles (although only after lengthy phaseouts of
existing protection in some cases). There *are* advantages to the United States in

trading more with Mexico, which buys a lot of U.S. exports, rather than with East Asia, which maintains more closed markets and buys relatively more Japanese exports. Allowing more foreign investment in Mexico could assist many U.S. corporations in "restructuring" efforts that could help make them more profitable. In making an honest case for NAFTA from an American viewpoint, these would certainly be the points to emphasize; but then it would be necessary to question whether the gains thus obtained would be shared with, or rather come at the expense of, workers in the United States.

The Bush administration negotiators did an excellent job (perhaps too good a job) of extracting concessions from Mexico in matters relating to foreign investment and property rights (both pecuniary and intellectual). If we think only of the interests of the U.S. business community, then Hufbauer (1993, p. 2) is right when he says that "NAFTA represents a stunning success for U.S. commercial diplomacy." Certainly, when it came to intellectual property rights, capital controls, and government procurement policies, Mexico's sovereignty was sacrificed on the alter of trade and investment liberalization. However, unless we seriously believe that "what is good for General Motors is good for America," then we have to recognize that the U.S. negotiating agenda that produced this NAFTA agreement was incredibly one-sided. Business interests got virtually a wish list of their trade policy objectives; labor and other citizen interests (environmental, consumer, etc.) were frozen out of the original negotiations and were offered little more than window dressing in the side agreements.

This contrast lies at the heart of the controversy over NAFTA. It is not a matter of "special interest politics"; the AFL-CIO is no more a "special interest group" than is the U.S. Chamber of Commerce. More to the point, the unequal treatment of business and labor in NAFTA largely explains the great disparity between elite opinion (which generally favored NAFTA) and mass public opinion (which was much more distrustful). The average businessperson looks at NAFTA and sees investment opportunities; the average citizen or worker looks at it and sees little but potential losses of jobs and incomes. To put it bluntly, what made the NAFTA debate so divisive was the fact that it revived class politics in the United States as no other issue had done in recent decades.

While the evidence on the jobs front seems mixed, it is clear that significant dislocation can be expected and that the wage effects are most likely to be negative. In fact, the distributional implications of NAFTA are almost exactly the reverse of what free trade economists usually claim for trade liberalization. For the most part, the losses (in average wages) will be widespread and diffuse, although small in proportional terms (although there will also be large, concentrated gains or losses for workers who either gain or lose specific jobs). However, the gains (mainly in corporate profits, and to some extent in salaries of professional and technical workers) will be more narrow and concentrated. There is no "representative consumer" who will benefit from cheaper imports due to NAFTA, unless the representative consumer is defined as a member of the upper-middle class whose livelihood will not be threatened by heightened international capital mobility. The truly representative consumer, if there is such a person, is a median worker with average skills and training whose wages are likely to fall in real terms, no matter how many imported consumer goods he or she buys.

Now that NAFTA is in effect, the question is what can or should be done to redress the distributional inequities that this trade-and-investment liberalization agreement threatens to worsen. One solution, proposed by Chimerine and Cohen (1992), is to seek modifications in the implementation of NAFTA that would lessen the negative impact on U.S. manufacturing employment. In particular, these authors urge acceleration of Mexican market-opening measures to keep U.S. exports expanding, and inducements for firms that invest in Mexico to export more to countries outside North America rather than to the United States and Canada. Alternatively, Leamer argues that the United States needs to increase the supply of skilled labor and capital in order to reap more gains from trade, as in the following quotation:

> We are getting ourselves in trouble in the international marketplace because we have too few scientists and managers, and too little capital. We need to invest more in both physical and human capital if we are to benefit collectively from the increasingly intense international competition in the markets for labor-intensive goods. (Leamer 1993, p. 120)

While these responses are important, they are not enough, and to some extent they may not even work without deeper changes in the U.S. and world economies. For example, the use of Mexico as an export platform to third countries (other than the United States or Canada) is limited by the tendency of other regions (especially Europe and East Asia) to form trading blocs of their own. In addition, while it is all well and good to improve the education and training of the U.S. labor force, it is risky to assume that better-prepared workers will automatically find better jobs that utilize their higher skills. Supply does not necessarily create its own demand. Moreover, Mexicans and other low-wage workers can be trained better too, and they will continue to compete with U.S. workers even if the latter increase their skills.

It is too late to turn back the clock and re-erect large barriers to trade with Mexico and other low-wage countries. Global integration is an inevitable tendency in a world where technological revolutions have virtually eliminated barriers to international communications and transportation. The challenge that lies before us is how to make this process work in the interest of the majority of the people in the United States, Mexico, Canada, and other countries. The solution to this challenge is not easy, but the ways to achieve it are fairly clear. The first key is to harmonize social standards upward across countries at the same time as trade and investment flows are liberalized; the second is to ensure a macroeconomic environment of sustainable growth with full employment.[52] While the tendency toward greater integration is probably inevitable, this does not mean that the integration process cannot be slowed down and regulated so as to minimize the impact on people's lives.

Standard economic theory implies that international trade and investment flows can sometimes be *socially excessive* in the presence of various sorts of "market failures" that make the private returns to those flows exceed the social net benefits. One important area of market failures is the inadequate provision of needed public goods (such as sanitation or education) in Mexico. By failing to tax foreign investors to pay for such needed public goods in export zones, the government of Mexico effectively subsidizes the foreign investors, as compared to the costs they would have to bear if they made similar investments in the United States or Canada. Another important area of market failures is environmental externalities. If Mexico either lacks or does not enforce adequate environmental regulations, firms producing for export do not pay the full social costs that are created by their production activities, and this again is an implicit subsidy vis-à-vis production located in the United States or Canada. (Even though environmental protection in these countries is far from perfect, it is generally conceded to be better enforced there than in Mexico.) Last but not least, the lack of adequate workplace safety and health regulation, the tacit allowance of child labor, and the failure of Mexican minimum wages to rise in proportion to productivity growth all effectively subsidize the transfer of jobs to Mexico. In this regard, the tight control of the Mexican ruling party over the labor movement, and the consequent inability of Mexican workers to freely organize independent trade unions, while not itself a "market failure," nevertheless contributes to the low wages and working conditions that have been so attractive to foreign investors (see Friedman 1992).

Based on these considerations, it is reasonable to conclude that an agreement that significantly liberalizes trade and investment, without raising or harmonizing international social standards in all these other areas, promotes a socially excessive amount of increased economic integration. For this reason, it is entirely appropriate to reopen discussion of the social dimension of NAFTA and to move toward a more comprehensive form of social and political integration in North America. Of course, we cannot expect Mexico to upgrade its wages or standards to U.S. or Canadian levels overnight, and ultimately any decisions about social conditions in Mexico should be for the Mexican people to make through freely elected representatives (a step that in turn requires political reform to establish true multiparty democracy). But agreements should be reached, with the same force as NAFTA itself, on long-term goals for the harmonization of social standards and human rights in North America, and for short-term measures to move in that direction on a definite timetable (and in parallel with the removal of barriers to trade and investment). As an example, it is certainly infeasible to raise Mexico's minimum wage to current U.S. or Canadian levels in the immediate future; but there is no reason real minimum wages in all three countries could not be indexed to productivity growth, after being rebased at levels that would eliminate any real reductions that occurred during the 1980s (under Ronald Reagan in the United States and during the debt crisis in Mexico).[53]

The discussion of the macroeconomic problems of Mexico earlier in this chapter also highlights the importance of reversing the excessively contractionary biases of fiscal and monetary policies in all three NAFTA countries in recent years.[54] The adjustments and dislocations that economic integration inevitably causes are certainly easier to bear in an economy in which full employment and rapid growth allow workers who lose jobs to find new ones quickly, and without significant losses in pay. While economists traditionally like to separate issues of trade liberalization and macroeconomic policy, in political economy terms (and in reality) they cannot be separated. Certainly, public support for integration schemes like NAFTA would be much higher if unemployment and wage cuts were not chronic fears of average workers. Even the budgetary ability of the NAFTA governments to pay for the social costs of adjustment and to remedy the market failures discussed above would be much greater in an atmosphere of high employment and robust income growth.

Shifting macroeconomic policy making in a more pro-growth direction would not be easy to achieve, given the present hegemony of financial interests in determining monetary policies in all the NAFTA member countries. At the time of this writing (1994), the U.S. Federal Reserve Board was raising interest rates as a supposed preemptive strike against an as yet imperceptible threat of future inflation—and higher U.S. interest rates were putting pressure on the Mexican peso as foreign investors began to move funds out of Mexico and back to the United States. If anything, the NAFTA provisions that liberalize financial movements and financial services in North America will only heighten the veto power of big financiers, who can threaten to pull capital out of any country whose policies they do not like. Nevertheless, it is imperative for industrial and labor interests to recapture control of macroeconomic policy making in order to restore emphasis on the goals of full employment and sustained growth.

Finally, it is important to redefine the concept of sustainable growth to incorporate environmental and other social concerns, as well to imply the absence of accelerating inflation. In this respect, the harmonization of North American labor and environmental standards is consistent with the goal of achieving sustainable economic growth, not opposed to it. NAFTA as it stands will probably be disappointing even in terms of conventional growth criteria, and it promises to impose a lot of painful adjustments on the populations of all the countries involved. NAFTA accompanied by the kinds of reforms advocated here could bring true benefits to all three countries.

Notes

1. According to the U.S. International Trade Commission, "in 1989 under the Generalized System of Preferences, about 9 percent of the value of Mexican exports to the

United States entered free of duty and some 45 percent of Mexico's exports to the United States . . . [was] subject to duties only on the portion of their value not produced in the United States" (1991, p. 2-2).

2. In principle these provisions apply equally to all three nations, but in practice they are mainly intended to force Mexico to revise its laws so as to provide more favorable treatment for foreign investors (and to prevent Mexico from changing those laws again in the future).

3. The liberalization of so-called trade in services is largely an opening up of the Mexican service sector to foreign investment by U.S. and other foreign corporations. Foreign multinationals will be able to enter into Mexican sectors, including communications, transportation, insurance, banking, and other financial services. These types of "exports of services" do not necessarily generate as many jobs in the United States as equivalent amounts of exports of merchandise.

4. Since the FTA with Canada was already in effect, and most of the controversy focused on the consequences of extending the FTA to incorporate Mexico, this chapter will focus mainly on the U.S.-Mexican relationship.

5. The labor side agreement in particular has enforcement provisions only for a limited range of issues, not including union organizing rights, and these provisions contain so many cumbersome procedures and wide-open loopholes that effectively no country could ever be penalized unless it volunteered to be penalized. See Levinson (1993) for details.

6. First and foremost was the spectacle of Bill Clinton winning approval of an agreement originally negotiated by the man he had defeated for the presidency. In addition, the pro-NAFTA forces included major corporate lobbyists, some Latino community groups, mainstream environmentalists, and many intellectuals concerned with Mexico's development. On the other side, labor unions were strongly opposed, as were more activist environmental groups and many consumer advocates. Some of the most prominent opponents were Ralph Nader and Jesse Jackson on the left and H. Ross Perot and Patrick Buchanan on the right. For a more detailed survey of the NAFTA political debate, see Cohen, Paul, and Blecker (1995, chapter 13).

7. See chapters 1 and 2 in this book for critical perspectives on these theories and alternative views.

8. See, for example, Bhagwati (1994), who also argued that the U.S. negotiating agenda in the NAFTA negotiations was often driven more by corporate interests than by free trade principles.

9. For detailed surveys of this literature, see Brown, Deardorff, and Stern (1992b); Lustig, Bosworth, and Lawrence (1992); Schoepfle (1993); Spriggs and Stanford (1993); U.S. Congress, Congressional Budget Office (1993a); U.S. Congress, Joint Economic Committee (1993); and U.S. International Trade Commission (1992a, 1992b).

10. Although Hufbauer and Schott (1992, 1993) put a lot of emphasis on their separate estimates of how U.S. exports to Mexico and imports from Mexico will increase as a result of "NAFTA and related reforms," a careful reading of their method shows that they basically force the exports to increase by exactly $9 billion more than the imports.

11. Mexico has had a large negative change in its current account balance since 1990, which would appear to confirm the hypothesis of large "excess" net capital inflows. However, since Mexico's overall current account deficit is more than double its bilateral deficit with the United States, it is evident that much less than three-quarters of the increased net capital inflows is being used to purchase imports from the United States. For further discussion of Mexico's current account deficit, see the next section of this chapter.

12. The first estimate of the direct foreign investment outflow is based on the analogy that Mexico's joining NAFTA resembles low-wage European countries' (such as Ireland

and Spain) joining the European Community (EC). The second estimate comes from a multivariate regression analysis of the determinants of U.S. direct foreign investment in a sample of twenty-three countries. These two methods give Koechlin and Larudee their "high" and "low" estimates of the increased direct foreign investment due to NAFTA, respectively.

Then, two alternative methods are used to deduce the employment effects of the direct foreign investment outflow. First, the authors use an employment multiplier of one job for every $108,500 of investment, based on the capital/labor ratio in U.S. manufacturing. Second, the authors use a figure of one job lost for every $120,000 of outward direct foreign investment, derived from estimates in Glickman and Woodward (1989). Each of these methods is then applied to both the high and the low estimates of the direct foreign investment effect.

13. In their technical working paper, Koechlin and Larudee justify this assumption by arguing that "when the elimination of trade restrictions allows firms to serve a large market from a low cost site abroad, it is reasonable to assume that DFI [direct foreign investment] is a substitute for investment at home . . ." (1992b, p. 9). Koechlin and Larudee do not present any empirical estimates of the relationship between investment outflows and domestic investment to back up this assertion.

14. However, these authors do not consider the diversion of U.S. exports to other countries or U.S. domestic shipments into exports to Mexico, which reduces some of the gains from increases in the latter.

15. All the predicted employment effects in Chimerine and Cohen (1992) assume a jobs multiplier of 25,000 jobs per $1 billion of exports or import-competing production. The ranges of estimates come from high and low alternative scenarios of the trade effects of NAFTA.

16. This discussion relies on the summary of the INFORUM model by Shiells and Shelburne (1992).

17. A CGE model represents an entire economy through a series of equations representing supply and demand for different goods and factors of production, as well as equilibrium conditions in which supplies and demands must be equalized. If factor prices are assumed to be flexible, then factor markets will clear with all resources (including labor) fully employed. However, it is also possible to have factor price rigidities, such as for wages, in which case factor markets can clear by quantity adjustment (e.g., of the level of employment).

18. In order for NAFTA to cause U.S. employment to increase by 2.8 million jobs, the U.S. trade balance with Mexico would have to increase by about $112 billion, assuming the jobs multiplier of 25,000 jobs per $1 billion of traded goods used by Chimerine and Cohen (1992). This figure ($112 billion) is almost as large as the entire U.S. trade deficit with all countries in 1993 ($132 billion), and far more than the total amount of U.S. trade with Mexico (about $82 billion for exports and imports combined in 1993).

19. Note that, for scenarios 1 and 2, which assume the same market structure (perfect competition with constant returns to scale), the jobs created by NAFTA jump from a mere 92,000 to 2.161 *million* merely by adding NTB removal into the simulation. The U.S. International Trade Commission report remarked, with some understatement, "It would therefore be inappropriate to place great emphasis on the upper-bound U.S. employment effects from this study" (1993, chapter 2, p. 3, n. 12).

20. The credible estimates do not include those of Choate (1993), who claims that 6 million U.S. manufacturing production workers are "at risk" of losing jobs as a result of NAFTA simply because their industries have a large proportion of labor costs. See Schoepfle (1993, pp. 120–22) for a critical evaluation of this study.

21. This figure is obtained by assuming that the increase in Mexican exports due to

NAFTA can be predicted from the difference between the average export growth of countries that relaxed "previously severe restriction" and of countries that had "collapsed liberalization" experiments, according to an influential World Bank study (Michaely, Papageorgiou, and Choksi 1991), and assuming that three-quarters of the additional Mexican exports thus predicted will be sold in the United States.

22. At the time when NAFTA was proposed in 1990, Mexico already had a relatively open trade regime for a developing country, and there is no reason to believe that all its liberalization efforts would have collapsed if NAFTA had been rejected. Most of the cases considered in the World Bank study cited in note 21 were cases of unilateral trade liberalizations by developing nations, not cases of such countries joining free trade areas with more developed neighbors. Thus, the historical analogy upon which Hufbauer and Schott rely is likely to understate the potential export gains for Mexico from gaining preferential treatment in the U.S. market.

23. It should be noted that the Hinojosa-Ojeda and McCleery model (1992) contains a specification of labor migration that heavily influences the results. In the case of the Faux and Spriggs simulation (1991), the outflow of capital to Mexico induces some Mexican migrant workers to return to (or remain in) Mexico, thus causing a shortage of low-wage workers in the United States. Apparently, this accounts for a large part of the shift of 550,000 U.S. workers from the high-wage to the low-wage category. However, this result at least demonstrates the sensitivity of CGE models to alternative assumptions imposed by the researchers. See below for further discussion of CGE models that do not allow for capital mobility.

24. Manufacturing employment was just under 18 million workers as of 1993, according to data in U.S. Council of Economic Advisors (1994, table B-44, p. 318).

25. In this theory, the "scarce factor of production" is defined as the input that is *relatively* least abundant in a country. Even though nonprofessional, nontechnical workers are actually a majority of the U.S. labor force, they are relatively scarce in the United States because the United States has relatively more of other factors of production (including physical capital, professional and technical workers, and certain natural resources) than Mexico.

26. Leamer (1993) also estimates probable income gains for professional and technical workers and capital owners, but these gains are smaller than the losses to other workers, indicating a net loss to the United States. Leamer attributes this net loss to a fall in the U.S. terms of trade, rather than to trade liberalization per se.

27. Technically, what Leamer (1993) does is estimate the factor intensities of various goods for three factors (capital, professional and technical labor, and other labor) in these thirteen countries, and then use these factor intensities to estimate how the factor prices are affected by changes in the goods prices as labor-intensive products become relatively cheaper.

28. Brown, Deardorff, and Stern have published several versions of their results, with slight differences, but none that affect the points discussed here. The Bachrach and Mizrahi (1992) model is essentially the same as the KPMG Peat Marwick (1991) study. See Schoepfle (1993) for a comprehensive survey.

29. To realize just how small these wage increases are, consider a worker who works 2,000 hours per year at an hourly rate of $15, for an annual salary of $30,000. Using the highest estimate from the INFORUM report of a 0.28 percent increase, this would add up to $84 per year (after ten years). Using the lower estimate from Bachrach and Mizrahi of 0.02 percent, the increase would be only $6 per year.

30. In fact, the wage gains from trade liberalization (tariffs and NTBs) with Mexico alone are zero; only when direct foreign investment to Mexico is added into the model does a positive wage gain (of 0.1 percent) emerge without Canada included in Brown et al. (1992a).

31. In another context, one of these authors (Brown 1988, p. 354) has admitted that CGE models often imply implausibly large terms-of-trade effects, which swamp other effects of trade liberalization.

32. Brown et al. (1992a) assume that all the increased direct foreign investment in Mexico as a result of NAFTA comes from the thirty-one other countries (non–NAFTA members) in their model, but not from the United States, with which Mexico has three-quarters of its trade and with which it is signing a free trade agreement. Bachrach and Mizrahi (1992) assume a 10 percent increase in the Mexican capital stock, part of which represents additional U.S. direct foreign investment in Mexico, but all of this increase is assumed to be diverted from U.S. direct foreign investment in other countries; none comes out of U.S. domestic investment. The INFORUM report does not consider direct foreign investment flows.

33. Brown et al. state that "the existing models are poorly designed to analyse international and intersectoral capital flows . . ." (1992b, p. 1509). This begs the question of why greater efforts were not made to remedy this deficiency when the issue of foreign investment effects is so central to the subject of the studies—and when so much ingenuity was devoted to other aspects of the models (such as incorporating Krugman-style monopolistic competition with scale economies). For models that do consider capital flows from the United States to Mexico, see Faux and Spriggs (1991), McCleery (1992), Stanford (1993), and U.S. Congress, Congressional Budget Office (1993b).

34. Stanford's model also includes other innovative features, such as a variable measuring labor standards, a bargaining-strength approach to wage determination, Keynesian independent investment functions, and less than full employment.

35. In what he calls his "neoclassical" case, Stanford (1993) assumes full employment with flexible, market-clearing wages; investment determined by savings; and no capital outflows from the United States or Canada to Mexico (but Mexico gets additional foreign capital from other countries). In this scenario, there is a small but positive wage gain of 0.12 percent for U.S. workers. Interestingly, Mexico gains less in this scenario than in the NAFTA base case (Mexican GDP rises by only 2.8 percent, and wages by only 3.8 percent). These are qualitatively similar to the predictions of Brown et al. (1992a) and Bachrach and Mizrahi (1992).

36. All these changes are comparative static effects in a model calibrated with 1988 data.

37. One could thus say that Stanford's model shows very substantial gains for Mexico at the expense of fairly minimal sacrifices for American workers (although the losses for Canadian workers are somewhat larger, as their wages fall by 1.67 percent).

38. However, one should recognize that Mexican real wages did fall by as much as 30 to 50 percent in the debt crisis of the early 1980s, so that swings of this magnitude would not be unprecedented there. See Lustig (1992).

39. For other related models, see Hinojosa-Ojeda and McCleery (1992) and Hinojosa-Ojeda and Robinson (1991).

40. Like Brown et al. (1992a) and Bachrach and Mizrahi (1992), Robinson, Burfisher, Hinojoso-Ojeda, and Thierfelder (1993) assume away the possibility that Mexico could attract some investment out of the United States as a result of NAFTA. In Robinson et al., NAFTA is said to generate extra investment in Mexico, but the extra investment does not come from anywhere—not from the United States, not from thirty-one other countries, and not from U.S. direct foreign investment in other countries.

41. For an account of Mexico's economic restructuring in the 1980s, see Lustig (1992).

42. Comparing Table 5.3 with Table 5.5 below, it is evident that there is significant underreporting of exports in Mexico, since the *total* value of exports reported by Mexico

(to all countries) in recent years is often less than the value of the imports that *the United States alone* reports receiving from Mexico.

43. Portfolio investments are increases in Mexican financial liabilities to foreigners, such as through bank loans and foreign purchases of Mexican stocks and bonds. Direct investments are acquisitions of controlling interests in business firms operating in Mexico, which may be either in manufacturing, in services, or in other activities.

44. Although that regime began to falter in the mid-1970s, it was temporarily rescued in the late 1970s by the exploitation of newly discovered oil deposits at a time when world oil prices were at a record high. Mexico also borrowed heavily in the late 1970s to finance government deficits, counting on future oil export earnings to service the debt.

45. InterPress Service/Spanish (1994), quoting statistics from the Mexican National Statistics Institute also showing a 14.9 percent decline in the number of salaried workers in manufacturing between 1992 and 1993.

46. The following argument was suggested by Ros (1993).

47. I am indebted to Jaime Ros for suggesting this point.

48. According to the World Bank (1993, table 27, p. 291), Mexico's birthrate fell from 48 per 1,000 population in 1970 to 28 in 1991. Also, Mexico's total fertility rate—the number of children born to a typical woman if she lives to the end of her childbearing years—fell from 6.5 in 1970 to 3.2 in 1991, and is projected to fall further, to 2.4 in 2000.

49. These figures jumped up in the early 1990s as the Mexican peso appreciated in real terms (see Table 5.5, above). A few years earlier, Mexico's per capita GNP was on the order of one-tenth of U.S. GNP, and its manufacturing hourly compensation was as low as one-twelfth in 1988. If the peso depreciates in the future, Mexican relative wages will fall again.

50. The traditional theory discussed here is based on the Ricardian theory of trade, as expounded, for example, in Krugman and Obstfeld (1994, chapter 2). Critiques of this theory can be found in Brewer (1985) and in Daly and Cobb (1989). See chapter 3 in this book for further discussion of the connection between trade and wages.

51. See Blomstrom and Wolff (1994), who found that labor productivity in many manufacturing industries in Mexico was well over half of U.S. productivity by 1984, well before the recent boom in export-oriented foreign investment in Mexican manufacturing.

52. The "social NAFTA" package described above, in the discussion of Stanford (1993), is a good example of how progressive social policies and expansionary macroeconomic policies can be combined to cushion the shocks of economic integration in North America and to generate mutual benefits for workers in all three NAFTA countries.

53. For a specific proposal on minimum wage regulations for NAFTA, see Rothstein (1993).

54. While the large U.S. budget deficits are frequently interpreted as a sign that U.S. fiscal policy is highly expansionary, in fact the real impact of fiscal policy on the U.S. economy has been quite contractionary in the early 1990s. See Eisner (1994) for a thorough account of these issues.

Bibliography

Alliance for Responsible Trade, Citizens Trade Campaign, and the Mexican Action Network on Free Trade. 1993. "A Just and Sustainable Development Initiative for North America." Washington, DC: Development GAP (September).

Bachrach, Carlos, and Lorris Mizrahi. 1992. "The Economic Impact of a Free Trade Agreement between the United States and Mexico: A CGE Analysis." In *Economy-*

Wide Modeling of a FTA with Mexico and a NAFTA with Canada and Mexico. USITC Publication No. 2508. Washington, DC: U.S. International Trade Commission (May).

Bhagwati, Jagdish N. 1994. "Interview: Which Way? Free Trade or Protection?" *Challenge,* Vol. 37 (January–February), pp. 17–24.

Blecker, Robert A. 1993. "Effects of the North American Free Trade Agreement on American Labor." Testimony before the U.S. Senate, Committee on Labor and Human Resources, October 13.

Blecker, Robert A., and William E. Spriggs. 1992. "Manufacturing Employment in North America: Where the Jobs Have Gone." Briefing Paper. Washington, DC: Economic Policy Institute (October).

Blomstrom, Magnus, and Edward N. Wolff. 1994. "Multinational Corporations and Productivity Convergence in Mexico." In William J. Baumol, Richard R. Nelson, and Edward N. Wolff, eds., *Convergence of Productivity: Cross-National Studies and Historical Evidence.* New York: Oxford University Press.

Brewer, Anthony. 1985. "Trade with Fixed Real Wages and Mobile Capital." *Journal of International Economics,* Vol. 18, pp. 177–86.

Brown, Drusilla K. 1988. "Trade Preferences for Developing Countries: A Survey of Results." *Journal of Development Studies,* Vol. 24, No. 3 (April), pp. 335–63.

———. 1992. "The Impact of a North American Free Trade Area: Applied General Equilibrium Models." In Nora Lustig, Barry P. Bosworth, and Robert Z. Lawrence, eds., *North American Free Trade: Assessing the Impact.* Washington, DC: Brookings Institution.

Brown, Drusilla K., Alan V. Deardorff, and Robert M. Stern. 1992a. "A North American Free Trade Agreement: Analytical Issues and a Computational Assessment." *World Economy,* Vol. 15, pp. 11–30.

———. 1992b. "North American Integration." *Economic Journal,* Vol. 102 (November), pp. 1507–18.

Business Week. 1994 (April 11).

Caves, Richard E., Jeffrey A. Frankel, and Ronald W. Jones. 1993. *World Trade and Payments: An Introduction,* 6th ed. New York: HarperCollins.

Chimerine, Lawrence, and Robert Cohen. 1992. *NAFTA: Making It Better.* Washington, DC: Economic Strategy Institute.

Choate, Pat. 1993. *Jobs at Risk: Vulnerable U.S. Industries and Jobs under NAFTA.* Washington, DC: Manufacturing Policy Project (April).

Cohen, Stephen D., Joel R. Paul, and Robert A. Blecker. 1995. *Understanding U.S. Foreign Economic Policy.* Boulder, CO: Westview Press.

Daly, Herman E. 1993. "The Perils of Free Trade." *Scientific American* (November), pp. 24–29.

Daly, Herman E., and John B. Cobb. 1989. *For the Common Good.* Boston: Beacon Press.

Davis, Bob. 1992. "Sweetheart Deals: Pending Trade Pact with Mexico, Canada Has a Protectionist Air." *Wall Street Journal* (July 22), p. A1.

Dornbusch, Rudiger. 1991. "US-Mexico Free Trade: Good Jobs at Good Wages." Testimony before the Subcommittee on Labor-Management Relations and Employment Opportunities, Committee on Education and Labor, U.S. House of Representatives, April 30.

Eisner, Robert. 1994. *The Misunderstood Economy: What Counts and How to Count It.* Boston: Harvard Business School Press.

Faux, Jeff, and Thea M. Lee. 1992. "The Effect of George Bush's NAFTA on American Workers: Ladder Up or Ladder Down?" Briefing Paper. Washington, DC: Economic Policy Institute (July).

Faux, Jeff, and William Spriggs. 1991. "U.S. Jobs and the Mexico Trade Proposal." Briefing Paper. Washington, DC: Economic Policy Institute.

Friedman, Sheldon. 1992. "NAFTA as Social Dumping." *Challenge,* Vol. 35 (September– October), pp. 27–32.

Glickman, Norman J., and Douglas P. Woodward. 1989. *The New Competitors: How Foreign Investors Are Changing the U.S. Economy.* New York: Basic Books.

Grossman, Gene M., and Alan B. Krueger. 1993. "Environmental Impacts of a North American Free Trade Agreement." In Peter M. Garber, ed., *The Mexico-U.S. Free Trade Agreement.* Cambridge, MA: MIT Press.

Hinojosa-Ojeda, Raúl A., and Robert K. McCleery. 1992. "U.S.-Mexico Interdependence, Social Pacts and Policy Alternatives: A Computable General Equilibrium Approach." In Jorge Bustamante, Clark W. Reynolds, and Raúl A. Hinojosa-Ojeda, eds., *U.S.-Mexico Relations: Labor Market Interdependence.* Stanford, CA: Stanford University Press.

Hinojosa-Ojeda, Raúl A., and Sherman Robinson. 1991. "Alternative Scenarios of U.S.-Mexico Integration: A Computable General Equilibrium Approach." Working Paper No. 609. Berkeley: University of California, Department of Agricultural and Resource Economics (April).

Hufbauer, Gary Clyde. 1993. "NAFTA & U.S. Jobs." Paper presented at NAFTA Summit: Beyond Party Politics, Conference sponsored by The Brookings Institution, The Center for Strategic and International Studies, and The Fraser Institute, Washington, DC, June 28–29.

Hufbauer, Gary Clyde, and Jeffrey J. Schott. 1992. *North American Free Trade: Issues and Recommendations.* Washington, DC: Institute for International Economics.

———. 1993. *NAFTA: An Assessment.* Washington, DC: Institute for International Economics.

Interindustry Economic Research Fund, Inc. (INFORUM). 1990. *Industrial Effects of a Free Trade Agreement between Mexico and the USA.* Research Report. Washington, DC: U.S. Department of Labor, Bureau of International Labor Affairs, Clopper Almon, principal investigator.

International Monetary Fund. 1993. *Balance of Payments Statistics Yearbook.* Washington, DC: IMF.

———. 1994. *International Financial Statistics.* Washington, DC: IMF (April, May, October).

InterPress Service/Spanish (Peace Net). 1994. "More Than a Half Million Workers Lost Manufacturing Jobs in 1993." Mexico City (March 10).

Koechlin, Timothy, and Mehrene Larudee. 1992a. "The High Cost of NAFTA." *Challenge,* Vol. 35 (September–October), pp. 19–26.

———. 1992b. "Effect of the North American Free Trade Agreement on Investment, Employment and Wages in Mexico and the U.S." Unpublished paper. Saratoga Springs, NY: Skidmore College and University of Massachusetts—Amherst, August.

KPMG Peat Marwick, Policy Economics Group. 1991. "The Effects of a Free Trade Agreement between the U.S. and Mexico." Washington, DC: U.S. Council of the Mexico-U.S. Business Committee.

Krugman, Paul R. 1979. "Increasing Returns, Monopolistic Competition, and International Trade." *Journal of International Economics,* Vol. 9 (November), pp. 469–79.

Krugman, Paul R., and Maurice Obstfeld. 1994. *International Economics: Theory and Policy,* 3d ed. New York: HarperCollins.

Leamer, Edward E. 1993. "Wage Effects of a U.S.-Mexican Free Trade Agreement." In Peter M. Garber, ed., *The Mexico-U.S. Free Trade Agreement.* Cambridge, MA: MIT Press.

Levinson, Jerome I. 1993. "The Labor Side Accord to the North American Free Trade Agreement: An Endorsement of Abuse of Worker Rights in Mexico." Briefing Paper. Washington, DC: Economic Policy Institute (September).

Lustig, Nora. 1992. *Mexico: The Remaking of an Economy.* Washington, DC: Brookings Institution.

Lustig, Nora, Barry P. Bosworth, and Robert Z. Lawrence, eds. 1992. *North American Free Trade: Assessing the Impact.* Washington, DC: Brookings Institution.

McCleery, Robert K. 1992. "An Intertemporal, Linked, Macroeconomic CGE Model of the United States and Mexico Focusing on Demographic Change and Factor Flows." In *Economy-Wide Modeling of a FTA with Mexico and a NAFTA with Canada and Mexico.* USITC Publication No. 2508. Washington, DC: U.S. International Trade Commission (May).

Michaely, Michael, Demetris Papageorgiou, and Armeane M. Choksi. 1991. *Lessons of Experience in the Developing World,* Vol. 7 of *Liberalizing Foreign Trade.* Oxford, England, and Cambridge, MA: Basil Blackwell for the World Bank.

Mishel, Lawrence, and Jared Bernstein. 1993. *State of Working America, 1992–93 Edition.* Armonk, NY: M. E. Sharpe.

Nasar, Sylvia. 1993. "A Primer: Why Economists Favor Free-Trade Agreement." *New York Times* (September 17), pp. A1, D5.

Pastor, Robert A. 1993. "The North American Free Trade Agreement: Hemispheric and Geopolitical Implications." Working Paper No. WP-TWH-21. Washington, DC: Inter-American Development Bank and United Nations Economic Commission for Latin America and the Caribbean (January).

Prestowitz, Clyde V. 1993. "NAFTA: Why We Hafta; How I Overcame My Doubts and Learned to Like the Pact." *Washington Post* (September 19), p. C1.

Robinson, Sherman, Mary E. Burfisher, Raúl Hinojosa-Ojeda, and Karen E. Thierfelder. 1993. "Agricultural Policies and Migration in a U.S.-Mexico Free Trade Area: A Computable General Equilibrium Analysis." *Journal of Policy Modeling,* Vol. 15, Nos. 5–6, pp. 673–701.

Roland-Holst, David, Kenneth A. Reinert, and Clinton R. Shiells. 1992. "North American Trade Liberalization and the Role of Nontariff Barriers." In *Economy-Wide Modeling of a FTA with Mexico and a NAFTA with Canada and Mexico.* USITC Publication No. 2508. Washington, DC: U.S. International Trade Commission (May).

Ros, Jaime. 1993. Presentation at Third Conference on New Directions in Analytical Political Economy, University of Vermont, Burlington (October).

Rothstein, Richard. 1993. "Setting the Standard: International Labor Rights and U.S. Trade Policy." Briefing Paper. Washington, DC: Economic Policy Institute.

Schoepfle, Gregory K. 1993. *A Review of the Assessments of the Likely Economic Impact of NAFTA on the United States.* Economic Discussion Paper No. 44. Washington, DC: U.S. Department of Labor, Bureau of International Labor Affairs (December).

Shaiken, Harley. 1990. *Mexico in the Global Economy: High Technology and Work Organization in Export Industries.* Monograph Series, No. 33. San Diego: Center for U.S.-Mexican Studies, University of California.

Shiells, Clinton R., and Robert C. Shelburne. 1992. "Research Summary: Industrial Effects of a Free Trade Agreement between Mexico and the USA." In *Economy-Wide Modeling of a FTA with Mexico and a NAFTA with Canada and Mexico.* USITC Publication No. 2508. Washington, DC: U.S. International Trade Commission (May).

Spriggs, William E., and James Stanford. 1993. "Economists' Assessments of the Likely Employment and Wage Effects of the North American Free Trade Agreement." *Hofstra Labor Law Journal,* Vol. 10, No. 2, pp. 495–536.

Stanford, Jim. 1993. *Estimating the Effects of North American Free Trade: A Three-*

Country General Equilibrium Model with "Real-World" Assumptions. Ottawa: Canadian Centre for Policy Alternatives (September).

Swoboda, Frank. 1994. "Xerox Workers Take a Wage Cut: Union Makes Other Concessions to Gain Job Security at N.Y. Plant." *Washington Post* (June 9), p. D11.

U.S. Congress, Congressional Budget Office. 1993a. "Estimating the Effects of NAFTA: An Assessment of the Economic Models and Other Empirical Studies." CBO Paper. Washington, DC: CBO (June).

————. 1993b. *A Budgetary and Economic Analysis of the North American Free Trade Agreement.* Washington, DC: U.S. Government Printing Office (July).

U.S. Congress, Joint Economic Committee. 1993. *Potential Economic Impacts of NAFTA: An Assessment of the Debate.* Staff Study. Washington, DC: JEC (October).

U.S. Congress, Office of Technology Assessment. 1992. *U.S.-Mexico Trade: Pulling Together or Pulling Apart?* Washington, DC: U.S. Government Printing Office.

U.S. Council of Economic Advisors. 1994. *Economic Report of the President, 1994.* Washington, DC: U.S. Government Printing Office.

U.S. Department of Commerce, Bureau of Economic Analysis. *Survey of Current Business* (various issues). Washington, DC: U.S. Government Printing Office.

U.S. Department of Labor, Bureau of Labor Statistics. 1992. "International Comparisons of Hourly Compensation Costs for Production Workers in Manufacturing, 1991." Report No. 825. Washington, DC: BLS (June).

U.S. International Trade Commission. 1991. *The Likely Impact on the United States of a Free Trade Agreement with Mexico.* USITC Publication No. 2353. Washington, DC: USITC (February).

————. 1992a. *Economy-Wide Modeling of the Economic Implications of a FTA with Mexico and a NAFTA with Canada and Mexico.* Report on Investigation No. 332-317. USITC Publication No. 2516. Washington, DC: USITC (May).

————. 1992b. *Economy-Wide Modeling of the Economic Implications of a FTA with Mexico and a NAFTA with Canada and Mexico.* Addendum to the Report on Investigation No. 332-317. USITC Publication No. 2508. Washington, DC: USITC (May).

————. 1993. *Potential Impact on the U.S. Economy and Selected Industries of the North American Free-Trade Agreement.* USITC Publication No. 2596. Washington, DC: USITC (January).

World Bank. 1988. *World Development Report 1988.* New York: Oxford University Press.

————. 1993. *World Development Report 1993.* New York: Oxford University Press.

PART III
Macroeconomic Perspectives

CHAPTER SIX

The Trade Deficit
and U.S. Competitiveness

Robert A. Blecker

Introduction

The U.S. merchandise trade balance soared to $132 billion in 1993, the highest level since the record of $160 billion in 1987.[1] Although the large trade deficits of the late 1980s were widely attributed to an overvalued dollar, the dollar has depreciated substantially since that time. In this context, the persistence of relatively large trade deficits once again raises the question of whether there is an underlying structural decline in competitiveness about which American policy makers should be concerned.

While mainstream economists are divided on whether the U.S. economy has suffered a decline in competitiveness in any sense, they almost unanimously deny that any such decline could be related to the origins and persistence of the trade deficit. Competitiveness cannot matter to the trade balance, we are told, because "the trade deficit is a macroeconomic phenomenon." Based on this premise, economists generally attribute the trade deficit to the fiscal deficit, the (allegedly) low private saving rate, the exchange value of the dollar, mismatched business cycles at home and abroad, the attractiveness of the United States for foreign investment, and virtually any other macroeconomic cause—anything, that is, but the competitiveness of the nation's industries.

All these conventional macroeconomic causes of the trade deficit are genuine and important, although the precise degree to which each of them matters can be debated. Indeed, it is correct that the trade balance is a macroeconomic variable. Where the conventional wisdom has a blind spot, however, is in denying that "structural" factors such as industrial competitiveness

This chapter summarizes and extends the arguments in the author's previous Economic Policy Institute book (Blecker 1992a); portions of that book are reproduced by permission of M. E. Sharpe, Inc. The author would like to thank participants in conferences at Columbia University and the University of Notre Dame for comments on earlier drafts of this chapter.

can have a macroeconomic impact. This chapter argues that macroeconomic and structural explanations of the trade deficit are not inconsistent with each other, and that the conception of macroeconomics should be broadened to incorporate those structural problems that have some impact at the aggregate level.

When economists say that any explanation of the trade deficit must be macroeconomic, then, they are right, but that does not necessarily mean that the causation of the trade deficit can be attributed entirely to macroeconomic *policies* (especially just U.S. budget deficits) or even to national saving and investment *behavior,* more broadly defined. Macroeconomics is simply the study of economic aggregates and economywide averages. It includes such factors as productivity growth, labor cost trends, prevalence of trade barriers, preferences for home versus foreign products, and other aspects of what most people would consider competitiveness. "Structural" explanations of the trade deficit are therefore not antithetical to macroeconomic explanations and, indeed, must ultimately find expression in a coherent macroeconomic model.

Indeed, a nation's structural characteristics determine the parameters that influence how any given set of macropolicies (both domestic and foreign) impacts on the trade balance. The point, then, is that *structural and macroeconomic explanations of the trade deficit are not mutually exclusive,* and must be combined in order to achieve a complete understanding of current trade imbalances in the U.S. economy and elsewhere.

The argument that there is no connection between the trade deficit and competitiveness is often based on the assertion that macroeconomic problems cannot be explained by microeconomic phenomena. Since the trade balance is a macroeconomic variable, it is claimed, it must be explained by macroeconomic factors such as saving and investment rates, fiscal policies, and exchange rates. These macro-level forces supposedly determine a nation's trade balance independently of industry-level performance, which merely influences the composition of the nation's exports and imports.

Such an attitude is curious in a profession in which the reigning theoretical paradigm prides itself on its methodological individualism: the view that everything in the entire economy ultimately reduces to the optimizing decisions of individual agents (such as households, workers, and business firms). Surely such a theoretical tradition should admit the possibility that structural changes at the micro level, if sufficiently widespread, could influence aggregative outcomes to some extent. Stated this way, indeed, the proposition is one that virtually all economists would be forced to accept. The question, then, is: Why is it so hard for economists to admit that the behavior of the aggregate trade balance (which surely is a macroeconomic variable) may be influenced by the shifting competitive positions of the individual business firms that either sell exports or compete with imports?

Implications of the Equilibrium Method

The reluctance to link trade balances to competitiveness rests fundamentally on the other cornerstone of the neoclassical paradigm: the insistence on using a general equilibrium model in which all markets clear via price adjustment as the benchmark for making welfare judgments and policy recommendations. Among other things, most general equilibrium models assume full employment and balanced trade. The latter assumption is justified by the notion of some sort of automatic adjustment mechanism that eliminates absolute competitive advantages and disadvantages and forces trade to follow comparative advantages. Usually, the story is told in terms of the real exchange rate's settling at a value that balances the nation's trade.

In this view, competitive problems may exist (e.g., if a nation's relative rate of productivity growth falls, or if other countries have more rapid qualitative improvement in the quality of their products), but what they affect is *the standard of living at balanced trade* (as determined by the income levels and exchange rates that would prevail in a balanced trade equilibrium).[2] For example, Hatsopoulos, Krugman, and Summers argued that the United States has a serious competitiveness problem, defined as the inability of the country to balance its trade while "achieving an acceptable rate of improvement in its standard of living" (1988, p. 299). The logic is that, if a country is not competitive, it can balance its trade only by depreciating its currency or, equivalently, by cutting its workers' real wages. Competitiveness thus influences the real income level (the purchasing power of consumers) that is consistent with balanced trade.

If a country with a trade deficit improves its competitiveness, then the degree of real currency depreciation (or wage cuts) required to balance trade in the long run is reduced, and hence the sacrifice of domestic living standards necessary to restore external balance is diminished. As three influential economists have written,

> The macroeconomic adjustment that the United States faces over the years ahead [in order to reduce the trade deficit] is *linked to the microeconomic issues of competitiveness* in particular products and the general performance of U.S. exports and import-competing industries. How well we compete will determine how far the dollar needs to fall, which in turn makes a major difference to the costs in terms of our standard of living of bringing our trade deficit down. (Dornbusch, Krugman, and Park 1989, p. 9, italics added)

In this view, micro-level policies are *essential* to alleviate the future costs of adjustment to the United States external imbalance. The more the United States can enhance the competitiveness of its own industries, as well as open up markets for its products abroad, the less the dollar and real wages will have to fall in order to eliminate the trade deficit, and the higher will be the sustainable standard of living associated with balanced trade in the long run.

To be sure, this view of competitiveness is not only logical on its own terms but actually represents a significant concession to economists who worry about the problem. Nevertheless, this approach still begs the question of what happens if the adjustments required to achieve and maintain balanced trade do not take place. What determines the trade balance in real historical time, when the actual values of economic variables are not at their hypothetical, general equilibrium levels, and there can be both unemployed resources and imbalanced trade? This question is simply ignored by economists who insist on viewing a disequilibrium phenomenon through the lens of an equilibrium theory. We need to analyze the actual causality involved in determining trade balances in economic systems that are not in a full-employment, balanced trade equilibrium, and that often show little or no persistent tendency in that direction.

Nevertheless, it is important not to lose sight of the fundamental truth that is found in the economists' view of the trade deficit. Since the trade balance *is* a macroeconomic variable, any argument that it is affected by competitiveness must show how competitive problems manifest themselves at the aggregate level. Moreover, any logically consistent theory of the trade balance must respect the famous "national income identity." This dictates that a nation's trade balance must be equal to the difference between what it saves and what it invests at home,[3] as shown in the following identity:

(1)   Trade balance = national saving – domestic investment

"National saving" in turn is the sum of private saving (of households and corporations) plus public sector saving (the government's budget surplus). If the government is running a budget deficit, then public saving is negative, and national saving is less than private saving. By separating the government budget from private saving, we can rewrite identity 1 as:

(2)   Trade balance = private saving – budget deficit – domestic investment

By itself, this identity says nothing about the *direction of causality*—which of the variables (if any) are independent causes of changes in the other variables, or whether all these variables are responding to some underlying causes that are not incorporated in the identity itself. As Richard N. Cooper has written,

> This relationship is an after the fact identity. It represents an important check on the consistency of any proposed policy, since in order to reduce the current account deficit the policy actions must also affect savings and investment in the required way. *But this accounting identity says nothing about the dynamics of the impact of policy actions on the economy.* (1987, p. 12, italics added)

Cooper's point about logical consistency is well taken: if we want to argue that structural changes in a nation's international competitive position can affect its trade balance, we must have a convincing explanation of how such changes affect national saving (relative to domestic investment) so as to satisfy identity 1 or identity 2.

Two-Way Causality

At the most general level, all the variables in the national income identity are endogenous variables that are simultaneously determined in the short-run equilibrium of the macroeconomy (which should not be confused with the long-run, full-employment, balanced trade equilibrium). Exports, imports, personal and business saving, domestic investment, government expenditures, and tax revenue are all functions of various combinations of macroeconomic variables, such as income levels, prices, exchange rates, and interest rates. These in turn are influenced, but not exclusively determined, by government fiscal and monetary policies. Even the level of the government deficit is not determined by tax and spending policies alone; it also depends on the levels of income and employment (which influence tax receipts and entitlement expenditures), as well as on the monetary policies of the Federal Reserve Board, which determine the interest rates at which the government can finance its debt (not a trivial consideration in a country with a $4 trillion debt!).

What all this means is that causality essentially runs both ways in the macro identity. Changes in domestic saving and investment behavior and fiscal policies do, of course, affect the trade balance. These factors operate partly through the level of national income, which strongly influences import demand, and partly through net foreign capital flows and exchange rate fluctuations. Changes in the competitiveness of a nation's tradable goods also affect national saving and investment, as well as exports and imports. More competitive nations earn higher incomes and employ more people, ceteris paribus, than less competitive nations, and these higher levels of income and employment translate into greater private saving and tax revenue. Competitiveness matters precisely because it affects both sides of the macro identity, not just the trade balance side.

Suppose, for example, that a country's trade performance improves as a result of innovations that give domestic products a greater competitive advantage in either quality or cost, or as a result of the opening up of a new foreign market. The immediate effect will be to increase the country's exports or reduce its imports, and thus to improve the trade balance, for any given exchange rate and level of national income. Let us trace out exactly how this will affect national saving and domestic investment.

Assuming that the country has some excess industrial capacity and less than full employment, as is normally the case, higher net export demand increases domestic output and employment. As output and employment rise, national income grows. The increased national income will be divided between higher capital and labor incomes; in general, both will increase to some extent. Now these higher incomes in turn result in higher private saving, both corporate and personal. Since corporate saving accounts form the lion's share of gross private saving in the United States, the increase in corporate profits is especially important for total saving to rise.

In addition, higher private incomes imply higher tax revenue for the government, since most taxes are proportional to either income or spending (and spending tends to rise with income). Since government expenditures are unlikely to rise when private incomes increase (and are likely to fall if higher employment lessens social welfare costs), the government budget surplus should increase (or the deficit should decrease). Thus, both parts of national saving, private and public, should benefit from greater international competitiveness.

It is also likely that business investment will be stimulated to some extent by increased consumer demand and higher capacity utilization in industry, as well as by increased corporate profitability (which provides incentives to invest and relieves potential financing constraints). Since increased domestic investment will absorb some part of the increased national saving, the net improvement in the saving-investment balance will be diminished to the extent that investment also rises. However, in a stable macroeconomic system,[4] the induced increase in domestic investment will normally be less than the induced increase in national saving (private saving plus the government surplus). This implies that the right-hand side of identity 1 should increase to some extent as national income adjusts to its new, higher level.

At the same time, some part of the increased national income will be spent on imports. This "leakage" to imports reduces but does not eliminate the positive gain in the trade balance from improved competitiveness (or access to foreign markets), since only a fraction of every dollar of increased income will be spent on imports. The greater the competitiveness of domestic products, the smaller this fraction should be.[5] Thus, an improvement in competitiveness should be expected to raise the equilibrium trade balance *and* national saving relative to domestic investment—thus increasing *both* sides of identity 1—although the net increase in the trade balance will be somewhat less than the hypothesized initial increase in exports (or decrease in imports).

In the case of a deterioration in competitiveness, this mechanism will work in reverse. Domestic output and national income will be reduced, employment will fall, and both corporate profits and workers' wages will be lower. Both private saving and government tax revenue should then be expected to fall, thus reducing national saving (by relatively more than investment falls). The trade balance will worsen, although this effect will be partially mitigated by reduced demand for imports due to lower national income. The government budget surplus will also tend to fall (the deficit to rise), creating an apparent "twin" relationship between the trade and budget deficits—but without a change in fiscal policy's being responsible.

Many analyses of trade imbalances implicitly assume full employment. For example, this is evidently assumed by McCulloch and Richardson (1986, p. 51) when they assert that improved competitiveness would mean "higher-productivity jobs" but "not necessarily more jobs." If full employment is assumed, then of course "more jobs" are ruled out. In spite of the tendency among economists to assume that there is always full employment in the "long run," however, actual advanced capitalist economies tend to oscillate between periods of relatively high and relatively low employment rather than to stay at full employment unless disturbed. In this case, better trade performance can help provide "more jobs" as well as "better jobs."

Exchange Rate Adjustment and Living Standards

In theory, the positive effects of improved competitiveness described above could be completely offset by a sufficient appreciation of the nation's currency. Indeed, this is exactly what is argued by economists who claim that competitiveness does not matter to the trade balance. Here is an example:

> The ingredients of industrial competitiveness cannot be regarded as *independent* determinants of trade performance. In particular, induced movements in exchange rates tend to offset the aggregate consequences of any improvement in industrial competitiveness. Unless national saving rises relative to the demand for funds for private investment, any increase in the competitiveness of an industry will be accommodated mainly through a *further appreciation* of the dollar. . . . (McCulloch 1986, p. 26, italics in original)

The qualifying phrase "Unless national saving rises . . ." in the last sentence of the above quotation is crucial; as explained above, this is exactly how an increase in competitiveness (or opening up of foreign markets) can improve the trade balance.

While McCulloch implies that exchange rate movements immediately offset changes in competitiveness, Robert Z. Lawrence takes the more defensible position that such adjustments occur only in the long run:

> Changes in the relative trade performance of American industries will only affect the trade balance in the short run. The trade deficit may rise temporarily, but the loss of foreign markets will put downward pressure on U.S. wages and prices, and, more important, will tend to depress the exchange value of the dollar . . . to the point where the trade deficit turns around and moves back to an equilibrium determined by the country's fundamental spending-saving behavior. (1989, p. 29)

In spite of his efforts to emphasize the long-run adjustment mechanism, however, Lawrence effectively concedes that the trade balance *is* affected by industrial competitiveness in the "short run"—defined as the period in which exchange rates have not sufficiently adjusted. Once the problem is posed in this way, however, it becomes relevant to ask: How long is the short run? How long will it take for the exchange rate to settle at its new, long-run equilibrium level, following a change in competitiveness?

In order for the exchange rate to adjust to a level that would offset competitive advantages (or disadvantages), it is necessary for exchange rate changes to be driven by the need to restore balanced trade. That is, when a country's trade balance improves, its currency will have to appreciate; when a country's trade balance worsens, its currency will have to depreciate. Before flexible exchange rates were adopted in the early 1970s, this is generally how economists anticipated that a system of flexible rates would work, but the reality has turned out to be quite different. Flexible exchange rates are determined by the conditions for *overall* balance-of-payments equilibrium, not by balanced merchandise trade or even a balanced current account (which includes trade in services, net interest payments, and unilateral transfers). This means that capital account transactions—that is, international investment, borrowing, and lending—play an important role in determining currency fluctuations.

In fact, international capital flows have turned out to be far *more* important than current account transactions (trade in goods and services) for determining exchange rates. The sheer volume of international financial flows dwarfs the value of trade flows. According to Levich, foreign exchange transactions in the three largest trading centers (London, New York, and Tokyo) alone totaled $188 billion *per day* as of March 1986, and "worldwide foreign exchange could possibly exceed $250 billion per day or more than $60 trillion per year" (1988, p. 220). In contrast, the total value of U.S. merchandise trade (exports plus imports) in 1986 was $592 billion for the entire year, or less than $2 billion per day.

It is now generally recognized that the main determinants of fluctuations in currency values, at least in the short run, are located in international financial markets, not in international goods markets. This insight led economists in the 1970s to develop theories in which underlying macroeconomic "fundamentals" (such as money supplies, budget deficits, interest rates, and inflation rates) explain changes in exchange rates. By the end of the 1980s, however, international economists had to admit that even these theories could not explain much of the volatility of exchange rates over the preceding two decades. In particular, a number of economists (e.g., Dornbusch 1988, 1989; Frankel 1990; and Krugman 1989a) have concluded that the sharp rise in the U.S. dollar in the mid-1980s went far beyond anything that could be explained by such fundamentals.

The assertion that, in the long run, the value of the dollar must adjust to offset any change in real competitive advantages seems to be based on outmoded a priori reasoning rather than on any evidence on the actual behavior of exchange rates in recent years. Certainly the experience of the 1980s suggests that the dollar can stay above a level that would be consistent with balanced trade for at least a decade. If exchange rates do not do their job, then the "short run" can be quite long in practice. If the dollar does not adjust to its hypothetical long-run equilibrium value faster than the underlying competitive conditions themselves change, then actual trade deficits can be continuously affected by those conditions for an indefinite period of time.

Moreover, *even if the nation's currency does eventually adjust to its new equilibrium value, this new value will reflect the changed competitive conditions.* This point is crucial, because the value of the nation's currency is an important determinant of its cost of living, and therefore of the purchasing power of domestic incomes. To the extent that people consume imported products, or products that are manufactured with imported inputs, a higher value of the currency means a higher standard of living for domestic residents, and a lower value means the opposite. Therefore, even if economists are optimistic about the effectiveness of exchange rate adjustment, they should still be concerned about a nation's underlying competitiveness.

That it can take a long time for the exchange rate adjustment process to work is especially significant because of its dynamic implications. *By the time the exchange rate eventually adjusts, a country is not starting from the same initial conditions as when the competitive improvement (or deterioration) originally occurred.* In the intervening years, the more competitive nation will have invested in more new capital and R&D, increased its labor productivity faster, and raised its technological advantages further, while the less competitive nation will have fallen behind in all these respects. The eventual appreciation or depreciation of the currency will not necessarily be sufficient to reverse these dynamic gains or losses, and therefore will not generally return a country's economy to the position it was in before the change in competitiveness.

The Fiscal and Trade Deficits: Twins or Cousins?

In the 1980s, it became popular to argue that the U.S. trade deficit could not result from competitive problems because it was merely a result of the federal government budget deficit. Using the macro identity, it was argued that the fiscal deficit caused a decrease in national saving, which in turn caused a nearly equal decline in the trade balance. This view was promulgated by many prominent economists, such as former Reagan economic adviser Martin Feldstein. It also appeared to be supported by some theoretical models, such as the Mundell-Fleming analysis,[6] in which a fiscal deficit crowds out an equal amount of net exports in a small country with perfect capital mobility and a flexible exchange rate.

While this so-called twin deficits view found its way into newspaper editorials and pundits' columns, in fact it always rested on shaky empirical grounds. Not that there was no connection between Reagan's budget deficit and the trade deficit in the early 1980s, but the relationship was far less than the $1 for $1 implied by the "twin deficits" terminology. A number of studies attempted to quantify the twin deficits relationship by estimating how much the increased budget deficit contributed to the increased trade deficit in the early 1980s. While some of these were advertised as supporting the twin deficits view, in fact most of the studies found at most only a partial causal connection between the rise in the U.S. federal government budget deficit and the increased U.S. trade deficit in the early 1980s.

A systematic comparison of international macroeconomic models revealed that different models constructed according to different assumptions yielded very different quantitative (and sometimes even qualitative) results about the effects of shifts in fiscal policies (see Bryant, Henderson, Holtham, Hooper, and Symansky 1988). For example, while most of the models in the study agreed that a 1 percent of GNP fiscal stimulus in the United States would lower the current account balance, estimates of the magnitude of this effect (cumulated over six years) ranged from $3 billion to $53 billion.

The model that generated the *largest* estimated effect of fiscal expansion on the trade deficit in the study by Bryant and his coauthors was the multicountry model (MCM) of the Federal Reserve Board. Helkie and Hooper (1988, p. 48) applied this model to analyze the underlying macroeconomic causes of the increased U.S. current account deficit from 1980 to 1986.[7] They estimated that U.S. fiscal expansion accounted for about a $70 billion rise in the current account deficit, or just under half of the actual increase of $143 billion, holding domestic monetary and foreign fiscal policies constant.[8] Thus, a *high-end* estimate of the twin deficits relationship is that *less than half* of the 1980–87 rise in the trade deficit can be explained by the rise in the U.S. budget deficit. Most of the other macro models surveyed by Bryant and his coauthors (1988) yielded substantially *smaller* estimates of this relationship. As Hooper concluded elsewhere,

> Fiscal policy, or the twin deficit relationship, is a significant part of the story, but evidently explains *no more than half* of the decline in our net foreign saving [i.e., current account balance]. The remaining half must be explained by fundamentals other than macroeconomic policy that led to a decline in private domestic saving relative to investment. (1989, p. 38, italics added)

In another study of international imbalances, Sachs found that "a sustained, bond-financed U.S. fiscal expansion (an increase in federal spending on goods and services [of 1 percent of gross national product]) . . . worsens the U.S. trade [current account] balance . . . by an average of 0.31 percent of GNP over three years" (1988, p. 645). Although Sachs's result is obtained from simulations of a large-scale general equilibrium model of the world economy (the McKibbin-Sachs global model; see McKibbin and Sachs 1989), an almost identical result is obtained in a much simpler econometric exercise by Bernheim (1988). Using a single-equation model in which only the budget deficit and the gross national product (GNP) growth rate (current and lagged) are used to explain the current account, Bernheim finds that "a $1 increase in government budget deficits leads to roughly a $0.30 rise in the current account deficit" (1988, p. 2) in the United

States. Sachs's and Bernheim's results imply that a $100 billion reduction in the budget deficit would eliminate only about $30 billion of the current account deficit—even assuming an offsetting monetary expansion, as Sachs does. On this basis, Sachs concluded that,

> The U.S. fiscal expansion was only *one* of the reasons for the widening of the U.S. current account deficit. Completely *eliminating* the U.S. budget deficit, other things being equal, would remove no more than half the current external gap.... Balancing the U.S. current account will therefore require policy actions or other economic events . . . beyond balancing the U.S. budget. (Sachs 1988, pp. 646–47, italics in original)

Curiously, even some economists who claim to have evidence for the twin deficits hypothesis in fact have evidence against it. For example, the study by Rosensweig and Tallman (1993) found that about 30 to 40 percent of the variation in the U.S. trade balance in the 1980s could be explained by variations in the fiscal deficit. Although these authors assert that their evidence is "consistent with . . . the typical twin deficits explanation" (Rosensweig and Tallman 1993, p. 590), it requires an incredible stretch of the English language to label a 30 to 40 percent connection "twins." To be sure, the fiscal and trade deficits were probably at least "cousins" in the mid-1980s, when both increased notably. This is the period emphasized in the studies just cited. Taking a longer historical view, these two deficits have not always been as correlated as they seemed at that time. In the next section, I examine what the longer-term record shows.

Evidence for a Secular Decline in Competitiveness

A Retrospective on the 1980s

Table 6.1 gives some perspective on the changes in the U.S. trade balance and its macroeconomic determinants in the 1980–90 period, ending before the trough of the recent recession in 1991. Data are given for 1980 and 1990, and for one intermediate year, which is either 1985 (for national income and exchange rate data) or 1987 (for trade balance data). These different break points are chosen because of the different timing of the trends in U.S. and foreign growth, in the value of the U.S. dollar, and in the trade balance. In particular, the trade balance seems to respond with a lag especially to changes in relative prices.

From 1980 to 1987, the trade balance fell by almost 4 percent of GNP by any of the three measures shown (a bit less for the total merchandise balance in current dollars, which was aided by the fall in prices of oil imports in the mid-1980s). Undoubtedly, the primary direct cause of this deterioration was the enormous rise in the real value of the dollar between 1980 and 1985,[9] which averaged about 56 percent by the Federal Reserve Board index (which empha-

Table 6.1

U.S. Trade Balance and Related Macroeconomic Indicators, 1980, 1985 or 1987, and 1990 (index numbers, 1980 = 100, except as noted)

	1980	1987	1990
Trade balance (percent of GNP)			
Merchandise[a]	−0.8%	−3.5%	−1.9%
Nonoil, nonagricultural[a]	0.5	−3.2	−1.5
Current account[b]	0.5	−3.4	−1.6

	1980	1985	1990
National incomes			
United States[c]	100	115	133
Other industrial countries[c,d]	100	112	133
Western Europe	100	108	126
Japan	100	121	153
Developing countries[e]	100	114	135
Latin America[e]	100	102	112
Real exchange rate (value of dollar)			
Federal Reserve Board G-10 Index[f,g]	100	156	102
Dallas Fed 101 Countries Index[g,h]	100	135	110
IMF Wholesale Price Index[i]	100	136	94
IMF Unit Labor Cost Index[i]	100	139	77

Sources: Trade balance data are taken from U.S. Department of Commerce, Bureau of Economic Analysis (1986), and updates in the *Survey of Current Business* (various issues). Other sources are as noted below.

[a]Trade balances measured in current dollars on a national income and product account basis.

[b]Measured by net foreign investment in the national income and product accounts.

[c]Measured by gross domestic product (GDP) in constant 1985 dollars. From Organization for Economic Cooperation and Development (1991, p. 172).

[d]Total OECD minus the United States and Turkey. Includes some countries not listed separately (Canada, Australia, New Zealand).

[e]From index in International Monetary Fund (*1991 Yearbook*, p. 163). Indexes extrapolated to 1990 at average annual rates for 1980–89. Latin America is defined as all developing countries in the western hemisphere.

[f]From U.S. Council of Economic Advisors (1991, p. 410), based on data from the Board of Governors of the Federal Reserve System.

[g]Nominal exchange rates are adjusted by CPI.

[h]Unpublished data from Federal Reserve Bank of Dallas.

[i]From International Monetary Fund (*1991 Yearbook*, pp. 110–11). The normalized unit labor cost index was used.

sizes the G-10 industrial countries and uses consumer price indexes [CPIs] to adjust for inflation), and about 35 to 38 percent by the other indexes shown. However, sluggish growth in foreign countries—especially those that traditionally bought the largest volumes of U.S. exports (Western Europe and Latin America)—also contributed substantially to the increased trade deficit in the early 1980s.

By 1990, these proximate causes of the large trade deficits had been largely reversed or eliminated. In general, foreign income growth speeded up (especially in Western Europe, but also to some extent in Japan and the developing countries). The gross domestic product (GDP) of all other industrialized countries in 1990 was 33 percent above its 1980 level—exactly the same as the U.S. GDP. Latin America, depressed by "stabilization" and "structural adjustment" policies adopted in response to the debt crisis, was the only major region (in terms of U.S. export markets) that lagged far behind U.S. growth over the whole decade (although Latin America has recovered considerably since 1990).

At the same time, the dollar fell just about as far in real terms in the late 1980s as it had risen in the early 1980s. The Federal Reserve Board's CPI-adjusted G-10 index shows the dollar back to a mere 2 percent above its 1980 level in 1990, while the broader Dallas Fed 101 Countries Index (which includes many developing country currencies, and is also CPI-adjusted) shows the dollar about 10 percent higher in 1990. Both of the International Monetary Fund (IMF) indexes show the dollar lower in 1990 than in 1980, especially when the nominal exchange rates are adjusted by normalized unit labor costs rather than by wholesale prices.

In spite of these reversals, the trade deficit remained about 2 percent of GNP worse in 1990 than it had been in 1980 by two of the measures shown (nonoil import, nonagricultural export merchandise trade—which is mostly trade in manufactures—and the current account), and about 1 percent worse for the total merchandise balance (which was helped by the declining trend in oil import prices over the whole decade). This suggests a notable structural deterioration in the U.S. trade position, centered in trade in manufactures.

Table 6.2 shows the trends in U.S. real wages and unit labor costs relative to major competitor nations from 1975 to 1990. Throughout this period, real hourly compensation in manufacturing was stagnant or falling slightly in the United States, while real hourly compensation in the other nations shown[10] continued to rise steadily. That U.S. real hourly compensation declined absolutely without achieving balanced trade suggests a particularly grave competitiveness problem by the Hatsopoulos, Krugman, and Summers (1988) definition. The United States has not been able to balance its trade in spite of *substantially reducing its standard of living* in terms of hourly labor compensation in manufacturing.[11]

U.S. (nominal) unit labor costs in manufacturing rose slightly relative to foreign unit labor costs from 1975 to 1980 in own-currency terms, but fell relatively in dollar terms due to the depreciation of the dollar in the late 1970s. U.S. unit labor costs fell relative to foreign costs throughout the 1980s in own-

Table 6.2

U.S. Real Hourly Compensation and Unit Labor Costs in Manufacturing Compared with Major Competitor Nations
(indexes, 1975 = 100)

	1975	1980	1985	1990
Real hourly compensation				
United States	100	101	102	96
Canada	100	109	115	117
Japan	100	101	107	122
Germany (West)	100	118	122	140
France	100	118	134	142
United Kingdom	100	109	116	127
Italy	100	105	111	117
Korea (South)	100	167	222	428
Nominal unit labor costs (U.S. relative to other countries)				
In own currencies				
Industrial countries[a]	100	103	98	87
Industrial countries[a] plus Korea and Taiwan	100	101	95	84
In U.S. dollars				
Industrial countries[a]	100	95	128	75
Industrial countries[a] plus Korea and Taiwan	100	94	124	73

Sources: Hourly compensation in national currency is from U.S. Department of Labor, Bureau of Labor Statistics (1991). Compensation in national currency was deflated by CPI from International Monetary Fund (*1991 Yearbook*, October 1991). Relative unit labor cost indexes are taken from unpublished BLS data in "Trade Weighted Output per Hour, Hourly Compensation, and Unit Labor Costs in Manufacturing, 1970–90," August 1991.

[a]Industrial countries included are Canada, Japan, Denmark, France, (West) Germany, Italy, Netherlands, Norway, Sweden, and United Kingdom.

currency terms. U.S. unit labor costs rose relative to foreign unit labor costs in dollars from 1980 to 1985 while the dollar was rising, but, by 1990, U.S. unit labor costs had fallen relative to those of the other countries in dollar terms beyond where they were in 1980. The fact that the U.S. trade balance remained in deficit by nearly 2 percent of GNP in spite of *falling* U.S. relative labor costs suggests an especially acute qualitative competitiveness problem.

The Falling Trend of the Dollar

Another perspective on U.S. competitive decline can be gained by comparing the trends in the trade balance with the trends in the exchange rate. Since the collapse of the Bretton Woods system of fixed exchange rates in 1973, the dollar has had to depreciate in real terms in order to prevent growing trade deficits—and these deficits have grown precisely whenever the dollar did not depreciate or did not depreciate sufficiently.

Figure 6.1 shows the merchandise trade balance and the current account balance, both measured as percentages of GDP.[12] Note that the current account remained balanced throughout most of the 1970s, in spite of some fluctuations. The merchandise trade balance worsened notably in the late 1970s, but this was mainly due to the rising price of oil imports (the nonpetroleum trade balance, not shown in Figure 6.1, did not have a downward trend in the 1970s). The current account balance was higher than the merchandise balance as a result of a trade surplus in services, including positive net investment income from abroad. In the 1980s, however, both balances turned sharply negative together, and the gap between them shrank as net investment income from abroad dried up (due to increasing U.S. foreign debt). By both measures, the trade deficit peaked in 1987.

In the late 1980s and early 1990s, both measures of the trade balance showed improvement as a result of two factors: the slowdown in U.S. economic growth (culminating in the 1990–91 recession), and the post-1985 depreciation of the U.S. dollar (see Blecker 1991b). However, the apparent current account surplus in 1991 was the spurious result of transfer payments received from foreign nations (especially Germany, Japan, and Saudi Arabia) to pay for Operation Desert Storm and did not reflect any permanent improvement in the U.S. trade position. Once the U.S. economy recovered from the recession (and the transfer payments ceased), the trade balance worsened again by both measures in 1992–93, with the merchandise trade deficit again reaching about 2 percent of GDP.

Figure 6.2, on page 195, shows two indexes of the real value of the dollar (these are two of the indexes also shown in Table 6.1, above). The first is the Federal Reserve Board index of the trade-weighted value of the dollar against the G-10 industrial country currencies, corrected for consumer price inflation. The second index is the IMF real effective exchange rate index, covering sixteen industrial countries and based on relative normalized unit labor costs. Both measures show the same strong rise in the dollar in 1981–85 and the same sharp decline thereafter, but the IMF index shows a more pronounced decline in the early 1990s (due to the fall in U.S. relative wages discussed earlier), while the Fed index shows the dollar stabilizing at that time.

Comparing Figure 6.2 with Figure 6.1, we see that the dollar was more or less continuously falling while the current account remained essentially balanced (or in surplus) throughout most of the 1970s. To be sure, there were current account deficits in 1971 and again in 1977–78, but they were relatively small and more than offset by surpluses in the rest of the decade—thanks to the continued depreciation of the dollar. *That a continuous real depreciation of the dollar was necessary to maintain current account balance and to keep the merchandise trade deficit from worsening indicates an underlying declining trend of U.S. competitiveness in the 1970s.*

The problem in the early 1980s was not simply that the dollar rose, but more

194

Figure 6.1. **Alternative Measures of the U.S. Trade Balance, 1970–93**

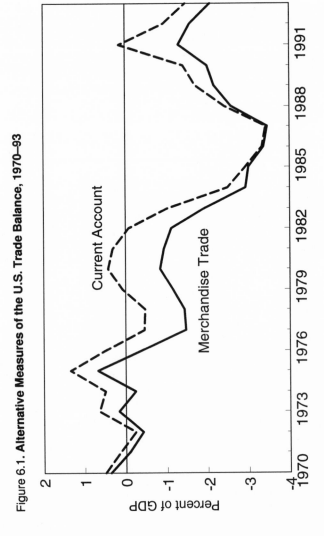

Sources: U.S. Department of Commerce, Bureau of Economic Analysis, and author's calculations.
Note: Both trade balances are measured on a national income accounts basis.
The current account is measured by net foreign investment.

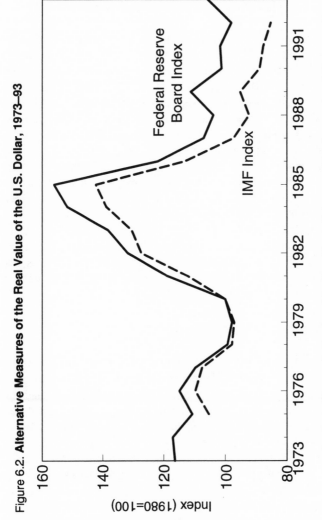

Figure 6.2. **Alternative Measures of the Real Value of the U.S. Dollar, 1973–93**

Sources: Economic Report of the President, February 1994; International Monetary Fund, *International Financial Statistics, 1994 Yearbook; and author's calculations*

precisely that *it rose when it needed to fall further.* To make this point, Figure 6.3 extrapolates the 1973–79 trend of the Fed index into the 1980–93 period, assuming a constant proportional rate of change.[13] Along this trend line, the dollar fell at an average rate of about 3 percent per year from 1971 to 1980. Extending this trend line to 1993 gives a rough indication of the exchange rate adjustment that would have been required to maintain current account balance in the 1980s.

Viewed against this benchmark, the rise in the dollar in the mid-1980s is truly astounding. From 1980 to 1985, the dollar moved in the *opposite* direction from that which would have been necessary to offset declining competitiveness. Moreover, this way of viewing the problem shows that relying on dollar depreciation to solve the trade deficit is like shooting at a moving target. Although the dollar fell to about its 1980 level in the early 1990s, it was still far above the extrapolated 1970s trend line; the dollar would have to fall by about 40 percent in real terms in order to return to that trend.

It is also important to realize that these exchange rate indexes, which emphasize industrial country currencies, do not give a complete picture of the value of the dollar. This is because a rising share of U.S. imports and of the U.S. trade deficit is accounted for by the developing nations, especially the newly industrializing countries (NICs) of East Asia and Latin American countries like Mexico. On the whole, the dollar has not depreciated as much against these countries' currencies since 1985 as it has against the industrial country currencies, and that difference may account for the shift in the composition of the U.S. trade deficit toward the NICs, as discussed below.

Income Elasticities and Time Trends

Economists have developed more rigorous methods for detecting the presence of structural competitive problems. These methods involve the statistical estimation of what are called import and export demand functions. These are mathematical expressions that show how a country's imports and exports depend on other variables such as the relative prices of home and foreign products (which are heavily influenced by exchange rates) and the income that domestic or foreign residents have to spend on imports or exports, respectively. Other variables that are thought to explain the quantities of imports and exports can also be included in these demand functions, if desired.

The use of import and export functions yields estimates of the income elasticities of U.S. import and export demand. These elasticities are the percentages by which the quantity of our imports or exports rises for a 1 percent rise in domestic or foreign income, respectively. If the income elasticity is higher for imports than for exports, this implies that the United States can maintain balanced trade only by either (1) continuously depreciating the dollar in order to keep the U.S. demand for imports from growing too fast (and to make U.S. exports grow

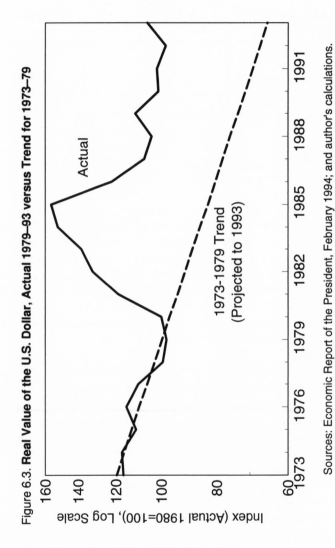

Figure 6.3. **Real Value of the U.S. Dollar, Actual 1979–93 versus Trend for 1973–79**

Sources: Economic Report of the President, February 1994; and author's calculations.

Table 6.3

Estimates of Income Elasticities of U.S. Export and Import Demand

Author(s)	Exports	Imports
Krugman and Baldwin (1987)	2.42	2.87
Helkie and Hooper (1988)[a]	2.19	2.11
Cline (1989)	1.70	2.44
Lawrence (1990)[b]	1.60	2.47
Blecker (1992b)	1.67	2.68
New estimates for this chapter[b]	1.38	2.22

Sources: See the bibliography for references to older studies. See the appendix to this chapter for an explanation of new estimates for this chapter.

[a]This model includes another variable (the ratio of U.S. to foreign capital stocks) that picks up structural trends in competitiveness.

[b]This model includes an adjustment for computer price measurement.

faster), or (2) keeping the U.S. income growth rate lower than the rest of the world's, by about the same proportion as the ratio of our income elasticities for exports and imports, if the dollar is not allowed to fall (Thirlwall 1979).

Table 6.3 gives the estimates for the income elasticities of imports and exports from a variety of recent studies, including ones done expressly for this chapter. Most of the estimates show a notably higher income elasticity of U.S. demand for imports compared with foreign demand for U.S. exports, thus confirming the existence of a competitiveness problem in the U.S. case. Of the two studies that do not find a large difference in income elasticities, at least one (Helkie and Hooper 1988) includes another variable that picks up the effects of structural competitive decline (it uses the ratio of U.S. to foreign capital stocks to represent "supply-side" conditions). The other exception (Krugman and Baldwin 1987) is the oldest of the studies in the table, and does not include data from the late 1980s.

Of the studies that do find a difference in the income elasticities, the work of Cline (1989) is especially noteworthy because it is based on a disaggregated study of U.S. trade with several other specific countries and regions. Also, Lawrence's (1990) results are important because he corrected for biases in the measurement of the "real" (inflation-adjusted) quantity of computer imports and the prices of computers. These biases are thought to exaggerate the real volume of U.S. imports to some extent.[14] For this reason, the new estimates prepared for this chapter, which are given in Table 6.3, are done with a computer correction as well.[15]

Another econometric approach involves the estimation of "time trends" in the import or export demand function. That is, it is possible to test whether imports (or exports) tend to rise (or fall) over time by a greater amount than can be explained by the observable variables such as relative prices (including exchange rate effects) and relative incomes. According to the results in Blecker (1992a, 1992b), there is fairly robust evidence for a positive time trend in U.S. demand for nonpetroleum imports. The real volume of U.S. imports (in inflation-adjusted terms) tends to grow by about 2 percent per year more than can be explained by the observable problems. Statistical problems, however, preclude any firm conclusions about a time trend for U.S. exports. These findings suggest that the greatest U.S. competitive problems lie on the import side, where qualitative improvements in foreign productive capabilities have caused a structural shift toward imports in U.S. consumers' and firms' purchasing patterns.

Income Adjustment and Absolute Advantages

What are the implications of the declining tendency of U.S. competitiveness that was identified in the previous section? One approach is to focus on the implied need for the dollar to depreciate in real terms in order to maintain balanced trade in the long run, as discussed earlier. If these hypothesized long-run adjustments do not take place, how declining competitiveness manifests itself in actuality remains to be analyzed. In this vein, another approach emphasizes the adjustment of national income levels and growth rates, assuming that real exchange rate adjustment does not take place. This alternative approach was pioneered by British Keynesian economist A. P. Thirlwall (1979) in his theory of "balance-of-payments constrained growth." The income-adjustment view has been extended recently by Dosi, Pavitt, and Soete (1990) in their work on "technological gaps" and "absolute competitive advantages." What follows is a brief effort to explain this alternative view of the international adjustment process.

Assuming that countries cannot maintain trade deficits (or surpluses) indefinitely, and that exchange rate adjustments do not necessarily operate, then relative income levels (or growth rates) are constrained in the long run by the requirements of balancing trade. The crucial constraints are the income elasticities of demand for a country's exports and imports, as discussed in the preceding section. If a country like the United States has an income elasticity of demand for its imports that is higher than its trading partners' income elasticity of demand for its exports, then the country must grow at a slower rate in order to prevent growing trade deficits with its trading partners. While macro policies can foster an "adjustment" to such a problem, they cannot overcome it. On the contrary, macro-policy responses designed to cure trade deficits—such as contractionary fiscal policies—are only likely to reinforce the tendency for slower growth in the less competitive country. Only direct efforts to address problems of relative costs and quality, as well as market access barriers, can overcome this kind of constraint.

The concept of a trade balance constraint on national income implies that the most important question for the United States is not whether it can balance its trade, but *how* it should balance its trade. One way to balance trade is to make domestic incomes and expenditures grow sufficiently slowly in order to hold down the growth of imports from the rest of the world. This is the "belt-tightening" or austerity path, and it will cut domestic living standards just as surely as a continuous real depreciation of the dollar (perhaps even more surely). Yet this is exactly what a reduction in the government budget deficit accomplishes, unless accompanied by other measures to stimulate demand. The alternative is for the United States to adopt industrial and trade policies that can relieve the trade balance constraint, combined with expansionary foreign macro policies and market-opening measures to increase demand for U.S. exports.

In their study *The Economics of Technical Change and International Trade,* Dosi, Pavitt, and Soete (1990) concluded that much international trade in manufactures is determined by the technological innovativeness of the various national firms rather than by comparative cost factors. Technological innovation includes the development of new and improved products as well as more efficient production processes (which lower costs). Countries with superior technologies in sectors such as computers, aircraft, chemicals, machinery, and scientific or medical instruments can export these goods in spite of high wages. The income-adjustment view says that such absolute technological advantages determine whether a country will have a tendency to run overall trade surpluses or deficits, and thus whether it will have a relatively loose or tight trade balance constraint on its income level and its growth rate. The wider the range of sectors in which a country has such absolute superiority, the higher are the real wages, per capita income, and growth rate that are consistent with balanced trade.

Even in this new view, adjustments of relative wages and exchange rates can still permit much trade to take place according to comparative advantages. Thus, for example, the United States will be a net importer of goods like textiles and steel in which it has lost comparative advantages (although the more productive and high-end segments of these domestic industries will remain viable). These same adjustments also allow countries with superior technologies to have higher real wages and living standards. It is precisely because their wages are higher that these countries must be net importers of goods in which their absolute productivity advantage is relatively low (i.e., in which they have a comparative disadvantage). To this extent, the "new view" accepts part of the "exchange rate adjustment view" discussed earlier. The new view adds that there is a second type of adjustment process, which is the adjustment of relative national incomes. A country that has absolute competitive advantages in a wide range of manufacturing industries will be able to grow faster with balanced trade, while a country with absolute competitive disadvantages will have to grow more slowly in order to have balanced trade.[16] Furthermore, there are positive feedbacks from rapid growth and negative feedbacks from slow growth, which tend to reinforce the initial gaps in absolute competitiveness. For example, a rapidly growing country will generally be able to sustain higher rates of saving and investment, and will thus be able to upgrade its capital equipment and raise its productivity faster. A slowly growing country will generally have low saving and investment rates, and will therefore be saddled with an aging capital stock and sluggish productivity growth. These self-reinforcing mechanisms in international competitiveness are examples of what is called *cumulative causation*—which essentially implies that it is harder for a country to catch up once it has fallen behind.

Alternative Interpretations of Declining Competitiveness

Factor Costs

The declining trends in U.S. competitiveness suggest an agenda for research to determine their sources. Judging from the data on relative wage changes and unit labor costs in Table 6.2 above, it does not appear that the United States has lost out in comparative labor cost terms, at least not compared to other industrialized countries. If anything, the United States has gained ground in this respect—at the cost of reducing its workers' ability to improve their standard of living without working more jobs or longer hours. Some authors put the blame on high capital costs, not so much for their direct effect on overall costs, but rather for their allegedly large negative impact on investment and thus on productivity growth and qualitative improvement (see, e.g., Hatsopoulos, Krugman, and Summers 1988). However, this argument requires some extreme assumptions about the importance of the cost of capital versus other factors for explaining investment— assumptions that are not robust in empirical studies that separate cost of capital factors from accelerator, profitability, and internal financial variables (see, e.g., Fazzari and Athey 1987; Fazzari, Hubbard, and Petersen 1988; Fazzari 1993).

Moreover, the causes of high capital costs in the United States in the 1980s are subject to dispute. While the traditional view ascribes higher capital costs to a low saving rate and tax disincentives, the accuracy with which the U.S. saving rate is measured has been questioned by Eisner (1991), Block (1990), and Blecker (1990, 1991a), among others. It has also been argued (by McCauley and Zimmer 1989) that the higher cost of capital in the United States is explained by differences in financial institutions and a larger risk premium on investment in the United States as compared to Japan or Germany. In addition, new theories of investment (summarized by Dixit 1992) imply that investment should be less sensitive to the cost of capital and more sensitive to the stability of the economic environment when entrepreneurs are uncertain about future returns to current investment projects and when those projects involve sunk costs—problems that are ignored in the traditional view of investment.

A Product-Cycle View

An alternative hypothesis about declining U.S. competitiveness would focus first and foremost on changes in the global pattern of technological innovation, development, and diffusion. As Krugman (1979) showed in his formalization of the product-cycle model, a country like the United States that specializes in technologically innovative manufactured products has its equilibrium wage level determined by the difference between the rate of new product innovation and the rate of technology transfer to less developed countries (LDCs). Furthermore, in a world with more than one innovator nation, each innovator gets more rents from its new products when it has a greater monopoly over new innovations.

In recent decades, the U.S. position has eroded on every front. First, the United States has clearly lost its unique dominance in the field of technological innovation. Especially Japan, but also Germany and some other European countries, have been catching up with or surpassing the United States according to various measures of technological leadership. For example, the U.S. share of total business sector R&D spending among the industrialized countries has fallen from about two-thirds in 1967 to barely over one-half in 1987, while the Japanese share soared from less than one-tenth to over one-quarter (Dosi, Pavitt, and Soete 1990, p. 45). The share of GNP devoted to nondefense R&D in the United States is only about two-thirds of the same share in Japan or (preunification) West Germany (U.S. National Science Foundation 1990).

Furthermore, as Wright (1990) points out, the structure of American industry in the postwar period was geared to a previous era (before 1940) in which the United States had a comparative advantage in heavy industrial products that were intensive in complementary inputs of capital and natural resources (including energy). Thus, American firms have been struggling to emerge from being locked into a "technological trajectory" that left them uncompetitive in a world in which comparative advantages in such products have shifted to other nations, as more abundant natural resources have been discovered and exploited abroad. In the new era, countries like Japan and West Germany succeeded precisely by developing technologies (both processes and products) that economized on energy and other natural resources. In addition, Nelson and Wright (1992) point out that many U.S. manufacturers had emphasized large-scale mass-production techniques, while high-technology industries benefited from the U.S. lead in education, research, and development. In the last few decades, trade liberalization and economic integration generally have reduced or eliminated the U.S. special advantage in large-scale production methods, while greater educational and R&D efforts in some other countries (notably Germany and Japan) have enabled them to close the gaps in many high-tech sectors.

All these factors indicate a reduced ability of the United States to gain monopoly rents from technological innovation at the front end of the product cycle. At the other end, casual empiricism suggests a tremendous speedup in the rate of diffusion or "transfer" of new technology to low-wage developing countries. The lengthy maturity phase postulated by Vernon (1966) seems to have been squeezed out, as new products quickly become standardized and their production shifts rapidly to "offshore," low-wage areas. Thus, even though the United States retains its technological edge in many product lines, it is increasingly unable to maintain domestic production of the new products (or at least, of major components of the new products) for very long. Productivity in many NICs' export industries is well over half of U.S. productivity (see, for example, Blomstrom and Wolff 1994, on Mexico), in spite of wage rates ranging from 10 to 25 percent of U.S. wages (U.S. Department of Labor 1991). The presumption from Ricardian trade theory that international wage differentials merely reflect average productivity differentials—often asserted by economists on a priori grounds—is no longer valid, at least not for tradable goods in sectors in which capital and technology are mobile (low wages in LDCs may still reflect low productivity in domestic nontradables sectors due to "technological dualism").

In this kind of global competitive environment, U.S. producers have to run faster just to stay in place, and many are giving up the chase (or rather, choosing to run it elsewhere). The character of changing global technological competitiveness can account for why the United States' greatest problem lies in an accelerating structural tendency for imports to increase. In spite of the catch-up of other nations in technological leadership, the United States still retains enough of a lead in enough areas (e.g., aviation equipment, telecommunications, and advanced computers) to keep its exports growing relatively well, provided that foreign income growth is sufficiently rapid and the dollar is not too high. There is only a comparatively slow erosion of the U.S. share of industrial country exports. However, the United States is having increasing difficulty in retaining domestic production of existing import-competing products (without sectoral protection, that is), and is even importing more and more relatively high-tech products that it might formerly have exported.

Structural Problems with Particular Countries

As the preceding discussion suggests, U.S. structural trade problems are concentrated with two groups of countries. The first group consists of countries that have caught up to the United States (or are surpassing it) in technological innovation. The second group consists of the countries that have most successfully combined relatively low wages with relatively high productivity in manufacturing assembly operations (usually through some combination of technology transfers and direct foreign investment) to gain overall competitive advantages in unit labor costs in standardized products. Even then, as discussed above, there are macroeconomic adjustment mechanisms that could come into play but do not do so automatically. Structural trade deficits will emerge, therefore, with countries in which the requisite macroeconomic adjustments are effectively blocked by state policy or institutional barriers.

A look at the data on bilateral U.S. trade balances in recent years confirms that the most persistent deficits have been with countries that match these descriptions, especially Japan and some of the rapidly industrializing nations of East Asia. Table 6.4 gives data on U.S. merchandise trade balances with the

Table 6.4

U.S. Merchandise Trade Balances by Selected Country and Region, 1980 and 1987–92 (in billions of dollars)

Country	1980	1987	1988	1989	1990	1991	1992
Western Europe	21.1	−27.5	−16.2	−4.0	2.2	14.9	3.2
EC[a]	16.5	−22.0	−11.6	−1.0	4.9	15.6	6.7
Germany	−0.4	−15.4	−12.1	−8.3	−9.7	−5.3	−8.4
Canada	−1.5	−11.6	−10.3	−8.9	−9.6	−7.1	−9.7
Japan	−10.5	−56.9	−52.6	−49.7	−41.8	−44.3	−50.5
Mexico	2.6	−5.7	−2.7	−2.5	−2.4	1.6	4.9
Latin America[b]	1.2	−12.3	−7.8	−8.7	−10.1	0.3	6.2
OPEC[c]	−41.4	−13.7	−9.2	−17.4	−24.8	−15.0	−13.0
China	2.8	−2.8	−3.4	−6.2	−10.4	−12.7	−18.3
Korea	0.2	−9.3	−9.5	−6.7	−4.5	−2.1	−2.8
Taiwan	−2.8	−17.5	−12.8	−14.5	−11.5	−10.3	−10.1
All countries[d]	−25.5	−159.6	−127.0	−115.2	−109.0	−73.8	−96.1

Source: U.S. Department of Commerce, Bureau of Economic Analysis, *Survey of Current Business* (June 1993, p. 78).

[a]European Community.

[b]Includes all western hemisphere countries except Canada.

[c]Organization of Petroleum Exporting Countries.

[d]Total, including some countries not shown separately.

country's leading trading partners and major regions of the world. The data are presented annually for the years 1987–92, with data for 1980 included for purposes of historical comparison. Not surprisingly, when the overall trade deficit peaked in 1987, the United States had deficits with every country and region shown in this table. At that time, most of the deficit could have been attributed to macroeconomic policies and exchange rates, as discussed earlier. By the early 1990s, the overall deficit had been reduced substantially. There were essentially three reasons for this adjustment: the growth slowdown and recession in the United States, the falling value of the dollar, and more rapid growth abroad (at least up to 1991). The countries and regions with which the United States still had deficits in the early 1990s, after all these macroeconomic adjustments had taken place, are therefore the ones with which the greatest structural trade problems may be inferred.

Far and away the largest and most persistent deficit is with Japan, the nation that has clearly offered the greatest challenge to American technological leadership in the postwar period. The dollar fell from 238 yen in 1985 to 128 yen in 1988; the dollar then rose only to 145 yen in 1990 before falling again to 127 yen in 1992.[17] In spite of this massive appreciation of the yen, as well as the fact that the U.S. budget deficit shrank as a percentage of the national product during most of the period 1985–90, the trade deficit with Japan fell only slightly from $56.9 billion in 1987 to a low of

$41.8 billion in 1990, before rising again to $50.5 billion in 1992.

In contrast, the U.S. trade balance with Western Europe went from a deficit of $27.5 billion in 1987 (actually, the deficit with Europe peaked at $28.6 billion in 1986) to a *surplus* of $14.9 billion in 1991 (which then fell to a $3.2 billion surplus in 1992, as European growth slowed). To be sure, these small surpluses with Western Europe in the early 1990s are less than the surpluses that the United States enjoyed with that region as recently as 1980, and are significantly smaller in proportion to the level of GNP. Nevertheless, it is clear that among the industrialized countries, the Western European nations have borne the lion's share of the adjustment to the global trade imbalances of the United States, while Japan (which had a larger surplus to begin with) has borne relatively little of the adjustment burden in spite of massive currency appreciation.

There is still some room for macro-policy correctives with Japan. Surely a massive fiscal stimulus in Japan would help not only to end that country's recession but also to reduce its record trade surplus (which is global, not just bilateral with the United States).[18] Some economists have suggested that further yen appreciation might be more effective than the previous appreciation of 1985–88, because Japanese profit margins are now lower and could not be squeezed any further in order to prevent exchange rate pass-through.[19] It is difficult to believe that these measures would be sufficient, in the absence of correctives to the underlying sources of Japan's structural trade surplus. These sources include Japan's notoriously closed markets for manufactured goods, as well as the aggressive export-oriented strategy of its corporations (including their subsidiaries in other countries) (see Dornbusch 1990; Salvatore 1990; Lawrence 1987, 1991).

Since formal trade liberalization would be largely beside the point, the solution must lie either in the enactment of effective international antitrust agreements or in the negotiation of "results-oriented" managed trade agreements with allotted foreign shares of Japanese markets and restraints on their exports. The idea of an across-the-board surcharge on manufactured imports from Japan has also been suggested (see Dornbusch 1990; Salvatore 1990), if Japan fails to meet specified market-opening targets.

The other group of countries with chronic large trade surpluses with the United States in recent years has been a somewhat shifting group of low-wage East Asian exporters of manufactures. In 1987, the two largest offenders were South Korea and Taiwan, with which the United States then had a combined deficit of $26.8 billion—nearly as great as the U.S. deficit with all of Western Europe at that time! Since then, Korea has made great strides toward rectifying its trade surplus with the United States, helped by significant real depreciation of the won, and by major increases in domestic wages and aggregate demand. The advent of effective political democracy in Korea probably played an important part in making these adjustments possible, and shows that they are consistent with domestic economic gains.

In contrast, the deficit with Taiwan (Republic of China) has remained stuck at over $10 billion, and the deficit with the People's Republic of China has come out of nowhere to reach $18.3 billion in 1992. The two Chinas (the People's Republic and Taiwan) together had a combined surplus of $28.4 billion in 1992, even larger than the combined Korea-Taiwan surplus of 1987 (when the overall U.S. deficit was more than 50 percent larger), and more than half of the 1992 Japanese surplus with the United States. If the remaining deficits with Korea and Singapore (which are not shown in the table) are added, the total U.S. deficit with the East Asian industrializing countries is well over $30 billion.

The explanation of the huge U.S. deficits with China and Taiwan is simple: low unit labor costs due to the combination of low wages (which actually are much lower in China than in Taiwan) with high productivity in modern industries (but productivity is also higher in Taiwan, undoubtedly). To a trade theorist, this is a disequilibrium situation with a simple and natural remedy: if wages in China and Taiwan do not rise sufficiently, revaluation of the Chinese and Taiwanese currencies can raise their average unit labor costs in dollars and eliminate their overall competitive advantage. The problem is that there is no automatic mechanism in the international financial marketplace to compel this outcome. Both countries have heavily managed exchange rate regimes. Both nations' central banks have amassed enormous reserves as they have bought up excess supplies of foreign exchange, in order to keep their currencies undervalued.[20] And both nations have authoritarian political regimes that effectively keep the lid on domestic wages.

In this situation, unless the democratization movements in these countries succeed, the only solution is outside political pressure. The need to renew China's most favored nation (MFN) trading status with the United States could be used as an occasion to obtain commitments in this regard, including revaluing the yuan against the dollar. It is important to include a specific economic demand like this in U.S. negotiations with the Chinese government, as well as the broader human rights and political democracy concerns. While the latter are extremely important, as a practical matter the United States is much more likely to get the Chinese government to adjust its exchange rate than to change its political system. Similar pressures should be applied to Taiwan. In both China and Taiwan, political liberalization would undoubtedly help with trade adjustment, as industrial workers would claim higher wages consistent with their rising productivity, and citizens could win more consumption-oriented economic policies, both of which would help to reduce trade surpluses. However, revaluing undervalued currencies is something that can be demanded even of current political regimes.

The question then arises of what to do if these countries do not raise their average unit labor costs in dollars, through either wage increases or currency appreciation, to levels consistent with balanced trade. In Blecker (1992a), I have urged the threatened imposition of a "unit labor cost equalization surcharge" on manufactured imports from countries like China and Taiwan, which have large and persistent surpluses accounted for by low unit labor costs in dollar terms, and a record of exchange rate intervention to keep their currencies undervalued.[21] Clearly, revaluing the currency should be a preferable option for these countries, as compared to accepting a surcharge, since the revaluation brings improved terms of trade while the surcharge does not. Thus, with revaluation there is a gain in purchasing power over imports that offsets the lessened competitiveness of exports; with the surcharge there is no such offsetting gain. It seems, then, that countries like China and Taiwan should be willing to revalue in order to avoid actual imposition of the surcharge.

The issue of market openness also arises in regard to China and Taiwan. Both countries have maintained tight effective controls over the importation of manufactured goods that could compete with nascent domestic industries. Taiwan has used its import controls to create a hothouse environment favorable to the growth of small domestic firms, while China is now striking deals with foreign multinationals like McDonnell-Douglas to acquire state-of-the-art technology in advanced industries. While these countries have relied on open markets abroad, particularly in the United States, to fuel their export-led growth, they have not been willing to reciprocate by opening their home markets. This is mercantilism, pure and simple, and it has no place in a truly "liberal" trading system.

The United States, with its declining real wages and sluggish growth, can no longer afford to keep its market unilaterally open in exchange for geopolitical or strategic (but noneconomic) advantages. This is especially true in the case of the two Chinas, whose rivalry is a relic of the Cold War era, and whose ideological disputes are increasingly just a cover for two authoritarian regimes that have more in common than they would like to admit. What U.S. tolerance of their undervalued exchange rates and closed markets does is only to prop up these undemocratic states at the expense of American workers who lose jobs to artificially cheap imports. Even with balanced trade, of course, we would continue to import large amounts of labor-intensive manufactures from China, Taiwan, and other East Asian NICs. However, the current levels of imports go far beyond what can be justified by the principle of comparative advantages due to the enormous trade imbalances. In 1992, China's exports to the United States were *more than three times* the level of its imports from the United States ($25.7 billion versus $7.5 billion); Taiwan's exports to the United States were *nearly double* its imports ($24.6 billion versus $14.5 billion). This is not Ricardian comparative advantage trade!

Conclusions

The discussion of the Pacific rim surplus countries in the previous section points out the subtleties involved in trying to disentangle structural and macroeconomic causes of trade imbalances. Since Japan, China, and Taiwan together account for roughly 80 percent of the 1992 U.S. trade deficit, these three cases are clearly consequential to the aggregate outcome. In each case, it is possible to identify structural factors that contribute to large trade surpluses, including closed internal markets and highly competitive exports (Japan more in terms of rising technological sophistication and high product quality, China and Taiwan more in terms of low unit labor costs). Nevertheless, there are also macroeconomic factors at work, including undervalued currencies and insufficiently expansionary fiscal and monetary policies. In the cases of these countries, the structural and macroeconomic determinants of trade balances seem to be reinforcing each other in creating chronic surpluses, rather than offsetting each other and eliminating surplus tendencies. Macroeconomic correctives could be made but are impeded by political institutions and entrenched interests. Market forces alone do not automatically call forth such correctives.

As noted earlier, even allowing macroeconomic correctives to work can have its costs. Depreciating the dollar lowers the U.S. terms of trade and the purchasing power of domestic incomes. Slower income growth in the United States helps to keep the trade balance down but at tremendous social cost. For these reasons, it is imperative for the surplus countries to shoulder more of the burden of adjustment. Expansionary macro policies and market opening can both raise domestic living standards and cure external imbalances in surplus countries that are suppressing consumer welfare. This is the growth path, rather than the stagnation path, to restoring global trade balances.

In the end, this discussion shows that the structural and macroeconomic aspects of trade balances are closely intertwined. The structural characteristics (e.g., labor productivity, trade barriers, product quality, technological innovation) determine the parameters within which traditional macro policies (fiscal, monetary, and exchange rate) operate, while the latter determine the degree to which the structural factors are manifest in trade imbalances or in other variables. To ignore the macroeconomic relationships and policies would be naive and misleading. It is equally wrong to ignore the structural causes of trade imbalances, or to pretend that they are automatically and costlessly offset by macroeconomic adjustments. The precise way in which structural and macroeconomic factors interact will vary over time and between countries. Understanding the variety of ways in which they can interact and the full range of policy alternatives for dealing with imbalances when they arise is essential for sound policy formulation.

Appendix

The new estimates of income elasticites for U.S. exports and imports are based on a similar model that I used in Blecker (1992b). The main difference is that the new estimates make an adjustment for the overvaluation of the "real" volume of computers in the official U.S. data. These data, as published by the U.S. Department of Commerce, Bureau of Economic Analysis in the National Income and Product Accounts (NIPAs), measure the "hedonic" (qualitative) attributes of computers at constant, base-year prices. Given the rapid technical progress in computers in the past decade, this procedure results in an exaggerated picture of the volume of computer imports and exports. Essentially, the NIPA approach

Table 6.5

Econometric Estimates of Demand Functions for U.S. Nonagricultural Exports and Nonpetroleum Imports with Alternative Measure of Computers (sample period: 1978-I to 1990-IV)

Variable	Imports	Exports
Constant	−12.62	−3.28
	(−28.07)	(−5.03)
Relative price[a]	−1.27	−0.73
	(−9.48)	(−15.68)
Income[b]	2.22	1.38
	(40.43)	(22.15)
Adjusted R^2	0.99	0.96

Source: Author's calculations.

Note: The dependent variables are (respectively) nonagricultural merchandise exports and nonpetroleum merchandise imports in constant 1982 dollars, except for exports and imports of computers, which were revalued at current prices. All variables are measured in natural logarithms. All equations were estimated by ordinary least squares using quarterly data. Numbers in parentheses are *t*-statistics.

[a]For exports, this is the implicit price deflator for nonagricultural, noncomputer exports multiplied by the Federal Reserve Board index for the real value of the dollar, and divided by the U.S. CPI (so as to obtain an index of U.S. export prices relative to a trade-weighted average of foreign price levels). For imports, this is the implicit price deflator for nonpetroleum, noncomputer imports relative to the producer price index for nonfuel industrial commodities. Coefficients shown in the table are the sums for quarterly lags 0–8.

[b]For exports, the income variable is total GDP for all non-U.S. OECD countries, in constant 1985 prices, converted at 1985 purchasing power parity exchange rates. For imports, the income variable is U.S. gross domestic purchases in billions of 1982 dollars.

emphasizes the amount of computing power traded, rather than the number of computers. This is inconsistent with how all other goods in the NIPA are treated.

The alternative method chosen here was to value computers at their nominal prices in the "real" import and export series, which is equivalent to giving them a price deflator of 1.0. This is the actual practice in the German national accounts. This is essentially an agnostic procedure that admits that we do not have a very good way of measuring the real quantity of computers in a period when their quality is rapidly improving. In effect, the method used here treats a computer as a computer, regardless of when it was produced. The econometric results thus obtained are presented in Table 6.5.

In addition to the regressions reported in Table 6.5, a number of alternative specifications were estimated with the same data set in order to test the sensitivity of the results to the assumptions about computer prices. Using the official data results in higher estimates of both import and export income elasticities, very close to the estimates from Blecker (1992b) reported in Table 6.3. On the other hand, omitting computers entirely results in lower estimates of both. In all cases, the income elasticity is notably higher for imports.

Notes

1. All trade balance data in this paragraph are on a balance-of-payments basis, as reported in U.S. Congress, Joint Economic Committee (May 1994).

2. See, e.g., Hatsopoulos, Krugman, and Summers (1988) for a concise statement of this view.

3. Strictly speaking, the following equation applies to the *current account* balance, which equals the merchandise trade balance plus the services balance (including net inflows of investment income) and net transfers. In this context, the term "trade balance" should be understood to mean the current account.

4. The definition of *macroeconomic stability* used here refers to the output adjustment process in the goods market. Assuming that output increases when there is excess demand for goods and decreases when there is excess supply, then output will converge to its equilibrium level if and only if the propensity to save is greater than the propensity to invest out of additional income.

5. In particular, it is important to have a competitive domestic capital goods sector so that the import coefficient of investment is relatively low.

6. For an exposition of this analysis, see Bosworth (1993).

7. The Helkie and Hooper (1988) estimate of the effect of U.S. fiscal expansion is actually based on a rather crude extrapolation of the simulation results for the MCM model reported in the Bryant et al. (1988) comparison of models. Those results show a sustained 1 percent of GNP fiscal expansion in the United States, causing the U.S. current account to fall by about $10 billion after 1 year, $17 billion after 2 years, $23 billion after 3 years, and $53 billion after 6 years. Helkie and Hooper state that, based on these results, they "have chosen to estimate" the current account effect of U.S. fiscal expansion as a fall of $20 billion for each 1 percent of GNP of fiscal stimulus—apparently, the effect after 2½ years (since 20 is halfway between 17 and 23). Then they multiplied this figure by 3.5 (the approximate percentage of GNP by which the U.S. fiscal deficit rose in 1980–85) to obtain the estimate of a $70 billion fall in the current account. It should be noted that this procedure exaggerates the effects of the actual shift in U.S. fiscal policy, since some part of the 3.5 percent of GNP increase in the actual U.S. federal deficit must be attributed to the foreign demand contraction combined with U.S. competitive decline.

8. In addition, Helkie and Hooper estimated that "foreign fiscal contraction contributed another $25 billion to the deficit," so that domestic and foreign fiscal policies combined explain a total of $95 billion of the increased current deficit, or about two-thirds of the total increase (1988, p. 49). Most of the remainder of this increase is attributed to the "additional" dollar appreciation in 1980–85—i.e., the part of the dollar's rise that is not explained by fiscal policies (and is presumably due to monetary contraction plus the speculative bubble).

9. Note that the trade deficit peaked in 1987, two years after the peak in the real value of the dollar, due to the lagged effects of exchange rate changes on volumes of trade—the well-known *J*-curve effect.

10. The other nations shown are most of the United States' leading competitors, including all the other G-7 countries plus Korea representing the NICs. Other major NICs (such as Taiwan, Brazil, and Mexico) were omitted due to data problems.

11. It could be argued that, nevertheless, the nation kept its consumer standard of living rising by "living beyond its means" through public sector dissaving and private sector "overconsumption" (see, e.g., Hatsopoulos, Krugman, and Poterba 1989). While there is some tautological truth to this in regard to the federal budget deficit, the notion of a "consumption binge" by most private households has clearly been exaggerated (see Blecker 1990). It is also true that households have been able to keep their living standards from falling by having household members work more hours in order to compensate for falling hourly real wages, but the need to work more hours is itself evidence of a decline in the overall standard of living, including leisure time.

12. These series are taken from the NIPAs and thus differ slightly from the international transactions (balance-of-payments) series. The current account is measured by the NIPA concept of "net foreign investment."

13. The Fed index is used since it goes back two years earlier than the IMF index, which starts in 1975. The trend is calculated by a least-squares regression of the natural logarithm of the exchange rate index on the time period 1973–79, with the rest of the trend projected out of sample.

14. For further discussion of this issue, see Meade (1991) and Blecker (1992a).

15. See the appendix to this chapter for details on these new estimates.

16. Of course, if incomes do not adjust, then persistent trade imbalances will emerge, sustained by international capital movements (lending from surplus countries to deficit countries). This is what has happened to the United States in the last decade.

17. Averages of daily exchange rates from the U.S. Board of Governors of the Federal Reserve System, as published in U.S. Council of Economic Advisors (1993, table B-107, p. 470).

18. According to the International Monetary Fund in *International Financial Statistics* (March 1993, pp. 306–7), Japan had an overall merchandise trade surplus of $103 billion in 1991 and was running quarterly trade surpluses of over $30 billion for the first three quarters of 1992 (indicating an annual surplus approaching $125 billion for 1992).

19. Conversation with Rudiger Dornbusch, Anaheim, California, January 1993.

20. As of mid-1992, China's reserves totaled over $31 billion, while Taiwan's reserves surpassed $61 billion. These are among the largest reserves of any country in the world, and are much larger than those of most other developing countries (only Singapore comes close, with reserves of $26 billion in mid-1992). See International Monetary Fund (March 1993, pp. 29–31).

21. Note that this surcharge is designed to be applied only in these types of cases, and not in all instances of low wages. It is not, therefore, what is sometimes called a "scientific tariff" to equalize *wages* per se, and it would not be applied in any case to countries without undervalued currencies *and* chronic trade surpluses vis-à-vis the United States.

Bibliography

Bernheim, B. Douglas. 1988. "Budget Deficits and the Balance of Trade." *Tax Policy and the Economy,* Vol. 2, pp. 1–31.

Blecker, Robert A. 1990. *Are Americans on a Consumption Binge? The Evidence Reconsidered.* Washington, DC: Economic Policy Institute.

———. 1991a. "Low Saving Rates and the Twin Deficits: Confusing the Symptoms and Causes of Economic Decline." In Paul Davidson and Jan A. Kregel, eds., *Economic Problems of the 1990s.* Aldershot, England, and Brookfield, VT: Edward Elgar.

————. 1991b. "The Recession, the Dollar, and the Trade Deficit: Recent Trends and Future Prospects." Briefing Paper. Washington, DC: Economic Policy Institute.

————. 1992a. *Beyond the Twin Deficits: A Trade Strategy for the 1990s.* Economic Policy Institute Series. Armonk, NY: M. E. Sharpe.

————. 1992b. "Structural Roots of U.S. Trade Problems: Income Elasticities, Time Trends, and Hysteresis." *Journal of Post Keynesian Economics,* Vol. 14, No. 3 (Spring), pp. 321–46.

Block, Fred C. 1990. "Bad Data Drive Out Good: The Decline of Personal Savings Reconsidered." *Journal of Post Keynesian Economics,* Vol. 13, No. 1 (Fall), pp. 3–19.

Blomstrom, Magnus, and Edward N. Wolff. 1994. "Multinational Corporations and Productivity Convergence in Mexico." In William J. Baumol et al., eds., *Convergence of Productivity: Cross-National Stuides and Historical Evidence.* Oxford, England: Oxford University Press.

Bosworth, Barry P. 1993. *Saving and Investment in a Global Economy.* Washington, DC: Brookings Institution.

Bryant, Ralph C., Dale W. Henderson, Gerald Holtham, Peter Hooper, and Steven A. Symansky, eds. 1988. *Empirical Macroeconomics for Interdependent Economies.* Washington, DC: Brookings Institution.

Cline, William R. 1989. *United States External Adjustment and the World Economy.* Washington, DC: Institute for International Economics.

Cooper, Richard N. 1987. "Symposium on the Causes of the U.S. Trade Deficit." Report to Congressional Requesters. Washington, DC: U.S. General Accounting Office.

Dixit, Avinash. 1992. "Investment and Hysteresis." *Journal of Economic Perspectives,* Vol. 6, No. 1 (Winter), pp. 107–32.

Dornbusch, Rudiger. 1988. "The Adjustment Mechanism: Theory and Problems." In Norman S. Fieleke, ed., *International Payments Imbalances in the 1980s.* Boston: Federal Reserve Bank of Boston.

————. 1989. "The Dollar, U.S. Adjustment and the System." Unpublished MIT paper presented at American Economic Association Meetings, Atlanta, GA, December.

————. 1990. "Is There a Case for Aggressive Bilateralism and How Best to Practice It?" In Robert Z. Lawrence and Charles L. Schultze, eds., *An American Trade Strategy: Three Options for the 1990s.* Washington, DC: Brookings Institution.

Dornbusch, Rudiger, Paul Krugman, and Yung Chul Park. 1989. *Meeting World Challenges: U.S. Manufacturing in the 1990s.* Rochester, NY: Eastman Kodak Company.

Dosi, Giovanni, Keith Pavitt, and Luc Soete. 1990. *The Economics of Technical Change and International Trade.* New York: New York University Press.

Eisner, Robert. 1991. "The Real Rate of U.S. National Saving." *Review of Income and Wealth,* Series 37 (March).

Fazzari, Steven M. 1993. *Investment and U.S. Fiscal Policy in the 1990s.* Briefing Paper. Washington, DC: Economic Policy Institute (June).

Fazzari, Steven M., and Michael J. Athey. 1987. "Asymmetric Information, Financing Constraints, and Investment." *Review of Economics and Statistics,* Vol. 69 (August), pp. 481–87.

Fazzari, Steven M., R. Glenn Hubbard, and Bruce C. Petersen. 1988. "Financing Constraints and Corporate Investment." *Brookings Papers on Economic Activity,* No. 1, pp. 141–206.

Frankel, Jeffrey A. 1990. "The Making of Exchange Rate Policy in the 1980s." Working Paper No. 3539. Cambridge, MA: National Bureau of Economic Research (December).

Hatsopoulos, George, Paul Krugman, and James Poterba. 1989. *Overconsumption: The Challenge to U.S. Policy.* New York and Washington, DC: American Business Conference.

Hatsopoulos, George, Paul Krugman, and Lawrence Summers. 1988. "U.S. Competitiveness: Beyond the Trade Deficit." *Science,* Vol. 241, pp. 299–307.

Helkie, William L., and Peter Hooper. 1988. "An Empirical Analysis of the External Deficit." In Ralph C. Bryant et al., eds., *External Deficits and the Dollar: The Pit and the Pendulum.* Washington, DC: Brookings Institution.

Hooper, Peter. 1989. "U.S. Net Foreign Saving Has Also Plunged." *Challenge,* July–August, pp. 33–38.

Hooper, Peter, and Catherine L. Mann. 1989. "The U.S. External Deficit: Its Causes and Persistence." In Albert E. Burger, ed., *U.S. Trade Deficit: Causes, Consequences, and Cures.* Proceedings of the Twelfth Annual Economic Policy Conference of the Federal Reserve Bank of St. Louis (1987). Boston: Kluwer Academic Publishers.

International Monetary Fund. *International Financial Statistics.* Washington, DC: IMF (various issues).

Krugman, Paul R. 1979. "A Model of Innovation, Technology Transfer, and the World Distribution of Income." *Journal of Political Economy,* Vol. 87, No. 2 (April), pp. 253–66.

———. 1989a. *Exchange-Rate Instability.* Cambridge, MA: MIT Press.

———. 1989b. "Differences in Income Elasticities and Trends in Real Exchange Rates." *European Economic Review,* Vol. 33, pp. 1031–54.

———. 1991. *Has the Adjustment Process Worked?* Policy Analyses in International Economics, No. 34. Washington, DC: Institute for International Economics.

Krugman, Paul R., and Richard E. Baldwin. 1987. "The Persistence of the U.S. Trade Deficit." *Brookings Papers on Economic Activity,* No. 1, pp. 1–43.

Lawrence, Robert Z. 1987. "Imports in Japan: Closed Markets or Minds?" *Brookings Papers on Economic Activity,* No. 2, pp. 517–54.

———. 1989. "The International Dimension." In Robert E. Litan et al., eds., *American Living Standards: Threats and Challenges.* Washington, DC: Brookings Institution.

———. 1990. "U.S. Current Account Adjustment: An Appraisal." *Brookings Papers on Economic Activity,* No. 2, pp. 343–89.

———. 1991. "Efficient or Exclusionist? The Import Behavior of Japanese Corporate Groups." *Brookings Papers on Economic Activity,* No. 1, pp. 311–41.

Levich, Richard M. 1988. "Financial Innovations in International Financial Markets." In M. Feldstein, ed., *The United States in the World Economy.* Chicago: University of Chicago Press and National Bureau of Economic Research.

McCauley, Robert N., and Steven A. Zimmer. 1989. "Explaining International Differences in the Cost of Capital." *Federal Reserve Bank of New York, Quarterly Review* (Summer), pp. 7–28.

McCulloch, Rachel. 1986. "Trade Deficits, Industrial Competitiveness, and the Japanese." In Robert E. Baldwin and J. David Richardson, eds., *International Trade and Finance: Readings,* 3d ed. Boston: Little, Brown.

McCulloch, Rachel, and J. David Richardson. 1986. "U.S. Trade and the Dollar: Evaluating Current Policy Options." In Robert E. Baldwin and J. David Richardson, eds., *Current U.S. Trade Policy: Analysis, Agenda, and Administration.* Cambridge, MA: National Bureau of Economic Research.

McKibbin, Warwick J., and Jeffrey D. Sachs. 1989. "The McKibbin-Sachs Global Model: Theory and Specification." Working Paper No. 3100. Cambridge, MA: National Bureau of Economic Research.

Meade, Ellen E. 1991. "Computers and the Trade Deficit: The Case of the Falling Prices." In Peter Hooper and J. David Richardson, eds., *International Economic Transactions: Issues in Measurement and Empirical Research*. Chicago: University of Chicago Press.

Nelson, Richard R., and Gavin Wright. 1992. "The Rise and Fall of American Technological Leadership: The Postwar Era in Historical Perspective." *Journal of Economic Literature,* Vol. 30, No. 4 (December), pp. 1931–64.

Organization for Economic Cooperation and Development. 1991. *Main Economic Indicators*. Paris: OECD (February).

Rosensweig, Jeffrey A., and Ellis W. Tallman. 1993. "Fiscal Policy and Trade Adjustment: Are the Deficits Really Twins?" *Economic Inquiry,* Vol. 31 (October), pp. 580–94.

Sachs, Jeffrey D. 1988. "Global Adjustments to a Shrinking U.S. Trade Deficit." *Brookings Papers on Economic Activity,* No. 2, pp. 639–74.

Salvatore, Dominick. 1990. *The Japanese Trade Challenge and the U.S. Response: Addressing the Structural Causes of the Bilateral Trade Imbalance*. Washington, DC: Economic Policy Institute.

Thirlwall, A. P. 1979. "The Balance of Payments Constraint as an Explanation of International Growth Rate Differences." *Banca Nazionale del Lavoro Quarterly Review,* No. 128 (March), pp. 45–53.

U.S. Congress, Joint Economic Committee. *Economic Indicators*. Washington, DC: U.S. Government Printing Office (various issues).

U.S. Council of Economic Advisors. *Economic Report of the President*. Washington, DC: U.S. Government Printing Office (various years).

U.S. Department of Commerce, Bureau of Economic Analysis. 1986. *The National Income and Product Accounts of the United States, 1929–82: Statistical Tables*. Washington, DC: U.S. Government Printing Office.

―――. Various issues. Survey of Current Business. Washington, DC: Bureau of Economic Analysis.

U.S. Department of Labor, Bureau of Labor Statistics. 1991. "International Comparisons of Hourly Compensation Costs for Production Workers in Manufacturing, 1990." Report No. 803. Washington, DC: BLS (May).

U.S. National Science Foundation. 1990. *National Patterns of R&D Resources, 1990*. Report No. 90–316. Washington, DC: U.S. National Science Foundation.

Vernon, Raymond. 1966. "International Investment and International Trade in the Product Cycle." *Quarterly Journal of Economics,* Vol. 80 (May), pp. 190–207.

Wright, Gavin. 1990. "The Origins of American Industrial Success, 1879–1940." *American Economic Review,* Vol. 80, No. 4 (September), pp. 651–68.

CHAPTER SEVEN

Reforming the International Payments System

PAUL DAVIDSON

Introduction

The current international payments system does not serve the emerging global economy well. *The Financial Times* and *The Economist*, both previously strong advocates of the existing floating rate system, have acknowledged that the system is a failure and was sold to the public and the politicians under false advertising claims.[1] Can we not do better?

Too often, economic discussions on the requirements for a good international payments system have been limited to the question of the advantages and disadvantages of fixed versus flexible exchange rates. Although this issue is very important, historical experience indicates that more is required than simply choosing between fixed and flexible exchange rates if a mechanism is to be designed to resolve payments imbalances while simultaneously promoting economic growth with full employment and a stable international standard of value.

Since 1945, the free world has conducted several experiments with the international payments system. For a quarter of a century after World War II, there was a fixed, but adjustable, exchange rate system, which had been set up under the 1944 Bretton Woods Agreement. Since 1973, we have operated under a hybrid system of generally flexible exchange rates with varying degrees of exchange rate management across countries and over time.

The 1947–73 period of fixed exchange rates was "an era of unprecedented sustained economic growth in both developed and developing countries" (Adelman 1991, p. 15). The growth rate of real gross domestic product (GDP) per capita in the industrialized nations escalated to 2.6 times that of the interwar period (4.9 percent annually compared to 1.9 percent). Moreover, this real

The author would like to thank, without implicating, the following individuals, who gave comments and suggestions on earlier drafts: Philip Arestis, Janet Ceglowski, Sandy Darity, Sheila Dow, Alan Isaac, and John Williamson. An earlier version of the argument in this chapter appeared in Davidson (1992–93).

growth rate was almost double the previous *peak* growth rate exhibited by the industrializing nations during the period 1820–1914, while the growth in productivity during the Bretton Woods era was more than triple that of the period 1820–1914. Adelman (1991) observes that depressions disappeared, recessions were minor, and exports grew more than 50 percent faster than GDP during the Bretton Woods epoch.

This unprecedented prosperity was transmitted to developing nations through world trade, aid, and foreign investment. The growth rate of real gross national product (GNP) per capita for all developing nations rose to 3.3 percent, more than triple the growth experienced by the early industrializing nations between 1820 and 1914. Real total GNP growth in developing nations was almost the same as in developed countries (Adelman 1991, p. 17).

Thus, during the Bretton Woods epoch, both developed and developing economies experienced unprecedented real economic growth. Moreover, during this period, there was "a much better overall record of price level stability" vis-à-vis either the post-1973 period or the previous era of fixed exchange rates under the gold standard from 1879 to 1914 (McKinnon 1990, p. 10).

Historically, then, the 1947–73 epoch was truly a "Golden Era of Economic Development" (Adelman 1991, p. 24). Yet, in 1973, the free world abandoned the Bretton Woods system. At the time, this international payments system was blamed for importing inflation into the United States and reexporting it to others, and for draining gold reserves from the United States. The system was also blamed for trade imbalances, as the emerging surplus countries (West Germany and Japan) were not compelled to revalue their currencies.

The relevant question should have been whether it was possible to improve the existing system so that it could better cope with these newly emerging problems of inflation and increasing international demands for gold reserves for liquidity purposes. Instead, an emerging economic orthodoxy recommended the abandonment of the Bretton Woods system and the adoption of a flexible exchange rate system that would allegedly solve the U.S. current account deficit and prevent the United States from importing inflation due to rising foreign prices of its imports. It was claimed that a flexible exchange rate policy would permit each nation to pursue full-employment policies no matter what inflation rate the nation's trading partners experienced.

The dismal post-1973 experience of recurrent unemployment and inflationary crises, slow growth in the industrial countries, and debt-burdened growth and/or stagnation in most developing countries (and even falling real GNP per capita in some) contrasts sharply with the experience during the Bretton Woods period. The free world's economic performance in terms of both real growth and price stability during the Bretton Woods period was unprecedented. Moreover, even the record during the earlier period of fixed exchange rates under the gold standard was better than the experience during the post-1973 period of flexible exchange rates.

What can we surmise from these facts? First, this experience supports the thesis that a fixed exchange rate system provides an international environment that is more compatible with greater real economic growth and price stability than what has been experienced under a flexible exchange rate regime. Second, the significantly superior performance of the free world's economies during the Bretton Woods fixed rate period compared to the earlier fixed rate period of the gold standard suggests that there must have been an additional condition besides exchange rate fixity that contributed to the unprecedented growth during the period 1947–73. I shall argue that something more occurred, almost accidentally, during the first half of the Bretton Woods period, and that it was the failure of the Bretton Woods system to perpetuate this second necessary condition that led to its ultimate abandonment and the end of the golden era of economic development.

The Necessary Conditions for an Expansionary International Payments System

In 1941, John Maynard Keynes argued that no free market–oriented international payments system could be relied on to correct persistent current accounts imbalances without inducing recessions or depressions as part of the adjustment mechanism. He argued that:

> To suppose that there exists some smoothly functioning automatic mechanism of adjustment that preserves equilibrium if only we trust to methods of *laissez-faire* is a doctrinaire delusion which disregards the lessons of historical experience without having behind it the support of sound theory. (1980, pp. 21–22)

In developing his proposals for an international payments scheme, Keynes hoped to reduce entrepreneurial uncertainties and the possibility of massive currency misalignments by recommending the adoption of a fixed, but adjustable, exchange rate system. More important, however, Keynes argued that the "main cause of failure" of any traditional payments system—whether based on fixed or flexible rates—was its inability to foster continuous global economic expansion when persistent current account imbalances among trading partners occurred. This failure, Keynes wrote,

> can be traced to a single characteristic. I ask close attention to this, because I shall argue that this provides a clue to the nature of any alternative which is to be successful.
> It is characteristic of a freely convertible international standard that it throws the main burden of adjustment on the country which is in the *debtor* position on the international balance of payments—that is, on the country which is (in this context) by hypothesis the *weaker* and above all the *smaller* in

comparison with the other side of the scales which (for this purpose) is the rest of the world. (1980, p. 27, italics in original)

Thus, Keynes concluded, an essential improvement in designing any international payments system requires transferring "the *onus* of adjustment from the debtor to the creditor position" and aiming "at the substitution of an expansionist, in place of a contractionist, pressure on world trade" (Keynes 1980, p. 176, italics in original). In other words, to achieve a golden era of economic development requires combining a fixed, but adjustable, rate system with a mechanism for requiring the surplus trading nation or nations to initiate most of the effort necessary to adjust a payments imbalance, without removing all discipline from the deficit trading partner.

The Marshall Plan: An Illustration of the Surplus-Nation Adjustment Mechanism

The postwar experience provides support for Keynes's analysis. Almost immediately after the cessation of hostilities in 1945, the United States terminated its enormous exports of aid under the Lend-Lease Act, even though most of the productive facilities of Western Europe had been extensively damaged during the war. Moreover, as Kindleberger (1987, p. 13) noted, reparations by the Soviet army removed much of the remaining capital stock from Germany. Kindleberger characterized the early postwar period by stating that "given the fragile state of domestic production, country after country had to rely on imports, especially from the United States, but reserves of gold and dollars were being drawn down to the vanishing point" (1987, p. 99).

Under these circumstances, the economic recovery of the capitalist world required the European nations to run huge trade deficits in order to feed their populations and rebuild their stock of capital. Under the rules of free market economies, this implied that the United States would have to provide enormous credits to finance the required export surplus to Europe. The resulting European indebtedness would be so burdensome that it was unlikely that, even in the long run, the European nations could ever service this debt. Moreover, U.S. policy makers were mindful that reparation payments after World War I had been financed by U.S. investors lending Germany foreign exchange and that Germany had never repaid these loans (Kindleberger 1987, p. 95). Given these circumstances, it was obvious that private lending facilities could not be expected to provide the credits necessary for European recovery.

How could this problem be resolved? Under the fixed exchange rate system of Bretton Woods itself, the only mechanism available for redressing this potentially lopsided global import-export trade flow was for the debtors to accept the main burden of adjustment by "tightening their belts" and reducing their demand for imports to what they could earn from exports. The result would have been to depress further the standard of living of Western Europeans. This could have induced political revolutions in most of Western Europe.

Instead, the United States produced an innovative approach for financing the requisite export surplus to Europe without having to plunge Europe into a huge debt obligation—the Marshall Plan and other foreign grants and aid programs. The Marshall Plan provided $5 billion in aid in eighteen months and a total of $13 billion over four years (equivalent to over $100 billion in 1991 dollars).

Marshall Plan transfers represented approximately 2 percent of the annual GNP of the United States, yet no U.S. resident felt deprived of goods and services. Real GNP per capita in the United States during the first year of the Marshall Plan was still 25 percent larger than in the last peacetime year of 1940. Per capita GNP continued to grow throughout the 1950s. There was no real sacrifice associated with this export surplus. These exports were produced by employing what otherwise would have been idle resources in the United States. For the first time in its history, the United States did not suffer from a severe recession or depression immediately after the end of a major war.

Apparently as part of the emerging political Cold War, the world's major creditor deliberately chose to bear the burden of adjustment to a persistent current account imbalance with the rest of the world. As a result, U.S. firms found profitable export markets, while the trading partners of the United States obtained, without going into debt, the liquidity to finance the necessary food and material imports to help feed and shelter their populations while rebuilding their productive facilities. In the absence of such an innovative approach, the capitalist world would have suffered through a postwar recession at least as severe as the 1919–21 recession. Instead, a global postwar depression was avoided.

In sum, under the fixed exchange rate regime of the Bretton Woods system, enhanced by the leading creditor nation's accepting the major adjustment for trade imbalances, the economies of the free world experienced unprecedented rates of real economic growth for a decade after the war without inflation, despite the pressure put on available resources by rapidly growing demand. The world experienced an economic "free lunch," as both the potential debtors and the creditor nation gained from this "giveaway."

The Unraveling of the Bretton Woods System

In the late 1950s, foreign countries that had been accumulating dollar reserves began to be concerned about holding excessive dollar positions. No longer desperate for dollars to fuel their postwar recoveries, the European nations converted a portion of their dollar surpluses into gold. For example, in 1958, the United States lost over $2 billion in gold reserves. These trends accelerated in the 1960s, partly as a result of increased U.S. military and financial aid responses to the construction of the Berlin Wall in 1961 and later because of increasing U.S. involvement in Vietnam. At the same time, rebuilt Europe and Japan became important producers of exports, so that the rest of the world became less dependent on U.S. exports.

The United States maintained a positive merchandise trade balance until 1970, but this trade surplus was shrinking in the late 1960s and was more than offset by military and other unilateral transfers plus net capital outflows. In 1971–72, the United States had deficits on both the merchandise trade and current account balances. The Bretton Woods system had no way of automatically forcing the emerging surplus nations to step into the adjustment role that the United States had been playing since 1947. Instead, these nations continued to convert some portion of their annual dollar surpluses into calls on U.S. gold reserves. The seeds of the destruction of the Bretton Woods system and of the golden age of economic development were sown as surplus nations drained gold reserves from the United States.

When the United States closed the gold window and unilaterally withdrew from Bretton Woods in the Nixon administration, the last vestige of Keynes's enlightened international monetary approach was lost—apparently without regret or regard to how well it had served the global economy.

The oil price shock of 1973 created new and persistent current account imbalances between the deficit oil consumers and the surplus nations of the Organization of Petroleum Exporting Countries (OPEC). Nobel Prize–winning economist Wassily Leontief (1990) has indicated that if it were not for the recycling of petrodollars via bank loans, the free world's oil-consuming nations might have experienced another great depression after 1973, as they would have been forced to tighten their belts to relieve their huge payments deficits. Leontief has written that this petrodollar recycling was a

> private, improvised Marshall Plan for developing countries. Despite the absence of elegance in that plan, it enabled many less developed countries to advance. . . . The system grew quickly and then suddenly stopped . . . [as l]arge Western banks faced bankruptcies. . . . A second Marshall Plan is needed. . . . Unless the less-developed countries can increase their rate of development and improve their social and economic conditions, this explosive situation will get out of hand. (1990, pp. 58–59)

The conventional wisdom says that the post-1973 era of large bank loans to support oil imports created and recycled too much liquidity. This, it is averred, was the cause of the large inflationary experience of the decade. Implicit in Leontief's comments, however, is the notion that once Bretton Woods and the idea of the onus of the surplus nation initiating adjustments was lost, the real costs of preventing the 1973 oil price shock from producing the inflationary tendencies experienced during the 1970s would have been another worldwide great depression. Wasn't the great inflation of the 1970s less costly in real terms than another great depression would have been? In the two decades since 1973, neither the oil-consuming nations nor the oil-producing nations have, on average, exhibited the long-run growth rates associated with the earlier Bretton Woods period, while many less developed countries (LDCs) have suffered significant declines in real per capita income. What was needed then, and what is needed now, is a better system of current account adjustment without permitting price increases in any exporting nation to spill over into the international price level.

International Liquidity and Foreign Reserve Recycling

A necessary although not sufficient condition for a significant expansion of production to occur in any market-oriented, money-using entrepreneurial economy is a monetary payments system that automatically expands liquidity in order to meet the needs of trade. If entrepreneurs are not able to obtain sufficient additional financial commitments (i.e., increased working capital loans) today to finance planned expansion in productive activities tomorrow, no matter how profitable these production activities are expected to be in the future when output is sold to the final buyer, then enterprises will not be able to hire additional resources to expand their working capital positions. In an entrepreneurial economy, economic expansion requires meeting enlarged payroll and raw material obligations before additional output can be produced and made available for sale.[2]

A payments system should be capable of accommodating expanding entrepreneurial financial needs. There is also a need for institutions that can and will supply the necessary liquid reserves in order to maintain a full-employment level of effective demand. Such institutions must also soak up or absorb excess liquidity in order to prevent overspending. With appropriate institutions to regulate the availability of finance, the resulting economic system has the necessary and sufficient arrangements to assure economic prosperity.

In peacetime, there are two basic situations in which entrepreneurial systems can display a tendency toward a lack of effective demand to maintain full employment. These situations occur under the following conditions:

1. *The recessionary case.* Uncertainty about the future induces the private sector to hoard liquidity and/or to display insufficient optimism regarding future investment opportunities.

2. *The inability to expand production case.* The monetary authority provides inadequate accommodating monetary responses to entrepreneurial financial needs. In either case, the resulting liquidity shortage will induce private sector enterprises to limit employment opportunities unduly.

The recessionary case occurs when income earners allocate current "savings" into idle surplus liquid reserves and refuse either to spend these savings directly on the products of industry or to lend (or give) them to others who wish to spend these on current output. In other words, an uncertain economic environment prevents the necessary recycling of liquidity.

The inability to expand production case occurs when the payments system is unable, or unwilling, to expand liquid financial reserves as rapidly as profit-maximizing entrepreneurs need additional finance to increase real output. Without financial facilities to meet the inevitable increased payrolls and raw material costs associated with expansion, entrepreneurs are unable to increase production activity commitments, no matter how profitable they expect the sales from these expanded activities to be.

Accordingly, any well-designed international payments mechanism must provide for an accommodating financial system that not only supports but encourages spending to approach global full-employment levels by providing financial facilities at favorable terms. The system must be able to create and maintain an adequate volume and distribution of liquid assets as quickly as entrepreneurs are capable of expanding production flows for international trade. There must be a built-in mechanism for providing sufficient liquidity. This requires increasing nations' foreign reserves (i.e., liquidity) as global productive capacity grows, and recycling idle reserves (preferably at little or no cost to the user). As long as there is less than global full employment, those who use otherwise idle liquid reserves to finance additional purchase commitments are performing a useful function. They are paying otherwise involuntarily unemployed resources to produce goods. By definition, spending these liquid reserves provides additional utility in excess of the disutility involved in these productive activities. From a global standpoint, therefore, as long as there are people who are involuntarily unemployed, those with surplus credit accounts should not be permitted to either hoard liquidity or drain reserves from the system and therefore impose unemployment on willing workers in the global economy.

Given some initial level of global effective demand, the development of any trade imbalance between regions can induce liquidity (payments) problems that ultimately reduce production and thereby lower the real incomes of inhabitants of *both* the trade-deficit and the trade-surplus regions. A trade-deficit region's spending (cash outflow) on production from a trade-surplus region must exceed its earnings on sales (cash inflow) from those who have deposits in the surplus region's banks. Consequently, the deficit region finds itself without sufficient export earnings (and liquidity) to maintain its import purchases. In the absence of deliberate offsetting action by the monetary authority or the central government, these cash flow imbalances will create a loss of reserves (and therefore liquidity) from the deficit region's banks.

The deficit region can continue to finance the trade imbalance of imports over exports only as long as it is able either (1) to sell preexisting liquid reserve assets to residents of the trade-surplus region or their bankers; (2) to borrow funds from the surplus region by selling new debt contracts (or pledging other liquid financial assets) to foreigners; or (3) to sell the "family jewels," that is, to sell equity rights in the otherwise illiquid and unique assets of the deficit region to foreigners.

Most orthodox economists presume that the trade deficit cannot be expected to continue indefinitely, since the deficit region's holdings of family jewels, its liquid assets, and its creditworthiness are all limited. The surplus region's inhabitants are expected to be rational, self-interested agents who will not continuously give up currently produced real goods in exchange for promises that are never redeemed. In other words, there is a presumption that the deficit will not be financed indefinitely (or at least as long as necessary) either via unilateral transfer payments or through acceptance of promissory notes that are never called.[3]

Of course, if both regions are encompassed within the same national boundaries, then domestic monetary and/or fiscal policy may be used to recycle and even to create additional reserves to be used to finance the regional trade imbalance. The nation's central bank can rediscount the deficit region's promissory notes or even impose lower reserve requirements on the deficit region's banks to promote additional liquidity creation where it is needed. In recent years, however, the burden for maintaining reserves in deficit regions of a nation has been accepted by enlightened governments whose tax and spending policies can act as a unilateral transfer mechanism—even perpetually if desired or necessary. The magnitude of the finance of interregional trade deficits provided by central governments depends on the tax burdens imposed on each region, and on the central government's propensity to spend in the deficit region vis-à-vis the surplus region. Experience has shown that such regional transfers can create economic benefits for both the deficit and the surplus regions. Differential regional fiscal policy can promote economic expansion and therefore real income for the deficit region while maintaining and even expanding markets for the industries of the surplus region.[4]

National monetary and fiscal policy administered by public officials can therefore help to offset the deflationary pressures that interregional trade deficits can generate. Unfortunately, no global, supranational monetary and/or fiscal authority is likely to be created in the foreseeable future—although the U.S. Marshall Plan and U.S. government military and economic aid programs to LDCs have often played that fiscal role since World War II. In the days of Cold War politics, the superpowers provided unilateral transfers to LDC client states. As long as the Cold War did not escalate to actual hostilities, superpower politics played an important role in fostering economic growth in Europe and many LDCs. With the sudden end of the Cold War in 1989, the political requirement that the superpowers provide economic aid to client states diminished, thus tending to widen the gap between the rich and poor nations (holding other factors constant).

A New International Payments System

The following proposal for an international payments system builds on the elements that proved successful for producing the expansionist pressure on world trade and development during the 1947–73 period. Fifty years ago, Keynes provided a clear outline of what was needed when he wrote:

> We need an instrument of international currency having general acceptability between nations. . . . We need an orderly and agreed upon method of determining the relative exchange values of national currency units. . . . We need a quantum of international currency . . . [that] is governed by the actual current [liquidity] requirements of world commerce, and is capable of deliberate expansion. . . . We need a method by which the surplus credit balances arising from international trade, which the recipient does not wish to employ can be set to work . . . without detriment to the liquidity of these balances. (1980, p. 168)

Keynes's original "bancor" plan for the post–World War II environment was developed around the idea of a unionized monetary system (UMS) and a single supranational central bank. At this stage of the evolution of world politics, however, a global UMS with a supranational central bank does not seem feasible.[5] My suggestion is a more modest one aimed at obtaining an international agreement that would not require surrendering national control of local banking systems and fiscal policies.

What is required is a closed, double-entry bookkeeping clearinghouse to keep the payments score among the various trading regions, plus some mutually agreed upon rules to create and reflux liquidity, while maintaining the international purchasing power of the international currency. The eight provisions of the clearing system suggested in this section meet the criteria laid down by Keynes. The rules of my proposed system are designed (1) to prevent a lack of global effective demand due to any nation's (or nations') either holding excessive idle reserves or draining reserves from the system; (2) to provide an automatic mechanism for placing a major burden of payments adjustments on the surplus nations; (3) to provide each nation with the ability to monitor and, if desired, to control movements of flight capital;[6] and (4) to expand the quantity of the liquid asset of ultimate international redemption as global capacity warrants.

Such a clearing system would include the following elements:

1. The unit of account and ultimate reserve asset for international liquidity would be the international money clearing unit (IMCU). IMCUs would be held only by central banks, not by the public.

2. Each national (or regional UMS) central bank would be committed to guaranteeing one-way convertibility from IMCU deposits at the clearinghouse to its domestic money. Each central bank would set its own rules for making foreign monies available (through IMCU clearing transactions) to its own bankers and private sector residents.

Since central banks would agree to sell their own liabilities (with one-way convertibility) against the IMCU only to other central bankers and the international clearinghouse, while they would simultaneously hold only IMCUs as liquid reserve assets for international financial transactions, there could be no draining of reserves from the system. All major private international transactions ultimately would clear between central banks on their own account within the international clearinghouse.

3. The exchange rate between the domestic currency and the IMCU would be set initially by each nation, just as it would be if an international gold standard were instituted. Since enterprises that have already engaged in trade have international contractual commitments that would span the changeover interval, then, as a practical matter, the existing exchange rate structure (with perhaps minor modifications) would be expected to provide the basis for initial rate setting.

Provisions 7 and 8 below indicate when and how this nominal exchange rate between the national currency and the IMCU would be changed in the future.

4. Contracts between private individuals would continue to be denominated in whatever domestic currency the contracting parties agreed upon and the local laws permitted. Contracts to be settled in terms of a foreign currency would therefore require some announced commitment from the central bank (through private sector bankers) of the availability of foreign funds to meet such private contractual obligations.

5. An overdraft system would make available short-term, unused creditor balances at the clearinghouse to finance the productive international transactions of others who needed short-term credit. The terms would be determined by the clearinghouse managers.

6. A trigger mechanism would be developed to encourage any creditor nation to spend what was deemed (in advance) by agreement of the international community to be "excessive" credit balances accumulated by running current account surpluses. These excessive credits could be spent in three ways: (a) on the products of any other member of the clearinghouse; (b) on new direct foreign investment projects; and/or (c) to provide unilateral transfers (foreign aid) to deficit members. Spending via method a would force the surplus nation to make the adjustment directly by way of the balance on goods and services. Spending by way of method c would permit adjustment directly by the current account balance, while method b would provide adjustment by the capital accounts (without setting up a contractual debt that would require reverse current account flows in the future).

Consequently, this provision would provide the surplus country with considerable discretion in deciding how to accept the onus of adjustment in the way it believed was in its residents' best interests. It would not, however, permit the surplus nation to shift the burden to the deficit nation or nations via contractual requirements for debt service charges independent of what the deficit nation could afford.[7] The important thing would be to make sure that continual oversaving[8] by surplus nations could not unleash depressive forces and/or a building up of international debts so encumbering as to impoverish the global economy of the twenty-first century.

In the unlikely event that the surplus nation would not spend or give away these credits within a specified time, then the clearinghouse would confiscate (and redistribute to debtor members) the portion of credits deemed excessive. To reduce debit balances at the clearinghouse, the "excessive" credit balances that would be redistributed should be apportioned among the debtor nations in inverse proportion to each debtor's per capita income and in direct proportion to the size of its international debt. This last-resort, confiscatory action by the managers of the clearinghouse would make a payments adjustment via unilateral transfer payments in the current accounts.

Under either a fixed or a flexible rate system, nations may experience persistent trade deficits merely because their trading partners are not living up to their means— that is, because other nations are continually hoarding a portion of their foreign export earnings. By so doing, these oversavers are creating a lack of global effective demand.[9] The intention of this provision is to prevent deficit countries from having to deflate their domestic economies in order to adjust their payments imbalances because others are oversaving. Instead, the system would seek to remedy the payments deficit by increasing opportunities for deficit nations to sell abroad.

7. The long-term purchasing power of the IMCU in terms of each member nation's domestically produced market basket of goods would need to be stabilized. This would require a system of fixed exchange rates between the local currencies and the IMCU that would change only to reflect permanent increases in unit labor costs (wages in domestic currency divided by labor productivity). This would assure each central bank that its holdings of IMCUs as the nation's foreign reserves would never lose purchasing power in terms of foreign-produced goods, even if a foreign government permitted wage-price inflation to occur within its borders. Consequently, the nominal exchange rate between the local currency and the IMCU would change with inflation in the local money price of the domestic commodity basket.[10]

If, however, increases in productivity led to declining nominal production costs, then the nation with this decline in unit labor costs (say, a decline of 5 percent) would have the option of choosing either (a) to permit the IMCU to buy (up to 5 percent) fewer units of domestic currency, thereby capturing all (or most of) the gains from productivity for its residents while maintaining the purchasing power of the IMCU; or (b) to keep the nominal exchange rate constant. In the latter case, the gain in productivity would be shared with all trading partners. In exchange, the export industries in the more productive nation would receive an increasing relative share of the world market.

Altering the exchange rate between local monies and the IMCU to offset the rate of domestic inflation would stabilize the IMCU's purchasing power. Restricting use of IMCUs to central banks would avoid private speculation in IMCUs as a hedge against inflation. Each nation's rate of inflation for the goods and services it produces would be determined solely by the local government's policy toward the level of domestic money wages and profit margins vis-à-vis productivity gains. Each nation would therefore be free to experiment with policies for stabilizing its wages (relative to productivity and profits) to prevent inflation. Whether the nation was successful or not, the IMCU would never lose its international purchasing power. Moreover, the IMCU would have the promise of gaining in purchasing power over time, if productivity grew more rapidly than money wages and if each nation was willing to share any reduction in real production costs with its trading partners.

In such a system, the adjustability of nominal exchange rates would be used primarily (except as provided below) to offset changes in unit labor costs among trading partners. A beneficial effect that would follow from this proviso is that it would eliminate the possibility that a specific industry in any nation could be put at a competitive disadvantage against foreign producers (or secure a competitive advantage over them) solely because the nominal exchange rate changed independently of changes in the costs of production in each nation.

Consequently, nominal exchange rate variability could no longer create the problem of a loss of competitiveness due solely to the overvaluing of a currency as experienced, for example, by American industries during the 1982–85 period. Even if temporary, currency appreciation that is independent of changes in costs of production can cause significant permanent damage as industries abandon export markets and existing plant and equipment are cast aside as too costly to maintain. The mechanism proposed here would prevent such permanent damage, and also would prevent any nation from engaging in a beggar-thy-neighbor, unemployment-exporting policy by deliberately undervaluing its currency.

8. Although provision 6 above would prevent any country from piling up persistent excessive surpluses, this does not mean that it would be impossible for one or more nations to run persistent deficits. If a country at full employment still had a tendency toward persistent international deficits on its current account, then this country would not possess the productive capacity to maintain its current standard of living. If the deficit nation was a poor one, then surely there would be a case for the richer, surplus nations to transfer some of their excess credit balances to support the poor nation (see Davidson 1987–88). If it was a relatively rich country, then the deficit nation would have to alter its standard of living by reducing its relative terms of trade with its major trading partners. Rules, agreed upon in advance, would require the rich nation with a trade deficit to devalue its currency by stipulated increments per period until evidence became available to indicate that the export-import imbalance had been eliminated without unleashing significant recessionary forces.

If, on the other hand, the payments deficit persisted despite a continuous positive balance of trade in goods and nonfactor services, then there would be evidence that the deficit nation might be carrying too heavy an international debt service obligation. The officials of the clearinghouse should bring the debtor and creditors into negotiations to reduce annual debt service payments by lengthening the payments period, reducing the interest charges, and/or granting debt forgiveness.

Responses to Potential Objections

Many objections about the possible difficulties of installing this augmented fixed exchange rate system in the present circumstances could be raised. Without

Table 7.1

Comparison of OECD Estimates of Purchasing Power Parity and Actual Exchange Rates for the Japanese Yen and the German Deutsche Mark

	1985	1989
Yen–Dollar Exchange Rate		
PPP rate	222	204
Actual rate	238	138
DM–Dollar Exchange Rate		
PPP rate	2.48	2.41
Actual rate	2.94	1.88

Source: Organization for Economic Cooperation and Development (1991).

trying to provide a complete catalog of possible replies to potential critics, this subsection attempts to provide the reader with the kind of responses that can be offered to the most important types of objections that are likely to be raised.

1. Why not set the initial rate structure according to the purchasing power parity (PPP) of each currency?

The theoretical "ideal" exchange rate system, it is often claimed (e.g., by McKinnon 1988), would have exchange rates exactly reflecting PPPs so that the identical market basket of goods would cost the same (except for transportation costs) anywhere in the world, no matter what the money of contractual payment. Without necessarily accepting the notion that PPP exchange rates are ideal, as a practical matter, it would appear undesirable to set the initial rates based on estimates of PPPs whenever these estimates differed significantly from existing nominal parities at the time of conversion to the new system.

First, given the same historical facts, different so-called experts tend to provide significantly differing estimates of the "true" PPPs, although most agree that the existing rates are not generally PPPs. Consequently, any requirement that the initial setting must be based on a unique and commonly acceptable PPP will merely prevent any system from getting off the ground.

Second, and what is more important, the widespread existence of catenated money contracts in international transactions means that any sudden, major change in rates to set up PPPs would be highly disruptive of existing global international production and trade relationships, creating immediate windfall profits and losses. Such a change would, by fiat, alter the competitiveness of many industries in each nation. As already noted, such a change in competitiveness due to a change in nominal rates would create large real costs due to the sudden loss of markets and the loss of profitability of existing facilities.

Table 7.1 illustrates this problem. This table presents the estimates of PPP exchange rates and the actual exchange rates between the United States and Japan, and between the United States and West Germany, in 1985 and 1989 from the OECD. If these PPP estimates are taken seriously, then a movement toward a PPP rate system would require the United States to move back toward the exchange rates that existed in 1985. This would cause a severe loss of competitiveness for most of the reviving American industries, which, in the last few years, have made considerable investments to improve competitiveness. Imposing a system based on the OECD's estimates of PPPs would cause a windfall capital loss on recent capital investments and would simultaneously worsen the U.S. trade balance.

The purpose of introducing any new international payments system should be to improve trade, and not to disrupt it. As long as existing exchange rates do not reflect PPPs, the introduction of a payment system that imposes nominal rates equal to PPPs might kill the patient, even if the operation is successful. The simple expedient of permitting nations to start from close to the existing rate structure and then permitting realignments via provisions 7 and 8 above provides a better way of operating within a global full-employment environment without incurring significant and perhaps fatal real start-up costs.

2. Can any fixed exchange rate system be sustained if different nations pursue incompatible macroeconomic policies?

By definition, the pursuit of incompatible macroeconomic policies by large international trading nations involves disharmonies, incongruities, and antagonistic developments among nations. If trading partners are going to pursue disruptive and antagonistic macro policies, *no* international system can run smoothly, whether exchange rates are fixed or flexible. In other words, no system can automatically harmonize inconsistent macro policies among nations. In an interdependent global economy, if nations do not all hang together, they will surely all hang separately.

The real question is whether a fixed exchange rate system can be sustained if "different" (not incompatible) macro policies are instituted in different regions. The response to the latter query is definitely yes, provided that the different regions are experiencing different economic conditions. Suppose there were depressed and prosperous regions in different parts of the same nation. An enlightened approach would be expected to have deficit spending, easier credit terms, and so forth, in the depressed region, and less government spending, more tax collections, and possibly even a more restrictive monetary policy in the prosperous region. There is no reason such regional differential policies could not be pursued between nations operating with a fixed exchange rate system.

In any case, the proposals advanced here do allow for adjustments of exchange rates (parities between national currencies and the IMCU) to offset changes in relative unit labor costs (provision 7) as well as to help structural deficit countries balance their trade (provision 8). To the extent that these problems arise as a result of different macro policies in different countries, then, the system proposed here does allow for some flexibility of exchange rates in response to different macro policies.

Comparisons with Alternative Proposals

Two other alternative proposals for an international payments system have appeared in the recent literature: Williamson's (1987) target-zone, fixed real rate system and McKinnon's (1988) fixed nominal-PPP exchange rate system. While both of these proposals have some aspects in common with the proposal made here, there are also some important differences.

Both Williamson and McKinnon accept the argument that the existing flexible rate system is fundamentally flawed. McKinnon notes the tremendous "dissatisfaction with wildly fluctuating relative currency values, euphemistically called 'floating' or 'flexible' exchange rates" (1988, p. 83). Williamson argues that the post–Bretton Woods flexible exchange rate system "has proved unsatisfactory" for two major reasons. First, it has led to "recurring, and at times massive, currency misalignments ... [where a] misalignment is defined as a persistent deviation of the real exchange rate from the 'fundamental equilibrium exchange rate,' the level that can be expected in the medium term to reconcile internal and external balance" (1987, pp. 200, 200n). Second, according to Williamson, the flexible rate system fails to "pressure ... countries ... to coordinate their economic policies" (p. 200).

Williamson recommends a "target zone system" in which "a limited number of major countries negotiate a set of mutually consistent targets" for fixing exchange rates to maintain internal and external balance in the "medium term" (1987, p. 202). Williamson defines internal balance as "the lowest unemployment rate consistent with the control of inflation," without specifying what inflation rate and what unemployment rate are acceptable under this internal equilibrium concept. He defines external balance as "a current account balance that is sustainable and appropriate in light of thrift and productivity" (p. 202). Exchange rates would be permitted to fluctuate within a broad zone of plus or minus 10 percent around the target.

McKinnon recommends a system in which the central banks of the United States, Germany, and Japan would announce fixed nominal targets for exchange rates (within a narrow band) "set to approximate sustainable purchasing power parities" (1988, p. 87). Once these targets were set, McKinnon claims, all that would be necessary would be for the major central banks to "adjust their domestic money supplies to maintain these nominal exchange rate parities and, concomitantly, maintain roughly the same rates of domestic price inflation in internationally tradable goods" (p. 87).

Williamson would have central bankers negotiate a set of *real* exchange rates based on the amorphous idea of maintaining simultaneous internal and external equilibrium. Even Williamson admits that these equilibrium notions "involve an element of subjective judgment and will therefore permit obfuscation" (1987, p. 202). McKinnon, on the other hand, would have *nominal* rates fixed into the indefinite future based on current calculations of PPP. My proposal would start with existing nominal exchange rate parities, in order not to disrupt existing trade relations merely to start up a new system. Since both the Williamson and the McKinnon proposals envision significant changes in the existing exchange rates on the date of conversion to the new system, both proposals involve potentially large, real start-up costs. Since my proposal accepts the existing rate structure, no such start-up costs would be incurred.

Under what conditions should the fixed rates be changed? In essence, Williamson indicates that rates would not change as long as the authorities used coordinated interest rate policy to "manage the exchange rate." The targets, however, "should be regularly updated in the light of new data on differential inflation between countries ... [and] real shocks or new information" (1987, p. 202). Moreover, under Williamson's proposal a nation "need not accept an absolute obligation to keep its exchange rate within the target zone" (p. 202). Accordingly, changes would be permitted whenever the governmental authorities thought conditions warranted a change. No discipline would be imposed on the authorities to adopt policies either to control inflation differentials or otherwise to cushion the economy against real shocks.

Thus, Williamson's target-zone approach retains sufficient exchange rate flexibility to make the official target rates vulnerable to destabilizing speculation. McKinnon is therefore right when he says that, because Williamson's proposal "keep[s] open the option for occasional official adjustments in par values ... his system would remain vulnerable to speculative attack" (1988, p. 100). In addition, there is little discipline in Williamson's proposal to prevent the reemergence of beggar-thy-neighbor devaluations via discretionary changes in target exchange rates.

McKinnon argues that there would never be a need for the authorities to change the initial PPP rate, provided they followed the rules he suggests. In the McKinnon proposal, it is presumed that money wages and price levels would adjust to the nominal anchor of fixed PPP rates. Central banks would be forced to control money supplies to maintain these parities, and under strong monetarist assumptions the requisite monetary policies would have no "real" effects on output or employment (there would be a so-called neutrality of money). McKinnon assumes away speculative pressures by asserting that, as long as market traders *believed* that the authorities would keep the rates unchanged, there could be no reason to speculate. McKinnon does not deal with the case in which traders begin to doubt either the authorities' ability or their will!

What about trade imbalances? In McKinnon's fixed exchange rate scheme, trade deficits or surpluses could continually develop "depending on relative national imbalances between saving and investment" (1988, p. 98). Those whose saving exceeded domestic investment (assuming no government deficit) would, by definition, have to generate trade surpluses, and vice versa for nations with trade deficits.

Nevertheless, according to McKinnon, there would be no need for either trading partner to initiate an adjustment process to this trade imbalance. All that would be required would be a net transfer of real capital from the deficit country to the surplus country. This transfer would be accomplished by normal market processes under McKinnon's rules. The relative expansion of bank money in the deficit nation, because of the neutrality of money, would result only in a price increase of nontradables (relative to tradables) in the trade deficit nation. The oversaving (surplus) nation would experience "a slower increase in . . . nontradables prices" (McKinnon 1988, pp. 98–99).

If money were presumed neutral, there could be no change in the level of employment in the deficit (or the surplus) nation solely due to the alleged greater expansion (contraction) of bank credit money supply. Since the price of tradables would be, by hypothesis, kept in line in each nation through foreign competition and a PPP exchange rate, then the alleged relative rise in the money supply in the deficit nation could only induce a rise in the price of nontradables (and vice versa for the surplus nation). This differential, sectoral inflation rate—within a coordinated common aggregate inflation rate among the trading partners—would be the mechanism for transferring real wealth from the nation suffering from the deficit to the nation with a surplus.

McKinnon claims, but does not prove, that "[a]lthough these relative price movements within both countries would be modest, gradual, and need not be permanent, they would be sufficient to support the transfer of savings from one highly open economy to another" (1988, p. 99). Apparently, this wealth transfer could continue until either the deficit nation ran its stock of wealth down to zero or the rising real wealth of the surplus nation increased its demand for imports while the declining real wealth of the deficit nation reduced its demand for imports sufficiently to bring about a trade balance. Although the surplus nation would be becoming richer and the deficit nation poorer because of this hypothesized wealth transfer (induced by differential rates of money growth between the trading partners), global economic growth would be unaffected as long as the axiom of monetary neutrality was accepted. By presumption, therefore, no aggregate real economic losses would occur as nations adjusted to trade imbalances, in the McKinnon analysis.

In the absence of money neutrality, however, it cannot be demonstrated that the McKinnon proposal would resolve the problem of payments imbalances without imposing *real* contractionary consequences on all trading partners—at least in the short run.

To his credit, McKinnon recognizes that in his system, trade deficits could continually occur because of differential rates of savings, real income growth, and so forth. Williamson, on the other hand, denies the possibility of such occurrences under his proposal. Williamson explains away the problem by defining the targets in terms of a mutually consistent set of exchange rates that would maintain current account balances (a condition of external balance). There is, however, a fundamental logical flaw in Williamson's argument. It involves his assumption that there exists a unique set of real exchange rates that could maintain simultaneously both "the lowest unemployment rate consistent with the control of inflation" and "a current account balance that is both sustainable and appropriate in the light of productivity and thrift" (1987, p. 202). It is not logically possible to prove that there exists any set of exchange parities that would simultaneously assure a current account balance for all nations and fully employed workers in all nations. Consequently, it might be impossible for central banks to negotiate rates that would achieve the simultaneous equilibrium targets that Williamson has set for them.

Thus, a major problem with Williamson's proposal is that it would explicitly allow for the acceptance of high rates of unemployment if they were deemed necessary to control inflation and to achieve current account balance. Thus, a situation of chronically depressed demand could be defined as consistent with simultaneous internal and external balance. In this respect, Williamson's proposal would not eliminate the contractionary biases that are built into current international payments arrangements, which put most of the adjustment burden on the deficit countries to reduce their spending. In contrast, the proposals advocated here are designed to make the surplus countries bear a larger part of the burden of adjustment by stimulating global demand growth.

McKinnon, on the other hand, implicitly believes that trade imbalances would not create any global depressionary problem. McKinnon's neutrality of money presumption solves this problem by assuming it away. McKinnon (1988, p. 94) has argued that exchange rate flexibility does not facilitate balance-of-payments adjustment because trade balances depend more on savings and spending decisions and income effects than on relative prices and substitution effects. McKinnon argues that a trade imbalance could persist because of different income elasticities for imports and exports.[11]

These differentials in income elasticities could, through a "balance-of-payments constraint," force nations with trade deficits to reduce their growth rate of GNP.[12] Moreover, income elasticity differences could force the developing countries that specialized in the production of crops and/or minerals (except perhaps oil) to grow at a much slower pace than the more industrialized nations of the world.[13] Furthermore, since population growth is likely to be larger in LDCs than in industrialized countries, such a scenario could, under the McKinnon proposal, easily lead to a decline in per capita GNP for the poorest of the developing nations.

Unfortunately, McKinnon's plan, like Williamson's, does not explain how to deal with potentially disruptive forces, if they should arise. For example, what would happen under McKinnon's plan if social and political actions caused wages to rise more rapidly than productivity even as the nation faced a trade deficit? Under McKinnon's proposal, all countries' inflation rates would tend to converge, preferably to zero (1988, p. 97). If political and social powers forced wages to rise more rapidly than productivity in any major nation, the effect would be to force a convergence toward a common higher inflation rate, *unless* additional depressing pressures were applied to weaken workers' wage demands. The resulting increase in unemployment could lower import demands and therefore have spillover consequences to the country's trading partners. Severe and prolonged unemployment and business losses could be the necessary requirements for any nation (or group of nations, or even world economy) to make the necessary adjustments to bring about convergence to a zero rate of inflation.

Conclusion

My suggested provisions for a new international payments system are not unalterable either in principle or for practical reasons. Instead, they should provide the basis for the beginning of a sound analytical discussion of how to prepare for a twenty-first-century international monetary system.

The problems facing the international payments system are not easily resolved. If we start with the defeatist attitude that it is too difficult to change the awkward system in which we are enmeshed, then no progress will be made. We must reject such defeatism at this exploratory stage and merely ask whether these particular proposals for improving the operations of the international payments system to promote global growth will create more difficulties than other proposed innovations. The health of the world economic system will not permit us to muddle through!

Notes

1. The *Economist* magazine indicated that the decade of the 1980s will be noted as one in which "the experiment with floating currencies failed" (January 6, 1990). Almost two years earlier, the London *Financial Times* had admitted that "floating exchange rates, it is now clear, were sold on a false prospectus. . . . [T]hey held out a quite illusory promise of greater national autonomy . . . [but] when macropolicies are inconsistent and when capital is globally mobile, floating rates cannot be relied upon to keep the current accounts roughly in balance" (February 17, 1987).

2. This requirement of increased liquidity facilities for additional working capital loans is readily understood by every entrepreneur who has ever attempted to increase production to meet an expected increase in sales. This financial requirement for expansion has a long history in economics known as the *real bills* doctrine. The concept of "real bills" was written into the Federal Reserve Act, which gave the Fed the responsibility to provide an "elastic currency" to meet the needs of trade.

3. Yet, as suggested above, continuing unilateral transfers via the Marshall Plan were in the self-interest of residents of both the deficit and the surplus regions.

4. If, for example, the deficit region either is undeveloped or is an area of relatively high unemployment, then modern, nonconservative central government taxing and spending patterns are likely to permit the financing of regional deficits as long as these economic discrepancies between regions persist. Often it is recognized that such regional redistribution may have to continue indefinitely—if there are not sufficient regional devel-

opment opportunities to permit these government transfers to be the equivalent of self-liquidating loans.

5. This does not deny that some groups of trading partners may wish to integrate their central banks and banking systems into a regional UMS common market. Implicit in much of "Europe 1992" planning was the belief that ultimately there would be a single currency among the European Community (EC) of nations governed by a single supranational central bank. If some nations were willing to develop an interregional UMS, they would be free to develop their own UMS clearing mechanism, which would operate as a single unit in the larger global clearinghouse proposed below. For more on the UMS idea, see Davidson (1982).

6. This provision provides an added bonus by making tax avoidance and profits from illegal trade more difficult to conceal. Small-scale smuggling of currency across borders, etc., can never be completely eliminated. Such movements are merely a minor, but not debilitating, irritation. If, however, most of the residents of a nation hold and use (in violation of legal tender laws) a foreign currency for domestic transactions and as a store of value, this is evidence of a lack of confidence in the government and its monetary authority. Unless confidence is restored, all attempts to restore economic prosperity will fail.

7. Some may fear that if a surplus nation were close to the trigger point, it could short-circuit the system by making loans to reduce its credit balance *prior* to setting off the trigger. Since preventing unreasonable debt service obligations is an important objective of this proposal, a mechanism for monitoring and restricting such pretrigger lending activities might be required.

One possible way of eliminating this trigger-avoidance lending loophole would be to agree on sensible and flexible criteria for judging when debt-servicing burdens became unreasonable. Given these criteria, the clearinghouse managers would have the responsibility for preventing additional loans that would push debt burdens beyond reasonable servicing levels. In other words, loans that pushed debt burdens too far could not be cleared though the clearinghouse; the managers would refuse to release the IMCUs for loan purposes from the surplus country's account.

The managers would also be required to make periodic public reports on the level of credits being accumulated by surplus nations and to indicate how close these surpluses were to the trigger point. Such reports would provide an informational edge for debtor nations, permitting them to bargain more successfully regarding the terms of refinancing existing loans and/or new loans. All loans would still have to meet the clearinghouse's guidelines for reasonableness.

I do not discount the difficulties involved in setting up and getting agreement on criteria for establishing unreasonable debt service burdens. In the absence of cooperation and a spirit of goodwill that would be necessary to enable the clearinghouse to provide a mechanism assuring the economic prosperity of all members, however, no progress could ever be made.

Moreover, as the recent international debt problems of African and Latin American nations clearly demonstrate, creditors ultimately have to forgive some debt when they previously have encouraged excessive debt burdens. Under the current system, however, debt forgiveness is a last-resort solution acceptable only after both debtor and creditor nations suffer from faltering economic growth. Surely a more intelligent option would be to develop an institutional arrangement that would prevent excessive debt-servicing burdens from ever occurring.

8. *Oversaving* is defined as a nation's persistently spending less on imports plus direct equity foreign investment than the sum of the nation's export earnings plus net unilateral transfers.

9. Even Williamson recognizes that when balance-of-payments "disequilibrium is due

purely to excess or deficient demand," flexible exchange rates per se cannot facilitate international payments adjustments (1987, p. 201).

10. Technically, the rate of increase in unit labor costs will equal the rate of price inflation only if profit markup rates are constant, and, therefore, changes in unit labor costs should also be adjusted for changes in average markup rates. However, in the long run, changes in markup rates are likely to be proportionally small compared to changes in (nominal) unit labor costs.

11. The income elasticity of demand for a country's exports is the percentage by which demand for exports increases when foreign income rises by 1 percent; the income elasticity of demand for imports is the analogous percentage by which demand for imports rises when national income rises by 1 percent.

12. For further discussion, see Thirlwall (1979) and Davidson (1990–91).

13. This argument is developed in Davidson (1990–91).

Bibliography

Adelman, Irma. 1991. "Long Term Economic Development." Working Paper No. 589. Berkeley: California Agricultural Experiment Station (March).

Davidson, Paul. 1982. *International Money and the Real World.* London: Macmillan.

———. 1987–88. "A Modest Set of Proposals for Resolving the International Debt Problem." *Journal of Post Keynesian Economics,* Vol. 10 (Winter), pp. 323–38.

———. 1990–91. "A Post Keynesian Positive Contribution to 'Theory.' " *Journal of Post Keynesian Economics,* Vol. 13 (Winter).

———. 1992–93. "Reforming the World's Money." *Journal of Post Keynesian Economics,* Vol. 15 (Winter), pp. 153–79.

Keynes, John Maynard. 1980. *The Collected Writings of J. M. Keynes,* Vol. 25. London: Macmillan.

Kindleberger, Charles P. 1987. *Marshall Plan Days.* Boston: George Allen and Unwin.

Leontief, Wassily. 1990. "A Second Marshall Plan." In A. Cleese and A. C. Epps., eds., *Present at the Creation.* New York: Harper and Row.

McKinnon, Ronald I. 1988. "Monetary and Exchange Rate Policies for International Financial Stability: A Proposal." *Journal of Economic Perspectives,* Vol. 2 (Winter), pp. 83–103.

———. 1990. "Interest Rate Volatility and Exchange Risk: New Rules for a Common Monetary Standard." *Contemporary Policy Studies,* Vol. 8 (April).

Organization for Economic Cooperation and Development. 1991. *National Accounts,* Vol. 1, *Main Aggregates,* 1960–89. Paris: OECD.

Thirlwall, A. P. 1979. "The Balance of Payments Constraint as an Explanation of International Growth Rate Differences." *Banca Nazionale del Lavoro Quarterly Review,* No. 128 (March), pp. 45–53.

Williamson, John. 1987. "Exchange Rate Management: The Role of Target Zones." *American Economic Review Papers, Papers and Proceedings,* Vol. 77, No. 2 (May), pp. 200–204.

PART IV

Trade Policies in
the Developing Countries

CHAPTER EIGHT

Income Distribution, Trade, and Growth

LANCE TAYLOR

Introduction

Growth rates of output and movements in the distributions of income and wealth in developing countries have differed widely over the past two decades. In light of this diverse experience, it is reasonable to ask two questions. First, what factors beyond the control of policy makers helped produce these results? Second, do the results point to a need to take into account local history and institutions in formulating development strategy, or is there some royal policy road that inevitably leads to a rapidly growing, egalitarian Rome?

This chapter addresses these questions from several angles. Broadly speaking, its answer to the first question is that while policy errors certainly worsened some countries' problems,[1] there was also a massive withdrawal of external resources that held down Third World growth over the decade of the 1980s. This trend continued into 1990–91, when average growth rates of real gross domestic product (GDP) in two of the World Bank's four major regions (sub-Saharan Africa and the developing nations of Southern Europe, the Middle East, and North Africa)[2] were –1.4 and –3.8 percent respectively, while countries in Latin America and the Caribbean grew at –2.5 percent in 1990 and 0.5 percent in 1991, and Asian economies averaged 3.7 percent.

Scarce foreign exchange also contributed to faster inflations and more regressive income distributions. Small reversals of capital outflows and lower international interest rates helped create upticks in growth in a few places in 1991, but prospects for the immediate future are still not bright. In particular, at the country level they will be strongly affected by how the external constraint interacts with other key macroeconomic factors such as the fiscal constraint and flows of investment and saving.

This chapter describes these relationships quantitatively for a representative sample of developing countries, and sets up a simple "three-gap" model that

Comments on previous drafts by Robert Blecker, Gerry Helleiner, Desmond McCarthy, and Dani Schydlowsky, and support from the Economic Policy Institute, are gratefully acknowledged.

captures their salient features. The model was used to calculate the additional foreign resource inflows necessary to allow the countries to return to historical growth rates of per capita income. When these requirements are extrapolated to all developing economies, the total comes to $40 billion to $60 billion, or 1.5 to 2 percent of Third World GDP. At the moment, poor countries are transferring around $90 billion to industrialized nations via trade surpluses (World Bank 1991). Driving this transfer toward zero will be an important developmental goal for the 1990s.

With regard to the second question, the recent mainstream view, as enunciated in a "Washington consensus" (Williamson 1990) and the World Bank's *World Development Report 1991 (WDR)*, is that "market-friendly" policies ought to be applied in nearly all developing economies almost all the time. The counterargument is that while the importance of well-functioning markets cannot be denied, local economic structures and circumstances do matter. Sensible macroeconomic policy together with context-relevant trade, industrial, and agricultural interventions make far more sense than lunging for International Monetary Fund–style (IMF-style) stabilization and World Bank liberalization across the board. Each country has its *own* policy Rome; the trick is to map a road that gets there.

Since not all poor economies share the same structures and behavioral relationships, the discussion in this chapter is necessarily rather detailed. However, it does point to some generalizations about policy packages that are appropriate in given contexts. In the "Conclusions" section, these lessons are summarized in the form of contrasts between the market-friendly Washington consensus (WC) view and more realistic approaches.

Fiscal and Trade Positions

Recent patterns of financial intermediation and public saving and capital formation in less developed countries (LDCs) have characteristic features that are illustrated by the data in Table 8.1. These data are drawn from detailed country studies published by the United Nations World Institute for Development Economics Research (WIDER).[3] Five points stand out:

1. The public sector plays an important role in capital formation in all the countries, from free market bastions like Chile and Malaysia to statist India, Turkey, and Zimbabwe. Beyond public investment in infrastructure and resource extraction, additional considerations are involved.

As discussed more fully below, if there is any developing country rule, it is that state and/or foreign help is usually needed to get new industrial activities under way. The capital stocks in technically advanced branches may be publicly owned (the model in Turkey, India, and Brazil) or just publicly supported (as were the *Chaebol* in South Korea), but historically they have not been the product of private initiative alone (Shapiro and Taylor 1990). When new capacity

Table 8.1

Developing Country Trade, Investment, and Saving Flows
(in percentages of GDP)

	Investment						Saving		
	Intermediate imports	Imported capital goods	Domestic capital goods	Public sector	Private sector	Total	Public sector	Private sector	Trade deficit
Argentina (1988)	6.0	1.8	12.6	7.6	6.8	14.4	0.8	15.6	−2.0
Brazil (1987)	3.8	2.1	17.9	6.2	13.8	20.0	6.2	18.3	−4.5
Chile (1988)	14.9	6.8	11.6	7.9	10.5	18.4	5.7	15.6	−2.9
Colombia (1988)	5.4	3.5	14.6	7.1	11.0	18.1	4.0	16.7	−2.6
India (1987–88)	4.5	2.4	20.8	12.7	10.5	23.2	2.4	18.9	1.9
South Korea (1987)	24.7	15.7	13.9	6.2	23.4	29.6	11.1	28.5	−10.0
Malaysia (1988)	22.1	11.5	11.7	9.3	13.9	23.2	5.9	27.5	−10.2
Mexico (1988)	7.9	2.5	18.1	6.4	14.2	20.6	4.2	20.1	−3.7
Nicaragua (1989)	17.5	12.1	12.1	2.1	22.1	24.2	−2.0	9.5	16.7
Nigeria (1986)	1.7	3.8	8.1	7.6	4.3	11.9	3.1	8.9	−0.1
Philippines (1988)	11.4	4.4	13.8	3.0	15.2	18.2	0.0	19.2	−1.0
Sri Lanka (1987)	11.5	6.5	19.9	14.9	11.5	26.4	4.4	18.0	4.0
Tanzania (1986)	5.7	11.9	15.0	8.3	18.6	26.9	5.6	11.8	9.5
Thailand (1987)	9.8	8.6	15.0	6.7	16.9	23.6	5.4	19.7	−1.5
Turkey (1987)	13.5	1.0	24.4	13.3	12.1	25.4	8.2	19.5	−2.3
Uganda (1987)	5.6	8.6	8.4	3.9	13.1	17.0	−5.6	16.0	6.6
Zambia (1987)	30.7	8.0	2.7	7.7	3.0	10.7	−16.7	32.5	−5.1
Zimbabwe (1986)	11.1	7.1	15.4	11.9	10.6	22.5	−5.1	30.9	−3.3

Source: Taylor (1993).

creation relies on inputs from transnational corporations (TNCs), the state has to be active as well, in regulating and bargaining with these powerful economic actors. Otherwise, it has to help local producers hunt new technology along Japanese and Korean lines (Amsden 1989; Katz 1991). In a poor country, private entities generally lack the economic sophistication and clout to undertake these tasks.

An important aspect of this complementarity is that public capital formation can facilitate or "crowd in" private investment. This linkage was found in time-series analysis for the 1970s and 1980s in most of the country studies underlying Table 8.1 (Taylor 1993), and appears to be the rule in industrial countries as well.[4] For macroeconomic programming, public capital formation may be the only vehicle for stimulating investment after adverse shocks. Unless export growth bootstraps investment up in a cumulative process along Korean lines (certainly an outlying case among developing economies), it is hard to see how private capital formation will recuperate in and of itself.

2. Table 8.1 also illustrates that the public sector is typically a strong net saver. The only exceptions are macroeconomically distressed Nicaragua, Uganda, and Zambia, along with Zimbabwe, where for historical reasons the private saving rate is abnormally high. Saving by the public sector reflects its activity in capital formation, as well as the unique ability of the state to gather resources.

3. Private saving flows in Table 8.1 are also large, and their intermediation into capital formation and/or loans to the state to cover the public sector borrowing requirement (PSBR) poses questions about how to set up effective channels for financial intermediation, which are discussed later on.

4. Most economies in Table 8.1 have negative trade deficits, or surpluses (for trade in merchandise and nonfactor services), signifying net outflows of real resources. In many cases, these reflect foreign shocks suffered in the 1980s. Latin American and some other countries had to run surpluses in order to meet foreign interest obligations at the same time as their governments needed fiscal surpluses (apart from interest obligations) to meet overseas payments since they had nationalized foreign debts. This "double transfer" problem has crippled stabilization efforts and fiscal rectitude, as discussed further below.

Poor primary product exporters in Africa and elsewhere were hit by steady declines in their terms of trade and lagging export volumes. Countries such as Uganda, Tanzania, and Sri Lanka became highly dependent on foreign donors to make up the difference; their support produced trade deficits that will not be sustainable in the long run.

Finally, economies such as Malaysia and South Korea enjoy surpluses due to strong exports. Malaysia's positive trade balance may erode as exploitable resources such as timber and oil are depleted, while Korea's surplus results from decades of export-led growth that are virtually unparalleled in the modern era.

5. The last point to be noted in connection with Table 8.1 is the extreme

import dependence of developing economies: shares of both intermediate and capital goods imports in GDP are large, especially in East Asian economies such as Korea, Malaysia, Thailand, and the Philippines.

In all LDCs, capital goods and intermediate imports are essentially "noncompetitive" in the sense that they and similar products are not produced nationally, but they can play different strategic roles. Malaysia and Thailand, for example, increasingly are serving as platforms for assembly of exportable final goods by Japanese firms. Thai imports from Japan rose from $2 billion to $9 billion per year between 1986 and 1990; exports to the United States and Japan increased from about $1 billion to $4 billion each. Korea's big import shares reflect poor natural resource endowments and a hypertrophied industrial sector. Elsewhere, as in India and Brazil, intermediate import shares are low because they are large countries that have long pursued import-substituting industrialization (ISI).

A Three-Gap Model

Older economic models of the development process (e.g., Chenery and Bruno 1962) stressed the importance of two "gaps" that constrain capital accumulation (investment and growth) in developing countries: the saving and the foreign exchange gaps. The saving gap is the amount by which savings generated internally by private savers (households and businesses) plus the government budget surplus (or minus the deficit) fall short of the desired level of investment, requiring foreign capital inflows to bring in "foreign savings." The foreign exchange gap is the difference between needed imports of capital goods and raw materials plus debt service (all of which require outflows of hard currencies), and export earnings (which generate revenues in hard currencies). Foreign capital inflows can also fill this gap as foreign lending comes in hard currencies. Much analysis in economic development has centered on the relative importance of these two gaps and on alternative policies for relieving them.[5]

The foregoing discussion suggests that at least a third gap—the fiscal gap—should be added to these traditional foreign exchange and saving constraints in order to take into account the linked fiscal and foreign transfer limitations on policy choice that have become crucial in the Third World. I will discuss the fiscal, saving, and foreign exchange gaps in sequence.

Effects of fiscal deficits on inflation and/or on the public debt/output ratio are taken up in the following section; to ease cross-country comparisons, the PSBR is the focus of attention here. It is defined by the following accounting equation.

(1)   PSBR = government current spending – revenue from national sources
            + public investment + foreign interest payments
            – net transfers to the government from abroad

Following Taylor (1991, 1993) and many others, a minimally adequate country model has to incorporate five features, as follows:

1. The utilization and growth rates of capacity or potential output need not be closely linked. The experience of the 1980s amply demonstrates that output can fall below its potential when the economy is subjected to strong enough shocks. Both the *growth rate* of potential output or capacity and the rate at which that capacity is utilized (the *utilization rate,* measured by the ratio of actual output to full-capacity output) must be endogenous variables in a growth model; as we will see below, under a binding external constraint one of these variables may go up when the other goes down.

2. Another important question regards capital formation. The possibility that private investment is crowded in by public capital formation has to be included, and raises interesting questions about the fiscal role of the state.

3. The government's revenue from national sources net of current expenditure is usually an increasing function of the rate of capacity use; taxes and other receipts rise more rapidly than real spending when economic activity goes up. Public investment enters the fiscal accounts as shown in equation 1. It can increase as a function of capacity utilization and foreign transfers to the government, and decrease with interest payments to foreign countries. By crowding in private investment, more public capital formation raises the growth rate of capacity. An upward-sloping relationship results, via which a higher utilization rate can push up the growth rate by generating more net fiscal revenue, which is channeled to capital formation. This is shown by the schedule *GG* in Figure 8.1, which represents the fiscal gap or fiscal constraint.

4. Available saving also puts a limit on investment and potential output growth. Three sources can be considered: net government saving or the PSBR minus public investment, net foreign transfers from abroad (measured in the model's accounting by the trade deficit, and flowing to either the private or the public sector), and national saving by the private sector (assumed to increase with capacity utilization in standard fashion).

Such a saving function underlies another positive relationship between the utilization and growth rates, shown as schedule *SS* in Figure 8.1 (this is the saving gap or constraint). Depending on parameter values, the saving constraint on growth may rise more or less steeply than the fiscal constraint *(GG)* as a function of the utilization rate. A steeper saving schedule means that raising public investment to stimulate overall capital formation will land the government in fiscal difficulties, even though total saving in principle would be large enough to finance the additional investment demand.

Another, potentially troubling aspect of private saving is that it may not be directed toward investment at home; it can filter out via capital flight. Typical vehicles are overinvoicing of imports and underinvoicing of exports. Their outcomes in terms of national accounting conventions are lower national and higher foreign savings. Corresponding downward shifts of the *GG*

Figure 8.1. **A Three-Gap Model**

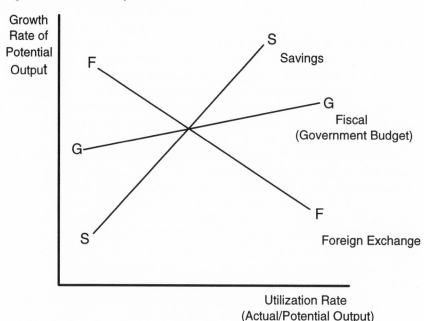

Utilization Rate
(Actual/Potential Output)

and *SS* schedules were notable in countries like Argentina and Mexico in the 1980s.

5. The last important linkage is the foreign exchange constraint. As noted above, production and capital formation depend crucially on imports of intermediate and investment goods. Especially for the small, open economies in the sample, these requirements at the margin can be large.

On the side of foreign sales, a common story (especially in economies with a manufacturing base such as Turkey or Brazil) is that producers cut back on exports as domestic demand rises. Especially if a firm is operating near full capacity, it often finds it easier to direct a given volume of output toward the local market. This response helps generate the following scenario: rising output pulls in intermediate imports and reduces export revenue; a higher utilization rate requires more foreign exchange. Since faster capacity growth also depends upon imports, an increase in one variable forces the other down. Thus, we get the negatively sloped relationship *FF* in Figure 8.1, which represents the foreign exchange constraint or gap.

This trade-off is central to macroeconomic decision making in the medium run. In Africa, for example, policy makers targeted measures such as import quotas and credit restrictions explicitly toward sustaining either capital formation or current production when external strangulation became acute. At the same time, aid donors imposed pressures to keep ongoing investment projects under way. The outcome in Tanzania was continued investment, while capacity utilization fell by 20 percent between 1976 and 1986. Other countries subject to import compression, such as Zimbabwe (which had fewer donor obligations), reacted the other way.

With these building blocks, the key questions relate to how a model should hang together. Which variables adjust to make *GG, SS,* and *FF* intersect at one point in the diagram? How should they be deployed in simulations to illuminate problems of policy choice? Answers to both questions rely on intimate understanding of the institutions and adjustment mechanisms of the economy at hand. The possibilities are discussed in the following section, but to wind up this discussion it makes sense to walk through one rather mechanical—although interesting—"closure" of the basic model.

Following Johansen (1960), the saving, foreign, and fiscal balances can be solved in a "planning" fashion to give cross-country comparisons of resource needs for faster growth. For a given target, say an increase in potential output growth of 1 percent, the foreign and saving gaps give corresponding values of capacity utilization and net foreign transfers to the government (or for extra taxes if the utilization rate is 100 percent). The fiscal gap then gives the required PSBR.

When such computations are extrapolated to all the developing world from the WIDER sample, the estimate of foreign resource transfers required to restore minimal, socially adequate growth rates is $40 billion to $60 billion per year in the early 1990s, and it rises steadily over the decade (Taylor 1993). Such an increased transfer can usefully be contrasted to the current net flow or trade surplus of develop*ing* countries to develop*ed* countries of nearly $100 billion annually. The industrial world seems unlikely to generate an equal transfer stream in the opposite direction, although it certainly had no qualms in coming up with payments of that magnitude during the 1991 war of the rest of the world against Iraq.

In a word, scarce external resources go a long way toward explaining the poor LDC growth rates mentioned at the outset. The interacting distributional and policy responses that mediated the slowdown are reviewed next.[6]

Income Distribution and the Adjustment Process

Three-gap models emphasize how an economy adjusts to shocks in the range of a few percentage points of GDP via variations in output and capital formation. Other channels are opened by changes in the national distributions of income and wealth induced by price and quantity fluctuations. For its own ends, the state also may seek to alter distribution. The change may be a primary goal—for example, an attempt to raise real wages on the part of a government with strong working-class support, such as Salvador Allende's in Chile in the early 1970s. Later in that decade, the successor Pinochet regime undertook massive wealth redistribution upward, favoring its own bourgeois "Chicago boy" clients by selling them the enterprises nationalized under Allende at knockdown prices. As described below, the subsequent financial speculation by these clients cost the country dearly in the medium run.

Alternatively, distributional changes may result from other policies. A program for ISI typically switches relative prices against agriculture by a variety of methods (import tariffs or quotas, an "overvalued" exchange rate,[7] etc.); pro-farmer strategies move sectoral prices and incomes the other way. As already mentioned, in the wake of the debt crisis most governments nationalized private, external obligations—a wealth transfer deemed essential to save local financial systems.

Distributional shifts—both endogenous and policy-induced—thus emerge as key linkages among shifts in capacity utilization, foreign transfers, the PSBR, and capital formation. Along lines set out in Taylor (1991), at least eight sorts of relationships recur in developing economies. These are summarized here:

1. If output is not limited by available capacity or other constraints, it may well be stimulated from the side of aggregate demand by progressive income redistribution in general and higher real wages in particular: "wage-led growth" appears to be a frequent occurrence, especially in the short to medium run.

Demand expansion due to real wage increases may crowd out exports and pull in intermediate imports, as described in the previous section, creating stabilization problems, which are discussed below. A positive wage/output linkage also complicates adjustments to rising labor productivity. If surplus labor is present, a productivity gain (or a fall in the labor/output ratio) is not likely to be accompanied by a higher real wage. At the initial level of output, total wage payments will decline, reducing consumption demand and ultimately also reducing investment and potential output growth via the accelerator. On the other hand, if exports are sensitive to local production costs that are reduced by the productivity increase, they may jump up enough to raise total output. The price elasticity of "our" exports becomes a crucial parameter, via which productivity and wage changes can feed into dynamic growth processes.

2. In the short run, currency devaluation drives up prices from the side of input costs (recall the large intermediate import component in developing country cost structures—an artifact of ISI—from Table 8.1). If money wages are not fully indexed to rising prices, real wages will fall and output will contract. This effect is reinforced if there is an initial trade deficit, for then devaluation raises exporters' incomes by a smaller absolute amount than importers' costs, again reducing local spending power.

An offsetting possibility is that devaluation, along with other moves to "get prices right," may boost exports enough to create net aggregate demand. This happened in the mid-1980s in Malaysia and Thailand, where devaluation in effect ratified a shift in comparative advantage in low-wage manufactures in their direction from countries like South Korea and Taiwan and encouraged their transformations into export platforms.

A third contingency is that depreciation may be accompanied by large incoming transfers from foreign donors, making the depreciation look expansionary and anti-inflationary as the foreign exchange constraint is lifted. Ghana early and Tanzania late in the 1980s are examples.

The obverse scenario takes over when, with a truly binding external constraint, a decrease in capital inflows accelerates inflation (for reasons to be discussed shortly). This leads to real appreciation of the domestic currency if the nominal exchange rate is fixed (or if the price of foreign exchange rises more slowly than domestic inflation relative to foreign), and further deterioration in the balance of payments then ensues. This potential problem applied in Ghana in the 1960s and 1970s and in Tanzania in the 1970s and 1980s before these countries got IMF–World Bank religion and reaped the foreign exchange rewards.

Finally, devaluation frequently makes sense as a complement to import liberalization, as in Colombia over the past decade. Conversely, attempting to liberalize when the exchange rate is still overvalued can lead to a flood of imports, deindustrialization, and a balance-of-payments crisis. Problems of coordinating such policy moves are taken up below.

3. This last possibility illustrates how getting the exchange rate badly "wrong" can be self-destructive, a point on which WC and nonmainstream economists now agree in the wake of Latin American and African policy disasters of the last decades. These disasters stemmed from the common temptation to let the local price of foreign exchange increase less rapidly than inflation, in the hope that real appreciation would hold down price increases and stimulate local demand.

The resulting overvaluation or income redistribution from foreigners toward nationals is a step down a primrose path. As in the classic Argentine and Chilean cases of the late 1970s, it leads ultimately to an unsustainable trade deficit and capital flight in anticipation of a maxi-devaluation that will surely follow—a clear example of how distributional changes constrain macroeconomic policy choice.

4. Another external problem can show up when there is a dollar bonanza, from oil discoveries, ample foreign aid, or other sources. Some of the extra foreign exchange will flow toward imports or a reduced export effort, but the balance is likely to spill over into demand for nontraded goods. As their prices rise, the real exchange rate will appreciate, leading to a further loss in export-industrial diversification, in an example of "Dutch disease." Mexico and Nigeria had severe cases after their oil discoveries, as did the Philippines under Marcos with foreign aid.

It is also difficult to prevent reserve gains from the extra foreign exchange from being monetized (open market operations not being available in most developing country financial structures).[8] Fiscal–monetary policy complications can arise as in Colombia with its recurrent coffee bonanzas. A possible offset is for either the state or the private sector to save the inflows from abroad. As noted above, capital flight was a frequent final voyage for the resources flowing toward developing countries in the 1970s, when they accumulated huge stocks of foreign debt.

5. Output may suddenly be bounded from above, often by foreign exchange shortfalls, as discussed earlier. Another contingency is that progressive redistribution (à la the Allende government in Chile) may drive production up against capacity limits. How can aggregate demand then be limited to available supply? One mechanism is via prices rising more rapidly than nominal wages, thereby cutting real wages and demand. This is the simplest example of inflation-induced "forced saving," which may also occur via shifts in prices favoring or harming groups with differential saving propensities from current incomes, for example, workers, capitalists, farmers, foreigners, and the state. Via such channels, real wage reductions during the 1980s have proved to be surprisingly large, ranging up to 50 percent and more in some Latin American and African economies.

6. Changes in the distribution of wealth may also influence aggregate demand. The most widely cited example is the "inflation tax" on money balances—a transfer from firms or people with cash (or unindexed deposits) to the state or other borrowers through the banking system that printed the paper in the first place. The value of money erodes with rising prices, usually leading to reductions in real producer and consumer purchases.

7. When inflation settles in, different social groups learn to protect themselves against its adverse distributional effects by continually bidding up the prices over which they have control, for example, oligopolistic firms via markups, labor via money wage increases, or wealth holders via higher nominal interest rates. As such informal or formal contract "indexation" spreads, eliminating inflation becomes correspondingly more difficult. Shortening the waiting periods between indexation steps makes the problem worse.

These "inertial" responses to ongoing price increases immensely complicated attempts to reduce inflation in places like Argentina and Brazil. By deindexing wages, Chile effectively braked inflation in the 1980s, with wage earners bearing the social cost. Outside the WIDER sample, the widely publicized Bolivian stabilization of 1985 also was built around massive real wage cuts and unemployment for government employees and erstwhile tin miners, as well as overvaluation and export stagnation when the nominal exchange rate was frozen as an anti-inflationary move (Pastor 1991). The latter outcomes are reminiscent of the late 1970s orthodox inflation-stabilization packages in Argentina and Chile. These packages helped to provoke financial crises, as described below.

So-called heterodox shock stabilizations were tried in the mid-1980s in Argentina and Brazil to attack inertial inflation where the orthodox approaches described above had failed. These stabilizations involved price freezes and deindexing contracts, and stopped inflation in the short run. But when the inflation tax and forced saving disappeared, real wages and aggregate demand rose. Internally, pressures for additional wage increases appeared, feeding in turn back into more demand. Externally, as imports rose, the foreign resource constraint began to bind, reintroducing forced saving, the inflation tax, and indexation. A few years later, Israel and Mexico made heterodox stabilizations stick, via fiscal discipline, social compacts to hold wages in line, and the use of foreign resources (from capital inflows and international reserves, respectively) to relax the foreign constraint.

8. Especially when low capacity utilization and slow potential output growth are accompanied by regressive redistribution and high interest rates, desired saving by the wealthy tends to exceed investment demand. Often in such circumstances, speculation in real estate, local financial paper, and foreign currency (especially if the exchange rate is overvalued) increases, since higher savings flows have no natural outlet into capital formation. The stage is then set for a speculative boom and crash, which can be worsened by the fetish of financial market deregulation. The U.S. economy, with its Savings and Loan crisis, junk bonds, and other forms of financial instability in the 1980s, provides a recent example, albeit in a developed country.

Chile in the late 1970s was a classic case: financial conglomerates organized themselves around the denationalized industrial firms mentioned above plus internally controlled banks. In a stock market boom, each one started borrowing from its bank to bid up its own share prices, until the banks became so extended that the scam fell apart. Transfers from foreign donors helped underwrite public sector bonds that were used to restructure the financial system during the 1980s. The external and internal debt burdens so created amount to over one-third of Chile's annual GDP.

All the foregoing points suggest that questions inevitably arise about the causal structure of a macro model appropriate to the economy at hand. Structuralist economists emphasize that causality often begins with demand injections such as exports and investment, subject to distributional processes of the sort just discussed and frequently binding foreign exchange restrictions on capacity utilization and growth.

More orthodox analysts—including many from the Bretton Woods institutions (BWIs), referring to the IMF and World Bank—often postulate supply-side determination of output with ample price responsiveness. They typically state (with straight faces!) that monetary and fiscal austerity will reduce inflation only, and not the level of economic activity, and that the primary impact of relative price changes will be on the relevant output levels, and not on the functional and sectoral income distributions.

The problem with this view is that it assumes away all the problems discussed in connection with Table 8.1. The output losses, regressive redistributions, and inflations that have plagued poor countries in the 1980s cannot occur in orthodox models by hypothesis. Nor does mainstream theory address transitions from austerity and price reform to renewed growth, since it does not permit exports to be unresponsive to price signals or investment to be stagnant in the face of lagging domestic demand. Prices are supposed to be flexible enough to assure that there are no unemployed resources in a neoclassical world.

The unreality of these notions is beginning to be recognized (see, e.g., Dornbusch 1990), but has yet to be corrected in standard practice. Market-friendly analysts remain impervious to the fact that the invisible hand plus a minimal government (especially in its fiscal, regulatory, and investment roles) do not necessarily act together to support sustained economic growth.

Boundary Conditions on Change

Beyond the points already raised, other factors shift the nexus among trade, growth, and distribution. In this section I discuss how these other factors delimit the medium-term economic space in which policy makers have room to maneuver. The discussion is set up in terms of "boundary conditions" on sensible policy interventions under specific circumstances that can be inferred from cross-country and historical comparisons.[9]

1. As already noted in the first section of this chapter, the size of a country, best measured by population, influences its trade and industrial prospects. Typical results from cross-country econometrics (Syrquin and Chenery 1989) suggest that a "big" country with a population exceeding, say, 20 million enters earlier into import substitution and has a higher manufacturing share of GDP than does a "small" country at the same per capita income level; the big country pursues import substitution further into intermediate and capital goods and producers' services. The statistically typical large country's import and export shares of GDP are likely to be about 10 percent (with a standard deviation of about the same size; e.g., South Korea, with import and export shares in the 30 percent range, is far more open than the norm), while a small country's shares may be more than 50 percent.

Both the regressions and (more important) country histories suggest that big countries exploit import-substitute-then-export (ISTE) strategies in manufacturing. The basic premise is that big, protected markets permit economies of scale and scope. At the same time, they allow the luxury of allocative inefficiency for extended periods of time. High-cost production does create a static economic loss but need not represent a binding restriction on inward-oriented growth. In a favorable context, a statically inefficient industrial sector may become the base for breaking into world trade with import-substituted products, as suggested by the Turkish example, which is sketched below.

Since small countries are far more open to foreign trade, they are likely to find the ISTE approach less fruitful. Sectoral inefficiencies can easily degenerate into a binding foreign resource constraint. With benefit of hindsight, it can be seen that now-prosperous small economies earned foreign exchange by exploiting niches in which they could be efficient producers for export trade. Some examples are the downstream expansion of forest products plus high-skill, high-tech manufacturing in Canada, Sweden, and Finland; shipping in Norway (before the discovery of oil); and industry and financial services in Switzerland.

Within the WIDER sample, Chile has been a successful small country in the recent period. Its trade shares have risen rapidly, buoyed both by public investment in the opening of new copper mines and by favorable world prices, along with the expansion of fishery, fruit, and forestry exports from $191 million to $2,134 million between 1972 and 1988. The latter successes were based on close collaboration between the public and the private sectors, despite the official laissez-faire rhetoric of the Pinochet government.

The Chilean production development corporation, known by its Spanish acronym of CORFO, created the base for the noncopper export push by instituting afforestation programs and promotion of pulp and paper production; by solving problems of transport, cold storage, quality control, and marketing for fruits; and by setting up a mixed public-private fish meal industry, rationalizing production from several preexisting plants. There were also subsidies for pine plantations, soft credits for fruit growers, significant devaluation (real wage reduction, in other language), elimination of export red tape, relaxation of labor legislation, ownership guarantees, and so forth. The state stood steadfastly behind these "liberal" initiatives designed to support private sector activity (United Nations Economic Commission for Latin America and the Caribbean 1990).

One final aspect of the Chilean case is of interest. The government's public investments in copper mines and promotion policies for other exports were kept on track even though the economy was reeling through a twelve-year sequence (1973–85) of disastrous stabilization experiments amply supported by the BWIs. Market-friendly economists usually recommend that stabilization should precede adjustment. In Chile, the sequence was exactly reversed (Meller 1991).

A special political economy may underlie long-term, small-country successes, as Katzenstein (1985) points out for the prosperous European economies. Historically, the private sector took the lead and absorbed the failures in opening export niches, but bankruptcies were cushioned by "oligarchic" politics (close linkages among large industrial firms, labor unions organized from the top down, and a stable state) plus publicly supported safety nets. Small, prosperous countries initially practiced protection but now maintain undistorted trade regimes and adjust to rapid technical change through close cooperation among public, corporate, and labor elites. Examples of this model have yet to become fully ensconced in the developing world, although Taiwan and Singapore may be moving in that direction.

2. The degree of "openness" of an economy has at least two interpretations: the levels of its trade shares (obviously affected by the nation's size), and the comparative absence of interventionist commercial policies. On both counts,

openness has implications for development strategy. How it influences industrialization and growth is a topic of intense debate.

The mainstream view is that high foreign trade shares—especially of exports—in GDP are associated with faster growth. This conclusion is based on the "average" experience reflected in cross-country regression equations. The methodology is compact, but easily misled by diverse country histories.

Syrquin and Chenery (1989) provide one example. They divide a sample of 108 countries according to size and whether they are more specialized in primary or manufactured exports. Within each of the four resulting groups, they then ask whether economies with higher export shares of GDP grew faster. In all cases, average growth rates were higher for the subgroup with more exports, especially for small countries. These arithmetic means hide skewed within-group distributions of growth that suggest specific explanations for the results:

a. By far the biggest difference in growth for the 1950–83 period was in small, primary exporting countries (a 1.4 percent gap between averages of GDP growth by high- and low-export subgroups, and 1.1 percent between subgroup median rates per capita). This relationship between slow growth and low exports reflects poor endowments or bad management more than failure to reap the benefits of openness per se. Poor small exporters like Chad, Ghana, or Madagascar (the three slowest growers) will both contract and have low observed trade shares when hit by adverse shocks. The policy implications are that somehow overcoming internal disruption and finding profitable export lines are prior conditions for economic viability, not that liberalizing an economy will miraculously "open" it to growth through trade.

b. Small economies with high shares of manufactured exports grew 1.0 percent faster on average than the primary exporters, in part because the former group includes ten European economies as well as Taiwan, Singapore, and Hong Kong. Among the manufactured export specialists, the more export-oriented economies had a 1 percent faster *mean* growth rate, but the difference in subgroup *medians* was only 0.2 percent. The three small Asian Tigers badly skew the mean.

c. A similar conclusion applies to large countries more specialized in manufactured exports. The outliers are Japan and South Korea, and they substantially raise the mean but not the median of the more open subgroup.

An agnostic conclusion about the benefits of openness follows from other studies. McCarthy, Taylor, and Talati (1987) find in another sample that fast-growing countries did not on average have either high or increasing shares of exports in GDP between 1962 and 1984. Nor is growth led by manufactured exports necessarily the rule: among middle-income countries, Jamaica (12 percent), Uruguay (5 percent), and Portugal (16 percent) have high industrial export shares of GDP and grow slowly, while Colombia and Brazil have shares of 2 or 3 percent and yet their growth has historically been fast. Poorer countries' growth rates are more subject to the vagaries of capital inflows and primary product trade, but similar observations hold. Cameroon and Egypt have grown fairly rapidly, with industrial export shares of about 1 percent, while traditionally slow-growing India and Honduras both have shares of 3 percent or more.

Despite these inconclusive results, the empirical literature does present a few boundary conditions that appear to apply fairly widely:

a. Least controversially, the ratios of manufactured to primary products both produced and exported tend to rise as per capita GDP goes up. In a broad sense, industrialization is concomitant to economic growth.

b. Trade and output data suggest that, at least at the two-digit level of industrial classification, import substitution usually precedes production for exports, as I have already observed. The lag may be very short, as in the case of South Korea (except for automobiles, where the transition took twenty years), but five- or ten-year periods are normal. Needless to say, this sector-average generalization does not rule out the possibility of a country's exporting a particular product the day it begins to be produced.

c. Both production and trade shares vary within narrower ranges in large countries than in small ones, emphasizing the importance of niche-seeking strategies for the great majority of economies in the world. The relatively few large economies that exist shape their industrial structures more in line with domestic demand.

d. Countries poor in natural resources tend to have high shares of industry in both exports and GDP, and vice versa. Japan and Korea are obvious examples of resource-poor countries, and the United States and Brazil are equally obvious examples of the opposite case.

Finally, recent experience has shown big increases in exports and reductions in imports in many countries as they have adjusted to external shocks (recall Table 8.1). Whether these adjustments over the past decade will cumulate into renewed growth is very much an open question.

3. Is there any reason to expect that *openness*, defined as a low degree of trade intervention, is associated with faster growth? What about internally oriented moves such as deregulation and privatization? Theoretical models in diverse contexts suggest that such questions have no clear answer (Taylor 1991). Nor is the empirical evidence conclusive. Among the WIDER countries, for example, trade liberalization has perhaps aided Chile's growth spurt since the mid-1980s (at least psychologically), but after its mid-decade devaluation, faster-growing Thailand raised tariffs for revenue purposes. Turkey's export boom was accompanied by real depreciation and export subsidies of up to one-third of sales value, combined with replacement of a baroque system of import quotas with arbitrarily manipulated levies. Meanwhile, Mexico liberalized conscientiously and grew slowly. Among the relatively poor performers, Argentina and Zambia dabbled with liberalization, while until very recently Brazil, Nicaragua, and Senegal did not.

Turkish experience with trade and industrial strategy is illuminating in this regard. The economy entered early into ISI, with an explicitly statist thrust under Kemal Ataturk in 1931. Waves of industrialization followed, in ten-year cycles, from "easy" to "hard" import substitution. Between 1950 and the late 1970s, GDP growth fluctuated about 6 percent per year, but there was less than full employment, and each cycle ended in an inflationary contraction as the saving, foreign, and fiscal gaps began to bind. Inefficiency as measured by the standard methods ran rampant. Indeed, Turkey was the launching pad for Krueger's (1974) generalizations about rent seeking, which often figure in the rhetoric of the BWIs.

In 1980, following a relatively mild but regressive IMF-style stabilization with ample capital inflows, Turkey broke from ISI and launched into state-sponsored export growth in *il*liberal fashion. Boratav's (1988) WIDER study shows that the export miracle rested upon the preexisting industrial base created by ISI, regressive redistribution, and other policies leading to contraction of domestic demand for manufactures, the export subsidies and import quota/levy manipulations mentioned above, and rapid growth in demand for products like cement and steel on the part of culturally compatible buyers in the region (as in the Persian Gulf region and the Iran-Iraq War). Had any of these factors been missing, the boom could well not have happened. It was clearly capitalist-led; perhaps providing the groundwork for a profitable private sector excursion is what liberalization rhetoric is all about.

4. Indeed, can we deduce any boundary conditions at all from liberalization exercises? A few observations are worth making, but they scarcely constitute a complete tool kit for policy choice.

a. The Chilean and Turkish vignettes suggest that one key to a growth spurt can be government-business collaboration appropriate to a given set of circumstances, while the longer-lasting success of small European economies implies that labor has to be brought into a social contract as well. If South Korea (another prime example of state-directed capitalist expansion) unravels politically, it will do so on the latter grounds.

b. Unless external liberalization is begun with a weak currency and ample foreign support, it can easily misfire. Moreover, effective protection rates have to be tuned to the local industrial structure. Colombia has recently been successful along these lines (with good "minor" export growth from industries previously nurtured under ISI and propelled by numerous stimulative measures), while the failed external liberalization attempts in Zambia and Argentina that were mentioned above suffered from misaligned sectoral effective protection rates, overvaluation, and inadequate external support.

c. While getting important prices "right" can be a major element in supporting growth, as for example with the devaluations in Chile, Colombia, Malaysia, Thailand, and Turkey in the 1980s, revising the price system is at best a necessary policy move. As the history of each country demonstrates, more fundamental structural changes were essential for growth as well. In addition, potential short-term adverse effects of liberalizing moves—contraction from devaluation, deindustrialization from reduced import protection—have to be factored into policy choice.

d. There are plenty of cases in which liberalizing moves were irrelevant or counterproductive. Uganda's and Zambia's foreign exchange auctions fed into luxury goods imports and capital flight. Mexico's frantic privatizations and deregulations throughout the 1980s underwrote slow growth (although the hope is that they will stimulate local "animal spirits" enough to reverse capital flight and stoke investment during the present decade). Kenya, Tanzania, and Zambia have tried hard to promote agriculture with price and other liberal policies with scant success, due to diverse causes such as poor weather and lack of transportation infrastructure.

e. Fast growth with widespread illiberal but pro-production public intervention and distorted prices is historically common. South Korea between the 1950s and the 1990s, Brazil between the 1930s and the 1980s, and Turkey between the 1930s and the 1970s are just three examples.

5. Besides market liberalization, financial restructuring is another broad plank in the market-friendly program. Neither Williamson's (1990) version of the consensus nor the 1991 *WDR* goes into much detail about the means by which saving flows are intermediated into capital formation through financial markets. Their basic policy suggestions are just to increase interest rates and deregulate the system. The goal is to enhance allocative efficiency, in the sense that returns on saving instruments and investment projects should tend toward equality, presumably with "the" marginal product of physical capital (see United Nations Conference on Trade and Development 1991).

Just as price liberalization does not ensure that firms will efficiently produce commodities, there is no particular reason to expect that removing wedges that separate rates of return will guarantee a low-cost supply of financial services. Usually when it has been applied, in fact, the WC reform package has reduced productive efficiency in finance, leading to increased credit costs. The outcomes also included stagflation (lower capacity utilization coupled with faster inflation), a fall in investment demand, and a speculative flurry ending in a financial crash.

The market-friendly model of finance has the same basic shortcoming as its counterpart for trade and industrial policy: it ignores existing market structures. In most developing economies, the "formal" financial sector comprises public institutions, large private enterprises, and banks. Financial claims typically have short maturities, and the ratio of the outstanding value of either assets or liabilities to GDP is a fraction (well less than ratios in the 1.0–1.5 range observed in industrialized economies). Although their size is difficult to judge, informal markets may account for as much as one-half of total credit outstanding. Loans to the private sector from both formal and informal intermediaries to a large extent pay for working capital; investment finance comes from internal funds, the state, or informal sources.

The typical initial conditions for a high interest rate–deregulation package include ceilings on nominal interest rates, and directed formal sector credit allocations by sector and form of use. Immediately imposing a reform gives the following sorts of results.

a. Getting rid of ceilings on bank deposit rates removes a nominal anchor on the pricing system. Particularly if the external capital account has been deregulated, the alternative to a bank deposit in a citizen's portfolio is a foreign holding, with a domestic return equal to the foreign interest rate plus the expected rate of exchange depreciation plus a premium for lower risk. Such an alternative puts a floor under the local deposit rate that is usually strongly positive in real terms. Deposit institutions have to pass along their higher costs into interest rates on their loans.

b. Eliminating credit targets in the absence of effective prudential regulation leads banks toward high-risk, high-return loans (a moral hazard made more acute if the government implicitly promises that failing banks will be rescued). The proportion of nonperforming loans in bank portfolios rises; the implicit cost has to carried by debtors still meeting their obligations.

c. Higher interest rates on loans for working capital tend to be passed along by firms into higher prices (especially if they have market power, common enough under ISI). Since production costs rise, supply may also be reduced, giving stagflation. Higher lending rates and lower output will constrict investment demand.

d. More attractive deposit rates can also pull funds from the informal market, reducing its credit flows and raising "curb" or "bazaar" borrowing costs with unfavorable effects on output and prices.

e. Although banks can (up to a point) protect themselves from these developments by raising the spread between borrowing and lending rates, the same is not true of their borrowers. The financial position of the private, productive sector becomes more precarious, while a higher proportion of the government's fiscal receipts must be dedicated to interest payments on its outstanding internal liabilities. Refinancing these flows can reach manic dimensions, as in the "overnight" market in Brazil during the 1980s. Profits on turning over the federal debt made bankers partisans of inflation in that country, a peculiar and risky situation.

f. The Brazil example suggests that with high rates and low investment, speculative holdings become attractive. Turkey had Ponzi schemes around bank certificates of deposit (CDs), Chile had a stock market boom for shares of prematurely privatized public firms (financed by loans from banks central to economic "groups" whose owners used the money to bid up prices of their own companies' equity), and Argentina had destabilizing flows of foreign exchange. In all cases, speculation went together with deteriorating enterprise balance sheets to pave the way for a crash. In each case, the taxpayers ended up with bills amounting to tens of percentage points of GDP in order to put the financial system back together.

During the past ten to fifteen years, scenarios along similar lines have played out in the countries just mentioned, as well as in the Philippines and Yugoslavia—a substantial list of neoliberal "mistakes" to be added to those involving trade policy. A more gradual reform in nearly industrialized South Korea avoided a debacle. After presiding over its stock market boom and crash around 1980, the Chilean government later took advantage of ample support from its donors to privatize once again, restructure its internal debt, and set up an effective pension fund program to capture savings flows. From these experiences and those of now-developed economies, can anything sensible be said about productively efficient directions for LDC financial evolution?

One option that immediately presents itself is modernizing the development bank institution with due care to avoid rent seeking and inflationary finance for the benefit of chronically derelict parastatals. Since (especially after fiscal restructuring) development banks can tap public savings flows, they fit naturally with the public-private patterns of saving and capital formation set out in Table 8.1.

Another idea worth pursuing is effective regulation and support of the bank-centered conglomerates that are common in the Third World, so that internal economies of scale and information flows can lead to low credit costs within the group. This model has been broadly followed in Germany and Scandinavia for well over a century, and similar market structures appear in Japan. Less appealing are attempts to create capital markets along Anglo-American lines. These have rarely taken hold in developing economies, except at best as subsidized speculative playgrounds with minimal capacity to efficiently intermediate financial resource flows.

6. The market-friendly approach also lays considerable store by privatization. According to the 1991 *WDR*, this approach "is necessary and highly desirable, even though difficult and time-consuming. It is not to be undertaken as [an] end in itself, but as a means to an end: to use resources more efficiently" (World Bank 1991, p. 144). Despite its laudable goal, the practical implications of privatization are difficult to judge.

As observed earlier, different historical divisions across nations among public, local private, and foreign ownership of productive enterprises have emerged. There is no solid evidence that firms of one stripe are consistently more efficient in static terms than those of another. Dynamically, scholars such as Amsden (1989) argue that Korea's home-owned but publicly subsidized private conglomerates are more adept at indigenizing technology than TNC affiliates, while in Brazil before the last decade public enterprises were effective motors for capital accumulation and technical change (Shapiro 1991; Carneiro and Werneck 1993).

In economic terms, the effects of privatization on savings and investment flows will be the only means of evaluation available for years. Improvements in productive efficiency will be difficult to trace, and in any case do not seem likely in the absence of financial market reforms and joint, public sector labor-management efforts to raise productivity growth. Moreover, outside Chile, Mexico, and Turkey, not much privatization has in fact taken place.

Even saving-investment calculations are tricky, when discounting is taken into account. Marcel (1989) argues, for example, that in Chile's 1985–88 second go at privatization, firms were sold below present value and half the receipts were allocated to uses such as tax reduction. In other words, there were probably no positive impacts on capital formation, along with a portfolio shift from public liabilities toward enterprise equity on the part of the private and external sectors.

More generally, local private sectors can finance acquisitions of public firms in just four ways: (a) an increase in private saving; (b) a fall in private investment; (c) a decrease in private sector flow demand for financial assets; and (d) an increase in private sector flow demand for credit.

Alternative a could be helpful for growth if accompanied by a jump in investment. The public sector would probably have to be the motor, taking into account the crowding-in effects discussed above. In other words, privatizing governments should reinvest the proceeds instead of following Chile's example of cutting the current fiscal deficit. This observation becomes doubly relevant if the private sector cuts its own capital formation to take over public firms.

Alternative c is more likely than alternative d, especially in countries where financial markets have contracted in the wake of adverse shocks. But then the government will find it increasingly difficult to place its own liabilities, provoking it to emit money or bear higher interest burdens or both. As in the Chilean paradigm case, there will be strong pressures to use the proceeds of privatization just to cover the PSBR with no spillover to capital formation.

Finally, if public firms are sold to foreigners, is their direct foreign investment "additional" to what would have arrived in any case? What about remittance obligations in the future? It *is* true that TNCs that are doing more than simple sourcing do not readily leave a country once they have entered and built up sunk capital, and that they can serve as vehicles for technology acquisition. Can the same be said of debt-swapping banks? Even in terms of current financial flows, privatization need not produce great benefits.

7. Labor skilling is also widely debated. There is no question that high skills are required of workers in industrial modes of production. Substantial literacy and numeracy are required to produce commodities ranging from green revolution wheat to computer code for microprocessors. Successful industrializers since World War II exemplify the pattern. Korea has virtually complete literacy and world-class ratios of engineers and technically trained persons to the overall population. Across countries, there is a positive correlation between education levels (especially of technical personnel) and output growth.

Despite this evidence, an obvious question is whether human capital acquisition is a more or less necessary or a sufficient condition for sustained development and growth. As usual, cross-country averages blur historical distinctions, with counterexamples running both ways. Sri Lanka has a healthy, well-educated population, but prior to the late 1970s, when its foreign aid inflows took a quantum jump, it had a slow rate of growth. Brazil's level of literacy is dismal, but its growth prior to the 1980s was extremely fast. The Sri Lanka example suggests that the direct economic benefits of education can be overemphasized, at least in some contexts. Nor is Brazil to be congratulated for having an undereducated population; its low average labor productivity underscores the point. As always, single-factor explanations of growth performance cannot be supported.

The same observation applies to the distribution of income: education is just one of a number of influential factors. For example, Thailand's recent increase in inequality can in part be associated with growing educational disparities among groups of the population, while Colombia's decrease in the 1960s and the 1970s was helped by the spread of public schooling. Sri Lanka's well-educated, egalitarian citizenry has been unable to avoid ethnic strife, in part because of rising unemployment. Both improved distribution and more widely spread education (especially for women) tend to slow the rate of population growth. These linkages may be essential for the economic salvation of nations throughout the Third World that are still passing through the demographic transition from a stable population with high fertility and mortality to an equilibrium with low rates of birth and death.

8. As noted previously, progressive income redistribution is likely to stimulate aggregate demand. Shifts in demand composition may also occur, although country-level evidence suggests that the new commodity basket may be either more or less labor-intensive (i.e., wealthier segments of the population that lose in the redistribution may bias their consumption toward either labor-intensive services or capital-intensive commodities, depending on context). There is also likely to be a reduction in the import intensity of demand.

These compositional shifts are all relatively weak, so that the short-run effect of redistribution on sectoral strategy can probably be ignored. The important conjunctural factor is the change in aggregate demand. It suggests that redistribution can be pursued only up to a certain point, beyond which balance of payments and/or inflation tax-forced saving problems arise.

Beyond the conjuncture, dynamic feedbacks become important. Real wages are central to the distributional process, and their secular growth may be necessary for industrialization in the long run. Now-popular efficiency wage models (see, e.g., Bowles and Boyer 1990) suggest that worker motivation and efficiency depend on good pay. Except in the few countries that successfully pursue import substitution of capital goods, the bulk of demand for advanced products must come from exports or wage income. These linkages mean that which classes gain from productivity increases is an important question.

If the economy is wage-led, worker motivation and internal demand require real wage increases, but another possibility is that if real wages rise more slowly than productivity, then unit labor costs fall, which can help trade. It is clear, though, that aiming for low wages alone is *not* a viable or sustainable strategy. South Korea would never have shifted its exports from human hair and cheap garments to automobiles and electronics had its wages stayed at the levels of 1955. The country prospered by learning to export commodities facing elastic world demand, so that falling unit labor costs as real wages lagged productivity growth translated into higher values of foreign sales. Selling to an increasingly sophisticated domestic market under ISI was an essential source of information in this process. The 1990s will reveal whether Thailand can follow this path.

As already noted, primary product exporters facing inelastic demand structures are likely to find productivity growth just feeding into lower terms of trade, to the benefit of consumers in rich countries but not at home. Part of Chile's and Malaysia's recent success with primary exports is tied to the fact that these countries chose (or stumbled into) commodities such as fruits and palm oil or latex, for which world demand was rapidly rising. Past ISI can pay off in this regard, since it at least teaches local industries how to produce products with high income elasticities. Industrial exports from Brazil, Colombia, Thailand, and Turkey (along with Korea) exemplify this observation.[10]

9. International competitiveness depends on steadily growing productivity and access to best-practice technology. Despite isolated exceptions (e.g., Korean and Brazilian design of new models of cars and armored personnel carriers), little technical innovation occurs in the developing world. New technology must be obtained through deals with international suppliers, involving licensing and royalty costs, or via direct foreign investment on the part of transnational firms (Helleiner 1989). Either route involves extensive bargaining between local public and private sector firms and external suppliers, under the aegis of the state.

The conditions of these bargains vary with a country's own industrial history and time. Dealing in the 1980s with Suzuki about setting up an automobile industry, India was in a weaker position than was Brazil when it dealt with Ford and Volkswagen thirty years before: the corporations were groping almost as blindly as their potential host at that stage. The main similarity is that a process beginning with assembly and leading toward rising domestic content is one policy goal. The time frame for such a change may be fairly short, since the industrial sophistication of the newly industrializing countries (NICs) has by now reached the point at which international productivity levels in greenfield plants can be achieved rapidly, as they were in production of automobile engines during the 1980s in Mexico.

Even this comfortable generalization breaks down, however, when new technologies like those based on microprocessors are at issue. Stimulating local applications rather than production of hardware has emerged as the relevant policy objective. Sweden, the most computerized economy in the world, does minimal local manufacture. In developing countries, pursuing computer literacy and computer familiarity emerges as the relevant policy goal. Traditional ISI strategies do not apply, but state and privately supported educational initiatives possibly may.

Conclusions

There is no single answer to the fundamental question of why nations grow at different rates, with diverse distributions of income and wealth. It is clear that policy must be tailored to the local situation and even to the particular conditions prevailing at the time.

This view contrasts with the Washington consensus (WC) about how a relatively uniform policy package can be applied with beneficial results almost everywhere. For the record as well as for comparisons with counterpoints to be set out below, the WC embodies the following notions:

W1. The fiscal budget should be balanced, with a deficit of at most a few percentage points of GDP, tight spending controls, and broad-based taxation programs with low marginal rates.

W2. Price reform should be aimed at positive (presumably moderate) real interest rates and a weak, stable exchange rate.

W3. Trade should be liberalized and direct foreign investment should be welcomed.

W4. State enterprises should be privatized.

W5. Markets should be deregulated, especially the labor market.

W6. There is a need for "sound" macroeconomic policy and at least a rudimentary social safety net.

W7. Accumulation of human capital has positive effects on growth and distribution.

W8. "Stabilization" or removal of macroeconomically disabling balance of payments and fiscal gaps as well as inflation has to come before "adjustment" or creation of conditions for sustainable growth; together with institutional changes, stabilization and adjustment are supposed to produce viable "reform."

W9. There is an implicit promise that pursuit of market-friendly policies will be supported by external donors, especially the World Bank and IMF.

Despite the appeal of these recommendations to the BWIs and the mainstream, "consensus" is too strong a word to apply to them. In particular, progressive (P) economists would on the whole agree with the following counterpoints to the WC:

P1. Fiscal equilibrium is desirable, but it can be devilishly difficult to attain. The fiscal, foreign exchange, and saving gaps are closely linked. Improvement in the first is not likely without gains for the other two as well. External support may well be required on all three fronts. It was certainly available in the (provisionally) successful reform cases of the 1980s. Reducing a fiscal deficit is always tricky in political terms; in some corners of the world, distributional conflicts make it well nigh inconceivable.

P2. Changing real macro prices, such as wage rates, exchange rates, and interest rates, is not easy. The required movements in their nominal counterparts may have to be large (tens of percentage points, or even more), with complicated, economywide effects and inflationary complications. Numerous orthodox programs based upon such changes in nominal exchange and interest rates have resoundingly failed. Gains in allocative efficiency when real macro prices are revised can be trivial, while losses in production may be painfully large (recent experiences in Eastern Europe are obvious examples).

P3. External liberalization programs have fared no better than packages based on intelligent use of quotas and controls. The advantages of the latter include the possibility of using the threat of withdrawing protection to extract efficient production from the private sector without having to estimate and impose a whole set of allocatively "correct" prices. Direct foreign investment bolsters the balance of payments and may help with acquisition of technology, but home-based firms may be able to do a still better job of acquiring technology.

P4. Privatization brings no obvious productivity gains, and if done in slapdash fashion it can adversely perturb saving, investment, and financial flows. The same observation applies to attempts to restructure a "repressed" financial system by raising interest rates and abdicating prudential control.

P5. Labor market deregulation may slash wage costs in the short run, presumably to some export advantage, but it may prove inimical to long-run socioeconomic development, and it can slow accumulation of productive human assets.

P6. Sound macroeconomic policy is always desirable, as are stable family relationships and apple pie. Whether it is feasible under LDC political and distributional conditions is another question. If "soundness" means austerity, it runs a grave risk of inducing secular stagnation.

P7. An increasingly educated, healthy, and well-paid population is necessary for long-run productivity growth. However, speeding up human capital accumulation is not a sufficient condition for raising actual or even potential output in the short run.

P8. Stabilization before (or concurrent with) adjustment sounds sensible but does not always work out. Maybe basic improvements in fiscal or balance-of-payments positions are required before macroeconomic difficulties can be overcome. There are recent examples both ways.

P9. As the macroeconomic analysis and country vignettes in this chapter indicate, there is no certainty that external support will be forthcoming in exchange for pursuit of a WC policy package. Again, there are examples to support both possibilities.

P10. Indeed, there have been successes and failures of both orthodox and heterodox policy initiatives more generally. The problem is how to invent and sequence policy changes effective in each economy's historical and institutional context. A little bit is known about how such factors as the structure of the existing capital stock, the size of the population, and natural resource endowments put somewhat flexible boundary conditions on policies aimed at raising productive efficiency, but the general solution to this problem is neither known nor likely to be found.

Notes

1. Grave policy "mistakes," incidentally, have also been committed by teams fully backed by the World Bank, the International Monetary Fund (IMF), and mainstream economists more generally. Latin America's Southern Cone around 1980 presents well-known examples.

2. The latter region includes only the middle-income countries of Europe, such as Portugal and Greece.

3. The WIDER country studies as well as other material appear in Taylor (1993).

4. Only in Chile and Colombia in the WIDER sample did public investment appear to reduce private investment overall. Even in those two cases, crowding out was less than one-for-one, so that total investment was an increasing function of its public component (as also appears to be the case in the United States, for example). Under austerity programs in the 1980s, both components tended to fall at the same time as real interest rates rose. In the future, conversely, any reduction in borrowing costs will complement higher public capital formation in stimulating private projects.

5. Much macroeconomic debate in developing countries takes place in terms of accounting balances; the "gap" usage reflects questions about the means by which they are satisfied ex post. As Sobhan (1990) puts it, discussion is organized ". . . essentially in terms of four sets of accounts—the balance of payments accounts, the fiscal accounts, the consolidated accounts of the banking system, and the national income and product accounts which usually offer only a pale reflection of what is going on in the real economy, out there. Now fairly simple models can be constructed using the . . . identities represented by the four sets of accounts just mentioned. . . ." Three-gap specification is one such simple model and IMF "financial programming" is another; both are widely used in practice.

6. Shifts in the three schedules in Figure 8.1 can also be used to explore how an economy adjusts to macroeconomic shocks. For example, with the parameters of its WIDER model, Mexico's output growth rate increase of about 2 percent per year in 1990–91 is consistent with the increment of 1.5 percent of GDP in net inflows that it received from direct foreign investment, repatriated flight capital, and lower interest rates. Contrary to a WC interpretation, no great improvement in the efficiency of aggregate resource use due to Mexico's drastic liberalization moves during the 1980s appears to have occurred.

7. Exchange rate "overvaluation" has at least two partially overlapping meanings. One is that nominal peso/dollar rate increases can lag inflation for a time, increasing costs of national exports to the rest of the world and cheapening imports at home. Overvaluation in this sense ranges from a few to a few thousand percentage points in developing economies worldwide. Second, the actual current rate—interpreted as a relative price between traded and nontraded goods—can be compared to a "shadow" rate that would lead to trade balance (or the current level of the trade deficit) if all import protection were removed. Calculations of shadow rates usually suggest that the actual rate is overvalued in the double-digit percentage range. The text reference invokes the latter definition; the former is taken up in the observations about distributional adjustment channels below.

8. Open market operations, which are purchases or sales of government bonds by the central bank, are the chief instrument of monetary policy in developed countries like the United States. When payments surpluses increase the reserve assets of the central bank, the domestic money supply will increase—with potential inflationary consequences—unless the reserve inflow is "sterilized" by the sale of government bonds (thus keeping total central bank assets from rising). The lack of developed private bond markets takes away this option in many developing countries.

9. Many of the arguments in this section are drawn from Shapiro and Taylor (1990) and from Fanelli, Frenkel, and Taylor (1992).

10. The point that productivity growth does not benefit a producer facing inelastic demand is an old one, recognized by economists as diverse as Prebisch (1959) and Houthakker (1976).

Bibliography

Amsden, Alice. 1989. *Asia's Next Giant: South Korea and Late Industrialization.* New York: Oxford University Press.

Boratav, Korkut. 1988. "Turkey." Country Study No. 5, WIDER Stabilization and Adjustment Policies and Programmes. Helsinki: World Institute for Development Economics and Research.

Bowles, Samuel, and Robert Boyer. 1990. "A Wage-Led Employment Regime: Income Distribution, Labor Discipline, and Aggregate Demand in Welfare Capitalism." In Stephen Marglin and Juliet Schor, eds., *The Golden Age of Capitalism.* New York: Oxford University Press.

Carneiro, Dionisio, and Rogerio Werneck. 1993. "Brazil." In Lance Taylor, ed., *The Rocky Road to Reform: Income Distribution, Politics, and Adjustment in the Developing World.* Cambridge, MA: MIT Press.

Chenery, Hollis B., and Michael Bruno. 1962. "Development Alternatives in an Open Economy: The Case of Israel." *Economic Journal,* Vol. 72, pp. 79–103.

Dornbusch, Rudiger. 1990. "Policies to Move from Stabilization to Growth." In *Proceedings of the World Bank Annual Conference on Development Economics.* Washington, DC: World Bank.

Fanelli, Jose Maria, Roberto Frenkel, and Lance Taylor. 1992. "The World Development Report 1991: A Critical Assessment." Mimeo. Buenos Aires: CEDES, and Cambridge, MA: Massachusetts Institute of Technology.

Helleiner, G. K. 1989. "Transnational Corporations and Direct Foreign Investment." In Hollis Chenery and T. N. Srinivasan, eds., *Handbook of Development Economics,* Vol. 2. Amsterdam: North-Holland.

Houthakker, Hendrik S. 1976. "Disproportional Growth and the Intersectoral Distribution of Income." In J. S. Cramer, A. Heertje, and P. Venekamp, eds., *Relevance and Precision: Essays in Honor of Pieter de Wolff.* Amsterdam: North-Holland.

Johansen, Leif. 1960. *A Multi-Sectoral Study of Economic Growth.* Amsterdam: North-Holland.

Katz, S. Stanley. 1991. "East Europe Should Learn from Asia." *Financial Times* (April 24).

Katzenstein, Peter. 1985. *Small States in World Markets: Industrial Policy in Europe.* Ithaca, NY: Cornell University Press.

Krueger, Anne O. 1974. "The Political Economy of the Rent-Seeking Society." *American Economic Review,* Vol. 64, pp. 291–303.

Marcel, Mario. 1989. "Privatización y Finanzas Públicas: El Caso de Chile." *Colección Estudios CIEPLAN,* No. 26, pp. 5–60.

McCarthy, F. Desmond, Lance Taylor, and Cyrus Talati. 1987. "Trade Patterns in Developing Countries, 1964–82." *Journal of Development Economics,* Vol. 27, pp. 5–39.

Meller, Patricio. 1991. *Review of the Chilean Liberalization and Export Expansion Process (1974–90).* Santiago: CIEPLAN.

Pastor, Manuel, Jr. 1991. "Bolivia: Hyperinflation, Stabilization, and Beyond." *Journal of Development Studies,* Vol. 27, No. 2 (January), pp. 211–37.

Prebisch, Raul. 1959. "Commercial Policy in the Underdeveloped Countries." *American Economic Review,* Vol. 49, pp. 257–69.

Shapiro, Helen. 1991. *The Public-Private Interface: Brazil's Business-Government Relations in Historical Perspective, 1950–1990.* Boston: Harvard Business School.

Shapiro, Helen, and Lance Taylor. 1990. "The State and Industrial Strategy." *World Development,* Vol. 18, pp. 861–78.

Sobhan, Rehman. 1990. "Introduction." In R. Sobhan et al., eds., *Structural Adjustment in Third World Countries.* Dhaka: Bangladesh Institute of Development Studies.

Syrquin, Moshe, and Hollis B. Chenery. 1989. "Patterns of Development, 1950 to 1983." World Bank Discussion Paper No. 41. Washington, DC: World Bank.

Taylor, Lance. 1991. *Income Distribution, Inflation, and Growth.* Cambridge, MA: MIT Press.

———, ed. 1993. *The Rocky Road to Reform: Income Distribution, Politics, and Adjustment in the Developing World.* Cambridge, MA: MIT Press.

United Nations Conference on Trade and Development. 1991. *Trade and Development Report 1991.* New York: United Nations.

United Nations Economic Commission for Latin America and the Caribbean. 1990. *Changing Production Patterns with Social Equity.* Santiago, Chile: UN ECLAC.

Williamson, John. 1990. "What Washington Means by Policy Reform." In John Williamson, ed., *Latin American Adjustment: How Much Has Happened?* Washington, DC: Institute for International Economics.

World Bank. 1991. *World Development Report 1991: The Challenge of Development.* New York: Oxford University Press.

CHAPTER NINE

Industrial Policy and Export Success: Third World Development Strategies Reconsidered

STEPHEN C. SMITH

Introduction

The great success stories of economic development in the last decade have been the newly industrializing countries (NICs) of East Asia, especially the so-called "Four Tigers" (South Korea, Taiwan, Hong Kong, Singapore) and, increasingly, Thailand and China. In these countries, rapid growth of manufactured exports has produced dramatic increases in income. Their successes have changed the prevailing sentiment in development policy from "export pessimism" to "export optimism." Throughout the 1980s, international development agencies such as the World Bank and the U.S. Agency for International Development (USAID) urged all less developed countries (LDCs) to follow the East Asian NIC model by adopting a development strategy based on export promotion.

These dramatic success stories are indeed important for development theory and policy, but to a large extent the wrong inferences have been drawn about the sources of their success. A conservative movement in development economics —referred to here as the "new orthodoxy" school—which dominated development policy discussions and practice in the 1980s, argues that the free operation of the market accounts for these East Asian successes. According to the new orthodoxy, the key to successful export-led development is simply for governments to abandon the trade protection and industrial policies that have been used in the past to promote domestic production of manufactured goods in many LDCs. This old strategy, known as "import substitution," is thus identified with government intervention, while the "new" strategy of export promotion is identi-

This chapter is an edited and revised version of a report previously published by the Economic Policy Institute (Smith 1991). The author would like to thank Robert Blecker, Michael Carter, Jeff Faux, Ira Gang, Larry Mishel, Timothy Nulty, Louis Putterman, Steve Quick, Lance Taylor, Michael Todaro, James Weaver, and Pan Yotopoulos for comments on earlier versions.

fied with laissez-faire policies (trade liberalization and domestic deregulation). By opening up domestic markets to international competition, it is claimed, producers are given the right "price signals" (incentives) to produce efficiently (see Krueger 1980 and 1990a). As production becomes more efficient, exports naturally expand, propelling the domestic economy to "take off" on a path of self-sustaining growth (although how greater static efficiency is supposed to ensure more dynamic growth is not clearly specified).

A growing body of scholarship, however, has begun to challenge the new orthodoxy as both empirically and theoretically flawed, as well as damaging to the LDCs that have strictly based their export policies upon it. The new orthodoxy in effect makes the logical error of assuming that, because the old import-substitution policies were highly interventionist, therefore the export-promotion policies must be largely noninterventionist. However, there is nothing that inherently links export promotion with a completely free market environment. Governments can and do promote their exports by making targeted interventions in the economy. Such interventions include, for example, subsidizing the acquisition of certain technologies and providing tax breaks to industries judged most likely to foster further economic progress. In fact, this is precisely the course that most of the East Asian NICs followed. The governments of South Korea, Taiwan, and most other NICs have undertaken a host of interventionist measures that have created powerful incentives for export-oriented manufacturing firms, often in particular targeted industries at particular stages of development.

There is no question that economic incentives are crucial to development success. However, this does not necessarily mean that the "right" prices are always the current international market prices. Development in the East Asian NICs has often been guided by price signals (incentives) that deviated from world market prices as a result of conscious government intervention. At the same time, in a policy reemphasized in the 1980s, many LDCs followed the incentives of current world market prices by specializing in primary commodities (agricultural and mineral exports), only to discover that the prices of those commodities subsequently fell as global supplies outstripped demand. While ultimately a country's products must become competitive at world market prices in order to be exported, it does not follow that strict reliance on the incentives given by those prices has been positively associated with development success. The "right" prices for guiding resource allocation in developing countries are not necessarily identical at all times and for all sectors with prevailing world market prices.

The contrasting experiences of the East Asian NICs and the commodity-exporting LDCs suggest two vital distinctions. First, it seems to make a big difference whether a developing country promotes exports of primary commodities or manufactured goods. It makes a difference not only because of the recurring problem of gluts resulting in falling prices in commodity markets but also because of the greater potential for raising technological capabilities and increasing productivity in manufacturing industries. Second, it is critical to distinguish a country's *static* comparative advantage (what it can produce relatively more efficiently and export successfully in the short run) from its *dynamic* comparative advantage (what it can develop the potential to produce relatively efficiently and export in the long run). All the evidence about the East Asian NICs supports the view that most of them deliberately altered the market incentives through trade and industrial policies that favored manufacturing activities of increasing technological content, and that placed long-run development goals over short-run comparative advantage.

This is not to say, of course, that any kind of government intervention, however inefficient, can be justified by appeal to long-run development objectives. As the history of import-substitution policies demonstrates, there is ample room for government intervention to overpromote certain industries to the detriment of long-run efficiency, competitiveness, and growth. This makes it all the more important to understand exactly what kinds of trade and industrial policies have worked and what kinds have not. To paraphrase Albert Fishlow (1987, p. 28), the key is "getting the inferences right" about the real sources of success or failure in export-led development efforts.

Competing Views of Exports and Development

Conservative trade and development economists of the new orthodoxy school have tended to use the terms "export promotion," "outward-looking development," and "free trade" (or at least "liberalizing trade regime") more or less synonymously. For example, Balassa (1988) explained the export and growth success of the East Asian NICs as a result of the "neutrality and stability of the incentive system." Little (1979, 1982) attributes the stellar success of Taiwan to a free labor market, high real interest rates, a virtual free trade regime for exports, and conservative government budgeting. Other economists seem to have concluded that any active export-promotion interventions in Korea, Taiwan, or Singapore merely had the effect of reversing the impact of any previous import-substitution policies, so that, in the end, the same price signals that would have prevailed under free trade emerged out of a set of mutually self-canceling policies (World Bank 1982, p. 82).[1] This interpretation has played an influential part in the development literature and in the perceptions of many American policy makers.[2]

The leading promoter of trade liberalization in the 1980s was the World Bank. It published a study of trade policy and industrial development that received widespread attention in the American and international press: the *World Development Report 1987* (World Bank 1987a). This study did much to reinforce the perception that liberalization and export promotion are logically and factually associated with each other. The report begins by distinguishing between what it calls "outward-oriented" and "inward-oriented" trade strategies.

For the outward-oriented strategy it was claimed that "trade and industrial policies do not discriminate between production for the domestic market and exports, nor between purchases of domestic goods and foreign goods . . ." (World Bank 1987a, p. 78). For the inward-oriented (import-substitution) strategy, "trade and industrial incentives are biased in favor of production for the domestic over the export market" (p. 78). The report classified forty-one countries as either strongly outward-oriented, moderately outward-oriented, moderately inward-oriented, or strongly inward-oriented in two periods, 1963–73 and 1973–85. This classification scheme has influenced some scholarly work and has subsequently appeared as an explanatory variable in empirical studies (e.g., Berg and Sachs 1988).

The World Bank study classifies South Korea, Singapore, and Hong Kong as strongly outward-oriented. In this category, according to the report, "trade controls are either nonexistent or very low. . . . There is little or no use of direct controls and licensing arrangements and the exchange rate is maintained so that the EERs [effective exchange rates] for importables and exportables are roughly equal" (1987a, p. 82). The study called its results inconclusive for the moderately outward- and moderately inward-oriented countries. Therefore, the report actually bases its conclusions on a comparison of growth rates for just three cases of strongly outward-oriented countries (South Korea, Singapore, and Hong Kong) with those of the strongly inward-oriented countries—as categorized by the report, a group composed mainly of low-income LDCs with a host of other problems. The study then concludes that outward-oriented countries have fared better than inward-oriented countries, and attributes the success of the former to policies that "do not discriminate."

There are several major problems with this conventional view of export promotion and development success. First, it is notoriously difficult to identify the causes of differences in growth performance in comparisons among countries that differ in many ways besides their external trade policies. Developing countries vary greatly in their political and economic institutions, demographic and ethnic composition, and other historical and cultural factors. Unless all these factors are controlled for, it is impossible to conclude with certainty that their international trade policies were the main determinant of the success or failure of their development efforts. Even in the strictly economic realm, macroeconomic (fiscal and monetary) policies, land tenure systems in agriculture (the concentration of landownership), and the honesty and efficiency of the government bureaucracy seem to matter at least as much as trade policies for development outcomes—in regard to both aggregate growth and distributional equity.

A more specific problem with the World Bank analysis is the fact that virtually all the low-income countries in the sample fell into the strongly inward-oriented category. According to data supplied in the appendix to the report, the middle-income countries grew at more than twice the rate of the low-income countries (excluding China and India) during 1965–80. The growth rate for industry in the middle-income group was nearly double the rate for the low-income group (World Bank 1987a, tables 1, 2, and 8; see also Singer 1988). Yet it is doubtful that this differential performance between low- and middle-income countries can be explained by a difference in their trade policies. The middle-income group for this period was dominated by the Latin American countries, which by and large exhibited excellent growth performance during that time, while typically pursuing strong import-substitution policies (see Fishlow 1987).

The identification of export orientation with neutral, noninterventionist trade policies almost seems to be based on an error of logic: because import-substitution policies are highly interventionist, it is often assumed that export-promotion policies must be *non*interventionist or at least *less* interventionist. This identification may also have taken its cue from abstract economic theory: the model of international trade in a world of "perfectly competitive" markets. Following this theory, across-the-board protection of importable goods through tariffs or quotas shifts domestic price incentives in favor of production for the domestic market and away from production for export. Since widespread protectionism thus has an "antiexport bias," trade liberalization is considered to be inherently export-promoting. Liberalization promotes exports because it increases the relative prices exporters receive for their products in comparison with import-competing and nontradable goods. This theory predicts that the market mechanism will then automatically shift resources away from protected import-substitution activities and direct them toward export activities.[3]

There are several problems with applying this abstract theory to actual developing countries. First, it is not necessarily correct to assume that countries end up exporting only the goods in which pure "free market" forces would have led them to specialize. Many of the NICs seem to be exporting manufactured goods that were deliberately (if not openly) subsidized or otherwise encouraged by government policies. Thus, it is logically as well as empirically wrong to identify trade liberalization with export promotion. The next section will show that two of the three countries identified as "strongly outward-oriented" in the 1987 *World Development Report* (South Korea and Singapore), along with another major East Asian NIC (Taiwan) that was not included in the study, followed active industrial policies that did indeed "discriminate" through the selective promotion of favored exports.

The view that import substitution and export promotion are mutually exclusive policy options is also misleading. The monumental study of Chenery, Robinson, and Syrquin concludes that "periods of significant export expansion are almost always preceded by periods of strong import substitution"[4] (1986, p. 178). In many cases, the leading industrial sectors did not change after the switch to export promotion (pp. 180–87). This fact strongly implies that the import-substitution phase had something to do with the export success that followed. How and when to make a transition from import substitution to export promotion is an important issue in itself, but it should not be thought that Korea's or Brazil's import-substitution phases were merely mistakes and did not contribute to their subsequent export success. Moreover, many of the major manufactures-exporting NICs simultaneously protect some infant industries while intervening actively to promote the exports of others. Sometimes an export industry also receives protection, as in the case of South Korean automobiles, which have had a prohibitive tariff. Such a tariff, either on an export product or on an exporting firm's other products, can constitute a hidden subsidy to exports. For this reason, it is misleading to classify a country such as South Korea as simply export-oriented, and especially to characterize it as "not discriminating" between different types of products.

Rather than classifying countries as more outward- or inward-oriented, and rather than trying to determine which type of orientation is more or less interventionist, it makes more sense to start by recognizing that some export promotion is all but universal among developing countries. Although some countries have emphasized exports more than others,[5] there is scarcely a single LDC that has not had some kind of active export-promotion program in the past few decades. Developing countries have, in fact, been forced to emphasize exports for a variety of reasons. For example, many LDCs had to expand exports in the 1970s because the rise in oil prices necessitated obtaining more foreign exchange. Also, the exhaustion of easy opportunities for import substitution and the saturation of domestic markets for manufactures led to searches for outlets for manufactured exports from the 1960s onward (although some countries lagged behind others). The debt crisis of the 1980s compelled debtor nations to push exports of all kinds very strongly. More fundamentally, economic development requires substantial imports from developed countries, including capital goods, intermediate inputs, some consumer goods, some more advanced services, and higher education.[6] All these imports, plus the servicing of any debts incurred to finance them, must be paid for with hard currencies (i.e., convertible foreign exchange). As these requirements expand with growth, LDCs must supplement traditional export activities, development assistance, and loans (which create a debt burden) with expanded exports in order to increase foreign exchange earnings.

The necessity to expand exports in the development process has long been recognized, even by economists who advocated a stage of import substitution. Indeed, the pioneering "structuralist" development economists of the 1940s argued as strenuously for export promotion as did any of the recent new orthodox economists.[7] This is true even of the structuralists who were criticized most for stressing "inward-looking growth," based on a strategy of import substitution. For example, Rosenstein-Rodan spoke of the need for "pushing exports" and to "create. . . export industries" (1943, p. 252). Nobel Prize winner Gunnar Myrdal, who has often been criticized for advocating inward-looking policies, actually concluded that "the underdeveloped country will have to do its utmost to increase its exports" (1958, p. 105). And Hirschman argued that export promotion "may often be the only practical way of achieving" import substitution (1958, p. 124).

Of course, some LDCs have been more successful at exporting than others. It is also true that export promotion was not *consistently* pushed in some countries with strong import-substitution policies, or with inconsistent macroeconomic, financial, and exchange rate policies. In spite of these exceptions, the evidence suggests that *it is sectoral promotion and not across-the-board trade liberalization that is crucial for dynamic growth and development.* One of the most important determinants of long-term development success from export promotion seems to be a focus on manufacturing as opposed to (or in addition to) primary products. There have long been important arguments in the development literature in favor of limiting dependence on exports of primary commodities, including the following:

- *Commodity price instability.* Prices of primary commodities are subject to much larger swings than prices of manufactures and services, and so risk-averse, credit-constrained LDCs will suffer from overspecializing in the former (Todaro 1989).
- *Strong agricultural trade barriers.* Agricultural trade barriers in the developed countries tend to be stronger than manufacturing barriers. Although various voices have called for removing these, including the United States in the Uruguay Round General Agreement on Tariffs and Trade (GATT) negotiations, as yet few concrete actions or guarantees of removal have emerged (see World Bank 1986 for a complete discussion).
- *Widespread benefits produced by manufactures.* The production and export of manufactures has been widely argued to foster economies of scale, intersectoral linkages, and positive externalities (benefits spilling over to other producers), resulting in accelerated technological progress and productivity growth in LDCs (see Pack and Westphal 1986). More broadly, industrialization generally brings about qualitative changes throughout the society, including improved education, increased labor skills, greater technical expertise, enhanced capacity for innovation, and more flexible management, which traditional agricultural and mining activities do not tend to generate.
- *Declining terms of trade for commodities.* Singer (1950), Prebisch (1950), and others argued that the terms of trade for commodity producers are likely to have a long-run falling tendency, due to the substitution of synthetic materials for natural products, the low income elasticity of demand for these items, and the structural characteristics of LDC and developed country labor and product markets.[8] While the long-term trend of the commodity terms of trade has been disputed ever since (see Spraos 1983), it is clear that commodity prices turned sharply downward (relative to industrial prices) in the 1980s—just after large investments in numerous primary commodities were undertaken in Africa, Latin America, and Southeast Asia (World Bank 1987–88).[9] New evidence, cited later in this chapter, now supports the Prebisch-Singer view.

Export Promotion in the East Asian NICs

The East Asian Four Tigers (South Korea, Taiwan, Hong Kong, Singapore) and their heirs apparent, such as Thailand, offer essential clues to the ingredients of successful development policies. Misinterpretations of the experiences of these countries have caused much confusion in policy discussions, particularly in the United States It is essential that debate about these countries turn on the facts of the countries' actual policies rather than on hypothetical models. The new orthodoxy school is correct in that the growth performance of the Four Tigers has been generally outstanding. What is in dispute is the *source* of this success and the implications that are drawn for development policy in other countries.

The successes of South Korea, Taiwan, and, to a large extent, the secondary East Asian NICs as well, cannot be attributed to reliance on free market policies. In fact, these countries have had among the most active industrial policy programs in the world, following and expanding on the example of Japan.[10] The existence of such programs does not prove that these policies caused the successes that followed. Assigning causality unambiguously in such cases is impossible, and some economists have even suggested that these NICs would have had even higher growth without them (see Lal 1985). It should be noted, however, that no countries have ever grown faster in recorded economic history.

In addition to having historically unprecedented growth rates, South Korea and Taiwan in particular seem to have fared quite well on other important development criteria, such as keeping inequality from increasing and even reducing it, virtually eliminating absolute poverty, maintaining rapid growth of industrial employment, and keeping underemployment in the "informal" sector (e.g., minimally paid street traders, hawkers, and petty service providers) from getting too high, among other things. In Korea, the education and skill levels of the labor force have steadily risen; however, labor rights were severely restricted until recently.[11] Taken as a whole, the development track record in Korea and the other East Asian NICs has indeed been stellar. This record warrants a close look at actual policies, however, rather than a reliance upon theoretical presumptions.

South Korea

Numerous studies have documented a truly prodigious array of incentives for exporting used by the Korean government since the early 1960s. One of the most complete accounts of Korean export subsidies and promotion efforts is given in the World Bank study by Rhee, Ross-Larson, and Pursell (1984).[12] Only some of these policies have been in effect in any one industry at any given time, and effective subsidies have been considerably scaled back (although not eliminated) in recent years. Nevertheless, the scope and pervasiveness of the nineteen major types of intervention listed here should dispel the myth that Korea succeeded by "allowing the free market to work."

1. *Periodic devaluations* of the Korean currency have been combined with other policies to keep the EER for exporters *higher* than that for importers. As early as 1964, South Korea's EER for exports was 281 and its EER for imports was 247 (Gillis, Perkins, Roemer, and Snodgrass 1987, p. 457)—reflecting not trade neutrality but a pro-export bias.[13]

2. *Preferential access to imports needed for producing exports* has been provided to manufacturers with unrestricted, guaranteed, and tariff-free access to imported intermediate inputs used in goods later exported, while other imports are severely restricted. "Wastage allowances" have often been relaxed further for exporters. Strict controls are in place to prevent abuse. Since 1975, industries have been allowed to collect rebates from the government only after documenting the completion of the exports.[14]

3. *Tariff exemptions* have been granted for imports of inputs of capital goods needed in exporting activities. This is a price incentive, while preferential access is a quantity restriction.

4. *Tax breaks* have also been given for domestic suppliers of inputs to exporting firms, which constitutes a domestic content incentive.

5. *Domestic indirect tax exemptions* have been provided for successful exporters.

6. *Lower direct taxes* have been charged on income earned from exports.

7. *Accelerated depreciation allowances* have been granted for exporters.

8. *Import entitlement certificates* (exemptions from import restrictions) have been linked directly to export levels. Korea has long maintained an extensive list of items generally prohibited from import, including both luxury goods and import-substitution targets. Profitable exemptions from this prohibition have often been available for firms exporting specified goods with low profit margins.

9. *Monopoly rights* have been granted to the first firm to achieve exports in a targeted industry.

10. *Loans at subsidized interest rates* have been made available to exporters.

11. *Preferential credit access* has been given to exporters, including automatic access to bank loans for the working capital needed for all export activities. Medium- and long-term loans for investment are rationed and often available only to firms that meet government export targets and pursue other requested activities.

12. *Reduced public utility taxes and rail rates* have been granted for exporters.

13. *A system of export credit insurance and guarantees,* as well as tax incentives for overseas marketing and postshipment export loans by the Korean Export-Import Bank, have been put in place.

14. *Free trade zones, industrial parks, and export-oriented infrastructure* have all been created.

15. *Public enterprises* have been created to lead the way in establishing new industries. Public enterprises produced the first Korean output of ships and refined petroleum products and petrochemicals (Amsden 1989, p. 275). Pack and

Westphal note that "the share of public enterprises in Korea's nonagricultural output is comparatively high, being similar to India's" (1986, p. 97). This is a striking comparison, because India's high share is often held to be symptomatic of an interventionist stance leading to lowered growth.

16. *Export sales promotion* is carried on by the Korean Traders Association and the Korea Trade Promotion Corporation (KTPC). These are publicly supported activities that promote Korean exports on behalf of Korean firms worldwide.

17. *Sectorwide efforts to upgrade the average technological level* have been orchestrated, encouraging the use of a new generation of machinery (Westphal 1990).

18. *Government coordination of foreign technology licensing agreements* has enabled the use of national bargaining power to secure the best possible terms for the private sector in utilizing proprietary American and other foreign technology.

19. *Export targets* have been set by firms themselves since the early 1960s, although they may be adjusted by the government.

The last point is perhaps the most surprising. Quantitative targeting in development planning has become particularly unfashionable in new orthodox development economics, perhaps because of its apparent similarity to "comprehensive development planning," or even the failed "central planning" of the Soviet Union and its former satellites. Why might quantitative targeting have been successful in the East Asian context? First, the countries of this area specifically targeted manufacturing exports of growing technological content. Such a planning yardstick automatically emphasizes targets with very strong development benefits. In addition, the world export market is an arena in which performance is clearly, quickly, and rigorously tested. This quick feedback tends to keep the development ministries, whose resources and information capacities are inherently limited, tightly focused on relevant and manageable problems. Consider, for example, the heavy and chemical industries push of the mid- to late 1970s, which is often regarded as a failure (e.g., by Collins 1990). Even though the target of 50 percent of exports coming from these sectors was not reached by the target year of 1980, by 1983 it had reached 56 percent (World Bank 1987b, p. 45). The slight dip in overall Korean growth in the late 1970s and early 1980s that resulted from this push may thus be understood as a kind of investment toward future growth and upgrading of the Korean industrial base. Econometric evidence suggests a clear link between industrial policy targets and later industrial structure in Korea (Mahidhara 1988).

In this regard, export targets hold a distinctive advantage over general output targets as a development policy mechanism because export levels are easier to monitor, making it harder for firms to gain benefits by cheating. This fact has long been understood by fiscal authorities, which have often taxed exports precisely because they are easily observable and therefore not subject to the tax evasion that is rampant in the developing world. This distortion produces a well-known and much criticized antiexport bias. The East Asian NICs appear to have been the first countries to put this observability insight to use as the centerpiece of a development planning system. They have done so in a way that reverses by 180 degrees the negative incentive effects of export taxes. Enforcement of export targets in the case of Korea is mostly moral in nature, relying on recognition of achievement more than on penalties and fines. The evidence seems persuasive that in Korea these have been among the most powerful of incentives.

In popular discussions, cultural explanations are commonly given for Korea's export success. These explanations generally cite the workforce's Confucian values of loyalty, discipline, hard work, respect for authority, and education. This argument is ironic, however, since the same cultural values were often cited in explaining East Asia's relative backwardness in the 1950s and early 1960s.

In practice, the corporate culture and business behavior of Korea may be much more important than the overall culture. In a study of corporate behavior, Deal and Kennedy concluded that companies with "clearly articulated . . . qualitative beliefs or values" were "uniformly high performers," while "we could find no correlations of any value among the other companies" (1982, p. 7). Without question, Korea as a whole has emphasized export expansion as both a corporate and a cultural value. Export performance is a relatively easy value to operationalize, through the instrument of export targets. In addition to the wide range of economic incentives to achieve these targets, Korea as a whole has an extensive pattern of rituals that reinforce these economic incentives with cultural ones.

A key ritual in Korean economic life is the Monthly National Trade Promotion Meeting, at which awards are presented for excellent export performance.

> Chaired by the president, the monthly trade promotion meetings are select gatherings of the ministers and top bureaucrats responsible for trade and the economy; the chief executives of export associations, research organizations, and educational institutions; and the heads of a few firms, mainly the general trading companies and other large firms. The prominence of those attending shows that the monthly meetings are far more than perfunctory meetings to improve coordination between the private and public sectors. (Rhee, Ross-Larson, and Pursell 1984, p. 29)

Such rituals are not limited to the business elite. One of the major national holidays in South Korea is Export Day, held on November 30 since 1964, when exports first topped $100 million.

To what extent is this cultural aspect of the Korean export experience transferable to other countries?[15] There is no obvious connection between Export Day and Confucianism. The love of public recognition through contests and competitions, medals and prizes, seems to be a universal human trait. It might be reasonable to conjecture that if Export Day were better known, the idea could be adopted by other developing countries. In fact, as shown later, Thailand is adopting a similar approach. On the other hand, it is reasonable to doubt the effectiveness of awards and recognition in the absence of reinforcing economic policies.

On the import side, South Korea maintained a very extensive system of import controls well into the 1980s (Luedde-Neurath 1986). What Luedde-Neurath terms the "Korean Kaleidoscope" includes restrictive trader licensing for importers, widespread quantitative controls on imports, domestic content requirements, systematic foreign exchange allocation under the Foreign Exchange Demand and Supply Plan, intervention in export-import settlements, required advance deposits (sometimes as high as 200 percent of the value of imports), and capricious customs practices.[16] For example, prospective importers must achieve a minimum level of earnings from exports before becoming eligible to import. These obligations began at $10,000 in 1962 and increased over time to $1 million in 1982 (Luedde-Neurath 1986, p. 91). Pack and Westphal conclude that:

> through import restrictions, selectively promoted infant industries were often initially granted whatever levels of effective protection were required to secure an adequate market for their output as well as a satisfactory rate of return on investment. Initial rates of effective protection were frequently in excess of 100 percent. (1986, pp. 94–95)

The country also utilizes an informal system of indicative planning-type protectionist measures (Pack and Westphal 1986, p. 95). Wade concludes that:

> it is misleading to use tariff revenue over total imports to indicate low tariff protection, because in Korea and Taiwan duties are collected mainly on imports for use in domestic-market-related sales rather than export sales, so that tariff revenue should be averaged over non-export-related imports only, giving a substantially higher average. (1988d, p. 100)

After 1971, the Korean government established the "Prior Import Recommendations" list, which "permitted certain imports [even] for export production only if the price advantage of the imported item exceeded a minimum level" and "prohibited the import of selected plant facilities in certain industries even if used for export production" (World Bank 1987b, p. 44). It also established minimum domestic content requirements for large plant facilities and for facilities built with foreign loans or foreign currency loans. Petri concludes that Korea has "an unusually protection-prone export bundle" based on overall industry data (1988, p. 1661).

In the Korean case, import controls have often been a handmaiden of successful industrial export promotion. As a result of the export-promotion reforms of the early 1960s,

> imports destined (either directly or indirectly as inputs) for the domestic market remained subject to tariffs and quantitative controls. However, the system

of controls on these imports was rationalized and thereby converted from a mechanism of socially unproductive rent seeking into an instrument of industrial promotion. (Pack and Westphal 1986, p. 93)

Many successful Korean export industries begin as infant industries requiring protection. For example, the electronics industry was the recipient of numerous special government benefits under the eight-year Electronics Industry Development Plan and subsequent five-year plans. These benefits included import protection as well as export incentives. As of 1984, there were 185 electrical and electronic goods imports that were still restricted in Korea (World Bank 1987b). Amsden (1989, p. 273) has pointed out that diversified Korean *Chaebol* firms are able to subsidize their entry into new export markets (such as shipbuilding) out of the monopoly rents created by import barriers on other products they produce, under government monitoring.

The developing industrial sector functions as a whole and benefits from externalities and linkages between firms, making a market failure case for more general protection, at least at the takeoff stage (Luedde-Neurath 1986).[17] *Widespread* protection may not be necessary for rapid technological progress, even at an early stage, but the *selective* promotion of infant industries with high training and technological progress externalities is probably necessary (Westphal 1982).

Unquestionably, by the late 1980s, South Korea substantially liberalized; but this had occurred only *after* the country had virtually joined the ranks of the industrially developed countries (Amsden 1989). As Pack and Westphal summarize the evidence, "something approximating neutrality" applies to "established industries.... But there has been substantial industry bias in favor of the promoted infant industries" (1986, p. 94).

It should also be noted that an active industrial policy continues to this day, encouraging Korean entry into high-technology fields (Borrus and Simon 1989). Research and development (R&D) expenditures are planned to reach a striking 5 percent of gross domestic product (GDP) by the year 2000 (Amsden 1989). The World Bank's International Finance Corporation (its private sector arm) has played a role in financing these developments. Recently, South Korea's Ministry of Trade and Industry targeted new areas for production, such as computer-controlled machine tools, bioengineering, microelectronics, fine chemistry, optics, and aircraft. The ministry predicted that Korea could catch up with the United States and Japan economically and technologically in these fields. The government would be centrally involved in the whole process (see "Seoul's High-Technology Push" 1989). Government-funded but industry-focused institutes, such as the Korean Electronics and Telecommunications Research Institute, the Korean Biogenetics Research Institute, and the Korean Automotive Systems Research Institute, are playing a major role. As South Korea becomes a candidate for developed country status, targeted industrial policies oriented toward technology enhancement are continuing to play a pivotal role.

Taiwan

Much less has been written about Taiwan than about Korea. Due to Taiwan's disputed status in relation to China, information on Taiwan does not appear in most official charts of statistics of the World Bank and many other international organizations. Nevertheless, Taiwan has had one of the world's fastest-growing economies, averaging nearly 10 percent annual growth in the 1965–80 period, and an incredible 8.7 percent average over the four decades from 1950 to 1990 ("Taiwan and Korea" 1990). Taiwan is also widely regarded in America as an outstanding example of a successful "free market" economy; but, like South Korea, Taiwan has put in place active industrial policy systems. The Taiwanese government has licensed exports, controlled direct foreign investment both to and from Taiwan, established export cartels, provided fiscal incentives for investment in priority sectors, and given concessional credit for favored industries. Indeed, Taiwan has used most of the same types of interventionist policies used by Korea.[18]

Taiwan's post–World War II economic history began with a very highly dirigiste, import-substitution–oriented approach to industrialization. The 1958 reforms switched intervention to export promotion and introduced greater reliance on market forces. What emerged was far from a free market—only a less thoroughly planned one.[19] For example, in Taiwan, all imports and exports have to be covered by a license, a fact not well known in the United States. Imports are classified into prohibited, controlled, and permissible. Luxury goods are controlled. So are some goods produced locally with reasonable quality, in sufficient quantities, and at prices that are not more than a narrow margin (about 5 percent) above comparable import prices (Wade 1988a, 1988c). A striking fact is that even the "permissible" items have been subject to strong controls. For example, until 1980, garments could be imported only from Europe and America—the least competitive sources. Other goods subject to "competitive origin restrictions" have included yarns, artificial fibers, fabrics, some processed foodstuffs, chemicals, machinery, and electrical apparatus.

Moreover, more items are controlled than appear on the published list, so that not all "permissibles" are automatically approved. As Wade shows,

> Typically, a would-be importer of an item on the hidden list will be asked to provide evidence that the domestic supplier(s) cannot meet his terms (on price, quality, delivery). He may be asked to furnish a letter from the relevant producers' association. (1988b, p. 50)

Wade explains that these policies form the "referral mechanism" of import control. These Taiwanese policies function as a dramatically innovative domestic content strategy, oriented toward technological progress. According to Wade, these policies:

provide strong domestic demand for the products of the industries which the planners consider important, especially new ones. . . . Petrochemicals, chemicals, steel, other basic metals . . . are covered by the referral mechanism. So are some machinery and components industries, including some machine tools, forklift trucks, and bearings. (1988b, p. 52)

Fransman (1986) provides more specific details on the active role of government in fostering the development of a machine tool industry—one of the keys to achieving a domestic capability for technological innovation (Rosenberg 1976).

Under this system, Taiwanese importers cannot import freely, even when producing directly for export. Trade liberalization has taken place since the 1960s but has never been neutral. Instead, liberalization has always aimed at shifting production steadily up the technological scale. Overall protection—measured by average tariffs and other aggregate measures—has decreased, but quantitative and qualitative intervention has remained pervasive in specific sectors. Clearly, this is not the pure free market, but is rather indicative of the type of planning pioneered by the French in the 1950s (see Meade 1970). Taiwan, however, has used indicative planning more systematically than the French ever dreamed of doing. All this clearly contradicts the arguments of the new orthodoxy school and the *World Development Report 1987* that the sine qua non of outward orientation is no discrimination between foreign and domestic goods or between production for the domestic market and production for exports.

Wade explains that this import-substitution program has been successful because it is consistent with an emphasis on incentives.

Because the government is able to control quantities of goods crossing the national boundary, it can use international prices to discipline the price-setting of protected domestic producers. It is very sensitive to the point that there must be good reasons why domestic prices of protected items are significantly higher than international prices, especially in the case of items to be used for export production. In this way domestic prices for goods covered by formal or hidden controls can be kept near international levels, without there being a free flow of goods. The threat of allowing in more goods can be sufficient to hold prices down. (1988b, p. 51)

This is analogous to the well-known argument that monopolists will keep prices low to the extent that they fear the entry of a rival firm seeking to take advantage of a prevailing high price in an industry. Moreover, the programs illustrate the Taiwanese government's clear understanding of the development benefits of producing and exporting a particular set of manufactures at a given stage of rapid development, especially in regard to externalities (benefits that spill over from one sector to another).

Wade argues that Taiwanese "state interventions have been very selective between firms and industries" and "subject to the criterion of international competitiveness" (1988b, p. 58). He states that these interventions meet both "the need to keep the economy exposed to efficiency-enhancing pressure from the world market," and "the need to modulate that pressure so as to capture more value-added and more of the cumulative benefits of technological change within Taiwan" (p. 58).

The China External Trade Development Council (CETDC) provides a particularly clear illustration of the way in which Taiwan utilizes programs that are actually restrictive, but that appear to be similar to the policies of more genuinely free-trading countries, in order to carry out industrial policy. Superficially, CETDC is just an overseas trade representative office, but in practice it does much more.

> Market research in CETDC's New York office as of 1980 was based on an active search for items that could be sold in the United States. The search began with an analysis of the size and origin of U.S. imports, followed by a preliminary study of the price and quality of the more competitive imported and U.S. products. From this the officers in New York reached an estimate of the likelihood of Taiwan, China firms competing successfully against offerings already on the market. (They claimed to understand the manufacturing capabilities of Taiwan, China firms well enough to do this.) Once a likely product was identified, the office asked firms in Taiwan, China to send it samples of the product and price lists. Representatives of the office would then visit importers, wholesalers, and other traders with samples and price lists, prospecting for sales. They would try to get reactions to the product. If the buyers were interested they would telex the manufacturers. If not, they would find out why and then suggest appropriate steps to the manufacturer. (Keesing 1988, p. 28)

Why might this type of "intervention," broadly similar to that practiced by South Korea (and Singapore), be capable of yielding results better than the free market outcome? Essentially, the improvement is due to the public-good properties of information, reputation, and sales-network-building activities. Active policies of CETDC, like the KTPC in South Korea, have raised the information standards of industry there generally to more efficient levels. Perhaps equally important, they have helped to transform the image of national quality—an enormously valuable asset, as onlooking manufacturers in South America and South Asia understand all too well. Supply and sales networks can often be of benefit to many firms from a given country and may thus hold something of the character of an externality. Moreover, in the presence of capital market imperfections, public activities of this kind can help firms surmount high fixed costs.

Taiwan's industrial organization differs from that of South Korea in one important respect: rather than having an industrial sector intentionally organized around a small number of large business groups (the *Chaebol*), Taiwan has intentionally fostered small- to medium-sized firms clustered together by industry (Bertoldi 1990).

While Taiwanese industry has been organized in this manner with the intention of facilitating exports, the effect has also been to create an "industrial district" form of economic organization, of the type that has won so much praise for productivity and innovation in such regions as Baden-Württemberg in Germany and the north-central area of Italy (Piore and Sabel 1984; Porter 1990). The productive externalities between firms that have been cited for such districts explain the productive effect of a government role in their creation, even if such externalities were not the primary target of the government at the time of their implementation.

Industrial districts are characterized by the presence of many small firms in the same or closely linked industries that interact not only in conventional markets but through a complex and flexible division of labor. They are common in high-tech fields as well as certain traditional industries. Industrial districts facilitate labor market information, promote training and mobility, and reduce transaction costs. These benefits are largely external to any one firm, and so there may be market failures in the initial establishment of industrial districts.

This characterization fits the Taiwan industrial organization, including the prevalence of extended family and "network" enterprise (Greenhalgh 1988). Tai-Li Hu's (1984, chapter 4) description of the flexible relationship between village job subcontracting shops and nearby "center factories" parallels the Italian industrial districts. Although these relationships were established without government support (in many cases illegally), the establishment of the center firms, their clustering together into industrial zones, and the development of foreign markets for the final product resulted from deliberate industrial policy.

To assist small firms with technological progress, the Taiwanese government has been setting up cooperative research institutes, such as the Industrial Technological Research Institute (Wade 1990). It is sometimes suggested that Taiwan's small-firm orientation reflects less intervention ("Taiwan and Korea" 1990). A more accurate way to characterize the difference is that Taiwan has a policy of relying on different technologies and a different industrial organization in different sectors. Still, it seems clear that firms in Taiwan's relatively informal districts are subject to much less direct government guidance than are otherwise comparable small firms in Korea.

Linnemman, van Dijck, and Verbruggen cite the importance of Taiwan's "broad package of fiscal incentives, subsidies, and other measures" to promote exports, including "cheap credit for exporters, income tax exemptions, cheap export insurance, and marketing support" (1987, p. 343). The Taiwanese combination of selective import controls with activist export inducements demonstrates that industrial policies and trade intervention need not be inimical to economic efficiency. As Wade concludes,

> We see from Taiwan that it is possible for a government both to maintain a substantial protection system and to constrain its use of that system by a determination to be competitive on world markets. Indeed, the government has tried—apparently with some success—to use that system as an aid to competitiveness on world markets. It has done so by reducing risk for new producers, helping them to reach economies of scale on the domestic market (including the market for export inputs), and helping them to protect capacity utilization;

all the while putting pressure on them to keep their prices at near international levels, especially via the threat to allow in imports . . . and vigorous efforts in export promotion, including export marketing, export cartels, and export quality control have (presumably) helped to offset disincentives to exports stemming from protection. (1988c, p. 54)

In addition to ensuring efficiency and competitiveness, Taiwan's industrial development strategy helps firms to enter fields with ever-greater technological sophistication, which is essential for eventually achieving developed country status (see Romer 1992). Linked with more informal industrial districts, which the state played at least some role in fostering, Taiwan's industrialization policy has proved itself to be one of the world's most effective development strategies.

With its considerable progress in economic development and its huge trade surpluses (over $13 billion surplus with the United States alone in 1989) (U.S. Department of Commerce 1990, p. 88), Taiwan is now in a position to liberalize large parts of its trade without endangering its hard-won footholds in advanced technology and high value-added sectors. The lesson for less advanced LDCs from Taiwanese liberalization is not that they should foreswear combined import-substitution–export-promotion programs. Rather, the lesson is that liberalization is a process that should be undertaken cautiously, consciously, and often selectively, only as formerly protected or subsidized sectors become efficient enough to be competitive in export markets.[20]

Now that Taiwan's extensive industrial policies are at last beginning to gain some notice, it is a safe prediction that a cottage industry based on criticizing them as inefficient will be growing up in the next couple of years. With a 9 percent growth rate maintained decade after decade, these policies have clearly had something going for them, though with different elements than those observed in Korea's *Chaebol*-oriented policies. One of the most productive directions for future research will be in regard to the externalities fostered by encouraging industrial districts of smaller firms in closely related sectors, both cooperating and strongly competing in a detailed division of labor, as in the case of the "Third Italy" economic miracle (see Piore and Sabel 1984). Industrial policies in Taiwan may well turn out to have actively fostered such districts. Even if the government were not intending to realize the external productive benefits of such organizations but only seeking to facilitate exports, it would nonetheless remain true that Taiwan's policy played an important role in creating these districts. This would suggest the viability of a new industrial development strategy that might be employed consciously elsewhere.

Thailand

Thailand is showing signs of turning a current boom in exports of manufactures into an industrial takeoff in the same way that Taiwan and Korea did in the

1970s. Thailand has an industrial policy that is less active than that of Korea and Taiwan, but its anything-goes free market image is misleading. Despite its casino stock market and widespread corruption, the country's trade and industrial policy incentives have had significant effects on its industrial development.

Thailand's industrialization began in the 1960s, under the highly protectionist import-substitution strategy of the First and Second Economic Plans (1961–71). Under this regime, average annual growth rates of total manufacturing reached 11 percent in the 1960s, while the share of primary process manufacturing in the total declined from 60 percent to 40 percent. Consumer goods, petroleum products, and some producer goods industries were established (World Bank 1989a). The Third Economic Plan (1972–76) inaugurated an active phase of export-promotion interventions. As a result, the growth of manufacturing continued at 10 percent per year throughout the 1970s. Clothing and electrical machinery gained in importance as well as producer goods in chemicals, transportation equipment, and textiles. In the turbulent first half of the 1980s, Thailand experienced uneven economic performance. But since 1986, an explosive growth in investment and exports has renewed the widespread speculation of the late 1970s that Thailand would become the fifth East Asian Tiger. In 1965, just 4 percent of Thailand's exports were manufactured goods, but by 1990 this figure had reached 64 percent (World Bank 1992, table 16).

Thailand led the world in GDP growth at the end of the 1980s, with over 11 percent annual growth in 1988, 1989, and 1990. In 1991–92, growth was a still-strong 7 percent, and growth of about 8 percent was forecast through the mid-1990s. Since 1986, the annual growth rate of merchandise exports has reached 25 percent. Despite much slower growth in the early 1980s, manufactured exports from Thailand to the United States grew at an average annual rate of 26.3 percent from 1980 to 1987 (World Bank 1989a), while the rate of growth of exports to Japan was 12.6 percent. Substantial diversification of manufactured exports has also taken place, with rapidly increasing exports in manufactures requiring higher skill and technology content.

Such movements up the ladder of comparative advantage, in which technological progress is key, are always complex. Undoubtedly, there were "pull" factors at work, as the first four East Asian Tigers were climbing to still higher rungs and establishing high value-added manufacturing. There was also a "push" from lower rungs by new low-wage manufactures exporters such as China and Indonesia. However, these favorable external conditions are not enough to guarantee sustained rapid growth. Just as in the cases of Korea, Taiwan, and Singapore, increasingly selective, interventionist industrial policies played an important role in this transformation.

Many Thai departments and institutions—including the Board of Investment (BOI), the Ministry of Industry, the Ministry of Finance, the Ministry of Commerce, the Fiscal Policy Office (FPO), the Bank of Thailand, and the Department of Customs (DOC)—are actively engaged in formulating and implementing industrial and trade policies.[21] These policies include the following:

1. *Domestic content regulations.* Automobiles and motorcycles, among other sectors, are subject to stringent domestic content regulations. Locally manufactured engines were required as of mid-1989 on all domestically assembled autos and motorcycles, in addition to previously established domestic content minimums of 45 percent for autos and 70 percent for motorcycles.

2. *Export promotion.* The Thai BOI offers a series of special arrangements to promote exports, including three- to five-year exemptions from corporate income taxes, reductions or exemptions from business taxes and import duties on imported raw materials and machinery, and additional tax reductions in Investment Promotion Zones. These measures are increasingly targeted toward specific sectors, following the Korean example, with an eye to moving into higher value-added and more technologically sophisticated exports. The BOI, the DOC, and the FPO also offer various extensive duty drawback and exemption systems for exports, as well as special export credit facilities.

3. *Foreign investment.* Very favorable tax holidays and other inducements are used to attract direct foreign investment. Thailand's export boom has been largely fueled by a massive inflow of direct foreign investment from Japan and the Four Tigers. These investors are believed to be responding to their own movement up the technological ladder of comparative advantage and to fear of protectionist retaliation against products produced at home. In recent years strong links have been forged between Thai and Japanese firms.

4. *Selective protection.* Tariffs on consumer goods and light intermediate goods rose dramatically in the 1970s, Thailand's pretakeoff period, generally to between about 35 percent and 60 percent. These goods continue to be relatively highly protected, despite reductions of nominal tariffs in 1986 and 1987 after industries had become established. The objective of recent reductions appears to be more a desire to reduce the incentive to smuggle in such products than liberalization per se. There were still about twenty published import bans in 1988—although this was down from forty-three in 1985—and another thirty-three products were still subject to import licensing.[22] Television sets are still protected with 40 percent nominal tariffs, and many other kinds of consumer electronics, including videocassette recorders (VCRs) and stereo equipment, still have 30 percent tariffs. Average effective rates of protection of manufacturing appear to remain at over 60 percent, and the World Bank (1987c) found Thailand to be one of the most protectionist countries in East Asia. This pattern of Thailand's strongly protecting the same goods it is pushing as exports duplicates the earlier patterns of Taiwan and Korea. Thailand publicly describes its motive as the raising of revenues rather than protectionism. Nevertheless, its recent experience argues against the purported ineffectiveness of import substitution. Instead, Thailand offers more evidence that import substitution is an essential complement to successful export promotion.

5. *Currency undervaluation.* The Thai baht, which is fixed to the U.S. dollar,

was devalued by 14 percent in 1984 and by 8.7 percent in 1987. These devaluations increased the competitiveness of Thai products in the U.S. market. The baht is now undervalued, in the sense that the dollar prices of Thai manufactured exports are lower across the board than are the prices of U.S. goods. Thai exports to other industrial countries have also benefited, as the U.S. dollar has fallen against other currencies since 1985 and the baht remains pegged to the dollar.

6. *Export culture*. Following the example of Korea, Thailand is working hard to establish an export culture in government and industry. The deputy prime minister chairs the Export Promotion Committee, an influential advisory body with private and public representatives. The prime minister chairs the similar Joint Consultative Committee.

One area in which the Thai experience differs from Korea's is that Thailand has been very open to an active role of multinational corporations; it has placed much less emphasis on promoting indigenous firms and regulating multinationals. This may lead to problems in the future and will bear watching closely.

There is much room for policy improvement in Thailand, where rent seeking *is* pervasive and costly, and where dedicated civil servants are much rarer than in South Korea. The results of Thailand's policies have nonetheless more resembled the successes of Taiwan, Korea, and Singapore than the failures of the countries that have actually implemented the pure market neutrality advice.

In sum, Thailand has had an active, export-oriented industrial policy that by and large seems to have approximated a response to market failures in technology upgrading. Its record on poverty, women, distribution, the environment, and inequality is not the best in its region, but Thailand's democratic revolt is bringing about demands for action on these problems as well.

Problems of Commodity Export-Oriented Growth

This section briefly examines the experience of developing countries that tried to use commodity exports as an engine of growth in the 1980s. LDCs that stressed commodity export expansion did so partly as a result of development advice to follow their traditional (static) comparative advantages. The need for foreign exchange to service large external debts also contributed to the breakneck speed with which, in the 1980s, commodities exports were expanded in Africa, in Latin America, in Southeast Asia, and elsewhere. Whether out of choice or necessity, this revival of primary commodity export-oriented growth provides a test of the criticisms of this strategy that were reviewed earlier.

In the 1980s, the World Bank encouraged LDCs to follow an export-oriented course through its project lending. In accordance with policies set at the Bank's highest level, its regional and country departments advised LDCs to cut trade protections and produce whatever goods would bring in immediate foreign exchange on the world market. Estimates of the economic returns on these projects were based on current conditions of supply and demand. Pushing so many countries to export more of the same types of commodities simultaneously inevitably undermined the very conditions that were assumed in projecting the returns.

At the World Bank, project analysis and funding are quite decentralized. A myriad of small, regional departments are charged with promoting exports for their assigned countries. The staff of each department apparently assumes that, since most of these countries are small in the context of the world economy, their extra output will be too small to have an appreciable impact on world prices. World Bank analysts usually assume that prices will hold up (that is, continue to follow the same path as given by existing predictions), rather than falling as the supply of promoted exports (e.g., coffee, cocoa, tropical oils, sugar cane, rubber, or minerals) increases. This approach may simplify the task of the analyst, but it is likely to backfire for the countries that follow the World Bank's advice.

Even if the assumption of a given price were valid for the individual country (and this is questionable for many of the countries that are large sellers of certain products), if all the expanded exports that the Bank was advocating were aggregated, it would be clear that they would tend to depress the prices of those goods. For example, considering all the sugar exports that the Bank was urging upon a number of countries around 1980, the fall in sugar prices that ensued over the following decade might safely have been predicted.[23] The same could be said for dozens of primary products that the World Bank and other agencies encouraged countries to export.

It should be emphasized that the World Bank is not without the *capacity* to undertake a serious analysis of price trends in the context of world supply and demand. The Bank's International Commodity Markets Division regularly reports price projections and offers a working paper series on commodities. The problems have been rather that: (1) each regional department almost always uses the assumption that its activities will not affect these projections; and (2) despite nominal reporting requirements, there is no systematic internal adding up of these separate activities within the Bank, let alone across the other various development agencies.[24]

The Commodity Markets Division conducted a retrospective survey of World Bank activities in a particular commodity—sugar—that is worth quoting at length.

> The Bank has played [a] significant role in the development of sugar production in many countries. . . . In 1974–85, when the average annual price of world market sugar reached an all-time high, 114 projects were approved which included assistance to increase sugar production . . . in the aggregate, the incremental production estimates in appraisal reports amount to more than four million tons per year at full development . . . an important share of traded sugar, which averaged only 20 million tons in the same period. (Brown 1987, pp. 5–6)

These efforts included completed projects in thirteen countries and projects still in progress in thirty-five countries in every developing region in the 1974–85 period. In 1984, the division projected that the world price of sugar would be $519 per metric ton in 1990, in current 1990 dollars; that is, about 23 1/2 cents per pound (World Bank 1984). A later update reported a spring 1990 price of 15 cents per pound, after a temporary price surge. The division then projected a decline, in constant 1985 dollars, to 10 cents per pound in 1995, with a rise back to 11.5 cents per pound in 2000 (World Bank 1989b). These changing forecasts show that the earlier optimism about sugar prices is now recognized to have been mistaken.

Figure 9.1 shows an index of "real" primary commodity prices (excluding fuels) for developing countries, constructed from IMF data.[25] This index measures the purchasing power of commodity exports over manufactured goods exported by the industrial countries—what economists call the "commodity terms of trade." The index, which is constructed to be representative of all LDC nonfuel commodity exports, shows a clear declining trend of commodity prices (the terms of trade) since the late 1970s. An econometric study by IMF economists Morrison and Wattleworth (1988) confirmed that rising supplies of food and larger production capacity of agricultural raw materials and metals were the major factors depressing primary commodity markets in the 1980s and particularly in 1984–86. More recently, the persistence of the downward trend in the primary commodity terms of trade has led staff economists at the IMF to reconsider the validity of the old Prebisch-Singer hypothesis of a secular declining tendency (see Borensztein, Khan, Reinhart, and Wickham 1994). As one new study concludes, "the recent weakness in real commodity prices is primarily of a secular, persistent nature and is not the product of a large temporary deviation from trend" (Reinhart and Wickham 1994, p. 180).

In the 1970s, the ability of the Organization of Petroleum Exporting Countries (OPEC) to raise petroleum prices dramatically appeared to refute the hypothesis of a chronic tendency for the commodity terms of trade to decline. In the 1980s, even oil proved to be no exception. As a result of oversupply by petroleum exporters (including non-OPEC producers as well as OPEC members exceeding their quotas) and conservation efforts by petroleum importers, oil prices collapsed in the mid-1980s. From 1982 to 1988, the real price of oil (in terms of developed country manufactured exports) fell by about *two-thirds,* or 66 percent (International Monetary Fund 1989b). Of course, the international oil market is very volatile, as evidenced by the surge in oil prices in the period following Iraq's invasion of Kuwait. Nevertheless, it is clear from the experience of the 1980s that countries that rely too heavily on commodity exports, whether fuel or nonfuel, are placing their economic development at risk. Though the World Bank has since moved away from commodity development projects toward structural adjustment projects, these lessons should be borne in mind the next time commodity export projects return to popularity in the Bank.

Figure 9.1. **Real Price Index for Nonfuel Primary Commodity Exports of Developing Countries, 1970–93**

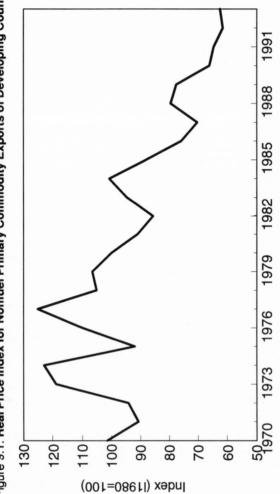

Sources: International Monetary Fund, International Financial Statistics, 1994 Yearbook; and author's calculations.

Note: The real price index is the non-fuel commodity price index for developing countries deflated by the index of export unit values for the industrial countries.

Implications for Development Policy

New orthodox doctrine to the contrary notwithstanding, the East Asian Four Tigers have not generally relied on free trade. South Korea and Taiwan in particular have employed an effective set of trade and industrial policy interventions. Most of the leading East Asian governments have purposefully undertaken protective actions to foster their capacity to produce manufactured exports of increasing technological content. These interventionist policies have played a major role, from early attempts at achieving technology transfers in relatively basic industries to the recent development of original innovative capacity in high-technology sectors. Such interventions have been crucial to overcoming the market failures endemic to technological progress. Many development experts have underestimated the importance and extent of such market failures in the transfer of product, process, and organizational know-how to developing countries.

The industrial and export policy approach followed by Taiwan, South Korea, and other successful NICs has been more effective than either extreme trade liberalization or primary commodity exporting. The systematic, well-planned promotion of manufactured exports of steadily increasing sophistication seems to lead to the greatest sustainable long-run growth. A number of factors contribute to making the manufactures export strategy more effective than a commodities export strategy, including the stimulus given to economywide technological progress, the absorption of advanced technology from abroad, the accumulation of "human capital" (labor skills as well as technical and managerial expertise), the construction of infrastructure that reduces future development costs, the ability to take advantage of scale economies, and the relatively stable terms of trade (relative prices) for manufactured exports. These factors have helped the East Asian NICs to realize the greatest possible benefits for growth from their high rates of savings and investments.

In addition, it appears that these gains can best be achieved when export promotion is accompanied by continued (but highly selective) government intervention to restrict imports of targeted products and to skew current private incentives in favor of long-run social benefits. Moreover, the targeting of manufactured exports as a development planning mechanism, as practiced in South Korea and Taiwan, holds a distinct advantage over general output targets: the outcomes are easily observable and face the immediate and rigorous test of world market competition.

All this points to the conclusion that real, sustainable development will, as a rule, require not just any exports, but manufactured exports. These findings are consistent with the thesis of Nobel Prize–winning development economist W. Arthur Lewis, who argued that "international trade became an engine of growth in the nineteenth century, but this is not its proper role. The engine of growth should be technological change, with international trade serving as lubricating oil and not as fuel" (1978, p. 74). The evidence from East Asian countries indicates that LDCs will better achieve this goal not through market forces alone, but through selective interventionist policies that use international competition as a disciplining device to ensure domestic efficiency. Such direction can come about only if government has the resources to make intelligent policy, the ability to implement it, and the will to act in the public interest. Thus, the government's industrial policies concerning production, exports, and imports will be significant determinants of development success.

Ultimately, the developing countries themselves are bound to recognize these facts on their own, given the preoccupation with imitating the success of the East Asian NICs that prevails throughout the developing world. The World Bank itself is in the midst of reevaluating these issues through its Asian Miracles project. This new research program was undertaken at Japanese instigation and with Japanese funding. Given that the tide of understanding is turning, the development agencies and the U.S. government should at least stop trying to block this recognition by insisting that developing countries adopt extreme trade liberalization in order to qualify for aid, loans, or debt relief. In a more positive vein, the World Bank and other development institutions should build on the Asian Miracles project by initiating research into effective government strategies for promoting industrial development that could avoid the pitfalls of either excessive import protection or pure trade liberalization.

Such strategies would emphasize facilitating technological and organizational innovation, both through transfers from developed countries and through the development of indigenous innovative capabilities. These strategies would use world market prices as guides to ensuring productive efficiency, but without allowing current price signals to cause LDCs to overspecialize in commodities that will be inferior in the long run. It is indeed sensible for LDCs to start with relatively simple, labor-intensive manufacturing activities, but the long-term goal should be to move progressively "up the technological ladder" to the higher value-added activities that are more likely to generate higher real wages and higher living standards.

The approach taken in this chapter should not be misread as antineoclassical. A more consistent neoclassical view would recognize the value of selective involvement of government in projects in which technological progress (product, process, or organizational) is a central concern. Such policies in the East Asian NICs can be traced from early attempts at achieving technology transfer in relatively basic industries to the current efforts of the Four Tigers to develop original, innovative capacity in high-technology sectors. The interpretation that seems most favored by the evidence is that the East Asian industrial policy mix has served to overcome market failures involved in the process of technological progress. That such market failures are endemic to original technological progress is one of the better-known propositions in economics, but there may have been a massive underestimation of the importance and extent of such market failures in the *transfer* of product, process, and organizational innovations to developing countries.

There is much that is not yet known, both about how to design effective policies to ensure that appropriate transfers occur and about how to construct the domestic organizational resources to develop and carry them out. This area should be a very high priority for the research agendas of the aid agencies.

Notes

1. See Wade (1988d) for an overview and detailed critique of this "market simulation" interpretation.
2. See also Krueger (1980, 1983, 1990a, 1990b) and Lal (1985). For a survey of the new orthodoxy school, see Todaro (1989, pp. 82–85, 530–36).
3. However, resource shifts rarely occur smoothly, swiftly, or without high costs. This itself necessitates some role for development policy and potentially justifies an interventionist version of shifting to export promotion.
4. Interestingly, the only exception that Chenery, Robinson, and Syrquin (1986) find is Japan. This does not mean that Japan was not protectionist but that it was a large and closed economy (the largest in these authors' sample), and one that therefore had little room to grow further through import substitution.
5. It is certainly true that many more LDCs have had average EERs biased against exporters than biased in favor of exporters, but in principle there are as many EERs in the economy as there are tradable goods. As discussed below, targeted export promotion at the individual commodity level may be more important than the economywide average EER level.
6. Most LDCs must also import energy and some raw materials, often from other LDCs, but generally with hard currency. For example, China and India, among the most self-sufficient of the LDCs, send tens of thousands of university students to the United States.
7. For a more complete discussion, see Luedde-Neurath (1986, pp. 8–15). Note that structuralist theories are not to be confused with dependency theories, which argue that developing country trade with developed countries is *inherently* antidevelopmental, and which therefore argue for nationalist or Third World economic autarky. This radical approach has not had much direct influence on economic policies and lies outside the scope of this chapter.
8. In particular, it has been argued that LDCs tend to have labor markets in which wages are held to a low level by the existence of large pools of "surplus," underemployed workers living at a bare subsistence level, while developed countries have labor markets that tend to be relatively tight and in which unions can win wage increases keeping up with productivity gains. This implies that workers in LDCs do not share in their industries' productivity growth as workers in developed countries do. Furthermore, it is often assumed that primary products sell in competitive markets where prices are flexible, while manufactured goods sell in oligopolistic markets where prices are set by a markup over unit labor costs. This implies a recurrent tendency for commodity prices to fall relative to industrial prices in periods of weak demand or excess supply.
9. Affected commodities include sugar, coffee, cocoa, natural rubber, palm nuts, kernels, and seeds; tropical oils such as cottonseed oil and coconut (copra) oil; ores of iron, copper, bauxite, lead, zinc, tin, and manganese; beef, certain cereals, certain citrus fruits, fresh vegetables for export in some locations, certain dried fruits, and wood (in various forms).

10. For an interesting comparison of the trade management policies of Japan in the postwar period and the more recent policies of South Korea and Taiwan, see Wade (1988d). For a discussion of industrial policy in Singapore and Hong Kong, see Smith (1991).

11. For a careful, succinct, and insightful economic analysis of the Korean labor market, see Park (1988). Restriction of labor rights may be proving to have been a single but very important strategic error in light of the extensive disruptive labor unrest in early 1990.

12. Additional key references (drawn on below) are Amsden (1989); Hong (1979); Frank, Kim, and Westphal (1975); Pack and Westphal (1986); Luedde-Neurath (1986, 1988); World Bank (1987b); Kuznets (1988); Petri (1988); and Park (1990).

13. In other words, exporters receive relatively high amounts of domestic currency for each dollar of exports, while importers must pay a relatively high amount of domestic currency (but not as high as exporters pay) to receive a dollar for importing.

14. South Korea has had high dispersion of effective rates of protection even with a relatively low average, again contrary to the advice of the new orthodoxy school and contrary to the implicit assumption in much new orthodoxy writing on South Korea.

15. Deal and Kennedy (1982) provided many examples of analogous award ceremonies or other special cultural rituals at the corporate rather than the national level.

16. The Luedde-Neurath (1986) study decisively refuted the well-known study of Westphal and Kim (1977), which had concluded that the Korean economy liberalized extensively in the 1960s.

17. This recalls arguments of the early structural development economists, such as Rosenstein-Rodan (1943).

18. See Wade (1988a, 1988b, 1988c, 1988d, 1990); Borrus and Simon (1989); Amsden (1979, 1984); Li and Yeh (1981); Yu (1988); Fransman (1986); Liang and Liang (1988); and Linnemman, van Dijck, and Verbruggen (1987).

19. See Amsden (1979). As Wade put it, the reforms "liberalized an exceptionally 'unliberal' economy and quite a lot of liberalization could take place without its becoming a recognizably liberal one" (1988b, p. 55).

20. While exports *have* been an important means of realizing economies of scale for Taiwan, there is some econometric evidence that economies of scale (made possible by trade) rather than expanded exports as such are better able to explain industrial development in that economy (Chen and Tang 1990).

21. In addition to Linnemman, van Dijck, and Verbruggen (1987), this section draws on numerous World Bank, United Nations, and other development agency reports.

22. This information is based on Sibunruang (1986) and World Bank (1989a).

23. The spot price of Caribbean sugar fell from 28.67 U.S. cents per pound in 1980 to 4.05 cents in 1985, before rising to just 12.81 cents in 1989. Similarly, Brazilian sugar fell from 21.79 U.S. cents in 1980 to 6.66 cents in 1985, and rose to only 12.19 cents in 1989. Philippine sugar peaked at 20.65 U.S. cents in 1981, fell to 12.70 cents in 1984, and then recovered to 19.16 cents by 1989. Prices are from International Monetary Fund (1989a, 1990).

24. Although today all projects are supposed to be summarized in a project database, and this repository is presumed to be referred to by World Bank commodity specialists in making price projections, this procedure at best suffers from lags and is loosely managed; moreover, there is no adding up across the Bank and the many other regional, bilateral, and private agencies lending to, or providing other support for, project development.

25. The index shown in Figure 9.1 is the ratio of the IMF index of nonfuel primary commodity prices for developing countries to the export unit value index for the industrial countries. Technically, it would have been preferable to use a *manufactures* export unit

value index for the industrial countries, but that index is not published in the IMF's *International Financial Statistics Yearbook*. However, in practice it makes little difference, since the vast majority of the industrial countries' exports consist of manufactures, and the trends are similar either way.

Bibliography

Amsden, Alice. 1979. "Taiwan's Economic History: A Case of Etatisme and a Challenge to Dependency Theory." *Modern China,* Vol. 5, pp. 341–80.
————. 1984. "Exports of Technology by Newly Industrializing Countries: Taiwan." *World Development,* Vol. 12, Nos. 5–6, pp. 491–503.
————. 1989. *Asia's Next Giant: South Korea and Late Industrialization.* Oxford, England: Oxford University Press.
Balassa, Bela. 1988. "The Lessons of East Asian Development: An Overview." *Economic Development and Cultural Change,* Vol. 36, Supplement, pp. S273–90.
Berg, Andrew, and Jeffrey Sachs. 1988. "The Debt Crisis: Structural Explanations of Country Performance." *Journal of Development Economics,* Vol. 29, pp. 271–306.
Bertoldi, Moreno. 1990. *Structural Development Policies: A Comparative Analysis of the Experience of Taiwan and South Korea.* Brussels: Commission of European Communities.
Borensztein, Eduardo, Mohsin S. Khan, Carmen M. Reinhart, and Peter Wickham. 1994. *The Behavior of Non-Oil Commodity Prices.* Occasional Paper No. 112. Washington, DC: International Monetary Fund (August).
Borrus, Michael, and Denis Fred Simon. 1989. "High Technology in the Pacific Basin: Analysis and Policy Implications." Paper presented at the State Department–NAS Conference on Foreign Competition in Science and Technology, National Academy of Science (May 11).
Brown, James G. 1987. "The International Sugar Industry: Developments and Prospects." Commodities Working Paper No. 18. Washington, DC: World Bank.
Chen, Tain-Jy, and De-Piao Tang. 1990. "Export Performance and Productivity Growth: The Case of Taiwan." *Economic Development and Cultural Change,* Vol. 38, pp. 577–86.
Chenery, Hollis, Sherman Robinson, and Moises Syrquin. 1986. *Industrialization and Growth: A Comparative Study.* New York: Oxford University Press.
"Clearing Practices Threaten Western Hemisphere's Air Quality." 1988. *Washington Post* (September 8), p. A3.
Collins, Susan M. 1990. "Lessons from Korean Economic Growth." *American Economic Review: Papers and Proceedings,* Vol. 80 (May), pp. 104–7.
Deal, Terrence E., and A. A. Kennedy. 1982. *Corporate Cultures: The Rites and Rituals of Corporate Life.* Reading, MA: Addison-Wesley.
Fishlow, Albert. 1987. "Some Reflections on Comparative Latin American Economic Performance and Policy." Working Paper No. 22. Helsinki: World Institute for Development Economics Research (August).
Frank, Charles R., Kwang Suk Kim, and Larry E. Westphal. 1975. *Foreign Trade Regimes and Economic Development: South Korea.* New York: Columbia University Press.
Fransman, Martin. 1986. "International Competitiveness, Technical Change, and the State: The Machine Tool Industry in Taiwan and Japan." *World Development,* Vol. 14, pp. 1375–96.

Gillis, Malcolm, Dwight H. Perkins, Michael Roemer, and Donald R. Snodgrass. 1987. *Economics of Development*, 2d ed. New York: Norton.

Greenhalgh, Susan. 1988. "Families and Networks in Taiwan's Economic Development." In Edwin Winkler and Susan Greenhalgh, eds., *Contending Approaches to the Political Economy of Taiwan*. Armonk, NY: M. E. Sharpe.

Hirschman, Albert O. 1958. *The Strategy of Economic Development*. New Haven, CT: Yale University Press.

Hong, Wontack. 1979. *Trade, Distortions, and Employment Growth in Korea*. Seoul: Korean Development Institute.

Hu, Tai-Li. 1984. *My Mother-In-Law's Village: Rural Industrialization and Change in Taiwan*. Taipei: IOE.

International Monetary Fund. 1989a. *International Financial Statistics, 1989 Yearbook*. Washington, DC: IMF.

———. 1989b. *Primary Commodities: Market Development and Outlook*. Washington, DC: IMF (July).

———. 1990. *International Financial Statistics*. Washington, DC: IMF (June).

———. 1994. *International Financial Statistics, 1994 Yearbook*. Washington, DC: IMF.

Keesing, Donald B. 1988. "The Four Successful Exceptions: Official Export Promotion and Support for Export Marketing in Korea, Hong Kong, Singapore, and Taiwan, China." Occasional Paper No. 2. UNDP–World Bank Trade Expansion Program.

Krueger, Anne O. 1980. "Trade Policy as an Input to Development." *American Economic Review: Papers and Proceedings*, Vol. 70 (May), pp. 282–92.

———. 1983. *Trade and Employment in Developing Countries*. Vol. 3, *Synthesis and Conclusions*. Chicago: University of Chicago Press.

———. 1990a. "Asian Trade and Growth Lessons." *American Economic Review: Papers and Proceedings*, Vol. 80 (May), pp. 108–12.

———. 1990b. "Government Failures in Development." *Journal of Economic Perspectives*, Vol. 4 (Summer), pp. 9–23.

Kuznets, Paul W. 1988. "An East Asian Model of Economic Development: Japan, South Korea and Taiwan." *Economic Development and Cultural Change*, Vol. 36, pp. 511–44.

Lal, Deepak. 1985. *The Poverty of Development Economics*. Cambridge, MA: Harvard University Press.

Lewis, W. Arthur. 1978. *The Evolution of the International Economic Order*. Princeton, NJ: Princeton University Press.

Li, K. T., and W. A. Yeh. 1981. "Economic Planning in the Republic of China." *Conference on Experiences and Lessons of Economic Development in Taiwan*. Taipei: Academia Sinica.

Liang, Kuo-shu, and Ching-ing Hou Liang. 1988. "Development Policy Formation and Future Policy Priorities in the Republic of China." *Economic Development and Cultural Change*, Vol. 35, pp. S67–102.

Linnemman, Hans, Pitou van Dijck, and Harmen Verbruggen. 1987. *Export-Oriented Industrialization*. Singapore: Singapore University Press.

Little, I. M. D. 1979. "An Economic Reconnaissance." In Walter Galenson, ed., *Economic Growth and Structural Change in Taiwan: The Postwar Experience of the Republic of China*. Ithaca, NY: Cornell University Press.

———. 1982. *Economic Development: Theory, Policy, and International Relations*. New York: Basic Books.

Luedde-Neurath, Richard. 1986. *Import Controls and Export-Oriented Development: A Reassessment of the South Korean Case*. Boulder, CO: Westview Press.

———. 1988. "State Intervention and Export-Oriented Development in South Korea." In

Gordon White, ed., *Developmental States in East Asia.* New York: St. Martin's Press.

Mahidhara, Ramamohan. 1988. "Cause and Effect: Industrial Policy and the Structure of Production in South Korean Manufacturing." Mimeo. Austin: University of Texas (October).

Meade, James E. 1970. *The Theory of Indicative Planning.* Manchester, England: Manchester University Press.

Morrison, Thomas, and Michael Wattleworth. 1988. "Causes of the 1984–86 Commodity Price Decline. *Finance & Development,* Vol. 25, No. 2, pp. 31–33.

Myrdal, Gunnar. 1958. *Economic Theory and Underdeveloped Regions.* Bombay: Vora.

Pack, Howard, and Larry Westphal. 1986. "Industrial Strategy and Technological Change: Theory versus Reality." *Journal of Development Economics,* Vol. 22, pp. 87–128.

Park, Se-Il. 1988. "Labor Issues in Korea's Future." *World Development,* Vol. 16, pp. 99–119.

Park, Yung Chul. 1990. "Development Lessons from Asia: The Role of Government in South Korea and Taiwan." *American Economic Review: Papers and Proceedings,* Vol. 80 (May), pp. 118–21.

Petri, Peter. 1988. "Korea's Export Niche: Origins and Prospects." *World Development,* pp. 1647–63.

Piore, Michael, and Charles Sabel. 1984. *The Second Industrial Divide.* New York: Basic Books.

Porter, Michael. 1990. *The Competitive Advantage of Nations.* New York: Free Press.

Prebisch, Raul. 1950. *The Economic Development of Latin America and Its Principal Problems.* Santiago: United Nations Commission for Latin America.

Reinhart, Carmen M., and Peter Wickham. 1994. "Commodity Prices: Cyclical Weakness or Secular Decline?" *IMF Staff Papers,* Vol. 41, No. 2 (June), pp. 175–213.

Rhee, Yung Whee, Bruce Ross-Larson, and Gary Pursell. 1984. *Korea's Competitive Edge: Managing the Entry into World Markets.* Baltimore, MD: John Hopkins University Press for the World Bank.

Romer, Paul. 1992. "Two Strategies for Economic Development: Using Ideas vs. Producing Ideas." Mimeo. Washington, DC: World Bank.

Rosenberg, Nathan. 1976. *Perspectives on Technology.* New York: Cambridge University Press.

Rosenstein-Rodan, Paul. 1943. "Problems of Industrialization of Eastern and Southeastern Europe." *Economic Journal,* Vol. 53, pp. 202–11.

"Seoul's High-Technology Push: South Korea Plans Major Investments in New Industries." 1989. *International Herald Tribune* (December 16).

Sibunruang, Atchaka. 1986. *Industrial Development Policies in Thailand.* Mimeo. Washington, DC: World Bank.

Singer, Hans W. 1950. "The Distribution of Gains between Investing and Borrowing Countries." *American Economic Review: Papers and Proceedings,* Vol. 50 (May), pp. 473–85.

———. 1988. "The World Development Report 1987 on the Blessings of Outward Orientation: A Necessary Correction." *Journal of Development Studies,* Vol. 24, pp. 232–36.

Smith, Stephen C. 1991. *Industrial Policy in Developing Countries: Reconsidering the Real Sources of Export-Led Growth.* Washington, DC: Economic Policy Institute.

Spraos, John. 1983. *Inequalising Trade: A Study of Traditional North/South Specialisation in the Context of Terms of Trade Concepts.* New York: Oxford University Press.

"Taiwan and Korea, Two Paths to Prosperity." 1990. *The Economist* (July 14), pp. 19–20.

Todaro, Michael P. 1989. *Economic Development in the Third World,* 4th ed. New York: Longman.

U.S. Department of Commerce, Bureau of Economic Analysis. 1990. "U.S. International Transactions, First Quarter 1990." *Survey of Current Business,* Vol. 70, No. 6 (June), pp. 66–109.

Wade, Robert. 1988a. "The Role of Government in Overcoming Market Failure: Taiwan, Republic of Korea and Japan." In Helen Hughes, ed., *Achieving Industrialization in East Asia.* New York: Cambridge University Press.

———. 1988b. "State Intervention in 'Outward-looking' Development: Neo-classical Theory and Taiwanese Practice." In Gordon White, ed., *Developmental States in East Asia.* New York: St. Martin's Press.

———. 1988c. "Export Promotion and Import Controls in a Successful East Asian Trading State." Mimeo. Washington, DC: Office of Technology Assessment.

———. 1988d. "The Rise of East Asian Trading States: How They Managed Their Trade." Mimeo. Washington, DC: World Bank (June).

———. 1990. *Governing the Market: Economic Theory and the Role of Government in East Asian Industrialization.* Princeton, NJ: Princeton University Press.

Westphal, Larry E. 1982. "Fostering Technological Mastery by Means of Selective Infant-Industry Protection." In Syrquin Moises and Simon Teitel, eds., *Trade, Stability, Technology, and Equity in Latin America.* New York: Academic Press.

———. 1990. "Industrial Policy in an Export-Propelled Economy: Lessons from South Korea's Experience." *Journal of Economic Perspectives,* Vol. 4 (Summer), pp. 41–59.

Westphal, Larry E., and Kwang Suk Kim. 1977. "Industrial Policy and Development in Korea." Working Paper No. 263. Washington, DC: World Bank.

World Bank. 1982. *World Development Report 1982.* New York: Oxford University Press.

———. 1984. "The Outlook for Primary Commodities, 1984–1995." Commodities Working Paper No. 11. Washington, DC: World Bank.

———. 1986. *World Development Report 1986.* New York: Oxford University Press.

———. 1987a. *World Development Report 1987.* New York: Oxford University Press.

———. 1987b. *Korea: Managing the Industrial Transition,* Vols. 1 and 2. Washington, DC: World Bank.

———. 1987c. *Trade and Industrial Policies in the Developing Countries of East Asia: Thailand.* Report No. 6925. Washington, DC: World Bank.

———. 1987–88. *Commodity Trade and Price Trends, 1987–88 Edition.* Baltimore, MD: John Hopkins University Press.

———. 1989a. "Thailand: Building on the Recent Success—A Policy Framework." Unpublished paper. Washington, DC: World Bank.

———. 1989b. *Price Prospects for Major Primary Commodities 1988–2000.* Vol. 2. Washington, DC: World Bank.

———. 1992. *World Development Report 1992.* New York: Oxford University Press.

Yu, T. S. 1988. "The Role of Government in Industrialization." In *Conference on Economic Development Experiences of Taiwan and Its New Role in an Emerging Asia-Pacific Area.* Taipei: Academia Sinica.

INDEX

Reinert, Kenneth A., 146
Reparations payments, 218
Research and development, 95, 118, 202, 279
Revenga, Ana L., 73
Rhee, Yung Whee, 274
Ricardo, David, 14–15, 20, 46, 47, 48
Richardson, J. David, 184–85
Risk, 110
Robinson, Sherman, 271
Roland-Holst, David, 146
Roosevelt, Franklin Delano, 8
Rosenstein-Rodan, Paul, 272
Rosensweig, Jeffrey A., 189
Ross-Larson, Bruce, 274
Roth, William, 22
Ruggie, John, 9, 11

Sachs, Jeffrey D., 62, 72, 77, 78, 89, 95, 188–89
Samuelson, Paul, 20
Savings, 182, 183–84, 244
  developing countries', 241
  gap, 243–46, 262
  and growth, 200–201
  private, 182, 242, 244
  U.S. rate, 16, 201
Savings and loan crisis, 250
Scale economies, 69, 77, 110, 140, 251
Scarce currency clause, 10
Schott, Jeffrey J., 142, 144, 146
Schuh, Scott, 66
Semiconductor industry, 17, 24, 30–31, 32, 33
Senegal, 254
Sengenberger, Werner, 64
Service sectors, 17, 63, 65, 111, 168n.3
Shatz, Howard J., 62, 72, 77, 78, 89, 95
Shiells, Clinton R., 146
Singapore, 270
Skills, 78, 259–60
Slaughter, Matthew J., 80–81, 89–90
Smith, Adam, 40, 48
Sobhan, Rehman, 264n.5
Social safety nets, 262
Social standards, 166
Soete, Luc, 199
South Korea, 242, 254, 255, 270, 291
  conglomerates in, 258
  culture of, 277
  export promotion in, 274–79

South Korea (continued)
  government intervention in, 274–76
  import controls in, 278
  imports, 243
  infant industries in, 279
  literacy in, 259
  mercantilism of, 4
  tariffs in, 272
  U.S. deficit with, 205
  wages, 261
Sovereignty
  hegemony and ideology, 12–19
  and interdependence, 45
  managed trade and, 3–34
Special interest groups. See Interest groups
Specialization
  and comparative advantage, 21, 46, 47
  and division of labor, 43, 51
  and market division, 53 ·
  and wage differentials, 50
Specific factors model, 70
Speculation, 231, 250, 257
Spriggs, William, 147
Sri Lanka, 242, 260
SS theorem. See Stolper-Samuelson (SS) theorem
Stabilization programs, 249–50, 262, 263
Stanford, Jim, 149, 152
"Statement on Trade Policy," 16
State planning. See National economic planning
Steel industry, 17, 26–29, 32, 33–34, 112, 130
  productivity growth in, 114
  and protectionism, 113–17
  trigger price mechanism, 28
Stegemann, Klaus, 21
Stern, Robert M., 148
Stolper-Samuelson (SS) theorem, 67–68, 69
  and NAFTA, 147–48
  test of, 89–91
Strategic trade policy, 21
Subsidies, 4, 17, 27, 272
  agricultural, 32–33
Sugar, 288–89
Summers, Lawrence H., 66, 79, 181
Supranational institutions, 11
Sustainable development, 291
Sustainable growth, 167
Sweden, 4, 261